COMPUTER-AIDED DESIGN AND DRAFTING

COMPUTER-AIDED DESIGN AND DRAFTING

CADD

Louis Gary Lamit and Vernon Paige

De Anza College

Illustrations by Brad Waldron and John Shull

MERRILL PUBLISHING COMPANY

A Bell & Howell Information Company
Columbus Toronto London Melbourne

Cover photos courtesy of Evans & Sutherland and Megatek Corp.

Published by Merrill Publishing Company
A Bell & Howell Information Company
Columbus, Ohio 43216

This book was set in Serifa.

Administrative Editor: John Yarley
Production Coordinator: Rebecca Bobb
Art Coordinator: Jim Hubbard
Cover Designer: Cathy Watterson
Text Designer: Michael Rogondino

Library of Congress Catalog Card Number: 86–63617
International Standard Book Number: 0–675–20475–5
Printed in the United States of America
1 2 3 4 5 6 7 8 9—92 91 90 89 88 87

To John Higgins, who has stood by me during many years of frustration and effort. No one could ask for a better friend.

Louis Gary Lamit

To my wife Gerri, for her support and encouragement, and to the memory of my father.

Vernon Paige

Preface

Integration of computers in all phases of industry, from design through production, is extremely important to the future technician, engineer, designer, or drafter. CADD (Computer-Aided Design and Drafting) and CAM (Computer-Aided Manufacturing) represent revolutionary technological changes affecting a wide variety of industries. The term CAD/CAM refers to the use of computers to improve productivity by integrating the design and production process. CAM includes NC (Numerical Control), CNC (Computer Numerical Control) machining, and the use of robotics in manufacturing. A relatively new term, CIM (Computer-Integrated Manufacturing), is being used to collectively describe CAD/CAM processes.

This text is primarily concerned with CADD (Computer-Aided Design and Drafting), although CIM, CAM, NC, and robotics concepts are introduced at appropriate places as they relate to and are affected by CADD. Also, this is an introductory text and is not written for a machine-specific system. Rather, basic skills, transferable across CADD systems, are thoroughly explained in a step-by-step manner. Numerous illustrations depict the most popular industrial hardware and software systems (AutoCAD, VersaCAD, IBM, Computervision, Megatech, Calma Co., McDonnell Douglas, Control Data, Evans and Sutherland), and a wide variety of industrial applications are provided.

The following special student-oriented features are included throughout the text to motivate student reading and understanding.

- a full-color section of 59 plates to show students actual CADD systems and their applications

- chapter-opening objectives

- end-of-chapter glossaries that provide excellent "memory joggers" of key terms and concepts

- a comparative glossary at the conclusion of the text comparing CADD to manual drafting methods

- a directory of CADD vendors

Part One introduces CADD hardware. The first chapter describes the typical CADD workstation and acquaints the reader with the associated capabilities of many types of CADD input devices: graphics tablet or digitizing table; electronic pen/stylus, light pen, puck or mouse; keyboard; image control devices or graphics manipulation device; graphics screen (CRT); and desktop printer. Chapter 2 introduces the major types of output devices, such as group plotters, and explains the reasons for using a specific type of plotter or printer for different applications. Chapter 3 then explains processors and storage devices, the "brain" of the CADD system that performs all the calculations, stores drawings, and controls the input and output devices.

Part Two focuses on CADD software principles. Chapter 4 begins this section by providing an introduction to software and an overview of the most widely used CADD software systems. Chapter 5 then covers the basic steps that precede the creation of geometry (drawing) and the basic options for creating single items of geometry; for example: points, lines, arcs, circles, splines, and simple two-dimensional drawings. Chapter 6 discusses how to modify the geometry via the four basic capabilities of a typical CADD system: view modification, geometry editing, geometry altering, and modifying geometry. Chapter 7 focuses on typical CADD special features, including capabilities to verify, list, measure, count, and request information from the system. Also discussed is the capability to display and organize geometry efficiently with colors, discrimination, and layer options. Lastly, an overview of three-dimensional simulation techniques is provided (isometric, oblique, 2 1/2-dimensional, and for surfaces).

Part Three introduces basic CADD techniques. The creation, storage, and recall of symbols is discussed in Chapter 8. This chapter also explains how a diagram is created on a CADD system and how this process differs from preparing a diagram manually on a drafting board. Data retrieval techniques, including a discussion of attributes for report preparation, are also introduced and explained. Chapter 9 discusses the graphic representation of an object in a CADD system, called modeling. Examples of three-dimensional modeling applications in electronics, mechanical, architectural, and piping design are presented. Chapter 10, on preparing the drawing, explains the difference between draw mode and model mode activity and how the availability of a three-dimensional system affects "drawing" preparation. Step-by-step methods used to dimension a part and the practice of cross-hatching are also discussed. Chapter 11 explains how to plot a drawing (saving it or recreating it on paper or plastic film) and archiving (placing infrequently used drawings/data in auxiliary storage).

Part Four introduces how CADD is being applied in a wide variety of industrial settings: electronic, mechanical, architectural, and piping design; as well as mapping. Chapter 12 discusses the specific role of CADD in the total manufacturing cycle. The advantages of using a common database for design, drafting, machining, and manufacturing processes are explained. Also, an understanding of the role CADD plays in NC part programming and in robot simulation and workcell management is presented. Chapter 13 explains why CADD has been widely accepted by industry and provides an overview of the major CADD industrial applications.

Part Five covers workstations: engineering workstations in Chapter 14 and personal computer–based systems in Chapter 15. How these systems work, how they differ from one another, and how they are being used are explained, and examples are provided.

In summary, this textbook thoroughly introduces the reader to all aspects of CADD, including hardware, software, techniques, applications, and systems.

Acknowledgments

The authors would like to thank the following persons for helping with this project: Angela Champagne Lamit, Gary's daughter, who typed the manuscript; Bob Pine, who wrote Chapter 3; and Brad Waldron and John Shull, who did a fine job on the CADD illustrations. Brad Waldron also helped coordinate the illustrations.

John Higgins, Pat Sheetz, and Carmen DiFede completed the manually drawn illustrations in the problem sections of the text. Mark Spear, Norman Robb, and Julie Newcomb helped with the many little tasks that take time when writing a text.

We also wish to thank Bob Hubbs, who was our dean at the time of the project, and De Anza College, for the professional encouragement and use of facilities.

In writing this text, the authors benefited from the assistance of a number of people from Merrill Publishing: Tim McEwen and John Yarley, administrative editors; Don Thompson, developmental editor; Rebecca Bobb, production editor; Bruce Johnson, art director; and Cathy Watterson, cover and color insert designer. The authors also thank the following reviewers, who provided many helpful, constructive suggestions: George Baggs, Augusta Area Technical School; Kermit Baker, Charles S. Mott Community College; Andrew Ford, Wahenaw Community College; James Kimmey, Elgin

Community College; Victor Langer, CAD Consultants; Kenneth Scott, Worcester Polytechnical Institute; Ken Weger, Sierra College; and Don S. Wills, Oklahoma State University.

Finally, we would also like to thank Houston Instruments for donating the use of a plotter and digitizer, and Kurta Corporation for use of a digitizer tablet. T&W Systems donated CADAPPLE and VersaCAD software, and Autodesk donated a copy of AutoCAD.

Most of the illustrations were completed on a Computervision system that was a gift to De Anza College.

All other companies are referenced in the text and with courtesy lines on the photographs and illustrations they provided.

About the Authors

Louis Gary Lamit is currently an instructor and CADD facility manager at De Anza College in Cupertino, California, where he teaches computer-aided drafting and design.

Mr. Lamit has worked as a drafter, designer, NC programmer, and engineer in the automotive, aircraft, and piping industries. A majority of his work experience is in the area of mechanical and piping design. Mr. Lamit started as a drafter in Detroit working for the automobile industry doing tooling, dies, jigs, and fixture layout, and detailing at Koltanbar Engineering, Tool Engineering, Time Engineering, and Premier Engineering for Chrysler, Ford, and Fisher Body. Mr. Lamit has worked at Boeing Aircraft, Remington Arms, Pratt Whitney Aircraft, Kollmorgan Optics, and Pacific Pipe Company as a designer and NC programmer.

Since leaving industry, Mr. Lamit has taught at the community college and university levels and has written a number of textbooks, including *Industrial Model Building* (1981), *Piping Drafting and Design* (1981), *Pipefitting and Piping Handbook* (1984), *Descriptive Geometry* (1983), and *Electronic Drafting and Design* (1985). He has also written a number of articles, booklets, and workbooks in technical areas associated with physical modeling, piping, electronics, and descriptive geometry. He owns a freelance technical illustration firm for industrial advertising.

Mr. Lamit received a B.S. degree from Western Michigan University in 1970 and did his master's work at Michigan State University. He has done graduate work at Wayne State University (Michigan) and the University of

California at Berkeley and holds an NC Programming certificate from Boeing Aircraft Company.

Vernon Paige has had over 30 years experience in the engineering field. Spending approximately the first half of his career as a designer and the second half developing computer-aided design (CAD) tools for designers and engineers has given him expertise in both the traditional manual methods of engineering design and CAD techniques. Mr. Paige has been associated with De Anza College for the past 14 years and has been instrumental in establishing the CAD courses in the drafting curriculum. Currently, Mr. Paige is a systems consultant at Lockheed in Sunnyvale, California. He is actively involved in the development and management of Lockheed's system. Mr. Paige has a B.A. and an M.A. in mathematics and teaches mathematics at De Anza College in addition to the CAD classes.

Contents

Color plates 1 through 16 are between pages 288 and 289.

Color plates 17 through 33 are between pages 320 and 321.

Color plates 34 through 46 are between pages 416 and 417.

Color plates 47 through 59 are between pages 448 and 449.

Introduction

Anyone wishing to enter industry as a drafter, designer, or engineer must understand the extent to which the computer is profoundly altering the factory floor and engineering office. *CAE* (computer-aided engineering), *CAM* (computer-aided manufacturing), and *CADD* (computer-aided design and drafting) are collectively called *CIM* (computer-integrated manufacturing), which is the integration of all phases of production, from design to manufacture, by means of the computer. The term CAD/CAM refers to the use of computers to improve productivity by integrating the design and production process. CAM includes *NC* (numerical control), *CNC* (computer numerical control) machining, and the use of *robotics* in manufacturing. All the above terms and concepts will be presented throughout this text. CAM, robotics, and NC applications are covered in Chapter 13.

Though this text is primarily concerned with computer-aided design and drafting, the integration of computers in all phases of the design-through-production process of industry is extremely important to the future engineer, designer, or drafter. CIM, CAM, NC, CNC, and robotics concepts are introduced at appropriate places in the text as they relate to and are affected by CADD.

Computer-aided design (CAD) is the use of a computer to develop, analyze, modify, or enhance an engineering design. CADD systems are based on interactive computer graphics, a user-oriented system in which the computer is employed to create, transform, and display data in the form of graphics or symbols. The user in the computer graphics design system is the engineer, designer, or drafter who communicates data and commands the computer through any of several input devices. The computer communicates with the user via a cathode ray tube (CRT). The operator creates an image on the CRT screen by entering commands to the computer. In most systems, the image is constructed from basic geometric elements, including points, lines, circles, arcs, fillets, and the like. The graphics can be modified according to the commands of the operator. They can be enlarged or reduced (zoomed), moved to another location on the screen (scrolled/panned), rotated, and transformed in other ways. Through these various manipulations, the required details of the graphic image are formulated.

Yet graphics is only one component of a CAD/CAM system. Interactive computer graphics is a tool used by the engineer, designer, or drafter to solve design problems. The system magnifies the powers of the designer by means of the *synergistic effect*: The operator performs the portion of the design process that is most suitable to human intellectual skills (conceptualization, independent thinking); the computer performs the task best suited to its capabilities (rapid calculation, visual display, storage of large amounts of data); and the resulting system exceeds the sum of its components.

Though the skill and knowledge of traditional manual drafting will still be needed and taught in the immediate future, by the end of the century, the ability to operate a CAD/CAM system will be an absolute necessity for those entering any field of engineering and technology. The student must, therefore, be familiar with the terms and capabilities of CAD/CAM in order to understand their applications to a specific area of design and drafting.

CAD/CAM

CAD/CAM is an effective way to apply computer power to drafting, design, manufacturing, documentation, and quality control tasks. It increases productivity, decreases costs, improves products, shortens product turnaround time, reduces product liability, and improves competitive position in the marketplace. It is being used in a wide range of applications, including integrated circuit (IC) and printed circuit board (PCB) layout (Figure I–1), mapping, plant design, piping, wiring diagrams, process design, numerical control, mechanical design (Figure I–2), and architecture (Figure I–3).

Just as business computers process alphanumeric data, CAD/CAM systems store, retrieve, manipulate, and display graphic information — all with unsurpassed speed and accuracy. Product quality and yield are also improved, and this permits optimal use of energy, materials, and manufacturing personnel. The primary benefit of CAD/CAM is that products can be far more accurately designed, tested, and manufactured than is possible by traditional methods. This minimizes errors and rejects and can thus lead to substantial cost savings. CADD alone can improve productivity 3:1 for product development. The ratios can range as high as 20:1 improvement over traditional methods of design and drafting.

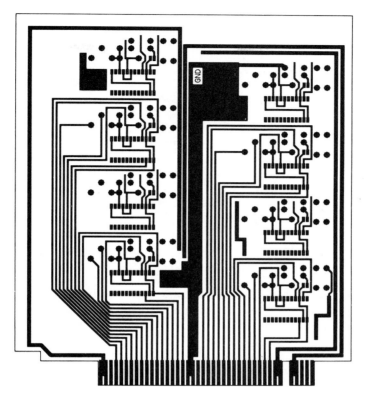

Figure I–1
Printed circuit board
artwork drawing.
(Courtesy Engineering
Systems Corp.)

Additionally, the CAD/CAM system can also improve drawing quality. For example, "original" ink drawings can be plotted in a few minutes. (Plotting is covered in Chapter 11.) Also, compliance with standards can be improved because standard parts, symbols, notes, and drafting practices can all be *locked into* the software.

CADD

This text is an introduction to two-dimensional and three-dimensional CADD systems. Its purpose is to acquaint the student with the many types of CADD systems, introduce the variations of output and uses being applied to interactive CADD, and, most important, enable the student to create simple-to-advanced drawings with the aid of this sophisticated automated drafting system. Specific industrial applications are presented throughout the text.

A CADD designer or drafter can perform mundane drafting tasks in a fraction of the time and with greater accuracy and repeatability than manual drawing methods ever afforded. Drafters create their designs electronically within the CAD system, view the designs on a TV-like display (monitor) (Fig-

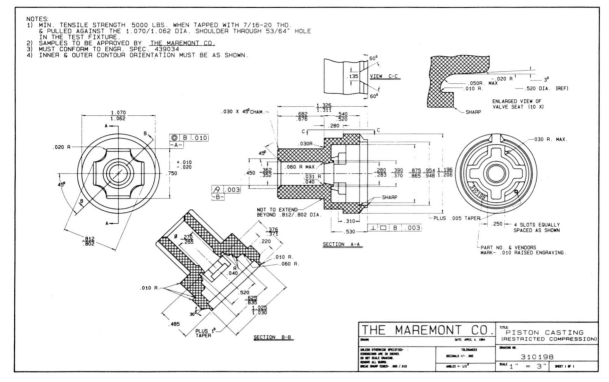

Figure I–2
Mechanical drawing completed with VersaCAD software. (Courtesy T&W Systems)

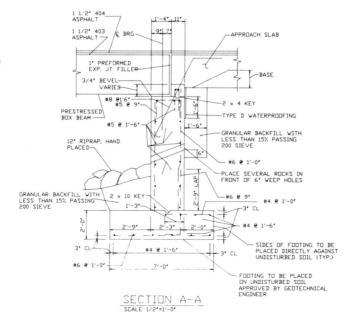

Figure I–3
Section of an architectural drawing done with AutoCADD software. Drawing is courtesy A/E Microsystems, Inc. (Courtesy AUTODESK)

ure I–4), make quick and easy revisions, and then command the system to draw the design on paper or clear film using a plotter. Figure I–5 shows a mechanical design that was created on a low-cost two-dimensional CADD system (AutoCAD) and plotted with a pen plotter on vellum.

It is important to understand that, in the CADD system, *design* refers to the establishment and definition of the database. *Drafting* primarily involves defining, refining, and manipulating the database to provide certain kinds of information, and *manufacturing* (or CIM, computer-integrated manufacturing) applies and utilizes the *same* database.

A typical interactive CADD system is an engineering design and drafting *tool*. It is *interactive* in that it works *with* the drafter/designer in the method and at the speed he or she chooses. The CADD designer/drafter need not be a computer programmer or typist. An efficient interactive CAD system operator directs the computer to do the mundane tasks in design and drafting. This leaves the designer free to try many design solutions.

The CADD system provides an electronic design/drafting capability that replaces a designer's or drafter's traditional set of tools; circle and ellipse templates; French curves; splines; pencils; pens; erasers; erasing shields; erasing machines; Leroy lettering templates; beam compasses; bow compasses; drop pens; protractors; 45, 30, and 60 degree triangles; pencil sharpeners; pencil pointers; various scales; and drafting machines.

The CADD operator also has constant access to processors and storage units that provide all the capabilities of a calculator and all the reference information of a math library; data are supplied for both trigonometric and geometric construction. Symbols, patterns, drawing segments, minidrawings, and even complete drawings can be stored and reused. The processors and storage units on some systems let the operator electronically erase selected portions, shrink or enlarge scalings, copy portions of other draw-

Figure I–4
CADD workstation may include dual CRT monitors, graphics digitizing tablet, and keyboard. (Courtesy Calma Co.)

Figure I–5
Pen plot of a mechanical assembly drawn with AutoCADD. Drawn by Leendert Versten, University of Nebraska–Lincoln. (Courtesy AUTODESK)

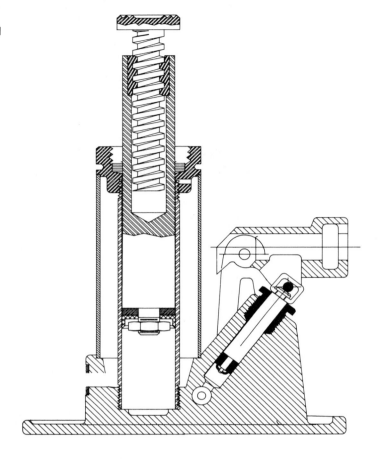

ings, and mirror or flop views for clarity. To accomplish all this requires an integrated combination of hardware and software.

Hardware and Software

The typical computer graphics system is a combination of *hardware* and *software*. The hardware includes a central processing unit, one or more workstations (including the graphics display terminal), and peripheral devices such as printers, plotters, data disks, and all other physical parts of the system (Figure I–6). The software consists of the invisible sets of instructions — the programs — that control the hardware and thus implement graphics processing on the system. The software typically includes additional specialized application programs to accomplish the particular engineering functions required by the application. Software is usually provided by the CADD manufacturer and is already stored on disk packs or magnetic tape, ready for use.

Figure I–6
Multiple CADD stations in a typical "drafting room." (Courtesy Lockheed-California Co.)

The input, output, and storage hardware elements are interconnected by cables or telecommunications. Interactive CADD is either a stand-alone system or a processor with remote input/output units attached. The complete system includes the interconnected hardware modules and the software.

Software programs are available for all areas of engineering and design. Most systems can be mastered in a short training period, but the specifics of the design area (piping, architecture, electronics, mechanical or structural design, etc.) must be learned through schooling and experience. Chapter 12 covers applications software for structural, piping, architectural, electronics, civil/mapping, technical illustration, and mechanical design.

Configuration

In addition to the computer (Chapter 3), CADD configuration includes the workstation (Chapter 14) with CRT display, function and alphanumeric keyboard, digitizer, and other operator input devices (Chapter 1); output devices such as pen plotter, electrostatic plotter, photoplotter, COM, and others (Chapter 2); software for high-level and other applications (Chapters 4, 5, and 6); and manufacturing applications such as CAM, NC, and robotics (Chapter 12).

A typical high-level three-dimensional CAD/CAM system configuration has a central processing unit. Large-scale host computers (Chapter 14) are equipped with mass memory as well as magnetic tape, line printers, card readers, and hardcopy devices. A large digital computer may be used to support, with its own memory and processing capabilities, various graphics programs running on the CAD/CAM system, as well as to do related engineering analyses.

A *turnkey* system—one that is functional, complete, and ready to operate as soon as installed (just turn the key) usually includes a variety of software. CAD/CAM software can include programs to perform graphic manipulation functions (such as scale, zoom, and rotate) and to perform graphic drawing functions, such as the creation of lines, arcs, and splines. Usually the software is written in a high-level language like *FORTRAN* or *Pascal*. The system may also include specific application software, such as automatic drafting. Software is covered in Chapters 4 through 7.

A CADD two-dimensional turnkey configuration is shown in Figure I–7. The computer used in such a configuration is generally a personal computer and contains its own CPU; therefore, it does not need an interface with a *mainframe*, or large central computer. Some personal computer–based CAD systems can be networked together and interfaced with a separate CPU providing the designer with access to a large database. An example of this configuration is the Computervision minicomputer–based CADDS 4 system. Computervision has migrated its software package down to the IBM AT and XT microcomputer. The IBM can be networked with the minicomputer–based CV system and its designer CAD stations. Personal computer–based CAD systems are discussed in Chapter 15.

Regardless of the type of system, the most common form of output remains the "drawing." In Figure I–8 the CAD designer is watching as his drawing is plotted on an electrostatic plotter.

Figure I–7
CADD plot of AutoCAD workstation drawn by Peter Barnet. (Courtesy AUTODESK)

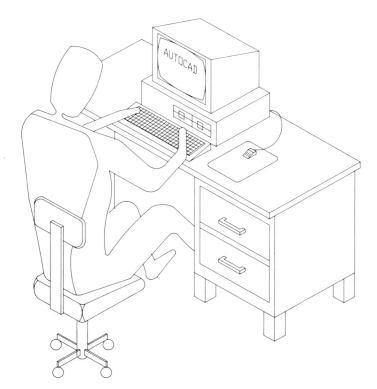

Figure I–8
CADD designer watching the plotting of his drawing on an electrostatic plotter. (Courtesy Lockheed-California Co.)

Capability

The heart of any CAD/CAM system is the design *terminal*, or workstation (Figure I–9). The CAD/CAM operator interacts with the system to develop a product design in detail, monitoring the work constantly on a TV-like graphics display screen. By issuing commands to the system and responding to system prompts, the user creates a design, manipulating, modifying, and refining it — all without drawing a line on paper or recreating an existing design element. Once the design is final, a command to the system will make a plot of the drawing or generate a computer tape to guide computer-controlled machine tools in manufacturing and testing the part. Plots can have any level of sophistication from a simple check copy to a full-scale ink plot of the drawing.

As a design is developed, the *computer graphics* system accumulates and stores physically related data — identifying the precise location, dimensions, descriptive text, and other properties of every element to help define the new part or product. With this design data, the system can help the designer do complex engineering analyses, generate special lists and reports, and detect and flag (note/indicate) design flaws before the part is manufactured. Not all CADD systems have these capabilities, however.

Most CAD/CAM systems are modular, both in hardware and software. Engineering firms can select the level of computational processing — from large mainframes to PCs — and graphic output that best serves their needs. The IBM system shown in Figure I–10 is an example of a low-cost personal computer-based CADD system. Some companies, such as engineering firms, use the system exclusively for drafting and design. Manufacturing companies also use CAD/CAM for analysis, fabrication, and testing.

Figure I–9
CADD terminal with function box, CRT, keyboard, and light pen. (Courtesy IBM Corp.)

Most stand-alone CAD/CAM systems include a central-processing facility with a *minicomputer* and mass memory (for programs and drawing storage), as well as system software. Computervision uses this configuration in its minicomputer-based system (Figure I–11). A terminal, shown in Figure I–4, typically consists of a *cathode-ray tube (CRT)*, a *graphics tablet* (data entry tablet) or digitizer, a *function box*, an *alphanumeric keyboard*, and possibly a hardcopy device (*printer*) for printing alphanumeric or graphic output. These and other hardware features are discussed in Chapters 1, 2, and 3.

A number of engineers and drafters can work simultaneously at various terminals, each on a different phase of development — such as design, engineering analysis, drafting, or manufacturing — for a single product or for

Figure I–10
IBM PC-based CADD system. (Courtesy Auto-trol Technology)

Figure I–11
Minicomputer–based CADD stations. (Courtesy Computervision Corp.)

many different products. Figure I–6 shows a typical CAD drafting and design room with multiple stations sharing a central CPU. It is not uncommon to have eight people working on different design tasks, all on the same system. This is possible because each operator can create his or her own design database. Productivity thus depends to a great extent on a very efficient interface between the computer and the engineer or designer at the terminal.

Operation

The workstation of a typical CAD/CAM system makes possible a simple yet powerful interaction between the designer and the computer. Just by pointing an electronic pen to a premarked, touch-sensitive drawing tablet, the designer gives the system drafting commands, such as *Insert Line* or *Zoom*. The designer creates, modifies, and refines the design interactively, viewing the emerging work on a graphics display. With a single stroke of the pen, the designer can move, magnify, flip, rotate, copy, stretch, or otherwise manipulate the entire design or any part of it.

In addition to the pen, the designer/drafter can communicate with the system through a typewriter keyboard. Using a combination of numbers and simple English phrases, the design types X-Y-Z coordinates, enters text for drawing annotation, and initiates graphics-processing commands, all of which can also be activated by the electronic pen.

The system lets the designer know, by a message or a flag on the screen, if there is a procedural error. Before the designer can begin creating, however, he or she must set the stage for computer-aided design. Using the keyboard, electronic pen, and drawing tablet, the designer asks the system to retrieve automatically any previously completed drawings needed for reference, as well as all the standard design symbols he or she expects to use. The designer then informs the system at what location on the drawing the symbol will be automatically placed, ready for assembling and incorporating into the emerging design.

Symbols and completed designs are all stored in the computer's data bank (memory or database) where they are instantly available to the designer. This online library speeds up the design process by eliminating unnecessary archival redrafting of commonly used components and subassemblies. Symbol creation is discussed in Chapter 8.

The designer can, with assistance from the computer, draw the outline of a simple part on the graphics *display*. Some systems can add depth automatically; produce a three-dimensional version at any desired angle; generate front, side, and top views of three-dimensional parts; rotate the parts; produce a mirror image; change the scale; and add text to produce a finished drawing. This drawing can be precise enough to meet the most exacting engineering standards, with all parts automatically dimensioned and labeled. Modeling is covered in Chapter 9. Figure I–12 is a simulated three-dimensional view of a mechanical design created with AutoCAD software.

Documentation

As a part is designed on the system, its physical dimensions are defined along with the attributes of its various components. These data, filed in the computer's memory, can later serve many other nongraphic needs. For example, the designer can use part number data of materials to help generate bills of materials for the purchasing department. (Data retrieval is presented in Chapter 8.) Computer tapes can guide NC machine tools and equipment for quality control of other product-testing uses. Other computer programs can help engineers check for interferences or tolerances; generate models for engineering analyses; and calculate areas, volumes, and weights of the product under development. All these nongraphic capabilities, sometimes called attributes, are automatic by-products of the CAD/CAM design process.

Designer Qualifications

Programming ability is not required for operation of today's *user friendly* CAD/CAM systems, but an operator of a CAD/CAM system must be able to

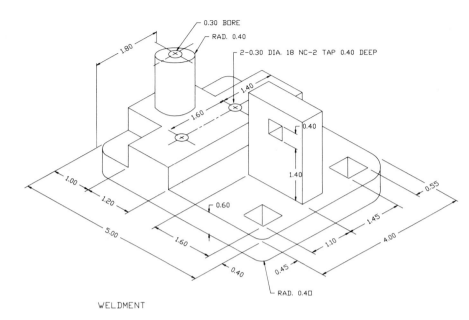

WELDMENT

Figure I–12
Simulated three-
dimensional (2½-
dimensional) mechanical
part drawn by Peter
Barnet. (Courtesy
AUTODESK)

understand the system's hardware configuration and its software capabilities. Additionally, the user must be familiar with:

1. Drafting standards

2. Specific engineering field conventions

3. Actual industrial applications

4. Software specifics for a particular CADD system package

The designer should be able to do all tasks efficiently, constantly prompted by the system to consider procedures, available functions, and sequence of steps.

Each designer should be able to communicate with the system in a natural way—for example, by pointing a pen or pushing labeled keys. Typing requirements are minimal. They basically involve entering text changes, numeric dimensions, or positional data, but not generally drawing commands. Ordinarily, a system lets the designer know that the instruction has been received and responds to it promptly.

It must be stressed that CADD is merely a drafting and design tool. A drafter or designer is still required to create the necessary graphics. Only the method of creating engineering graphics has changed, not the content. CADD frees the drafter or designer from the tiring, repetitious tasks of traditional manual methods. CADD makes lettering, linework, symbol construction, and dimensioning almost automatic. CADD also provides the user a new tool with which to expand and become truly creative.

Chapter

1

Input Devices

Objectives

Upon completion of this chapter, the reader will be able to:

- List the major types of input devices

- Discuss the differences in using various types of input devices

- Identify the types and discuss the operation of display screens

- Discuss the use of menus and digitizing tablets

- Explain the types and uses of keyboards used for CADD stations

- Describe the difference between a stylus and a light pen

Introduction

Most of the work of a drafter/designer is done at a **workstation** (Figures 1–1 and 1–2). This chapter discusses the hardware components of a CADD work-station and acquaints the reader with the associated capabilities of many types of CADD input devices.

   A workstation is an interactive computer graphics terminal, which may consist of any or all of the following:

- A graphics tablet or digitizing table with attached menu

- An electronic pen/stylus, light pen, puck, or mouse

Figure 1–1
IBM Graphics Display System. (Courtesy International Business Machines Corporation)

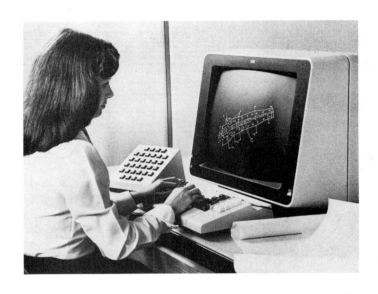

Figure 1–2
GSI task-oriented PCB CADD system includes color graphics, Winchester disk, on-screen design, and design rules checking. (Gerber Scientific Instruments Co.)

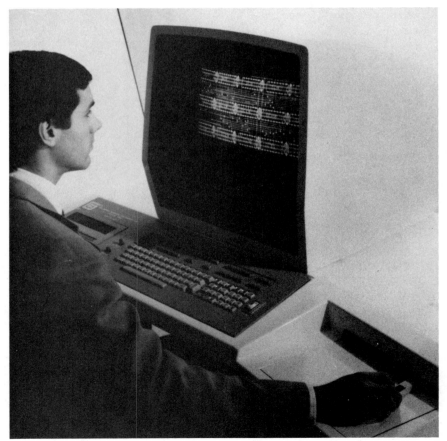

- A keyboard (alphanumeric keyboard and possibly a function keyboard)

- An image control device or other graphics manipulation device

- A graphics screen (CRT) that displays graphics and alphanumeric data, or possibly two CRTs, one for graphics and one for alphanumeric data

- A desktop printer or other "quick look" hardcopy unit

CADD systems are interactive graphics systems. A computer graphics system is said to be *interactive* if the drafter/designer can converse with it. If a system is interactive, the designer can "talk" to it and direct it to create designs and drawings using an English-based graphics command language. Input devices are used to communicate with the system.

CADD systems respond to commands by completing the graphic functions the drafter/designer directs and by displaying status information or requests for specific kinds of data on the screen.

Much of the drafter's/designer's communication with a CADD system is by means of the graphics tablet and electronic pen (Figure 1–3). The graphics tablet normally has two distinct areas on its surfaces:

Figure 1–3
Designer inputting data with a stylus and graphics tablet.
(Courtesy California Computer Products, Inc.)

The *graphics area* directly corresponds to the graphics area on the display screen. When the drafter/designer positions the electronic pen near the surface of the graphics area and presses the button (or pushes down on the pen), a corresponding location on the screen is identified by crosshairs.

The typical *menu area* is made up of many small squares or pads sometimes referred to as function keys (Figure 1–3). The menu provides a fast means of entering CADD commands. Instead of using the keyboard, the drafter/designer activates a square in the menu area with the electronic pen.

The electronic pen or stylus pen is the activating device that locates positions or identifies existing graphic entities. In Figure 1–4, the drafter/designer is using a stylus to input commands. This locating and identifying activity is called **digitizing**. On some CADD systems, the menu area also can be deactivated and the entire graphics tablet can be used for drawing. The positions located generally define construction of coordinate information. For example, when drawing a line the drafter/designer could locate (digitize) two points on the tablet. The system would then draw the line between these two points. The first point (location) would immediately be seen on the screen as a flashing **X**, box, or other marker (this flashing marker is called a **digitize mark**). The second point indicated on the tablet would also show as a flashing marker on the screen, and a line would appear between the two digitized, flashing points.

Figure 1–4
CADD station. (Reprinted with permission from Computervision Corporation, Bedford, Massachusetts)

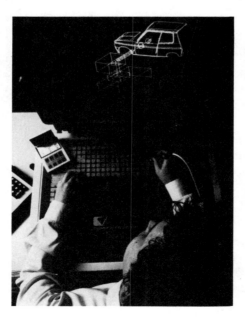

Workstations

The **workstation** (Figure 1–5) is usually composed of a smooth drafting table called a **digitizer**, which converts graphics to digits, and a TV-like **display** with an **alphanumeric keyboard**; this is the control center for input. The drafter/designer commands all system functions from this station. The digitizer is wired so that the location of each point on its surface can be sent electronically to the processor by pushing the input button on the crosshair device. In the processor, all information is in digits (0 or 1); the digitizer changes graphics (lines and points) to digits. The processor then uses its immense calculating power to create the lines as the drafter/designer indicates and reproduce them on the TV-like display.

At this station a drawing or a document can be created, revised, and annotated. **Annotation** is the process of inputting (keying in) numbers and letters for notes and other drawing information. Graphic items are specified on the display by pointing to an identical area on a companion **tablet** with

Figure 1–5
Networked CADD stations used for electronic design. (Reprinted with permission from Computervision Corporation, Bedford, Massachusetts)

a hand-held, pen-like **stylus** as in Figure 1–3. The display, capable of showing portions of a drawing enlarged to any scale, is like a TV camera, which can zoom and pan (scroll) images.

The digitizer can be used to input from a rough schematic or large layout drawing, to input and edit from checkplots, or to perform freehand edits of previously stored drawings. The drafting workstation provides access to the entire CADD system for input and editing of both graphics and text. Designers find the digitizer not unlike a drafting board. It can be tilted, raised, and lowered on systems configured with a large digitizing table. Some digitizers are available with backlighting for fast tracing.

CADD systems have different methods of operation, depending on the manufacturer. Here is a hypothetical example of what a drafter/designer might do at a workstation. He or she types two or three words on the keyboard or selects an area on the digitizer, and the drawing on which he or she had been working yesterday appears on the screen. As the crosshair device (or stylus) is moved across the digitizer surface, a little cross (cursor) following the movement is displayed on the screen. The drafter/designer pushes a button marked DEL (delete) and the line completely disappears. The drafter/designer then pushes the *LBP* (line between points) button, moves the crosshair device, and digitizes two points by pushing the input button when the cursor is at one end, then the other, of the desired line; a line appears on the screen. The drafter/designer then selects the zoom command and the picture expands. To flip the drawing, the drafter/designer simply pushes a few buttons. Satisfied with the revisions, the drafter/designer selects the save command, and the revised drawing replaces the previous drawing and is stored in the system. By pushing a few more buttons, the drawing is automatically copied onto paper.

Introduction to Graphic Display

The graphics display screen allows the drafter/designer to view model geometry and detail drawings as they are being constructed (Figure 1–6). Unless a separate CRT is used, the screen also displays the text of the commands that have been used to construct graphic elements. Both keyboard-entered and menu-entered commands appear on the screen and are referred to as *communications text* (Figure 1–7).

State-of-the-art technology provides all CADD systems with some form of **CRT** similar to that used in televisions, oscilloscopes, and radars. CRTs are available in many sizes and configurations and with various capabilities including dual screens (Figure 1–8).

The majority of CADD systems provide either a **vector** CRT or a **raster** CRT. In vector CRTs an electron beam "paints" the image on the screen by "stroking" vectors (Figure 1–9) on the screen's phosphor surface and a grid

Figure 1–6
Tektronix 25-inch computer display terminal is a direct-view storage tube display. This display is uniquely suited for displaying the highly complex graphics found in contour mapping, seismic analysis, and energy field modeling. Displayed here is a printed circuit board layout. (Courtesy Tektronix, Inc.)

directly behind the screen. Because the grid continuously energizes the image, resolution is very high and the lines remain clear and bright. This system is used in oscilloscopes and radars.

　　Raster CRTs operate by continuously sending a beam across the screen, left to right and top to bottom. The image is created by a system of

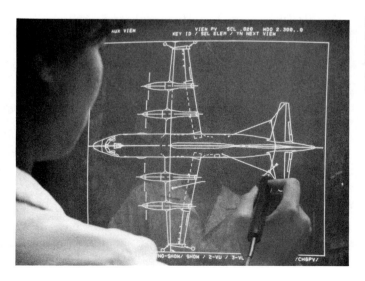

Figure 1–7
Operator using a light pen to redesign a tail configuration for an airplane. (Courtesy Lockheed-California Co.)

Figure 1–8
Calma CAE system is used primarily for VLSI design, including input, manipulation, and output of VLSI circuit masks. (Courtesy Calma Company, a wholly-owned subsidiary of General Electric Company, U.S.A.)

activating a light or dark dot at any given spot on the screen as the beam passes it (Figure 1–9). The process is called *rasterization*, and is the principle used in home television. Resolution is not as high with this system.

If the drafter/designer erases part of the image on a CADD system using the *storage vector* screen, the change will not be seen until the system is instructed to *"repaint" the entire image* with the reflected change. These systems cannot selectively erase within the image. The entire screen is always repainted when an item is erased. Depending upon the complexity of the image, repaint time can vary from one second to three minutes.

On CADD systems with refresh vector screens, the drafter/designer may also change the image on the screen, but he or she sees the change instantly since it is always being refreshed. Selective erasure is possible. However, because of the relatively slow refresh vector times associated with most refresh screens, flickering of the image is usually observed.

Raster systems offer a screen that combines the best aspects of vector refresh and storage CRTs while eliminating the disadvantages of both. This type of screen display offers a bright, flicker-free image, high resolution, and selective erasure (changes made to any portion of the drawing are shown immediately, as fast as they are made).

It is also possible to obtain systems with "dual screen capability," which incorporate two displays in one workstation. This offers a significant improvement over single display monitors since graphics information can be viewed on one screen while associated alphanumerics can be shown on the other. The advantage is an uncluttered view of the graphics, upon which most of the creating and editing is accomplished (Figure 1–8).

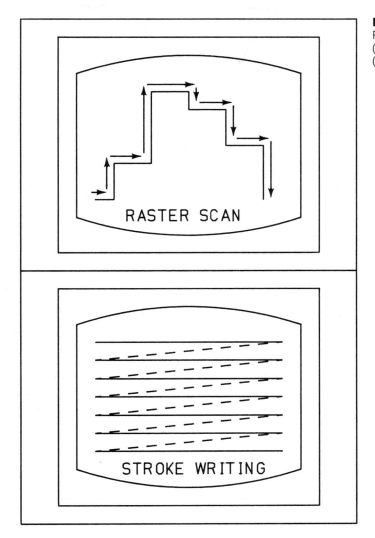

Figure 1–9
Raster display system (top) vs. stroke writing (bottom).

CRTs

Display Methods   Two basic picture-generation techniques are used in computer graphics systems: raster scan and stroke writing (refresh).

In *stroke writing* (refresh) the beam can be moved simultaneously in arbitrary X and Y directions along a curve or straight path, much like the line in the Etch-A-Sketch children's toy (Figure 1–9). Essentially, the beam is moved in the same way a pencil is used to sketch a picture. This method is commonly called random position, vector writing, stroke writing, line drawing, directed beam, cursive, or calligraphic writing. With this method the computer locates points and then connects the points with lines called vectors. Vectors are displayed on the screen by a process called **refresh**. Each vector in the picture is restroked so that it appears constantly in view. Thus, a picture is vector-refreshed with each change.

The **raster scan** technique is the familiar picture used in home television sets. It also is called digital TV or scan graphics. The electron beam is moved continuously in a fixed pattern, very rapidly in the X-axis, producing a single horizontal line in approximately 67 microseconds (Figure 1–9). The beam moves much more slowly in the Y-axis, scanning the entire screen vertically in about 16 milliseconds. At the end of a vertical scan, the beam resumes its horizontal scanning. This display uses a grid pattern of dots to create the picture. Each dot is called a **pixel**.

The **resolution** or sharpness of the raster picture is dependent on the spacing of the grid pattern of dots. The smaller and denser the dots, the greater the resolution.

Like the vector-writing CRT, the raster CRT refreshes the picture to keep it in view. The picture is refreshed by scanning the grid pattern of dots from left to right and from top to bottom very fast (30 to 60 times per second).

The **storage tube display** draws a line on the screen similar to the vector-writing CRT; however, the phosphor on the surface of the screen holds the picture for a very long time. There is no refreshing of the picture.

Color Display CRTs   CRT phosphors are available in black and white and a broad spectrum of colors, including green, blue, yellow, red, and orange. Most interactive CAD/CAM systems use single-color (monochromatic) CRTs. The color is determined by phosphor selection, not by the user's software. Color CRTs are made with three colors — red, green, and blue. The three colors of phosphors are scanned by three separate electron guns and the number of colors displayed on the screen is determined by the raster memory size. Four or eight colors are normally available on CADD systems. Color coding and color masking are important options in the design and layout of multilayer PC boards (Figure 1–10), mapping drawings and other types of projects.

Operator Input Devices

A variety of devices allows the CAD/CAM drafter/designer to communicate with a computer without having to learn programming. These devices allow the drafter/designer to pick a function, enter text and numerical data into the system, create and modify the graphics on the CRT (inputting, moving, deleting, expanding, rotating, dimensioning) and achieve the desired finished project.

Figure 1–10
GSI PCB CADD system includes a 19-inch color graphics display that enables the designer to display, simultaneously or separately, up to eight levels of data in seven colors. (Courtesy Gerber Scientific Instruments Co.)

All CAD/CAM systems have at least one **input device**. Many systems have several such devices, each for a different function.

This section discusses alphanumeric keyboards, function boxes, light pens, track balls, joysticks, stylus and data/graphics tablets, cursors, and digitizing tables.

The Keyboard

The **alphanumeric keyboard**, which is part of all CADD workstations, looks something like a typewriter keyboard (Figure 1–11). The drafter/designer communicates with the system by typing in the commands that tell it what to do. Location of coordinate information can be keyed as well.

The keyboard contains a number of key positions depending on the system, including a basic upper-case and lower-case alphanumeric group, special symbol keys, and a numeric pad (Figure 1–12). The numeric pad allows for high-speed entry of purely numeric data and is used instead of or in addition to the numeric keys on the top row of the keyboard. The menu can be used interchangeably with the keyboard.

Several kinds of alphanumeric keyboards are commonly used with CAD/CAM graphics terminals. The conventional typewriterlike alphanumeric keyboard, shown in Figure 1–11, allows the drafter/designer to enter commands, symbols, and text as well as to request information. One of the most important uses of the keyboard is for *annotation*, which is the process of inserting notes or text (words and numbers) on a drawing.

Figure 1–11
CADD keyboard.

The typewriter keyboard permits the drafter/designer to enter messages consisting of letters, numbers, mathematical computations, and other symbols into the computer storage. As the message or text is composed, it is displayed on the screen for verification or editing before the content is entered into the computer's main storage unit. The keyboard also controls the screen location of a movable **cursor** symbol (e.g., dash, blinking box, cross, or other marker) that is displayed where the next character will be entered.

Figure 1–12
Calma CAE workstation.
(Courtesy Calma
Company, a wholly-
owned subsidiary of
General Electric
Company, U.S.A.)

Keyboards also may include special graphics buttons, as shown in Figures 1–10 and 1–13, which move a cursor up or down and left or right, and transmit memory file content back to the host computer. Alphanumeric terminals often have keys to provide zoom, paging, and other functions.

In many cases, the CAD/CAM terminal is equipped with a separate box containing program-controlled pushbuttons (called a *function box* or button box). The function box can be integrated into the main keyboard or housed separately as shown in Figure 1–14.

The number of **function keys** varies from about eight to eighty. The function identified with each button is generally under computer control and can be changed as the program progresses or when a new application program is activated on the system. In some systems, the buttons can be labeled with an overlay, and the overlay can be changed with each application program. In other applications, the buttons are simply numbered and the function of each button is included in a user-selectable **menu**, which is part of the workstation. In a few systems, the pushbuttons are aligned along the edge of the CRT.

Sometimes buttons are illuminated, often under program control (Figure 1–15). A lighted button can tell the drafter/designer that the computer has received a command. The program also can illuminate buttons that are active for the portion of the program being worked on. This simplifies the task of determining which functions are active in a complex program.

An example of a function box is the CADAM system (Figure 1–16), which provides a function keyboard box with thirty-two keys, twenty-four for the CADAM program. A removable overlay template with applicable terminology is placed over these buttons. This overlay can be replaced for other programs.

Figure 1–13
CADD stand-alone station. (Courtesy Tektronix Inc.)

Figure 1–14
Graphics system using a
light pen and a function
box. (Courtesy
International Business
Machines Corporation)

Data Graphics Tablet and Stylus

The most common input device is the data graphics tablet with a stylus,
shown in Figure 1–17. The **data tablet** is an electronic unit that consists of
a rectangular grid of X and Y lines. Generators within the tablet pulse the
lines, producing discrete code signals in response to a pencillike stylus
moved by the drafter/designer (Figure 1–18). The computer determines the
location of the stylus by decoding the stylus signal. This decoded information
is displayed on the CRT in the form of a line or spot (cursor symbol) corresponding to the stylus position.

Figure 1–15
CADD system using
function box, stylus, data
tablet, and joystick.
(Courtesy Adage, Inc.)

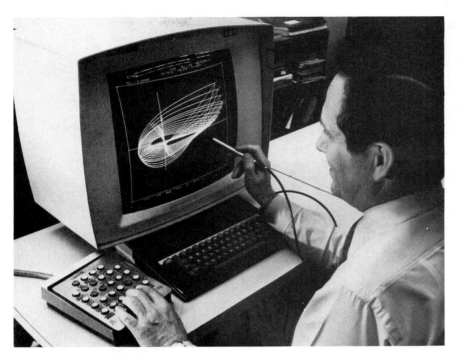

Figure 1–16
CADD operator design on the CRT with a light pen. (Courtesy Lockheed-California Co.)

Most data tablets allow some separation between the stylus and the tablet surface. That is, the stylus need not be in contact with the tablet surface. Therefore, a drawing can be placed on the data tablet to enable the drafter/designer to translate drawing coordinates into digital form, a process called *digitizing*. The digitizing feature is very important in many computer-aided

Figure 1–17
Data tablet. (Courtesy Houston Instrument)

Figure 1–18
Calma's CAE system uses a stylus and digitizing tablet for data input. (Courtesy Calma Company, a wholly-owned subsidiary of General Electric Company, U.S.A.)

design and data analysis applications. *Digitizers* are devices that convert coordinate information into numeric form readable by a digital computer. Some CAD/CAM systems use a sheet overlay to develop unique menus for program control. Designers do not need a separate button box or function box, nor do they have to list all the alternatives on the face of the screen; they simply draw a menu or a series of controls on a sheet of paper placed on the tablet, as shown in Figure 1–19. Tablets are available in sizes from 6 × 8 inches up to several feet in length and width, so the menu can either be very large or simply occupy a part of the area used to digitize drawings. A data tablet with menu digitizing capability is called a *digitizing tablet* if small (Figure 1–20) and a *digitizing table* if large.

Tablets without digitizing options are called **data/graphics tablets**. The graphics tablet shown in Figure 1–17 has a surface area that corresponds to the display area of the CRT. By moving a stylus, the drafter/designer can position the display cursor symbol on the CRT. Instead of a tablet menu, a **display menu** appears along the side or top portion of the CRT. Menu commands are entered with the stylus, which positions the cursor over the desired menu function displayed on the screen. Screen menus will be discussed in more detail later in this chapter.

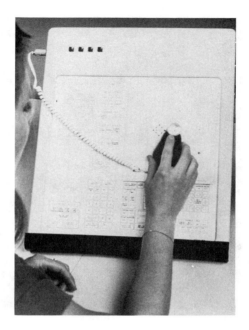

Figure 1–19
Graphics tablet with electronics menu. (Courtesy Bausch and Lomb)

Digitizing Tables

Digitizing tables are available for most CADD systems (see Figure 1–21). The cursor control for some tables is mounted on the drafting machine–like track guide, an arrangement that provides very accurate digitizing. Digitizer stations allow the drafter/designer to enter existing drawings and sketches into the system quickly and easily (Figure 1–22). A drawing is first taped to the digitizer board. The drafter/designer then defines the scale of the drawing

Figure 1–20
Bit pad. (Courtesy Auto-trol Technology Corp.)

Figure 1–21
Digitizing table.
(Reprinted with
permission from
Computervision
Corporation, Bedford,
Massachusetts)

Figure 1–22
Digitizing table.
(Courtesy Houston
Instrument)

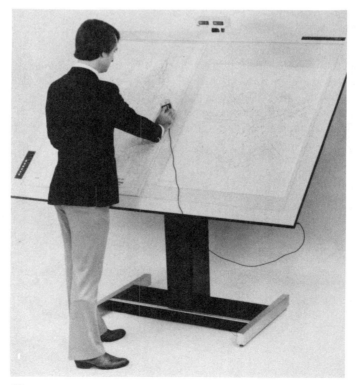

and enters it with the electronic cursor. The digitizer is commonly used to enter rough sketches into the system for later annotation and changes. The drafter/designer in Figure 1–23 is digitizing an electronic diagram sketch with a **puck**. The close-up view in Figure 1–24 shows the puck's control buttons and the **crosshairs** used for positioning. The buttons are used for X and Y data to be sent to the computer and for other "drawing" functions.

The digitizer can be used to input from a rough schematic or large layout drawing, input and edit from checkplots, or perform freehand edits of previously stored drawings. In conjunction with the interactive screen and the alphanumeric keyboard, the input/edit workstation provides complete access to an interactive CADD system for input and editing of graphical and textual information.

Light Pen

The **light pen** is a pen-shaped electrophoto-optical device that allows the user to identify a particular element directly on the display screen (Figure 1–25) or to select a particular function from the menu. A light pen also can be used to position dimensioning elements. In many ways, a light pen is more versatile than a stylus. A **stylus** is restricted to coordinate input or menu selection from a data tablet or digitizer table. A **light pen**, on the other hand, can be used to directly *draw on* the CRT display surface. *A stylus cannot be used to draw directly on the display device*. This means that the light pen can be placed against the display screen, whereas the stylus is limited to inputting from the digitizing tablet.

Figure 1–23
CADD operator digitizing a schematic diagram from a sketch. (Courtesy Houston Instrument)

Figure 1–24
12-button puck used to digitize a sketch. (Courtesy Bausch & Lomb)

Figure 1–25
CADAM system permits display screens like this one to be used simultaneously by designers in many scattered locations. Each display unit is connected to a central computer. Here, the operator makes changes in the design of a truck. She uses an electronic pen and a keyboard, instead of the traditional drafter's tools, to alter the drawing. (Courtesy Lockheed-California Co.)

The term *light pen* is a misnomer. The light pen does not write with light, but instead detects changing light as it appears on the screen. The pen may use a photodiode or a phototransistor as the light-sensitive element. It also may use a fiber-optics bundle to pipe the light to a higher-sensitivity, faster-response photomultiplier.

On refresh stroke-writing tubes, the events on the screen occur in time sequence even though to the eye they appear simultaneously. A light pen pointed on the screen, as shown in Figure 1–25, detects light at a discrete time and generates a computer interrupt command at that time. The computer software generally decides what to do about the interrupt command.

The light pen can be used for either pointing (selecting) or drawing. It can be used to point to information already on the screen, to designate a location on the screen where information is to appear, or to enter information directly (see Figures 1–7 and 1–14).

Before the light pen can be used to create graphics, a **tracking symbol** (cursor symbol, frequently a *plus* sign) must appear on the screen. The software makes the tracking symbol follow the pen as it moves across the screen. In effect, the hardware and software system is an optical tracking loop. By activating the appropriate function keys, the drafter/designer can designate what action the system is to take as a result of light pen motion — either to draw a series of dots along the light pen path or to connect the starting position with the present pen position.

In a random position, stroke-writing system, a light pen *hit* anywhere on an individual line or character completely defines that line or character, since no other graphic function can occur at the same time. Because of timing problems with the light pen, various kinds of position-detecting devices are often used with CAD/CAM systems. These devices let the drafter/designer simultaneously develop changing X and Y signals to direct a cursor on the screen. The drafter/designer indicates a particular point (e.g., the desired starting point of a line or arc) by pressing a button or other control when the cursor appears at that location on the screen.

Cursor Controls

The simplest way to generate cursor movement is by separate X and Y cursor control keys or knobs. Many special cursor controls are available for CADD systems, including the puck shown in Figure 1–26, the track ball shown in Figure 1–27, and the joystick shown in Figure 1–28. Each of these devices may be used by the drafter/designer to manually enter coordinates in specific X, Y, and Z registers.

The **track ball** (Figure 1–27) is a device that mechanically couples a control element to both the X and Y generators so that a single drafter/designer motion can drive both transducers simultaneously. The track ball uses a rolling ball to drive the transducers.

Figure 1–26
The HIPAD digitizer (11 inches × 11 inches) features a resolution of .005 inches and the ability to address up to 100 coordinate pairs per second. (Courtesy Houston Instrument)

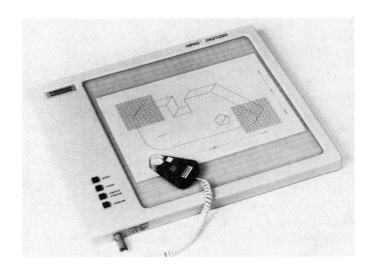

The **joystick** (Figure 1–28) is similar to the track ball except that it provides a small, batlike handle that the drafter/designer moves.

A few microcomputer-based CADD systems use a **mouse** as their primary means of input (Figure 1–29). A mouse is moved about a small pad or, in some cases, directly on any flat surface; its movement controls the position of the screen cursor. A digitizing tablet and menu are not used with this system. Buttons on the mouse allow the drafter/designer to quickly input screen menu commands or positions on the screen.

Two basic kinds of mice are available: mechanical and optical. *Mechanical mice* use rollers or two wheels mounted perpendicular to one another. *Optical mice* use LEDs and light detectors to detect motion and direction. Optical mice are moved on a reflector surface with a grid consisting of vertical and horizontal lines on a silver background.

Figure 1–27
Track ball. (Reprinted with permission from Computervision Corporation, Bedford, Massachusetts)

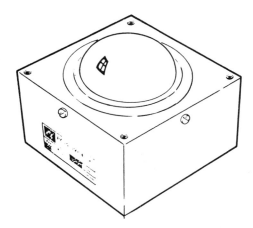

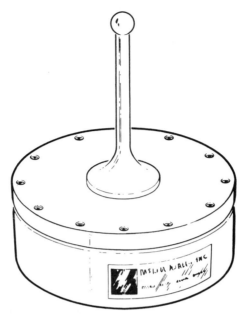

Figure 1–28
Joystick. (Reprinted with permission from Computervision Corporation, Bedford, Massachusetts)

Thumbwheels are also available on some systems. One thumbwheel controls the movement of the screen cursor in the X direction and the other in the Y direction. Movement of both wheels at the same time moves the cursor at an angle across the display screen.

Menus

A **menu** is an input device consisting of command squares (Figure 1–30) on a digitizing surface such as a tablet or table. The menu eliminates the need to use the keyboard for entering graphical or common command data. A menu tablet allows the selection of the most commonly used tasks for a par-

Figure 1–29
Mouse used as an input device. (Courtesy Mouse Systems Corp.)

Figure 1–30
Digitizing tablet menu with command squares used for allocation of menu commands.

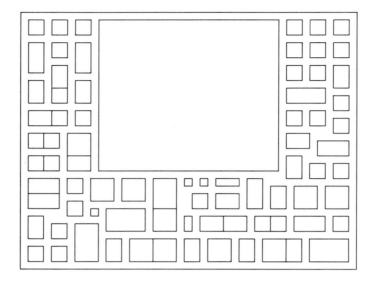

ticular design field. Menus are available for constructing simple to complex graphics (Figure 1–31). Specific engineering disciplines also have menus, such as the one shown in Figure 1–32 for electronic design, drafting, and engineering work and the mechanical design menu shown in Figure 1–33. Drafter/designers can change or create new menus as required.

Each square on the menu can represent a specific command. For example, instead of typing in the command to draw a line, the drafter/designer

Figure 1–31
General drafting menu.

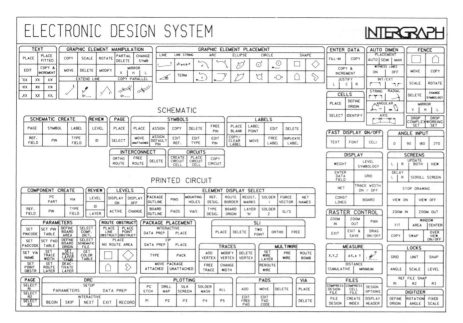

Figure 1–32
Menu for electronic
design. (Courtesy
Intergraph Corp.)

activates a menu square that performs this command. Each menu square
can be programmed to perform a particular function or a series of operations.
A menu also allows the drafter/designer to customize the CADD system
since commands can be defined to suit the needs of the drafter/designer or
company standards.

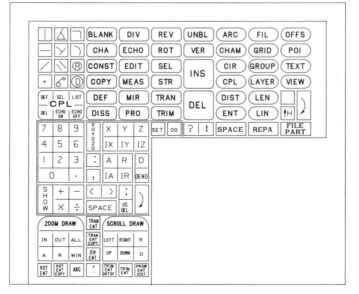

Figure 1–33
Mechanical drafting and
design menu.

To use a menu, the drafter/designer simply places the cursor crosshairs, stylus end, or light pen point over the desired command and presses the cursor button or function key (Figures 1–31 and 1–34). Most systems have commands that allow frequently changed parameter options such as letter heights and slant to be displayed on the alphanumeric screen for drafter/designer inspection or modification.

The menu shows the commonly used symbols and commands of a particular engineering field. Since not all symbols can be placed on a menu, a typical system has the capability to create and hold a large drafting library containing all the needed symbols, drawings, or figures — nuts, bolts, screws, electrical symbols, welding symbols, and component outlines. The library is basically a template; it can be added to or subtracted from as necessary. A drafter/designer typically collects and customizes figures or symbols from the drafting library, creates any special figures that will be used repeatedly, and assembles them into special menus.

As previously mentioned, **_screen menus_** are also available. The screen display menu shown in Figure 1–35 is used to initiate drawing functions, place symbols, and change menus. The graphics tablet and cursor control

Figure 1–34
CADD operator doing a stress test on a part. (Reprinted with permission from Computervision Corporation, Bedford, Massachusetts)

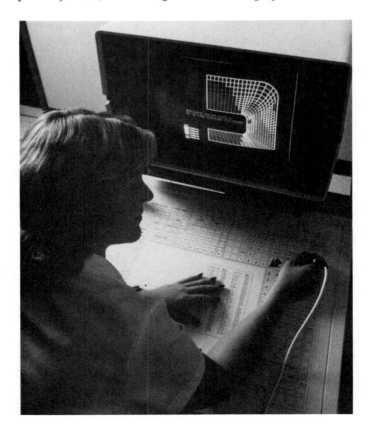

are used to enter the commands. This system does not use the digitizing tablet for a menu overlay.

Although the number of figures on a menu may be limited because of size and space, the number of menus is not. The typical menu item is inserted with a few keystrokes. Each symbol can be inserted at any angle or scale. The symbol or figure can be as simple as an electronic diagram symbol (Figure 1–36) or as complex as a complete printed circuit board. Once the menu symbol or part is created, it can be stored and used any number of times in other drawings. Figure 1–37 shows some common symbols available for an on-screen menu used in electronic design.

Function Devices

The following is a description of one type of function device and its capabilities. The image control unit (ICU) is part of Computervision's design workstation (Figure 1–38).

The Image Control Unit (ICU)

The ICU has twelve switches and eight buttons that perform various functions affecting the images displayed on the screen. The ICU allows the drafter/designer to control a variety of display characteristics for text and graphics. More important, it allows the drafter/designer to dynamically rotate, scroll, or zoom, making the construction and viewing of geometry easier. The following is a simple overview of one manufacturer's function-and-display device.

The eight buttons located on the bottom half of the image control unit control real-time dynamics capabilities (Figure 1–39). *Real-time dynamics* is

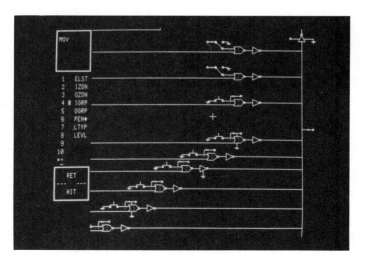

Figure 1–35
Drawing and screen menu displayed on the CRT. (Courtesy Bruning)

Figure 1–36
Calma's TEAGStation is an engineering workstation. (Courtesy Calma Company, a wholly-owned subsidiary of General Electric Company, U.S.A.)

a term that refers to the control and manipulation of the geometry that represents the model (part design). This geometry can be:

- Enlarged or decreased in size (ZOOM)

- Moved in any direction within the graphics area of the screen (SCROLL or PAN)

- Rotated about any one of several available axes (ROTATE)

The *real-time* aspect of this manipulation means that the drafter/designer sees the model geometry as if it were in a movie. That is, the movement is continuous and controlled entirely by pressing a particular sequence of buttons on the ICU.

Dynamics display buttons: There are four dynamics buttons labeled from left to right: RESET, ZOOM, SCROLL, and ROTATE (Figure 1–39).

- *ROTATE*: The ROTATE button, effective with three-dimensional models, rotates the model relative to its center.

- *SCROLL*: The SCROLL button allows the drafter/designer to move graphics around on the display screen to any location.

- *ZOOM*: The ZOOM button allows the drafter/designer to either enlarge or reduce the image on the display.

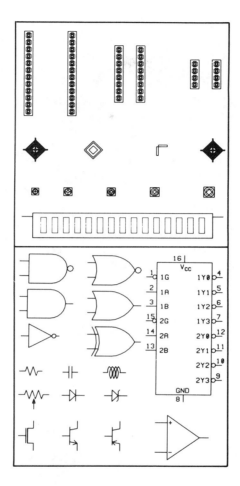

Figure 1–37
Display menu showing symbol options.

- *RESET:* The RESET button sets the image in the last position, which was defined using the other buttons. The RESET button is also used to stop the dynamic movement controlled by the ICU.

The dynamics display buttons control the *type* of motion that affects the image. To move between dynamics functions (e.g., change from ROTATE to ZOOM), simply press the desired dynamics display button and then use the directional buttons to control the motion of the graphics.

Directional buttons: Four buttons, located under the dynamics display buttons, control the *direction* of motion. Each button moves the image in a direction indicated by an arrow symbol (Figure 1–39). The dynamic effects of each button along with a particular function are shown in Figure 1–40.

When the up-arrow button is pressed in the

Figure 1–38
Image control unit (ICU) used on Computervision's design system.

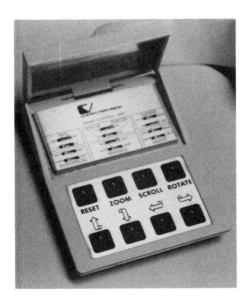

- ZOOM mode, it enlarges (zooms up) the size of the image.

- SCROLL mode, it moves the image up, toward the top of the display screen.

- ROTATE mode, it rotates or spins the image in place, bottom over top.

Figure 1–39
The ICU has four dynamics buttons and four directional buttons for control of its real-time dynamic capabilities. (Reprinted with permission from Computervision Corporation, Bedford, Massachusetts)

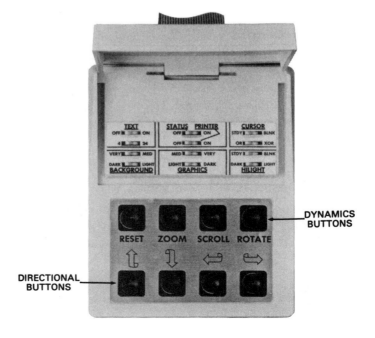

When the down-arrow button is pressed in the

- ZOOM mode, it decreases (zooms down) the size of the image.
- SCROLL mode, it moves the graphics down, toward the bottom of the screen.
- ROTATE mode, it rotates or spins the graphics in place, top over bottom.

When the left-arrow button is pressed in the

- SCROLL mode, it moves the image to the left.
- ROTATE mode, it spins the image in place, right to left.

When the right-arrow button is pressed in the

- SCROLL mode, it moves the image to the right.
- ROTATE mode, it spins the image in place, left to right.

The left-arrow and right-arrow buttons are not used in the ZOOM mode and will have no effect.

Figures 1–41, 1–42, and 1–43 show examples of the zoom, scroll, and rotate capabilities. The ICU also provides a means to control the *degree* of zooming, scrolling, and rotating for the displayed image. Parameters (controlling values) can be defined for each specific directional button. For example, each time the directional button is pushed in the ROTATE mode, the image will rotate five degrees (the default is ten degrees).

DYNAMICS FROM IMAGE CONTROL UNIT			
DIRECTION ⬆	⬇	⬅	➡
ZOOM ZOOM IN	ZOOM OUT	NO EFFECT	NO EFFECT
SCROLL SCROLL UP	SCROLL DOWN	SCROLL LEFT	SCROLL RIGHT
ROTATE ROTATE BOTTOM OVER TOP	ROTATE TOP OVER BOTTOM	ROTATE RIGHT TOWARDS LEFT	ROTATE LEFT TOWARDS RIGHT

Figure 1–40
This table illustrates the effects of activating the ICU's dynamics features and specified directional buttons. (Reprinted with permission from Computervision Corporation, Bedford, Massachusetts)

Figure 1–41
This series of panels illustrates the dynamic feature of zooming. Each panel represents the graphics area of the CRT. Panels 1 through 4 show a sequence of zooming up (increasing) the display size of a circle. Panels 5 through 8 show a sequence of zooming down (decreasing) the circle's display size. (Reprinted with permission from Computervision Corporation, Bedford, Massachusetts)

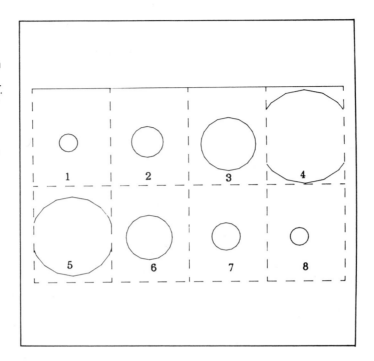

Figure 1–42
This series of panels illustrates the dynamics feature of scrolling. Each panel represents the graphics area of the CRT. Panels 1 through 4 show scrolling a rectangle to the right. Panels 5 through 8 show the rectangle scrolled up, scrolled down, and scrolled diagonally. (Reprinted with permission from Computervision Corporation, Bedford, Massachusetts)

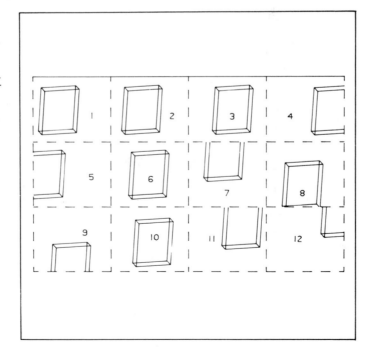

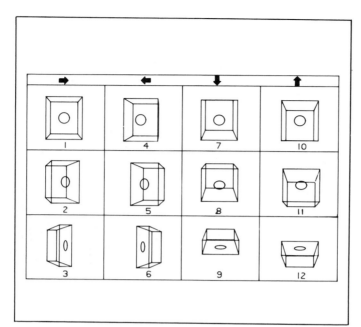

Figure 1–43
This series of panels illustrates the dynamics feature of rotation. Panels 1 through 3 show the geometry rotated to the left. Panels 4 through 6 show the geometry rotated to the right. Panels 7 through 9 show the geometry rotated bottom over top. Panels 10 through 12 show the geometry rotated top over bottom. (Reprinted with permission from Computervision Corporation, Bedford, Massachusetts)

This description of the image control unit is meant only to acquaint the CAD/CAM student with an example of a function device and its capabilities. All CAD/CAM systems are not alike, and in general, each has its own special functions and input device.

GLOSSARY

AIMING DEVICE   A pattern of light activated by a light pen on the display surface to assist positioning of the pen and to describe the pen's field of view. (See cursor.)

ALPHANUMERIC DISPLAY   A display that shows letters, numbers, and special characters. It allows the designer to enter commands and to receive messages from the system.

ALPHANUMERIC KEYBOARD   A typewriter-like keyboard that allows a designer to communicate with the system.

ANNOTATION   Text, notes, or identification on a drawing, map, or diagram.

CATHODE RAY TUBE (CRT)   A display device that creates images with a beam of electrons striking a screen.

CROSSHAIRS   On a cursor, a horizontal line intersected by a vertical line to indicate a point on the display whose coordinates are desired.

CURSOR   A special character, such as a small cross, on the screen that follows every movement of the stylus, light pen, or joystick.

DISPLAY   The part of the workstation that shows the image of the data so that a designer can view it; usually refers to a cathode ray tube.

DISPLAY DEVICE   A device capable of presenting, on a viewing surface or image area, the display elements that visually represent data (e.g., CRT).

DISPLAY MENU   An option listed on a display allowing a designer to select the next action by indicating one or more choices with an input device.

FLICKER   The flashing on and off of the image on the screen.

FUNCTION KEY   An area on the digitizing tablet or a key on a box or terminal that is used to enter a command.

FUNCTION KEYBOARD   A part of the workstation that contains a number of function keys.

FUNCTION MENU   The display or list of commands that the designer can use to perform a task.

GRAPHICS TABLET   A surface through which coordinate points can be transmitted using a cursor or stylus; another term for a digitizing tablet.

INPUT   To enter data or a program into the system.

INPUT DEVICE   Devices such as graphic tablets or keyboards that allow the designer to input data into the CADD system.

JAGGIES   The jagged or sawtoothed appearance of lines on the screen when it has low resolution.

JOYSTICK   A CADD data entry device that uses a hand-controlled lever to move the cursor manually on the screen to enter the coordinates of various points.

KEYBOARD   Resembles a typewriter and is used to enter instructions to the computer.

LIGHT PEN   A penlike device used in conjunction with a vector-refresh screen that identifies displayed elements from the light source on the screen.

MENU   A table of available commands, either on a digitizing tablet or on the screen, that can be selected instead of using the keyboard.

MONITOR   A display for computer output. Either monochrome or full color, a monitor is most often a cathode ray tube.

MOUSE   A hand-held data entry device, about the size of a cigarette pack, which can be used without a digitizing pad. It can be used like a puck.

NUMERIC KEYPAD   A calculator-type numeric input device that is generally part of the keyboard.

PIXELS   PICture ELements. Individual dots on a display screen that are illuminated to create an image. Pixels are evenly spaced on the display.

PUCK   A hand-held input device that enables the designer to digitize a drawing placed on the digitizer surface.

RASTER DISPLAY   A CADD workstation display in which the entire screen surface is a matrix of pixels and the image is scanned at a constant refresh rate. The bright, flicker-free image can be selectively written and erased.

RASTER SCAN   A line-by-line sweep across the entire screen surface to generate the image. The device can display a large amount of information without flicker.

REMOTE TERMINAL   An input or output peripheral located at a distance from the computer.

REPEATABILITY (OF DISPLAY DEVICE)   A measure of the hardware accuracy or the coincidence of successive retraces of a display element.

RESOLUTION   The smallest spacing between points on a graphic device at which the points can be distinguished.

SCREEN   A computer display device; also called a monitor or cathode ray tube.

STORAGE TUBE   A CRT that retains an image for a considerable period of time without redrawing. It allows no selective editing or erasing.

STYLUS   A hand-held object that provides coordinate input to the display device.

TABLET   An input device that a designer can use to digitize coordinate data or enter commands into a CADD system by means of a stylus or puck; also called a digitizing pad.

TERMINAL   A device equipped with a keyboard and some kind of display that sends and receives information over a communication channel to and from a computer.

THUMBWHEELS   A CADD input device that uses a manually controlled vertical wheel for locating a coordinate on the Y axis, and a horizontal wheel for locating a coordinate on the X axis.

TRACK   To cause the display device to follow and display or determine the position of a moving input device such as the writing tip of a stylus.

TRACKING   Moving a cursor across the surface of the screen with a light pen, stylus, or puck.

TRACKING SYMBOL   A symbol such as a cross, dot, angle, or square used for indicating the position of a stylus.

WORKSTATION   The hardware by which a designer interacts with the computer; also called a terminal.

QUIZ

True or False

1. Light pen and electronic pen/stylus are different names for the same device.

2. Raster CRTs paint the image on the screen by stroking vectors.

3. A stylus and a graphics tablet are the most common type of input devices used on CADD systems.

4. Menus can be used interchangeably with a keyboard.

5. A stylus must come in contact with the digitizing surface in order to input data.

6. Tablets without menu options are data tablets.

7. Thumbwheels are used to control the X, Y, and Z positions of the screen cursor.

8. A screen or display menu is activated with a stylus and graphics tablet.

Fill in the Blank

9. A stylus _____ be used to draw on the display device.

10. A _____ is normally displayed on the screen by a flashing _____ or other type of _____.

11. The two basic kinds of _____ that are available are _____ _____ and optical.

12. The number of _____ squares or figures is limited on a menu, but the total number of _____ is not.

13. A typical CADD _____ has a keyboard, _____ and _____, and a CRT.

14. A ____ ____ ____ is used to display graphics on a CADD system.

15. Raster CRTS operate by _____ sending a beam across the _____.

16. Dual screens are used to divide _____ from _____.

Answer the Following

17. Describe the differences between a stylus and a light pen.

18. What is a function box and what is it used for?

19. List the types of display devices and describe their operation.

20. Explain the difference between a digitizing tablet, digitizing table, and a data tablet.

21. What do the following input devices do and how are they similar in purpose: puck, joystick, track ball, thumbwheels, and mouse?

22. What are crosshairs and on what input device are they found?

23. What is a light pen and with what type of CRT is it used?

24. Define real-time.

Chapter

2

Output Devices

Objectives

Upon completion of this chapter, the reader will be able to:

- List the major types of output devices
- Group plotters by their method of operation
- Define repeatability and resolution as they relate to plotting devices
- Discuss the different types of pens used on electromechanical plotters
- Explain the reasons for using a specific type of plotter for different applications
- Identify the types of printers and explain their differences
- List the types of hardcopy units and how each type operates, why it is used, and for what application it is best suited

Introduction

Most graphical information will be drawn (**output**) in a form that is familiar and easy to use. In engineering, design, and drafting work, this output normally takes the form of a drawing. In the past, the design was sketched by the engineer or designer, laid out by the layout designer, and detailed by the drafter using paper as the drawing medium. Since CADD has eliminated hand-drawn graphics, the computer-aided design system must transfer the geometry to paper after it is created and stored by the operator. Output devices receive this graphic information via a communications link between the device and the computer. The hardcopy unit converts the **_soft copy_** (the engineering drawing saved in the computer) into a **_hard copy_** (a drawing). This drawing can be plotted by a variety of devices that _draw_ in ink. These devices create perfect _original_ drawings in a fraction of the time it takes to produce the same drawing by hand.

Printers are hardcopy units that can print out copies of alphanumeric data or make _quick look_ copies of screen graphics (i.e., what is on the CRT). Other types of output devices are also available. The choice of unit depends upon the engineering or design application, the quality of graphic output needed, and the quantity of drawings required. The quantity needed will influence the choice of plotter since plotters vary greatly in speed. This chapter provides an overview of the major types of equipment normally associated with CADD output.

Hardcopy Devices

Output from CADD systems can take many forms. The most common is a drawing just like the one created on a drafting board. This drawing is created

Figure 2–1
High-speed 14-pen plotter for C- and D-size plots. (Courtesy Houston Instrument)

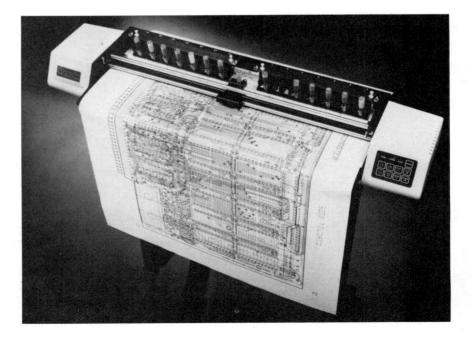

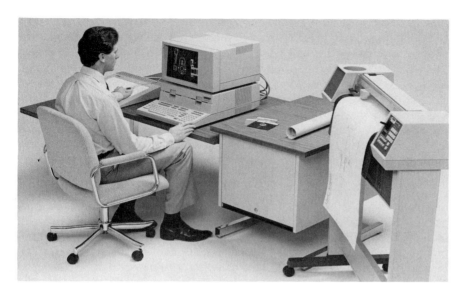

Figure 2–2
Bruning CADD system includes terminal, digitizer pad, and plotter.

by a **plotter** (Figures 2–1 and 2–2). Output also can be a simple copy of what is on the screen, called a **hard copy/screen copy**. A hard copy normally comes from a printer or plotter attached directly to the workstation. A drawing can be obtained from a plotter, or be "drawn" on microfilm. This is called **computer output microfilm (COM)**. Output is not always a drawing. Sometimes the output is a magnetic tape containing instructions for a particular machine to make the part that has been designed. This form of output is called *numerical control (NC)*. The output could also be a report produced on a line printer. Artwork for printed circuit design or integrated circuit design can be produced on a photoplotter.

Output devices include printers, plotters, and photocopy equipment. Printers provide the user with alphanumeric hard copy such as material lists. The plotter allows the user to produce drawings on paper, vellum, or drafting film in multiple colors. Some plotters are limited by the size of the plotting surface. Others can plot drawings of any length, although they are limited to standard paper widths. Pen plotters can use ballpoint pens, felt tip pens, or liquid ink pens. Check copies are normally run with inexpensive ballpoint pens. *Final* high-quality drawings are plotted with liquid ink pens. When plotting a drawing, the operator has many options: to scale the drawing, to rotate it, to select the colors to plot, and to select different line widths. Not all plotters have these options.

Plotters

A variety of plotters is used with CAD/CAM systems: pen plotters, electrostatic plotters, and computer output microfilm (COM). In the past, electrostatic plotters were used primarily for *quick look* capability. However, electrostatic plotters are now of such high quality that they are considered one of the primary hardcopy devices for CAD/CAM systems.

In a CAD/CAM system, plotters and displays complement each other. A display is capable of rapidly presenting a picture so that the user can react to it, perhaps making changes interactively. A plotter, on the other hand, can generally make large, highly accurate drawings, but more slowly. Displays are used to make the initial decisions, and plotters are used to make the record copies. A low-cost, two-dimensional CADD system is shown in Figure 2–3. This system is composed of a display (CRT), keyboard, digitizing pad, and a D-size pen plotter.

The accuracy of a hardcopy plot is considerably better than the accuracy and quality of the image on the display. A computer defines all graphics as coordinate points. Therefore, all graphics on a CADD system are made of straight-line elements. The closer the points of a curve are spaced, the greater a system's resolution. ***Resolution is the smallest spacing between points on a graphic device at which the points can be detected as distinct***. The degree of resolution influences the quality of the plotted drawing since curves appear as a series of straight lines if the resolution is poor. Since the holes, fillets, and other circular entities appear as curves and

Figure 2–3
Microcomputer based two-dimensional CADD system. (Courtesy T&W Systems)

not as straight-line elements, the resolution of the pen plotter used to plot Figure 2–4 can be considered good.

Pen Plotters

CAD/CAM systems use electromechanical **pen plotters** to plot data and make engineering drawings. Two basic kinds of pen plotters are currently used. The earliest and perhaps most widely used type is the **drum plotter** (Figure 2–5). Plot paper is wrapped around the drum, and the drum is rotated by a digital stepping motor. The rotation provides one deflection axis, while the pen, mounted on a gantry across the drum, provides the other deflection axis. The only other basic control, besides X and Y deflection, is the control to move the pen up and down. Drum plotters are available in sizes from $8\frac{1}{2}$ inches to more than 42 inches wide. They make plots of any length quickly. The smaller drum plotters make lines in incremental steps, approximately .005 to .01 inches apart, with plotting rates of around 5 inches per second. The less expensive drum plotters show steps similar to the *jaggies* on a digital TV displaying a diagonal line. Like most others, these plotters may operate on-line when directly connected to the CPU, or they may operate off-line through a remote magnetic tape unit. Either ballpoint, felt tip, or ink pens

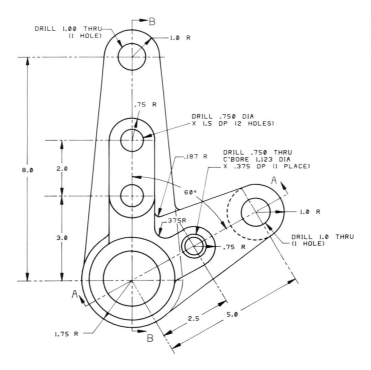

Figure 2–4
CADD plot of a mechanical drawing.

Figure 2–5
High-quality drum plotter
can make plots of
unlimited length.
(Courtesy Houston
Instrument)

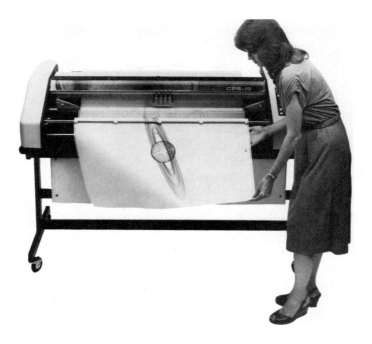

may be used. This unit is easy and convenient to use, placing lines on the paper or mylar at rates of up to 30 inches per second. In Figure 2–6, a close-up view of plotter pens shows four ink pens being used to plot a drawing. Figure 2–7 shows a multiple pen plotter capable of plotting in different colors and with a variety of pen widths.

Early drum plotters were excellent for plotting data, but because of their relatively poor line quality, they were not adequate for most engineering drawings. Later, high-speed drum plotters became available, which satisfied the image quality requirements. The pen plotter shown in Figure 2–8 plots drawings up to B size and is relatively inexpensive. The illustration of the plotter shown in Figure 2–9 shows the platen surface in relation to X and Y coordinates.

Flatbed plotters (Figure 2–10) also were marketed to satisfy the need for high-quality large drawings. Plotters ranging from about 11 × 17 inches to as much as 4 feet × 12 feet are available with repeatability of .001 inches. A small flatbed plotter is shown in Figure 2–11.

Repeatability is a measure of the hardware accuracy of successive retraces of a display element (e.g., a line) — *in other words, it is the ability of the device to retrace a given line exactly*. Flatbed plotters are suitable for the most exacting engineering requirements, including the making of templates and artwork for semiconductor chips. The plotter shown in Figure 2–12 is a precision flatbed plotter capable of extremely high repeatability and resolution.

Figure 2–6
Four-pen plotter.
(Reprinted with permission from Computervision Corporation, Bedford, Massachusetts)

Figure 2–7
Multiple-pen plotters can plot drawings with different colors and line widths. (Courtesy Houston Instrument)

Figure 2–8
Pen plotter. (Courtesy
Houston Instrument)

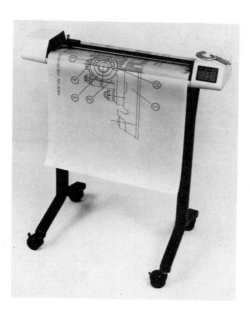

In electronic printed-circuit artwork applications, the pen may be re-placed by a light and the conventional drafting paper by photosensitive paper. Alternately, the pen may be replaced by a knife scriber and the paper by a peel-coat material such as rubylith. Flatbed plotting speeds range from about 4 to 40 inches per second. The price of these units varies from several thousand dollars to well over $150,000.

As the name suggests, a **flatbed plotter** has a flat horizontal drawing surface with the paper lying flat, suitable for highly accurate, top-quality drawings. On most flatbed plotters, the pens move and the paper remains stationary. A large flatbed plotter can accommodate up to six drawings at one time. Free-floating or carriage-driven drafting heads can reproduce lines at 20 inches per second at 0.005 inch (0.0125mm) accuracy and 0.002 inch

Figure 2–9
X and Y orientation on a
D-size pen plotter.
(Courtesy Houston
Instrument)

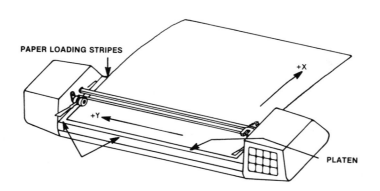

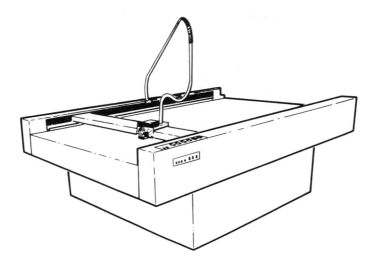

Figure 2–10
Flatbed plotter. (Reprinted with permission from Computervision Corporation, Bedford, Massachsetts)

(0.005mm) repeatability. In the large tables, a vacuum system is often used to keep the paper flat.

Many plotters are equipped with multiple pen heads, as shown in Figure 2–6, so that various line widths or colors can be plotted. A variety of pens may be used, including pencils, ballpoint pens, felt tip pens, and liquid ink pens with forced feeds.

Electrostatic Plotters

While it takes seconds (or even fractions of a second) to display an image on the CRT, the time required to plot that same drawing on a precision plotter may be several minutes.

All **electrostatic plotters** share a similar operating principle. Electric voltage is applied to an array of densely spaced writing nibs embedded in a

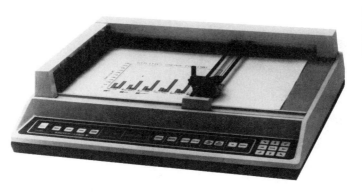

Figure 2–11
B-size format flatbed plotter. (Courtesy Houston Instrument)

Figure 2–12
Precision flatbed plotter.
(Courtesy Lockheed-
California Co.)

stationary writing head. The nibs selectively create minute electrostatic dots on the paper as the paper passes over the writing head. The paper is then exposed to liquid toner to produce a visible, permanent image. Plotting twenty to thirty times faster than pen plotters, electrostatics plot a square foot of data in a few seconds.

Figure 2–13
Electrostatic color plotter.
(Courtesy Versatec, a
Xerox Company)

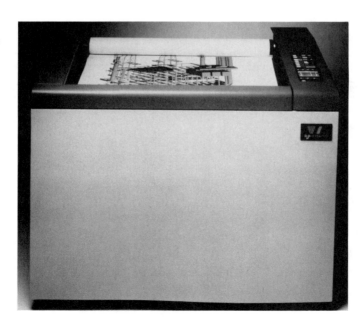

To reduce plotting time, even at the expense of some drawing quality, electrostatic plotters like the one in Figure 2–13 were developed. These plotters consist of wire nibs (styli) spaced from 100 to 400 styli per inch. As in the drum plotter, the paper's motion provides one axis of deflection. Instead of a pen moving along the other axis, however, the information is progressively *scanned* across the styli, and the styli needed to place a dot on the paper are activated.

The electrostatic plotter retains the advantage of the drum plotter — the drawing can be of unlimited length. Electrostatic plotters are available in widths of up to 6 feet. They can produce a drawing ten times faster than electromechanical plotters. A further advantage is that the electrostatic plotter can be used very effectively as a high-speed line printer. Color electrostatic plotters are also available.

Digitizer-Plotter

Just as current displays combine several techniques (storage and refresh, or stroke writing and TV), devices can combine the plotter and digitizer functions, as shown in Figure 2–14. Since the pen of the plotter is under computer control, some kind of pick-up is needed to indicate to the system the location of the pen. When a system has a digitizer, the pen can be positioned by the operator and the digital coordinates of its position can be entered into the system. Several digitizer-plotters are currently on the market.

Photoplotters

In electronics, printed circuit board artwork (drawings) is generated on a **photoplotter** (Figure 2–15). Photoplots (Figure 2–16) are extremely accurate drawings created by **plotting** the image on photosensitive film with a light beam. Photoplotters are extremely accurate since the drawing (artwork) is

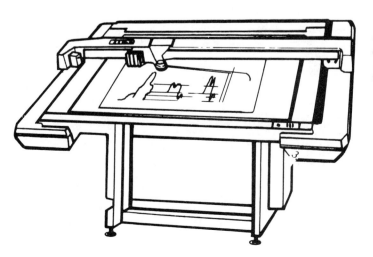

Figure 2–14
Digitizer-plotter.
(Reprinted with permission from Computervision Corporation, Bedford, Massachusetts)

Figure 2–15
Photoplotter. (Courtesy
Gerber Scientific
Instruments Co.)

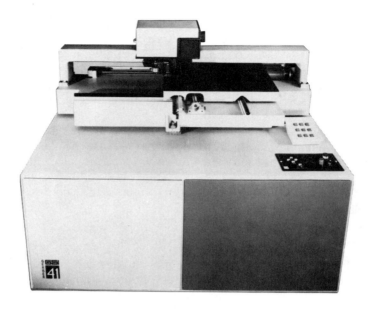

being created by a light beam whose thickness can be accurately controlled. Because of the cost associated with photoplotters, they are limited only to those applications that demand extreme accuracy.

Computer Output Microfilm (COM) Units

Drawing storage is a continual problem for large engineering facilities. Such companies may have 100,000 or more drawings that need to be stored and

Figure 2–16
Photoplot of a printed
circuit board.

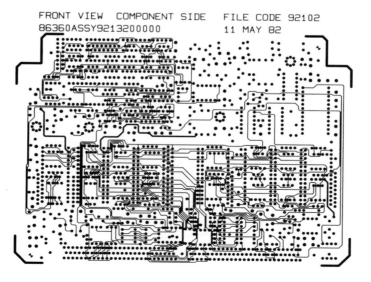

retrieved. One solution is the use of **computer output microfilm (COM)** units. Although relatively expensive, COM units provide fast and accurate plotting of drawings as large as 34 × 44 inches (E size). If the microfilm is mounted on an aperture card (Figure 2–17), drawings can be stored and retrieved easily. The operator in Figure 2–18 is viewing an aperture card on an enlarger-plotter.

The COM unit can be modified to include a color wheel (red, blue, and green filters through which the light beam is passed). This technique allows the production of high-quality, full-color animated films and 35mm slides.

COM devices operate in a manner similar to that of a photoplotter. The drawing is plotted on 35mm film with a light beam. The film is then developed to obtain a reversed negative.

Dry Silver Copies

The dry silver copier uses light-sensitive material exposed by a CRT. Dry silver hardcopy units are fast (about 12 seconds per print) and inexpensive, and they produce a dry copy. Copies are limited to $8^1/_2 \times 11^1/_2$ inches, and the copier can reproduce only what appears on the display. The copier cannot produce a hardcopy image directly from the digital display file. Dry silver copies are used for quick checks of the display graphics.

Printers

A **printer** provides the user with a hard copy of alphanumeric data, or a *quick look* rough copy of the screen graphics. A variety of printers is available. The quality of typeface and the speed of printing are two of the printer's most important features. Letter quality printers are slower and plot only character graphics. Dot matrix printers are extremely fast and plot limited-quality graphics, although the quality of the typeface is poor. Some systems use dot matrix graphic devices to obtain check prints, not for final copy drawings. Terminal/printers are used for communication with the computer (Figure

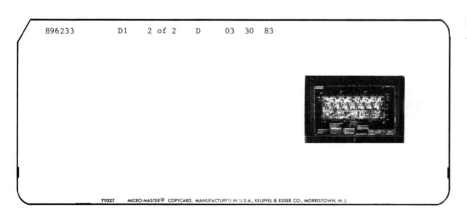

896233   D1   2 of 2   D   03 30 83

71027   MICRO-MASTER® COPYCARD, MANUFACTURED IN U.S.A., KEUFFEL & ESSER CO., MORRISTOWN, N. J.

Figure 2–17
Aperture card.

2–19). Printers are also available without an attached keyboard and are used solely for printing operations. Figure 2–20 shows a high-quality dot matrix printer and Figure 2–21, a letter quality printer. A typical dot matrix for numbers and letters is shown on a grid background in Figure 2–22. Ink jet and laser printers are now available for high-quality, high-cost printing requirements.

Output devices come in a variety of sizes and shapes, and may be matched to the output needs of the user. In general, the typical output of a CADD system will be a plotted drawing, similar to the section view of the assembly shown in Figure 2–23, the profile cut section of the flume canal shown in Figure 2–24, or the piping flow diagram shown in Figure 2–25.

Figure 2–19
Teleprinter used for
alphanumeric output and
communicating with the
CPU.

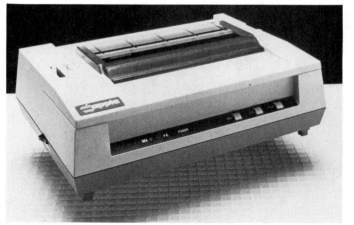

Figure 2–20
Apple Computer's dot
matrix printer. (Courtesy
Apple Computer, Inc.)

Figure 2–21
Apple Computer's letter
quality printer. (Courtesy
Apple Computer, Inc.)

Figure 2–22
Dot matrix character
formation.

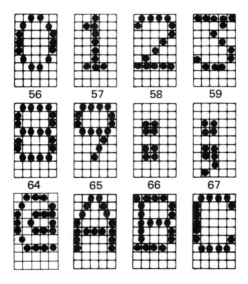

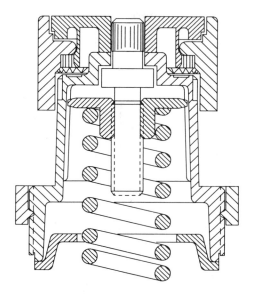

Figure 2–23
Mechanical assembly
created on a CADD
system and plotted with a
pen plotter.

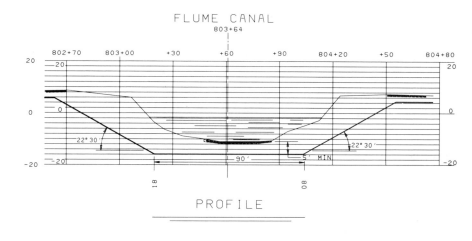

Figure 2–24
Plot of a flume canal.
(Courtesy ESI)

Figure 2–25
Piping flow diagram.
(Courtesy CALCOMP)

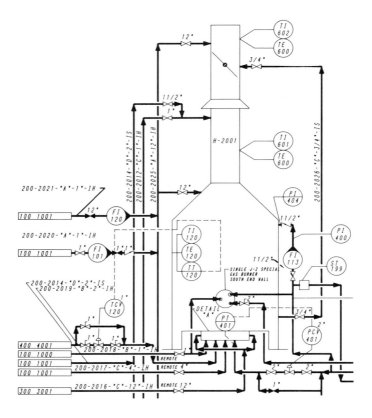

GLOSSARY

COMPUTER OUTPUT MICROFILM (COM)   The image of a drawing plotted on 35mm film at a small scale by a beam of light; microfilm containing computer-generated data.

DEVICE   A hardware item such as a cathode ray tube, plotter, printer, or hardcopy unit.

DRUM PLOTTER   An electromechanical pen plotter that draws a picture on paper or film mounted on a drum using a combination of plotting head movement and drum rotation.

ELECTROSTATIC PLOTTER   Wire nibs, spaced 100 to 400 nibs per inch, that place dots where needed on a piece of paper to generate a drawing.

FLATBED PLOTTER   An electromechanical pen plotter that draws a picture on paper, glass, or film mounted on a flat table. The plotting head provides all the motion.

HARD COPY   A copy on paper of what is shown on the screen. Hard copy is generated with an on-line printer or plotter.

HARDWARE   The computer, disk, magnetic tape, cathode ray tube, and other physical components that make up a system.

INCHES PER SECOND (IPS)   The number of inches of magnetic tape that can be recorded or read per second, or the speed of a pen plotter.

LINE PRINTER   A peripheral device that prints alphanumeric data one line at a time.

OUTPUT   The end result of a process or series of processes, such as artwork, hard copy, reports, and drawings.

OUTPUT DEVICE   Hardware, such as a printer or plotter, used to produce a copy of the results of the computer's processing operations.

PEN PLOTTER   An electromechanical output device that draws a picture on paper or film using a ballpoint pen or liquid ink.

PHOTOPLOTTER   A device used to generate artwork photographically for printed circuit boards.

PLOT   Drawing by pen or pencil of a design on paper or film to create a drawing.

PLOTTER   An automated device used to produce accurate drawings. Plotters include electrostatic, photoplotter, and electromechanical types.

PRINTER   A hardcopy unit used to produce "quick look" copies of screen graphics, alphanumeric data, or on-line documentation of commands as they were entered. Some printers have keyboards.

TELEWRITER   A typewriter-style keyboard device used to enter commands or to point out system messages. It can also be used as a printer.

QUIZ

True or False

1. Repeatability is a measure of a plotter's ability to retrace a given line exactly.

2. Electrostatic plotters output drawings of unlimited length and with high-quality line work.

3. Pen plotters using ballpoint pens are the fastest type of hardcopy device for creating drawings.

4. Printers can double as hardcopy units for alphanumeric output and "quick look" graphics.

5. Flatbed plotters are more accurate than drum plotters.

6. Photoplotters are the most accurate type of hardcopy units.

7. COM units eliminate the need for drawing storage cabinets.

8. Printed circuit board artwork can be output using a precision flatbed plotter or a photoplotter.

Fill in the Blank

9. Multiple pen electromechanical plotters can use different _____ and _____ pens.

10. Electrostatic, _____, _____, _____, and printers are hardcopy units.

11. A printer is used to output _____ data or to make quick _____ copies.

12. Photoplotters are the most _____ and expensive _____ units.

13. Flatbed and drum plotters are _____ plotters.

14. Electrostatic plotters can produce graphics of _____ length and very _____.

15. Electromechanical plotters are available with multiple _____ that can vary the line _____ and _____.

16. _____ plotters are the most common type used for engineering drawings.

Answer the Following

17. Name the two basic categories of printers and describe their uses.

18. What is a COM unit, and how can it save storage space and filing time?

19. What are the major differences between electrostatic plotters and electromechanical plotters?

20. Why would a ballpoint pen or felt tip pen be used on a pen plotter instead of a wet ink pen (technical pen) when plotting a drawing?

21. Describe the various types of electromechanical pen plotters.

22. What hardcopy unit can plot drawings of unlimited length?

23. Discuss the uses of "quick look" output devices.

24. Name the types of printers and explain the differences in their printing quality.

Chapter

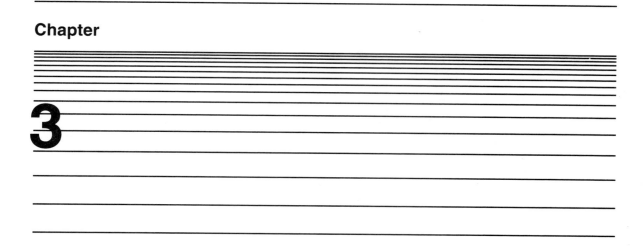

3

Processors and Storage Devices

Objectives

Upon completion of this chapter, the reader will be able to do the following:

- List the functions of the processors and the communication and memory devices

- Describe the main hardware elements of a computer system

- Describe software in general and the two types of software used in the processor

- Explain data

- Discuss the types of data used for a CADD drawing

- Understand the difference between a mainframe computer, a minicomputer, and a microcomputer

Introduction

The **computer system** is the portion of the CADD system that performs all the calculations, stores drawings, and controls the input and output devices. It is the "brain" of the system, directing all functions according to the designer's commands. A large computer system may appear very complex, but it can be easily described by comparing its functions to a hand-held electronic calculator.

The input devices, which were discussed in Chapter 1, are like the keys on a calculator; they are used to enter numbers and arithmetic commands to the calculator. The calculator adds or subtracts as requested; the computer system likewise processes commands and computations. The calculator displays the answer on the readout display; the computer system displays the results of an input command on the graphic screen or other output device. The calculator often has only one location to store a single value. Computer systems used for CADD have large-capacity storage devices to store many complex drawings. The computer system can range in size from a mainframe computer filling a room (Figure 3–1) to a desktop microcomputer containing the processor, input and output devices, storage devices, and a communication link (Figure 3–2).

In this chapter, you will learn that all computer systems have the same functions, regardless of the computer's size. There are, of course, differences in speed of computation, the number of drawings that can be stored, and the number of input and output devices.

The function of the computer system is to control the input and output devices, calculate the results of the designer's commands, and store the CADD models and drawings on a storage device for later retrieval. The communication link is used to transmit CADD information to other computers for analysis and storage. The architecture of the computer system is shown in Figure 3–3. Figure 3–4 shows a typical mainframe computer system; Figure 3–5 is a minicomputer; and Figure 3–6 is a microcomputer.

Figure 3–1
Computer input, processing, and storage devices. (Courtesy International Business Machines Corporation)

Figure 3–2
Microcomputer-based
CADD system utilizing
the Apple IIe. (Courtesy
T&W Systems, Inc.)

Computer System Hardware

The computer system hardware is the electronic equipment that is connected to the input and output devices to make up the CADD system. The computer system hardware includes the following elements:

- Central processing unit (CPU)

- Memory

- Input/output interfaces (I/O)

- Storage devices

- Data communication interface

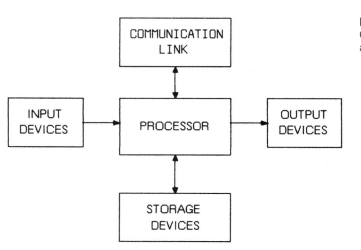

Figure 3–3
Computer system
architecture.

Figure 3–4
IBM mainframe-based system. Disk drives and storage devices are in the background. (Courtesy Lockheed-California Company)

Figure 3–5
Tektronix workstation. (Courtesy Tektronix)

Figure 3–6
Personal computer-based CADD system running VERSACAD software. (Courtesy T&W systems)

The processor element in Figure 3–3 contains the central processing unit (CPU), the memory, and the input/output interfaces. The **processor** consists of integrated circuit chips mounted on a printed circuit board. A mainframe computer has about 50 printed circuit boards; a microcomputer has only one printed circuit board. The storage devices store several hundred million characters on a mainframe computer, but only several hundred thousand characters are stored on a microcomputer. Each of the elements of the computer system will be described in detail in the following sections.

Central Processing Unit

The central processing unit, called the **CPU**, manipulates the information (data) that is entered with the input devices. In a CADD system, the command could be to draw a line — the data would be the coordinates of the ends of the line. A single command from a designer requires several hundred instructions to be performed by the CPU. Examples of instructions are add, subtract, multiply, and divide — just like a calculator. In a addition, there are instructions to compare numbers, retrieve information from storage, and to send information to the input/output devices. The instructions and data are stored in memory during a work session at a CADD station.

The instructions and data are brought into the CPU in "chunks" called a **computer word**. The length of a computer word can be compared to the number of lanes in a highway. Some highways have only two lanes, while a freeway may have eight lanes. The eight-lane freeway can handle more cars per hour, but both types of highway perform the same function. The same is true with computers. The 32-bit computer can add two numbers with one instruction, but the 8-bit computer must use four instructions because it can bring in data only in 8-bit words. The greater the word length, the faster a CPU can perform a command. This is one reason why a mainframe computer can support many CADD terminals, while a microcomputer can support only one terminal.

The function of the CADD system will be the same to the designer regardless of the word size of the CPU. The resulting CADD geometry and drawings will be the same no matter what type of CPU is used.

The CPU of a microcomputer is a single integrated circuit chip (**microprocessor**) as shown in Figure 3–7. A closer view of the microprocessor chip is shown in Figure 3–8, and Figure 3–9 shows the division of the chip into processor and memory portions. In Figure 3–10, the processor is a mainframe CPU that can accommodate multiple CADD stations. The minicomputer shown in Figures 3–11 and 3–5 is a typical stand-alone *turnkey system* with its own internal CPU.

Memory

Random Access Memory   Random access memory (RAM) stores instructions and data for use by the CPU. The instructions are the step-by-step sequences to perform each CADD input and output command. The data consist of all the items describing the CADD geometry or drawing.

Figure 3–7
Intel 8086 processor. (Courtesy Intel Corporation)

Figure 3–8
Motorola integrated circuit. (Courtesy Motorola Inc., Semiconductor Products Sector)

Figure 3–9
AMI integrated circuit. (Courtesy AMI)

Figure 3–10
Computer processors for
mainframe system.
(Courtesy Lockheed-
California Company)

Figure 3–11
Tektronix CADD station.
(Courtesy Tektronix)

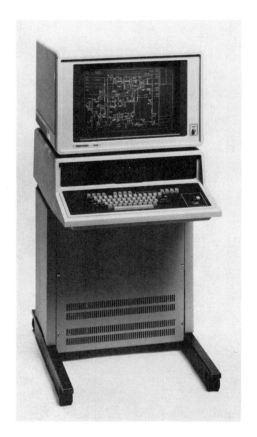

The basic unit of storage in a random access memory is the **bit**, which stands for *binary digit*. The bit is an on-off switch that has one of two values—0 (off) or 1 (on). The bits in a RAM are grouped into computer words that contain 8, 16, or 32 bits. In a computer word, numbers and letters are represented as patterns of the numbers 0 and 1 according to standard codes. One commonly used code is the American Standard Code for Information Interchange (ASCII). For example, in ASCII code an *A* is represented by the bit pattern 01000001; a *W* by 01010111.

The elements that actually store the bits are integrated circuits called chips. Each chip holds from 64,000 to 256,000 bits. Typical chips are shown in Figure 3–12. The chips are mounted in a printed circuit board (Figure 3–13) that has electrical connections to the CPU. The memory size is measured in **bytes**; and each byte consists of 8 bits. One byte is used to contain the code for a single character such as the *A* or *W* described previously. Large memories are measured in blocks of 1024 bytes, given the shorthand notation ''K.'' A 64K memory has 64 × 1024 bytes, or 65,536 bytes. Mainframe computer memories have about 4000K to 8000K bytes. Microcomputer memories have 64K to 512K bytes.

RAM will retain instructions and data as long as the computer is turned on but loses the information when the power is turned off. For this reason, a permanent storage device is used to store CADD information for future use. These permanent storage devices are described in subsequent sections.

Figure 3–12
Logic Board of Apple IIe showing 32 integrated circuits and the 8-bit 6502 microprocessor. (Courtesy Apple Computer, Inc.)

Read Only Memory   Read only memory (ROM) is similar to a RAM whose data are not lost even when the power is turned off. Data cannot be added to it, only read from it. The ROM has many uses. After the power is turned on, the computer must be given detailed instructions, that is, where to get the incoming data (from which peripheral). It must then be given specific information, that is, what to do with the incoming data and what kind of calculation or other process will be performed. These instructions can be in the ROM and thus are never erased.

Storage Devices   The data that describe the CADD geometry or drawing can be stored at any time by a command. These data can be retrieved the next day for further work or may be stored in an archive at the end of a project. The **magnetic disk** is used to store data that will be retrieved and updated frequently. There are two types of magnetic disks: *hard disks* and *floppy disks*. The hard disk unit consists of a set of platters, resembling long-playing records (see Figure 3–14, upper left-hand corner). On some disk units, the disk storage platters can be removed by the computer operator. Other disk units have nonremovable platters that are sealed in a dust-free enclosure (Figure 3–15). The nonremovable disks are known as Winchester disks (Figure 3–16).

The **floppy disk** (Figure 3–17) is used primarily in microcomputer systems. It consists of a flexible plastic disk with a magnetic coating, mounted in a square vinyl jacket. The disk rotates inside the jacket at about 300 revolutions per minute. Information is read through an opening in the jacket that exposes the disk. There are two popular sizes: the $5\frac{1}{4}$-inch diameter, called a minifloppy, and the $3\frac{1}{2}$-inch diameter, called a microfloppy. There are several storage standards for floppy disks, each storing varying amounts of data

Figure 3–14
Two-dimensional CADD
system. (Courtesy T&W
Systems, Inc.)

on the disk. Capacities range from 140 bytes to 1200 bytes. Figure 3–18
shows a dual disk drive.

A **magnetic tape** is used to store CADD data that are not retrieved frequently. The magnetic tape resembles a reel-to-reel audio tape. A copy of
the CADD data is transferred from magnetic disk to magnetic tape as a
backup in case the magnetic disk is damaged. The CADD data for a completed project are stored on tape for future reference. These data then can
be deleted from the magnetic disk to make space for new projects. The

Figure 3–15
Disk pack.

Figure 3–16
Disk drive.

Figure 3–17
Bruning CADD system
using floppy disks.
(Courtesy Bruning)

Figure 3–18
Floppy disk drive and
printed circuit board.

magnetic tapes can be stored off-site in fireproof storage vaults. CADD information and data are very valuable investments; magnetic tapes are used to protect this investment (Figure 3–19). The tape drive is used to read data from the tape and write data on the tape (Figure 3–20). In Figure 3–21, the computer facility manager is using a tape drive unit on a mainframe IBM system. A tape storage cabinet is shown in Figure 3–22.

Input/Output Interfaces

The input/output (I/O) interfaces are the electronic circuits that connect the CPU with the actual input and output devices. They are part of the processor as shown in Figure 3–23. The function of the input interface is to accept information from the input devices (e.g., the keyboard and digitizer tablet), to translate the information to a form the CPU understands, and to send the information to the CPU for processing. The output interface receives data from the CPU, translates the data into the proper form for the output device, and sends the data to the output device at the proper speed.

Data Communication Interface   The data communication interface is the portion of the computer that connects the CADD computer system with other computer systems. Data can be extracted from the CADD geometry or drawing and sent to another computer for further processing. One example of this is the extraction of lists of items appearing on a CADD drawing, such as the number of integrated circuit chips on a circuit board. The CADD system can collect this list of integrated circuit chips, then send the list through a *data communication interface* to another host computer that can collect data from all CADD systems on a project. The host computer can total all

Figure 3–19
Magnetic tape and disk pack.

Figure 3–20
Tape drive.

Figure 3–21
Computer tape drive and mainframe processor. (Courtesy Lockheed-California Company)

Figure 3–22
Magnetic tape storage cabinet and terminal.

Figure 3–23
Integrated computer
system.

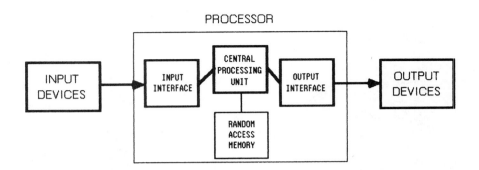

integrated circuit chips for the whole project. The data communication interface allows several computers to send data to each other.

Another common use of data communication is to send the input for a stress analysis to a host computer for an analysis. Typical CADD computer systems do not have the stress analysis programs. The CADD system can extract information from the geometry, format it for the host computer, and transmit the data to the host computer. The results come back to the CADD system and can be printed out or displayed on the graphic screen.

Data may be sent over telephone lines. A high-speed cable may be used for shorter distances. Data communications can be used to send an entire drawing to another computer such as a remote CADD system at a construction site. The remote CADD system can receive the latest drawings from engineers hundreds of miles away in a matter of minutes.

Computer System Software

Computer **software** is the set of instructions that tells the computer **hardware** what to do. Software consists of programs stored on magnetic disks; each program will perform a specific function or command. There are two types of computer software.

The *operating system software* controls the internal operation of the computer, such as sending data to the disk drive, controlling the data communication interface, and controlling the input/output devices. The operating system software may be different for computers from different vendors, but it is the same for all CADD applications on the same computer.

Application software is the set of instructions that tells the computer how to perform CADD operations. Examples are instructions to draw lines and add notes to a drawing. There are sets of application software for different applications (e.g., printed circuit board layout and the creation of mechanical parts). The application software will be described in detail in later chapters. The creator of the application software writes the set of instructions in a *programming language*. Popular programming languages used for CADD applications are FORTRAN, Pascal, and C. Once the program is written, it is *compiled*, that is, translated into instructions the computer can understand, and is then stored on magnetic disk.

The CADD system is sold with the operating system software included. The application software may be provided as separate packages.

Data Storage in Computers

There are three basic types of information that can be stored and processed by a computer system:

- Characters — These are the letters of the alphabet, numerals, and special characters.

- Integers — These are whole numbers such as 10, 3, −5, and 358.

- Decimal numbers — These are values such as 12.375 and 23.00544.

These types of information are arranged into groups called *records* and given special meanings when used in a CADD system. All three types of information are stored as patterns of zeros and ones as illustrated earlier in this chapter. The computer software interprets these patterns of zeros and ones, translating the designer's command to draw a line into a coded message to the computer for data storage and retrieval.

GLOSSARY

ACCESS To retrieve and use a specific program or data.

ACCURACY Generally used to denote the number of digits to the right of the decimal point that can be used by a particular algorithm or system.

ADDRESS The location of data or a program in storage.

ACSII American Standard Code for Information Interchange, a standard for representing characters in the computer.

APPLICATION SOFTWARE A computer program that assists a user performing a specific task.

ARCHIVE Placing infrequently used data in auxiliary storage.

ASSEMBLER The computer program that converts mnemonic instruction into equivalent machine language instructions.

ASSEMBLY LANGUAGE A computer-dependent language that corresponds one-to-one with the computer machine language instructions.

AUXILIARY STORAGE Storage devices other than the main memory; also called peripheral storage (e.g., disk drive or magnetic tape).

BACKUP COPY   A copy of a file that is kept for reference in case the original file is destroyed (i.e., safe keeping).

BAUD RATE   A measure of the speed of signal transmission between the computer and the workstations. It is measured in bits per second.

BINARY CODE   The representation of all characters by using combinations of 0 and 1.

BIT   A binary digit. The smallest unit of information that can be stored and processed by a digital computer. It can be a 0 or a 1. Computers are often classified by word size in bits, such as a 16-bit or 32-bit computer.

BITS PER INCH (BPI)   The numbers of bits in binary code that 1 inch of magnetic tape can store.

BOOT UP   To start up a computer.

BUFFER   A software program or hardware device used to hold data, when transferring data from one device to another, if there is a difference in the time it takes the devices to process the data.

BUG   A flaw in a software program or hardware design that causes erroneous results or malfunctions.

BUS   A circuit or group of circuits that provides a communications path between two or more devices.

BYTE   A sequence of 8 bits that are operated upon as a unit.

CATALOG   The directory of files contained in storage.

CENTRAL PROCESSING UNIT (CPU)   The brain of a CADD system. It controls the processing of information.

COMMAND   An instruction given to a processor using a menu and tablet, stylus, or alphanumeric keyboard.

COMMAND LANGUAGE   The language used by designers and drafters to operate a CADD system; varies with each system.

COMMUNICATIONS LINK   The physical connection, such as a telephone line, from one system to another or from one component to another.

COMPATIBILITY   The ability of a hardware module or software program to be used in a CADD system without modification.

COMPILER   A program that translates high-level language instructions to machine language instructions that can be understood by the CPU.

COMPUTER ARCHITECTURE   The internal design of the parts of a computer system.

COMPUTER PROGRAM   A set of software commands that instructs the computer to perform specific operations, often called a software program or software package.

COMPUTER WORD   A sequence of bits or characters treated as a unit.

CONFIGURATION   A particular combination of computer software, hardware, and peripherals at a single installation.

DATABASE   An organized collection of standard parts libraries, completed designs, documentation, and computer programs.

DATA MANAGEMENT   The control of access to information, information storage conventions, and the use of input and output devices.

DATA PROCESSING SYSTEM   A system that accepts information, processes it in a specific manner, and produces the desired results.

DEBUGGING   Detecting and removing programming errors (bugs) from programs.

DIAGNOSTICS   Computer programs that test a system or its key components to detect and isolate malfunctions.

DIRECTORY   The location on the disk where the names of files and information about them are stored.

DISK   A circular plate of magnetic medium on which information is stored.

DISK DRIVE   The device that reads data from or writes data on magnetic disks.

DUMB TERMINAL   A terminal that can only communicate with a host computer and cannot function in a stand-alone mode.

FILE   A name set of data on magnetic disk or tape; also to transfer the contents of working storage to permanent storage.

FLOPPY DISK   A flexible magnetic disk used to store data.

FORTRAN   FORmula TRANslation. A high-level language primarily for scientific applications that use mathematical formulae.

HIGH-LEVEL LANGUAGE   A programming language that is independent of any given computer and permits the execution of a number of subroutines through a simple command. Examples are BASIC, FORTRAN, Pascal, and COBOL.

HOST COMPUTER   The computer attached to a network providing services such as computation, database management, and special programs. The primary computer in a multiple computer operation.

INSTRUCTION   Line of computer programming telling the computer what to do.

INTEGRATED CIRCUIT (IC)   An electronic component that may vary in complexity from a simple logic gate to a microprocessor. An IC is usually packaged in a single logic substrate such as a slice or silicon. Also called a chip.

INTERPRETER   A software program that converts high-level language instructions to machine language instructions.

LOCAL AREA NETWORK (LAN)   A communications network in which all of the computers and workstations are in the same general area or building.

MACHINE LANGUAGE   The set of instructions, using combinations of the numbers 0 and 1, that is used directly by a computer.

MAGNETIC DISK   A flat, circular plate with a magnetic surface on which data can be recorded and from which data can be read. The data can be randomly accessed.

MAGNETIC DRUM   A cylinder with a magnetic surface on which data can be recorded and from which data can be read.

MAGNETIC TAPE   A tape with a magnetic surface on which data can be recorded and from which data can be read. The data can only be sequentially accessed. The access speed is constrained by the location of the data on the tape, the speed of the tape drive, and the density of the data on the tape.

MAINFRAME   In general, a central processing unit of a large-scale computer configuration.

MAIN MEMORY   The principal data storage device of a computer system — an integral part of the computer; generally, just called *memory*.

MAIN STORAGE   The general-purpose storage of a computer, program-addressable, from which instructions can be executed and from which data can be loaded directly into registers.

MASS STORAGE DEVICE   Auxiliary or bulk memory that can store large amounts of data readily accessible to the computer (e.g., a disk or magnetic tape).

MEGABYTE   One million bytes.

MICROCOMPUTER   A small, relatively low-cost computer that includes a microprocessor, memory, and all necessary interface circuits. Home or personal computers such as Apple, IBM PC, and TRS-80 are examples of microcomputers.

MICROPROCESSOR   A single integrated circuit that is the central processing unit of a microcomputer.

MINICOMPUTER   A computer that is between the mainframe computers and the microcomputers in size, power, complexity, and cost. Generally, a 32-bit computer.

OPERATING SYSTEM   The software that controls the execution of computer programs and all hardware activity; also called system software.

PERMANENT STORAGE   The location, outside the central processing unit, where completed data are stored, such as a disk or tape.

PROCESSOR   The hardware components that perform arithmetic and logic operations, often called the computer.

PROGRAM   The complete sequence of instructions to the computer to perform a task.

RANDOM ACCESS MEMORY (RAM)   A main memory storage unit that provides direct access to the stored information; memory from which data can be retrieved regardless of input sequence.

READ ONLY MEMORY (ROM)   A storage device (memory) generally used for control programs, the content of which is not alterable.

SECURITY   Safeguards and procedures that can be applied to computer hardware, programs, and data to assure that access to the system is controlled.

SEMICONDUCTOR   A material, such as silicon, that conducts electricity and is used for the storage and transfer of computer data.

SOFTWARE   The computer programs, procedures, rules, and instructions that control the use of the hardware.

STORAGE   The physical device or location that contains all of the information on a CADD system.

STORAGE DEVICE OR STORAGE UNIT   A peripheral component in which data can be stored and later retrieved.

WINCHESTER DRIVE   A combination of a disk drive and one or more hard disks permanently sealed in a case.

QUIZ

True or False

1.   The function of the computer system is to enter information to create a drawing.

2. The instructions and data are stored in a random access memory during a work session at a CADD station.

3. A microcomputer is used to support many CADD workstations at one time.

4. The basic unit of storage in a RAM is the byte.

5. The magnetic disk is used to store data that will be retrieved and updated frequently.

6. A common use for the data communication link is to perform stress analysis of a design.

7. Application software is the set of instructions that tells the computer how to perform CADD operations.

8. The operating system software explains to the designer how to use the CADD system.

Fill in the Blanks

9. Computer systems used for CADD have large _____ to _____ many complex drawings.

10. _____ stores instructions and data for use by the CPU.

11. The basic unit of storage in a RAM is the _____, which stands for _____.

12. There are two types of magnetic disks: _____ and _____.

13. A _____ is used to store CADD data that is not retrieved frequently.

14. Once a program is written, it is _____ into the instructions that the computer understands.

15. In the CADD system, information is arranged into groups called _____.

16. The _____ performs operations on data that are entered using the input devices.

Answer the Following

17. Describe the main hardware elements of a computer system.

18. What are the two types of software used in a CADD system? Briefly describe each one.

19. What are some of the uses for the data communication interface?

20. Discuss the primary difference between a mainframe, minicomputer, and microcomputer.

21. Explain how information is stored in the computer.

22. What is the function of the processor?

4

Introduction to Software

Objectives

Upon completion of this chapter, the reader will be able to do the following:

- List the various levels of software

- Describe machine language and binary representation

- Describe high-level languages and why they are needed

- Understand the difference between compiler and interpreter

Introduction to Software

Software is the programmed instructions that tell the processor what to do. It consists of *programs*, which are magnetic impulses usually stored on tapes or disks. Programming that is built into the chips (integrated circuits) and printed circuit boards of the computer is called *firmware*.

Most CADD systems come from the manufacturers preprogrammed. You do not need to know programming in order to use a CADD system: you just turn it on and the system is ready to use. Such a preprogrammed system is called a **turnkey system** (Figure 4–1).

Before the days of interactive workstations, software was kept on punched card decks. Today most interactive CADD systems keep software on their disks, where it is quickly accessible.

Software orders the computer to direct the flow of input data into working storage or to the disk for instant recall. Software also instructs the com-

Figure 4–1
CADD operator inputing
graphics using a menu
and digitizing tablet.
(Courtesy CALCOMP)

puter to retrieve input data for processing. Software ensures that the computer remembers the formula for volume and center of gravity of, for example, a truncated cone or an engine piston. Software enables the computer to create a drawing out of assorted bits and pieces of points, lines, arcs, circles, ellipses, text, and dimensions. It makes it possible to calculate square areas, volumes, and intersections of multiple curved surfaces in space. Software queues the plotter to plot different drawings of various sizes in specific order, without the user giving further instructions. Software remembers CADD-user passwords, a security measure, and prevents unauthorized use of the data.

In short, software is the internal operator of any interactive CADD system. It is a binary-based set of programs that operates the system and makes alphanumeric data, geometric data, and picture data all come together for the design and drafting process.

Machine Language

Programs written in binary strings using the numbers 0 and 1 (called **bits**) are known as **machine language** programs. Since these are the only kinds of instruction the computer can interpret, all programs must ultimately be placed in this form. Writing programs in this form is incredibly difficult. First, binary strings are cumbersome and unnatural to humans. Second, the programmer must assign binary **addresses** (a storage location for information) to all the data and instructions and, even worse, keep track of all these addresses.

Software was developed in a fairly natural and straightforward manner, but recently it has become quite complex. As noted, binary strings are inconvenient because they are so long. Thus, it was a natural first step to convert instructions to *octal* form, treating each group of 3 bits as a binary number, and replacing each group with the equivalent octal digit. It was a simple matter to equip the computer with the capability of converting each octal digit to the equivalent binary form.

Tables 4–1 and 4–2 provide an example of translating from hexadecimal (group of 4 bits) to a binary listing.

Assembly Language

Once we recognize that the computer can convert from one form to another, it is quite natural to replace the number codes with mnemonic names such as ADD, MULT, and DIV, and write a program to enable the computer to convert these names to the equivalent codes. Next, as we assign a name to memory locations, we create a table giving the addresses corresponding to the names. In the address portion of the instructions, we simply write the name instead of the actual address. When we feed the program into the computer, we also feed in the address table and let the computer replace names with the appropriate addresses.

Since assigning addresses is a routine bookkeeping job, it is a task that can be given to the computer. Now our programs need to contain only instructions consisting of operation names and location names. At this point, we have an **assembly language**. The program that assigns the addresses

Table 4–1

Hexadecimal to Binary Conversion

Decimal	Hex	Binary
0	0	0000
1	1	0001
2	2	0010
3	3	0011
4	4	0100
5	5	0101
6	6	0110
7	7	0111
8	8	1000
9	9	1001
10	A	1010
11	B	1011
12	C	1100
13	D	1101
14	E	1110
15	F	1111

Table 4–2

Machine Code (Hex)			Translates to	Machine Code (Binary)
B8	0000		:	1011 1000 0000 0000 0000 0000
BE	D8		:	1000 1110 1101 1000
9A	0000	0000	:	1001 1010 0000 0000 0000 0000
			:	0000 0000
81	EC	0000	:	1000 0001 1110 1100 0000 0000
			:	0000 0000
8B	EC		:	1000 1011 1110 1100
FC			:	1111 1100

and converts the instructions to machine language form is known as an **assembler.**

High-Level Language

Assembly language is an immense improvement over machine language, but there are still many problems. The main problem is that an assembly language is computer-oriented. Each assembly language statement corresponds to one machine language, so that the programmer must be familiar with the instructions and internal organization of the particular computer. Knowledge of how to program one computer will be of little value in programming any other computer. We would prefer a language in which we could write programs that could be run on virtually any computer. This leads us to the concept of **high-level languages**, such as FORTRAN, Pascal, COBOL, and BASIC.

The evaluation of a complicated formula will obviously require many machine language instructions. There are two distinct methods for converting high-level language programs into machine language programs within the computer. In one method, as the program is executed, each high-level language statement is converted into a corresponding set of machine language instructions, which are executed immediately, before proceeding to the next high-level language statement. A system functioning in this manner is known as an **interpreter.**

Interpreters are inefficient for programs with repetitive loops. For example, in FORTRAN we use a "DO" loop to apply the same set of instructions over and over to a whole set of data. An interpreter has to translate the instructions in the "DO" loop on every pass throughout the loop, which is clearly inefficient since the translation is the same on every pass. This fault is corrected by **compilers**, which translate the entire high-level language program into a machine language program before it is executed.

Since interpreters and compilers translate into machine language, they must be written separately for each computer. However, the compiler or interpreter for a given language may be written for any computer having adequate memory capacity to hold the software. Thus, programmers writing in a popular language, such as FORTRAN, can run their programs on any computer.

High-level languages permit us to write programs in forms as close as possible to the natural, "human-oriented" languages that might be appropriate to the particular problems. Thus, a program for drawing a box may be executed by a single statement (see below).

FORTRAN, High-Level Language

```
 1               PROGRAM BOX
 2   C
 3   C      FORTRAN PROGRAM TO DRAW BOX
 4   C
 5   C      COORDINATES OF LOWER LEFT CORNER
 6   C
 7              XLEFT = 1.0
 8              YBOT = 0.5
 9   C
10   C      WIDTH AND HEIGHT OF BOX TO BE DRAWN
11   C
12              WIDTH = 4.0
13              HEIGHT = 2.0
14   C
15   C      CALCULATE COORDINATES OF UPPER RIGHT CORNER
16   C
17              XRIGHT = XLEFT + WIDTH
18              YTOP = YBOT + HEIGHT
19   C
20   C      DRAW BOX ON GRAPHICS SCREEN USING X, Y COORDINATES
21   C
22              CALL MOVETO (XLEFT, YBOT)
23              CALL MOVETO (XRIGHT, YBOT)
24              CALL MOVETO (XRIGHT, YTOP)
25              CALL MOVETO (XLEFT, YTOP)
26              CALL MOVETO (XLEFT, YBOT)
27   C
28              STOP
29              END
```

Command Language

In order to interact with the computer, the designers and drafters must communicate their desires via a special **command language**. The words that make up this language are called **mnemonics**. Mnemonics are short words that can represent complete sentences or phrases of instruction needed to achieve the desired results. The command language is determined by the system manufacturer and can be augmented as the designer's needs dictate. For example, a user calling up a drawing from storage can direct the system to display all of the lines and curves of the drawing with the mnemonic *DIS-LIN*.

A typical CADD system may use English language sentences or portions of sentences to input a command. For example, to draw a horizontal line with a Computervision software-based system (Figure 4–2) we could enter the command:

INS	LIN	HORZ:
(INSERT)	(LINE)	(HORIZONTAL):
(VERB)	(NOUN)	(MODIFIER)

After the command is entered, the designer/drafter must give an explicit coordinate location or digitize the location of the end points. Since the command stated it was to be a horizontal line, the second digitize is used to establish the direction and the length of the line. The first digitize located the starting point and position of the line. If the coordinate location was specified for the first location, the first digitize would be used to establish the length and direction.

The following list gives a few examples of commands:

```
LINES:
        INS   LIN              VERT              :
                            (VERTICAL)
        INS   LIN              PAR               :
                            (PARALLEL)
        INS   LIN              LNG               :
                            (LENGTH)
CIRCLES:
        INS   CIR              RAD               :
                            (RADIUS)
        INS   CIR              DIAM              :
                            (DIAMETER)
        INS   CIR              DIAM 3            :
                        (DIAMETER 3 INCHES)
ARCS:
        INS   ARC   :
        INS   ARC   RAD   :
        INS   ARC   DIAM  :
```

Mnemonics can be specified from either the workstation keyboard or digitizer menus. The workstation keyboard is arranged like that of a typewriter. The designer types in the mnemonic and hits the "Return" button instructing the computer to execute the command. The digitizer **menu** consists of several areas on the digitizer to which mnemonics have been assigned. By digitizing a location within a menu area with the cursor, the designer initiates the specified command. In Figure 4–3 a training menu is used to help the operator learn the command structure by requiring the input of each word, noun and modifier.

BEFORE

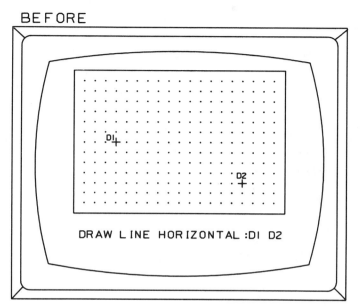

DRAW LINE HORIZONTAL :DI D2

Figure 4–2
Inserting a horizontal line.

AFTER

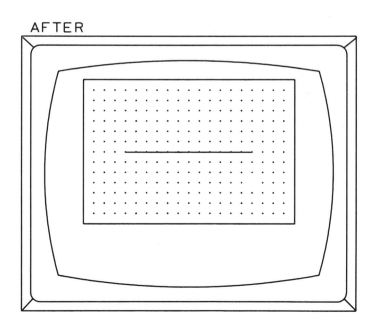

Figure 4–3
Portion of MATC training
menu used to teach input
of commands from a
digitizing tablet. Each
command is built with a
verb, noun, and modifier.

VERB			NOUN			MODIFIER			
INS	MOV		LIN	PNT		INTOF	TANTO	PPNT	•
ERS	ROT		CIR	ARC		PRL	PRP	R	•
TRIM	COPY		FIL	TXT		HOR	VER	D	'
DIV	MIR		LAY	ALL		SUP	AI	AO	;
SEL	CHG		DIM	GRD		LNG	PREC	TOL	
VER	ECHO		LDIM	ADIM		HGT	ANG	ON	
LIST			RDIM	DDIM		WDT	SLT	OFF	LAY USED

Special Features

The following are a few special features available with most CADD systems.

- *Macros*—Macros are custom commands that can be created and as-signed to a menu. Macros, consisting of sequences of standard graphics commands, allow repetitive, standard, or highly specialized operations to be preprogrammed and executed with single instructions. The sequence of commands required to perform a task is entered in the precise order as in the interactive mode. This sequence is then given a unique name that is used as a custom command.

- *Design languages*—To develop advanced software features, the design-ers need a design language with which they can call up and execute pro-grams to be used during a design process to reduce repetitious efforts. The design language is a high-level language that is easy to use and un-derstand.

    The design language allows the designer to write programs in a lan-guage such as BASIC or FORTRAN. These programs can access the stored information, read the digitizer, and drive the graphics display.

- *Analysis capabilities*—The types of analyses needed by the designer are as varied as the applications for which the system is being used. Most of the analyses can be done using the high-level language that is available with the system. This will enable the designer to customize the system.

- *Accounting*—The system keeps a log of time spent on the system by the user, project number, or drawing number. This information is determined automatically from the log-on, log-off times.

- *File security*— File protection is inherent within the system. The protection features include the following: entry into the system is not allowed unless the proper password is used, some data can be viewed but not modified, and certain commands will not be executed until the designer has a chance to verify their intentions.

GLOSSARY

ADDRESSES   The location of data or a program in storage.

ASSEMBLER   The computer program that converts mnemonic instructions into equivalent machine language instructions.

ASSEMBLY LANGUAGE   A computer-dependent language that corresponds one-to-one with the computer machine language instructions.

BASIC   Beginner's All-purpose Symbolic Instruction Code. A high-level algebraic programming language.

BINARY SYSTEM   The mathematical system used by all digital computers. The only two numbers used are 0 and 1.

BIT   A binary digit. The smallest unit of information that can be stored and processed by a digital computer. It can only be a 0 or 1. Computers are often classified by word size in bits, such as a 16-bit or 32-bit computer.

BYTE   A sequence of 8 bits that are operated upon as a unit.

COBOL   Common Business-Oriented Language. A high-level language oriented to business applications.

COMMAND LANGUAGE   The language used by designers and drafters to operate a CADD system; varies with each system.

COMPILER   A program that translates high-level language instructions to machine language instructions that can be understood by the CPU.

COMPUTER WORD   A sequence of bits or characters treated as a unit.

DIGIT   Either 0 or 1 in binary notation; 0 through 9 in decimal notation.

DIGITAL   The representation of data as a combination of the numbers 0 and 1.

FORTRAN   FORmula TRANslation. A high-level language primarily for scientific applications that use mathematical formulae.

HIGH-LEVEL LANGUAGE   A programming language that is independent of any given computer, easy to use, and permits the execution of a number of subroutines through a simple command.

INSTRUCTION   Line of computer programming telling the computer what to do.

INTERPRETER   A software program that converts high-level language instructions to machine language instructions.

MACHINE LANGUAGE   The set of instructions, using combinations of the numbers 0 and 1, that are used directly by a computer.

MENU   A table of available commands, either on a digitizing tablet or on the screen, that can be selected instead of using the keyboard.

MNEMONIC   Short words that represent complete sentences or phrases of instructions.

SOFTWARE   The computer programs, procedures, rules, and instructions that control the use of the hardware.

TURNKEY SYSTEM   A CADD system for which the vendor assumes total responsibility for building, installing, and testing all the hardware and software required to do a specific application.

QUIZ

True or False

1. Programming that is built into the chips is called hardware.

2. Software is the internal operator of any interactive CADD system.

3. Programs written in binary strings using the numbers 0 and 1 are called bits.

4. The program that assigns the addresses and converts the assembly language instructions to machine language form is called a compiler.

5. An assembly language is computer oriented.

6. High-level language programs can be run on any computer.

7. Mnemonics are numbers that can represent complete sentences or phrases of instruction.

8. Macros are custom commands that can be created and assigned to a menu.

Fill in the Blank

9. _____ is the programmed instructions that tell the processor what to do.

10. Since most CADD systems come from the manufacturer already programmed, they are called _____ systems.

11. All programs must ultimately be placed in _____ language form.

12. Programs that contain little more than instructions consisting only of operation names and variable names is called an _____ language.

13. Each _____ language statement corresponds to _____ machine language statement(s).

14. The two distinct methods for converting high-level language programs into machine language programs are _____ and _____.

15. The words that make up a command language are called _____.

16. By digitizing a location within a _____ with the cursor, the designer initiates a specific command.

Answer the Following

17. Describe the function of the software.

18. What is machine language and how is it represented inside the computer?

19. Why are high-level languages preferred when writing programs?

20. Describe the difference between a compiler and an interpreter.

21. Explain the distinction between a high-level language and a command language.

Chapter

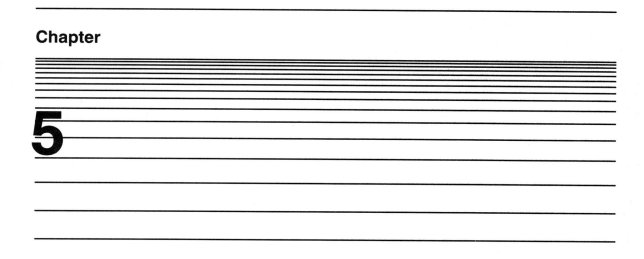

5

Creating Basic Geometry

Objectives

Upon completion of this chapter, the reader will be able to:

- Create simple geometry including points, lines, arcs, circles, and splines.

- Understand and use two-dimensional and three-dimensional Cartesian, polar, and incremental coordinates to create geometry.

- Define and select grids to use when creating geometry.

- Use menus on the CRT or on the tablet for creating basic geometry.

- Complete simple two-dimensional drawings with a CADD system.

- Understand how to isolate the various types of geometry to reference existing geometry while creating a part.

Introduction

CADD systems provide an easy, efficient, simple, and accurate means of creating designs and drawings, as shown in Figure 5–1. This chapter covers the steps that precede the creation of geometry (drawing), such as starting the CADD system, initiating a drawing, establishing a coordinate system and using it, selecting and using a grid, and using menus to create geometry. It also covers the basic options available for creating *items*, or single pieces of geometry that the designer or drafter can create with CADD. These include points, lines, circles, arcs, splines, and ellipses. And, finally, this chapter covers the *tools* of the CADD system used to create, modify, or enhance a design, just like the pencils, T-squares, protractors, and other manual tools the designer would use on the drafting table. They consist of:

- Geometric items

- Line fonts

- Layers, colors, and grids used for organization and presentation

- Automatic dimensions

- A symbol library

- Graphic text

- Text fonts

- Tablet and screen menus

Figure 5–1
Isometric projection of a part and a CRT display showing a side bar menu. (Courtesy Tasvir Corp.)

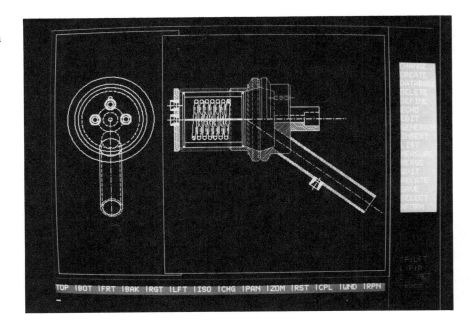

Logging In

Since most workstations and personal-computer-based systems are used as stand alone design tools, their start-up procedures are similar. When using a hard disk, the designer will turn on the system and key in the name of the CADD program to start working. With a floppy disk, the designer must load the floppy containing the CADD program into one disk drive and use another floppy in the second drive to save the drawings he or she creates.

Single and Dual CRT Configuration

Figure 5–2 illustrates a typical dual-CRT configuration. The geometry is confined to one CRT and the text to the other. This configuration is advantageous since the graphics area can cover the whole CRT instead of sharing it with the text.

On most systems, the graphics and the text or screen menu will be shown on the same CRT, Figure 5–3. This is the CRT for VersaCAD. In Figure 5–4, which illustrates a Computervision system, the STATUS TEXT area indicates:

1. The currently active PARTNAME.

2. The currently active DRAWING.

3. The current mode (MODEL (three-dimensional) or DRAW (two-dimensional)).

4. The active CONSTRUCTION PLANE (CPL).

5. The active CONSTRUCTION LAYER.

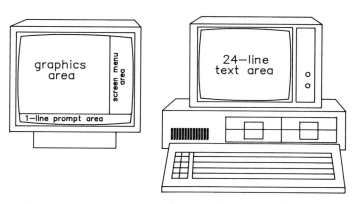

Figure 5–2
Dual-CRT configuration.
(Courtesy Autodesk, Inc.)

TYPICAL DUAL–SCREEN CONFIGURATION

Figure 5–3
CRT. (Courtesy T & W Systems)

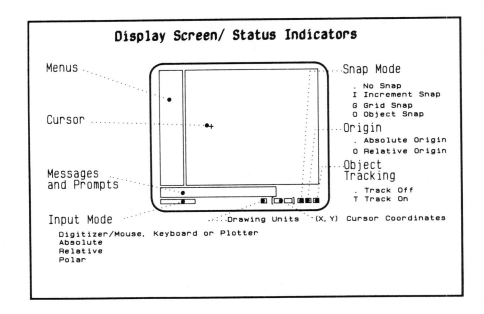

Starting a Drawing

After the CADD software has been loaded into the system, the designer first requests the system to start a new drawing. The system then asks the de-

Figure 5–4
Computervision graphics display and text areas of screen. (Reprinted with permission from Computervision Corporation, Bedford, Massachusetts)

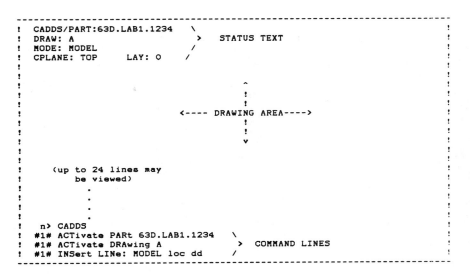

signer to enter a name for the drawing. The final step in beginning a drawing is to establish its initial defaults. On most systems, the defaults are constant until changed by the designer. A typical list of drawing defaults is shown below.

Defaults

APERTURE	10 pixels
ATTDISP	Normal (controlled individually)
AXIS	Off, spacing (0.0, 0.0)
BASE	Insertion base point (0.0, 0.0)
BLIPMODE	On
CHAMFER	Distance 0.0
DRAGMODE	On
ELEV	Elevation 0.0, thickness 0.0
FILLET radius	0.0
FILL	On
GRID	Off, spacing (0.0, 0.0)
ISOPLANE	Left
LAYER	Current/only layer is "0," On, with color 7 (white) and linetype "CONTINUOUS"
LIMITS	Off, drawing limits (0.0, 0.0) to (12.0, 9.0)
LINETYPE	Only loaded linetype is "CONTINUOUS"
LTSCALE	1.0
MENU	ACAD
ORTHO	Off
OSNAP	None
PLINE	Line-width 0.0
QTEXT	Off
REGENAUTO	On
SKETCH	Record increment 0.0
SNAP	Off, spacing (1.0, 1.0)
SNAP/GRID	Standard style, base point (0.0, 0.0), rotation 0.0 degrees
STYLE	Only defined text style is "STANDARD," using font file "TXT," with variable height, width factor 1.0, and no special modes
TABLET	Off
TEXT	Style "STANDARD," height 0.20, rotation 0.0 degrees
TRACE	Width 0.05

Modes for Creating Geometry

Free Digitizing Mode

CADD systems allow the designer to create geometry in two different modes. Most CADD systems start in the *free digitizing mode* that allows the designer to see and immediately change the relationships among the various parts of a drawing. This mode uses one of four devices for specifying the X,Y (or X, Y, and Z in a three-dimensional system) coordinate input:

- Digitizer

- Mouse

- Plotter

- Keyboard arrow keys

The particular model of input device must be specified. To move the cursor across the CRT, the designer moves the stylus (electronic pen) on the digitizer tablet, moves the mouse, moves the pen holder on the plotter, or presses the arrow keys on the keyboard.

When the designer digitizes, the system stores the corresponding coordinate information. If an incorrect coordinate is entered, the designer can usually override the mistake and re-enter the correct coordinate. The same capability is available when the designer digitizes the wrong location or item. The use of grids and isolation options (discussed in detail later in this chapter) also help to improve the accuracy of freehand digitizing.

Coordinate Entry Mode

The *coordinate entry mode* allows the designer to enter the actual coordinates of an object from the keyboard or menu. There are three types of coordinate entry, as shown in Figure 5–5 and listed below:

- Absolute

- Relative (incremental)

- Polar

Figure 5–5
Relative, Absolute, and Polar Coordinates. (Courtesy T & W Systems, Inc.)

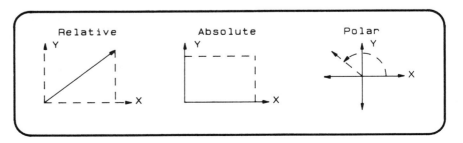

Absolute coordinate entry is the easiest to use. The designer types in the absolute X and Y coordinates (and Z for a three-dimensional system). The program uses these coordinates to do its calculations.

Relative (incremental) coordinate entry is a little more complicated. In this mode, the designer must type in the *relative* X and Y coordinates, that is, the difference between the desired location and the existing reference point.

Polar coordinate entry allows the designer to specify X,Y points (and Z for three-dimensional) by entering the angle (in degrees) from the horizontal and the distance of the point from the origin.

Cursor Controls

A CADD system often receives coordinates from either the digitizer (sometimes called the graphics tablet) or a mouse. In this text, the word *stylus* or *electronic pen* refers to the object that is moved across the digitizer, whether it is shaped like a pencil or a puck. The stylus position on the digitizer is represented on the CRT by crosshairs, called a *cursor*. As the stylus moves, the crosshairs will also move across the CRT.

The cursor is used to create lines, circles, rectangles, and other geometry. It is also used for the graphic manipulation of an entire picture or any part of it. To perform these tasks, it is necessary to select the appropriate function, position the stylus, and then press down on it (or on a button, if appropriate).

The cursor can be moved not only from the digitizer, which is the most common method, but also with the arrow keys on the keyboard. In the *arrow entry mode*, the designer must press the up, down, left, or right arrows to move the cursor in the desired direction.

The bottom line on the CRT may be used as the status line. It indicates the X, Y (or X, Y, Z) position of the cursor on the screen and provides information about the features that have been selected.

Coordinate Systems

As a vector-based system, CADD relies heavily on Cartesian and polar coordinates, as well as relative and absolute coordinates, to establish point locations. If these terms are unfamiliar or if you have doubts about their meaning, it is important to study these pages carefully.

Cartesian Coordinates

The *Cartesian coordinate system* allows the designer to locate points on his or her drawing (e.g., to position items). An X coordinate specifies horizontal location, and a Y coordinate specifies vertical location. Thus, any point on a drawing can be indicated by an X and Y coordinate pair, written as (X,Y). The (0,0) point is normally at the lower lefthand corner of the drawing on a two-dimensional system. A three-dimensional system allows for the entry of Z coordinates, and the (X,Y,Z) origin is positioned relative to the part in space.

The use of Cartesian coordinates, Figure 5–6, is similar to the process of locating an object on a map that has letters down the side and numbers along the top, Figure 5–7. The index shows that the location being sought is at B,3. To find B,3, follow B across until it is under 3, as indicated above. The Cartesian coordinate system used in CADD establishes a two-dimensional location in a slightly different way. Instead of using letters and numbers, it uses X and Y values to indicate horizontal and vertical locations, respectively. The crossed lines representing these locations are called *axes* and are pictured in Figure 5–8.

At the point where the two axes cross, both X and Y are equal to zero (0,0). Any movement to the right of the Y axis assigns positive values to X, and any movement above the X axis assigns positive values to Y. Because the origin generally is in the middle of the CRT, Figure 5–8, the CADD system may place drawings in only the upper righthand quadrant of the axes, which is the only quadrant where both X and Y are positive numbers. Alternatively, the origin may be repositioned to the lower lefthand corner, Figure 5–9, to make the entire CRT in the righthand quadrant. In this case, the CADD CRT, when set up to be an "A" size (8½ × 11 inches) drawing, would thus contain only the upper right quadrant of the X and Y axes as shown in Figure 5–10. The points (10,7), (3,4), and (6,1.5) are located by following the dotted lines from the points on the axes. The X value is always listed first, followed by a comma, then the Y value. Some systems require a X, Y, or Z before the value, as in (X10, Y7).

Figure 5–6
Cartesian Coordinate System. (Courtesy Autodesk, Inc.)

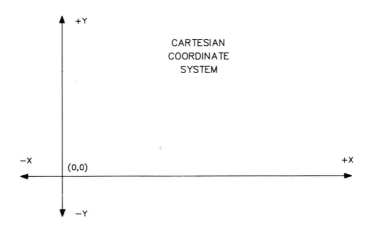

CARTESIAN COORDINATE SYSTEM

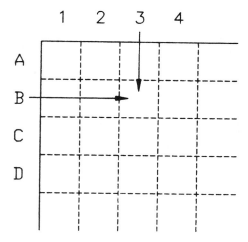

Figure 5–7
Finding a location on a map. (Courtesy Autodesk, Inc.)

Polar Coordinates

Polar coordinates also use axes but, unlike Cartesian X and Y axes, they form the quadrants of a 360 degree arc, starting from the right horizontal axis and rotating counterclockwise, Figure 5–11.

All polar-determined lines must have a point of origin, to which the coordinates relate. The line itself is determined by *radius* and *angle*. For example, AutoCAD requires an @ in front of the entry, which means "from the last

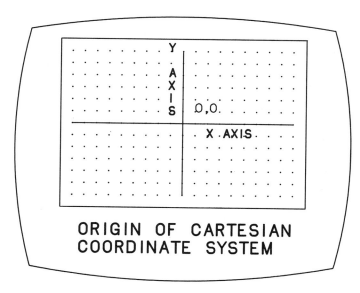

Figure 5–8
Origin of Cartesian coordinate system.

Figure 5–9
Two-dimensional
coordinates.

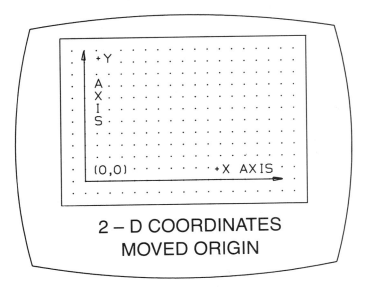

point." Thus @5 < 90 would mean "from the last point, draw a line 5 units long at an angle of 90 degrees." Figure 5–12 shows this line starting from point (2,2) and a second, @7 < 35, from point (5.5,3). In other systems, the designer must first enter the starting point and then give the polar coordinates, (R5, A90) (radius of 5 at a 90 degree angle).

Figure 5–10
Locating points with
coordinates. (Courtesy
Autodesk, Inc.)

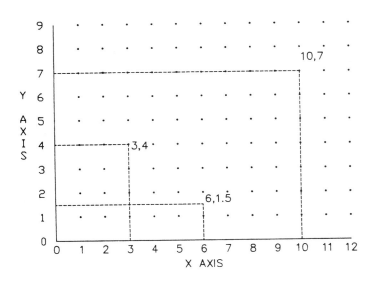

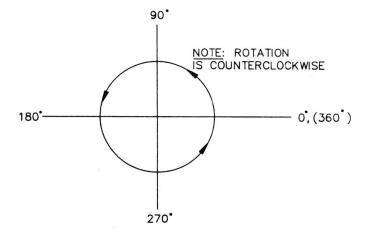

Figure 5–11
Degrees are calculated
for 0 degrees (3 o'clock
position) coun-
terclockwise. (Courtesy
Autodesk, Inc.)

Absolute and Relative or Incremental Coordinates

Absolute coordinates are established by measuring from the (0,0) point. All
points established in this way are measured from the crossing of the X and
Y axes.

   Relative or incremental coordinates (Figure 5–12) are established relative to some point other than (0,0). This is customarily the last point established. For example, on the AutoCAD system (Figure 5–12), relative or incremental coordinates must always be preceded by an @, as in (@17, 35.5).

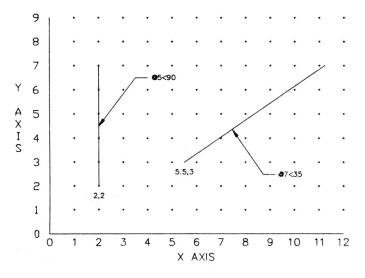

Figure 5–12
Creating lines using polar
and Cartesian coordi-
nates. (Courtesy Au-
todesk, Inc.)

AutoCAD interprets this to mean "from the last established point, establish a new point 17 units in the X direction and 35.5 units in the Y direction." Entering @16 < 105 would be interpreted to mean "from the last point, establish a new point 16 units away at a counterclockwise angle 105 degrees from the horizontal." Other systems use different prompts for the same purpose. Computervision's system simply uses *incremental* coordinates that can be entered directly from a tablet menu, Figure 5–13. IX means the last X position input. IY means from the last Y position. In a three-dimensional system, IZ means from the last Z position.

Three-Dimensional Coordinates

The third dimension (depth) can be entered on a three-dimensional system by coordinates just like X and Y. In Figure 5–14, which shows the origin of a three-dimensional system, the positive Z axis comes forward, out from the CRT. Figure 5–15 and Figure 5–16 show a three-dimensional part on an IBM-based system.

Fonts

Display Fonts

The numerous available *display fonts* may be composed of one solid line or variations of dashed and dotted lines (Figure 5–17). The size and spacing of the display fonts may be fixed and may not change when the designer zooms in or out of the drawing.

Figure 5–13
Digitizing area of menu.

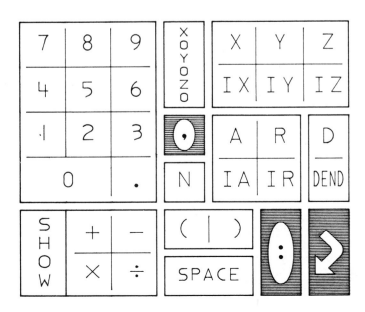

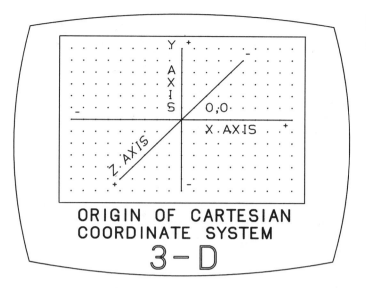

ORIGIN OF CARTESIAN COORDINATE SYSTEM

3-D

Figure 5–14
Three-dimensional
coordinate system.

Figure 5–15
Three-dimensional
IBM-based system
showing a three-
dimensional part in
isometric.

Figure 5–16
Three-dimensional part
with coordinate axes
shown.

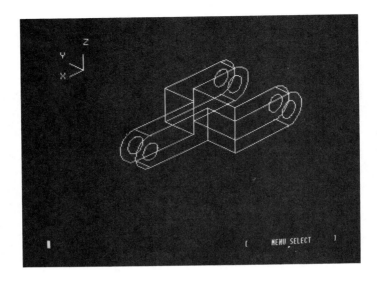

Plotting Fonts

The designer or drafter can define many plotting fonts. A *plotting font* responds to zooming in or zooming out and plots exactly what appears on the CRT. The plotting fonts are displayed on the CRT when a drawing is ready to be plotted and the size and spacing of the font needs to be checked for clarity and effective presentation.

Figure 5–17
Display fonts.

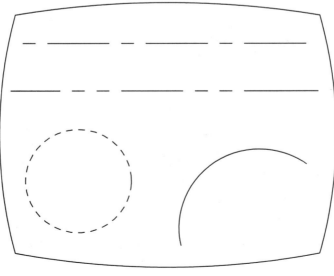

DISPLAY FONTS

Drawing Limits and Extents

CADD systems require the designer to work within a rectangular area, the borders of which he or she specifies in drawing coordinates. These borders comprise the *drawing limits*, which LIMITS allows the designer to designate and check. These limits perform three functions:

1. When the limits check is on, they specify the range of coordinates that can be entered without causing an "Outside limits" error.

2. They specify the portion of the drawing covered by the visible grid.

3. They help determine how much of the drawing is displayed by ZOOM All.

Setting Units of Measure

The distance between two points in the coordinate system is measured in units. Thus a line drawn between the points (1,1) and (1,2) is one unit in length. As Figure 5–18 shows, the grid unit and the drawing unit can be the same (left) or different (right). A unit can correspond to whatever form of measurement the drawing requires, whether it be inches, feet, centimeters, or meters. The designer merely specifies the relevant scale to plot each unit in the exact size needed. For example, in drawing a circuit board that is 8 inches high by 10 inches wide, the designer may wish to make each drawing unit correspond to one inch, with the lower lefthand corner of the board having the coordinates (0,0). Drawing limits would then be set as:

> Lower left corner: (0,0)
>
> Upper right corner: (10,8)

The standard units of measure are user-defined, inches, inches as feet, inches decimal, feet, feet as inches, feet decimal, miles, millimeters, meters, and kilometers. The default unit of measure is generally inches decimal.

The following chart illustrates each of the unit options available:

Drawing Unit

Inches:	in	[17.3/ 4",	13.15/16"]
Inches as feet:	in	[1'–5. 3/ 4",	1'–1.15/16"]
Inches decimal:	in	[17.7500	13.9375]
Feet:	ft	[16'–0.3/4",	12'–11.3/16"]
Feet as inches:	ft	[192.3/4",	155.3/16"]
Feet decimal:	ft	[16.0625,	12.9323]

Miles:	mi	[16.0625,	12.9323] (decimal format)
Millimeters:	mm	[16.06625,	12.9323] (decimal format)
Meters:	m	[16.0625,	12.9323] (decimal format)
Kilometers:	km	[16.0625,	12.9323] (decimal format)
User-defined:	ud	[16.0625,	12.9323] (decimal format)

Grids

Grids, Figure 5–18, are construction aids that provide points at specified intervals, just like graph paper, but with any desired spacing. They can be designated from a menu, Figure 5–19. Grids give the designer a "feel" for the sizes and relationships of individual geometry items, and, most important, they allow the designer to enter items at precise coordinate points with relative ease.

Grids are not considered part of the drawing. They are visual aids only and are never plotted. In most systems, grids may be used without actually appearing on the CRT.

Specifying Grids

Grids can be turned on and off at will. The desired grid is "specified" by entering SELECT GRID. After the grid is selected, it must be turned on (ECHO GRID ON). REPAINT shows the grid on the CRT.

AutoCAD has a variety of options for defining grids. These options are described below.

On
: The "On" option defines the grid, using the previous dot spacing.
For example:
Command: GRID
On/Off/Value(X)/Aspect: ON

Off
: The "Off" option allows the reference grid to be erased from the CRT.
For example:
Command: GRID
On/Off/Value(X)/Aspect: OFF

Value
: The "Value" option allows the designer to supply a numeric value to set the dot-to-dot grid spacing.
For example:
To set the grid spacing to 0.75 units, enter:
Command: GRID
On/Off/Value(X)/Aspect: 0.75

In Figure 5–20, the "before" illustration shows a blank display with options for selecting a grid, turning it on, and displaying it:

```
SELECT GRID   X.5   Y.5
ECHO GRID ON
REPAINT
```

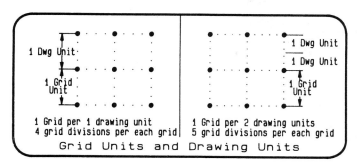

Figure 5–18
Grid and drawing units.
(Courtesy T&W Systems,
Inc.)

SELECT GRID ON X.5 Y.5 activates a rectangular 1/2 inch grid; *ECHO GRID ON* turns the grid on; *REPAINT* displays the grid. The "after" illustration in Figure 5–20 shows the grid itself. Figure 5–21 illustrates a rectangular grid with different X and Y values.

Snap Features

The ability to precisely position an object with a cursor depends upon the resolution of the CRT and the manual coordination of the designer. As a result, the CADD program will usually include a "snap" feature, which automatically snaps or pulls points digitized freehand to the nearest grid point.

Several different types of snap, Figure 5–22, may be selected:

1. *Increment snap* positions the cursor to the nearest previously defined increment. With increment snap, the coordinate display always shows the snapped cursor value, i.e., the values displayed are multiples of the smallest increment. For example, if the increment has been defined as 0.5, the cursor will snap to 0.5, 1.0, 1.5, …

2. *Grid snap* positions the cursor on the nearest grid intersection point. Here, too, the coordinate display always shows the snapped cursor value, i.e., the values displayed are grid intersection points.

3. *Object snap* positions the cursor on any selected geometry item as well as text.

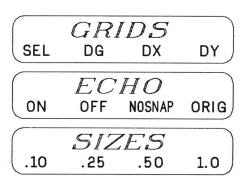

Figure 5–19
Grid menu area.

Figure 5–20
Selecting and showing a grid.

BEFORE

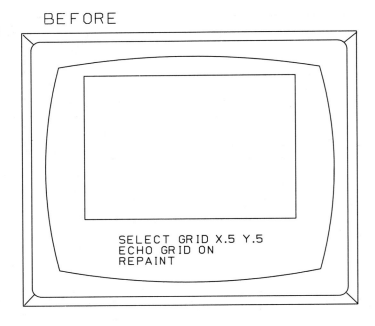

SELECT GRID X.5 Y.5
ECHO GRID ON
REPAINT

AFTER

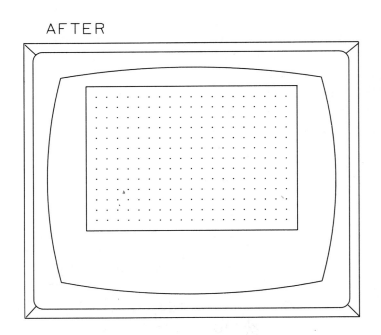

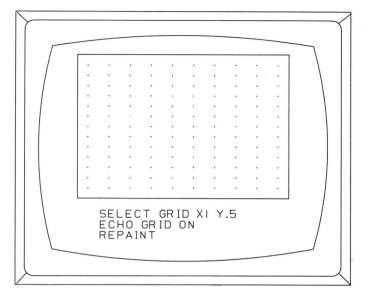

Figure 5–21
Selecting a grid with
varying X and Y spacing.

Some programs also allow the designer not to use the snap feature, as
in the NOSNAP option available in the menu illustrated in Figure 5–19.

Entering Instructions from Menus

The CADD system allows instructions to be entered in a variety of ways:
from a menu on the CRT, from a tablet menu, from a button menu, and from
the keyboard.

The CRT Menu

Some CADD systems provide a list of available options directly on the CRT
in the form of a menu that appears along the side of the screen, Figure 5–3.

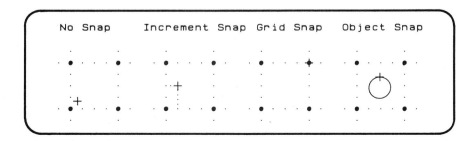

Figure 5–22
Grid capabilities.
(Courtesy T&W Systems,
Inc.)

Each menu item represents a specific instruction. For example, the FILER square allows the designer to enter instructions to save or retrieve drawing files, while the OUTPUT square allows him or her to send the drawing to an output device such as a plotter or graphics printer.

A pointing device (stylus) simplifies the entry of an instruction from the menu on the CRT. The designer moves the pointer until the crosshairs reach the edge of the CRT, then moves it up and down to highlight the desired menu item. The choice is made by pressing the "pick" button on the stylus or pressing down on the pen. If there is no pointing device, the selection can be made by moving the cursor from the keyboard.

Menus that appear on the CRT usually begin with a *main menu*, as in Figure 5–23 (VersaCAD). Some menus, however, may contain so many items that it is impossible to display them all at once. In such cases, the main menu is divided into *submenus*, usually arranged in a treelike format with the main menu as the trunk and the submenus as branches. The designer can then choose to have any of these displayed in full. This feature allows the designer to know exactly what options are available at any given time.

For example, to add some new object onto a drawing, the designer selects the ADD menu item, which displays a list of geometric items (line, rectangle, circle, arc, text) from which the designer can select and then position his or her selection on the drawing. To change something on the drawing, the designer selects MODIFY, which provides a list of the options that include copying, rotating, deleting, or moving an individual object on the drawing. The GROUP menu allows the designer to define and modify entire groups of items simultaneously. As on the MODIFY menu, groups of objects can be copies, rotated, deleted, or moved. The FILER menu item saves or retrieves drawings. The WINDOW menu item allows the designer to move in for a closer look (WINDOW IN) or back away from the drawing (WINDOW OUT). The LIBRARY menu item creates and maintains libraries of commonly used symbols or parts of drawings that the designer can retrieve instantly when needed.

The Tablet Menu

The CADD system typically employs a stylus or electronic pen and a tablet, which provides an efficient means of entering instructions and coordinates and identifying geometry. The tablet is divided into two areas: a geometric construction area and the *tablet menu* (see Figure 5–24). Usually, a printed form placed over the menu area assists in locating menu items. To select an item, the designer places the stylus over the place where it appears on the tablet and presses down. The tablet menu contains small squares called menu keys, as shown in Figure 5–25. Each key is labeled with the name of the option, letter, number, instruction, or set of instructions that it represents. The designer depresses the tip of the stylus on a menu key to give an instruction to the system, then manipulates the stylus as if it were a pencil

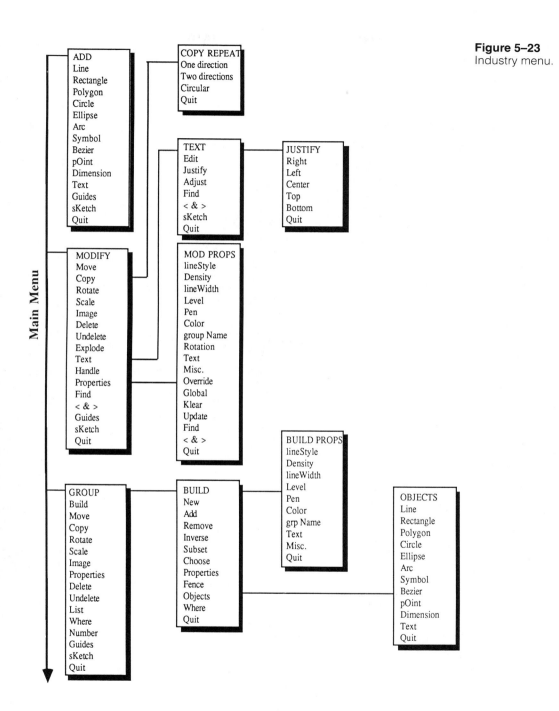

Figure 5–23
Industry menu.

Figure 5–24
Instruction squares for a user-defined area on a menu.

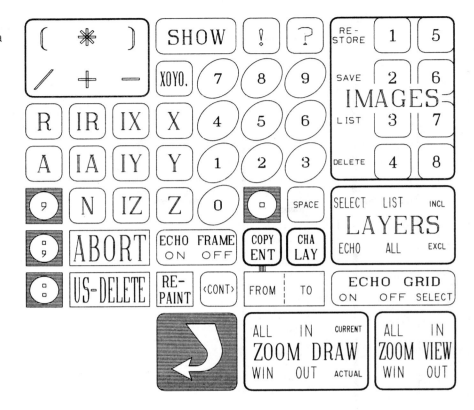

Figure 5–25
Main menu for a CRT menu-driven system. (Courtesy T&W Systems, Inc.)

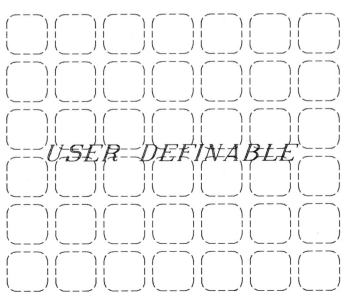

that could automatically draw, modify, and reposition the lines that compose the drawing. The process is called "digitizing." As the stylus is moved over the graphics portion of the tablet, a crosshair on the screen indicates its position.

Some CADD systems may have a predefined tablet menu specially designed to suit the need of the majority of designers. Figure 5–24 illustrates such a predefined menu. It is possible, however, to create a new format for the tablet menu or modify the existing one to specify the size of the area assigned to graphics digitizing, the size of the area assigned to menu keys, and the size and shape of the menu keys. Once the format of the tablet menu has been established, the designer can then assign functions to the different menu keys. Figure 5–25 illustrates a designer-defined menu area.

The tablet menu format and the tablet menu key assignments are stored in the *key file*, which may be predefined, Figure 5–24, but can be altered by the designer. A key file specifies the amount of space reserved for the graphics and menu areas as well as the size and shape of the menu keys. On most systems, the key file will include:

- Number of characters that can be entered when defining or editing a key.

- Size of the tablet's active (or total) area.

- Size of the graphics or digitizing area

- Size of an individual menu key

The system subtracts the digitizing area from the active area to determine the menu area.

Button Menus

If the tablet stylus or mouse has numerous buttons, commonly used instructions can be selected from the buttons not used for point selection.

Keyboard Entry

To enter an instruction from the keyboard, the designer simply types in the instruction name.

The Structure of Instructions to the System

Some CADD systems use English-based instructions that describe what they do in the form of phrases. The left half, or *verb-noun* portion, is separated from the right half, or *GETDATA* portion, by a colon. Each phrase begins with a verb. Although Computervision, Tasvir, CADDIS, ZERACAD, and MATC all use this basic format, it is important to remember that each CADD system has its own particular structure for instructions. The structure presented here is intended only to introduce and teach CADD in a generic way. Many of the instructions, for example, have been altered to use common drafting terms such as *DRAW* instead of *INSERT*.

Punctuation

The following punctuation is included in instructions throughout this text:

Punctuation mark	Use
:	Separates the verb-noun from GETDATA in an instruction. If it is used after input in GETDATA, it allows the modifiers to be changed in GETDATA and new data to be entered.
;	If used after input in GETDATA, it tells the system to process the instruction and to return to the beginning of GETDATA so new information can be entered.
,	Separates explicit coordinates in a series. If used in an instruction that requires the selection of both geometry items and locations, it tells the system that item selection is complete and location will be entered.

The Verb-Noun Command

A typical system — Computervision — employs the following form for the verb-noun portion of its instructions:

VERB — tells the system what action to take. It is usually a word like *trim* or *draw*.

NOUN — Specifies the item affected by the verb. It is usually a geometric term like *line* or *circle*.

MODIFIER — Focuses and refines the action, usually by describing a quality, value, or condition. Some modifiers require that a specific value be given.

Modifiers often have submodifiers arranged in a treelike structure as shown in the instruction line that follows.

#n# INSERT LDIM VERTICAL ARROWS OUT TEXT LOCATION AUTOCENTER:

The tree-structure would be as follows:

It is especially important to understand how modifiers work in the instruction phrase because they give the geometry item its specific characteristics. For example, the noun LINE can be linked to modifiers that explicitly define the kind of line to be constructed. The modifiers HORIZONTAL and VERTICAL create horizontal and vertical lines; the modifier ANGLE, with a value, creates a line at a specific angle; the modifier LENGTH, with a value, creates a line of a specific length; the modifiers PARALLEL and PERPENDICULAR create lines that are parallel and perpendicular to a defined line. The noun CIRCLE also has modifiers that define the size of the radius or the diameter.

Modifiers are flexible enough that they can even define text. TEXT modifiers control the type of text font (or style) and the desired height, width, thickness, slant, or location (justification).

The GETDATA Command

The GETDATA, or right half of the instruction phrase indicates three types of data—a *location*, an *item*, or a *view*—on which the verb-noun-modifier will act. GETDATA options can also isolate items on a menu as in Figure 5–26. In this portion of the instruction, after the colon, the system will ask the designer which of the three data types he or she wishes to enter. To increase the flexibility and accuracy of his or her response, the designer uses *references* to specify location and *isolation options* to specify items and views. The designer can also manipulate the display in GETDATA and use GETDATA punctuation to enter compound instructions.

Specifying Location by Reference

A designer can indicate a location by either digitizing it or entering explicit coordinates. In the latter option, the designer can:

- Specify absolute coordinates.

- Specify incremental coordinates.

- Specify incremental coordinates relative to existing geometry.

Figure 5–26
Menu area for selecting
isolation options.

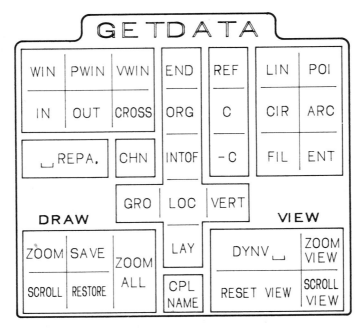

References specify a location that is relative to a point on the existing geometry. This is sometimes necessary for geometric constructions such as angled, parallel, perpendicular, or tangent lines. For example, the coordinates of either the END or the ORIGIN of an existing item can be used as reference points, or the INTERSECTION of two items can be used, as shown in Figure 5–27.

Specifying Items and Views by Isolation Options

A designer selects an existing geometric item by digitizing it. The isolation option allows the designer to select a specific type of geometric item — as Figure 5–27 shows — and insure its accurate identification. Especially when items are placed close together, therefore, isolation options help to avoid selection errors. An isolation option can also be used to specify the types of items *not* to be selected.

The WINDOW capability is an isolation option that can be used to specify a view. A WINDOW is a rectangular frame that is used to define the viewing area of the drawing on the CRT. With the WINDOW option, the designer can move, shrink, and magnify the viewing window, thus changing the portion of the drawing seen at any given time.

Geometric Items

In this text, the term *item* applies to any element of a drawing, including groups, figures, text, labels, dimensions, crosshatching, and *geometric*

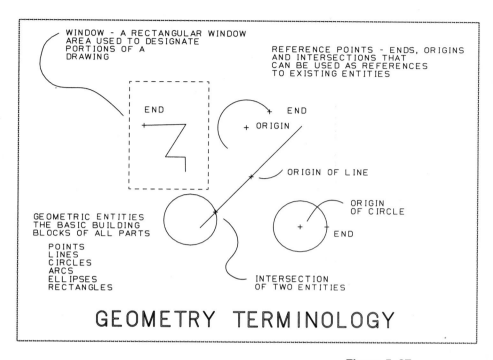

Figure 5–27
Geometry terminology.

items, which are the building blocks of a drawing. There are five basic geometric items, as defined in the table below and illustrated in Figures 5–28 and 5–29.

Geometric item	Definition
point	A location.
line	The connection between two points. The origin of a line is its midpoint.
circle	A complete 360 degree arc. The origin of a circle is its centerpoint.
arc	A segment of a circle. The origin of an arc is the centerpoint of the circle of which it is a segment.
string	A series of connected lines and arcs.

Points, lines, circles, and arcs are simple items: strings, on the other hand, are compound items composed of several simple ones, either new or existing. The use of strings reduces construction time, since the system can manipulate a single, compound item more quickly than it can a number of

Figure 5–28
Geometry for VersaCAD.
(Courtesy T&W Systems,
Inc.)

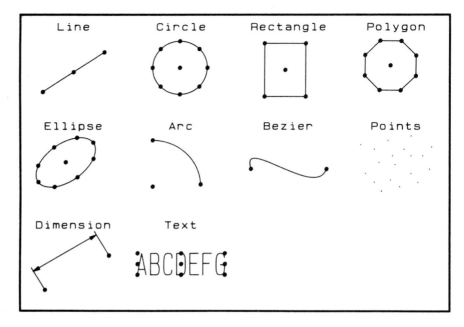

simple ones. The use of simple items, however, gives the designer more editing flexibility, because single items are easier to change than compound ones. Figure 5–28 illustrates a variety of geometric items available on VersaCAD.

In finalizing their drawings, designers and drafters using the CADD system often enhance the appearance of their design by adding *crosshatching*, *text*, *notes*, and *dimensions*. *NC toolpaths* are another group of geometric items, which are used by manufacturing engineers. All these distinct types are illustrated in Figure 5–29.

Basic Construction

The first step in drawing a part, whether on a two-dimensional or three-dimensional system, is creating individual geometric items. Items can be created by typing in the instruction; by selecting from a menu on the CRT, as on an AutoCAD or VersaCAD system; or by using a menu designed so that instructions could be entered with a digitizer, such as the one shown in Figure 5–30. Among the instructions included in this example are ones that create a circle, line, spline, crosshatching, rectangle, and chamfer.

While there are basic construction commands that will create geometric items, the system must first know their location, size, and appearance. As

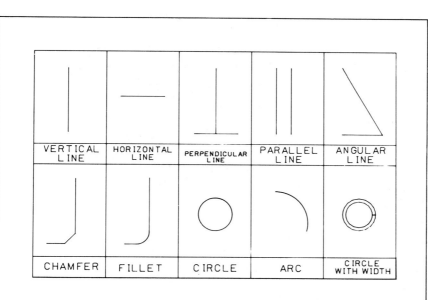

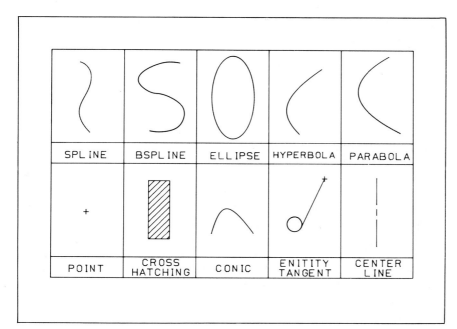

Figure 5–29
Geometry items. (Reprinted with permission from Computervision Corporation, Bedford, Massachusetts)

Figure 5–30
Creating geometry from a
menu.

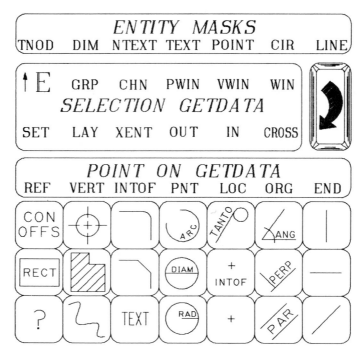

mentioned previously, an item's location can be specified by explicit coordinates or by freehand digitizing. Size is specified by a modifier, and its explicit coordinates are either typed in or defined by freehand digitizing.

There are two ways of giving basic geometric items the correct size, shape, color, and font: (1) by adding modifiers that determine the size and appearance of the item being created or (2) by creating basic geometric items with only the location specified and then using editing capabilities to modify the geometry, thus separating design decisions from presentation choices.

Most of the remainder of this chapter will deal exclusively with the basic construction of specific geometric items.

Points

Points are geometric items that are very useful as references or as placement coordinates for other items. They can be created either by *freehand digitizing* or by *coordinate entry* on or at the intersection of other items. The command DRAW POINT places a point at a specific location, using X, Y, and Z coordinates (in a three-dimensional system).

In Figure 5–31, three points (D1, D2, and D3) have been created by freehand digitizing. The BEFORE illustration shows that each digitized location is marked with an **x**, while in the AFTER illustration each is marked with a cross (+).

Figure 5–32 illustrates points that have been created by coordinate entry of X and Y values.

Figure 5–33 illustrates a point that was created at the intersection of two existing lines (D1 and D2), not by digitizing the point but by selecting the lines and allowing the system to determine the exact coordinates of their intersection.

Lines

Lines are geometric items that connect two points, each of which has an X, Y, and Z coordinate (in a three-dimensional system). The points may be specified either separately or relative to existing geometric items. The endpoints of connected lines are also the starting points of the lines to which they are connected. A line's origin is its *midpoint*.

The command DRAW LINE, accompanied by the appropriate values and modifiers, will create the following types of lines or line groups:

- A series of connected lines

- A closed region with connected lines

- A horizontal or vertical line

- A line at an angle to an existing line

- A line parallel to an existing line

- A line tangent to a circle and a line or point

Some of the modifiers necessary to create such items include:

- HORIZONTAL — parallel to the X axis

- VERTICAL — parallel to the Y axis

- PERPENDICULAR — perpendicular to a specified line

- PARALLEL n — parallel to a specified line, n units away

- ANGLE n — at an angle of n degrees from a specified line

- TANGENT to — tangent to a circle

- LENGTH n — n units long

The color, font, and layer of the line can also be specified in the DRAW LINE command.

Figure 5–31
Creating a point by free digitizing.

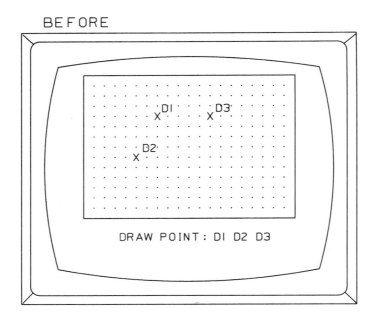

BEFORE

DRAW POINT: DI D2 D3

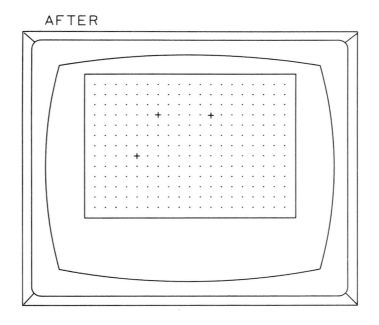

AFTER

BEFORE

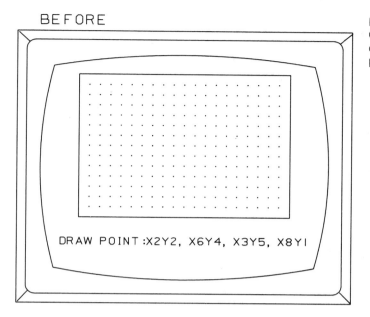

DRAW POINT :X2Y2, X6Y4, X3Y5, X8YI

AFTER

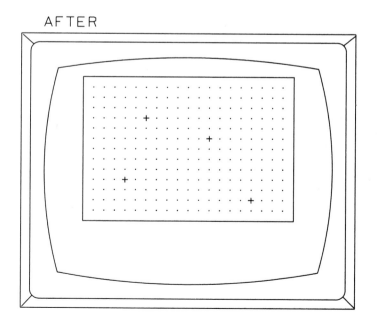

Figure 5–32
Creating points by
defining coordinate
positions.

Figure 5–33
Creating a point using
existing geometry.

BEFORE

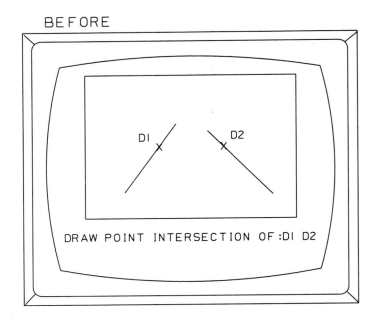

DRAW POINT INTERSECTION OF :DI D2

AFTER

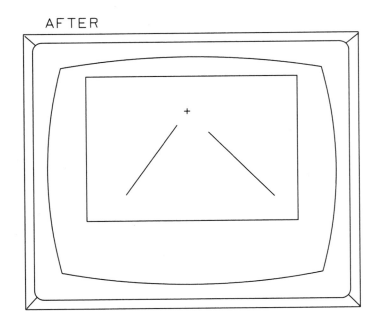

In specifying location, the designer can automatically align freely digitized points with explicit grid coordinates by using the grid option. In this case, the designer can then choose whether or not to have his or her freehand digitizing pulled to the appropriate grid point by the snap option. The start and endpoints are always entered *after* the DRAW LINE command and appropriate modifiers.

Creating Connected and Separate Lines

To create separate or connected lines, the designer must:

1. Select DRAW LINE and modifiers.

2. Digitize or enter exact coordinates of the start and endpoints of the line.

When the LENGTH modifier is used, the endpoint in Step 2 indicates only the direction of the line. Connected lines are created by digitizing the endpoint of the next line. This process is then repeated for each additional line segment. Additional separate lines are created by entering a semicolon and repeating Step 2.

Figure 5–34 illustrates the selection of DRAW LINE and the location of endpoints (D1 and D2). Figure 5–35 illustrates three individual but connected lines (D1, D2, D3, and D4). And Figure 5–36 two separate lines created by the same instruction (Step 2; Step 2).

Creating Horizontal and Vertical Lines

To create horizontal and vertical lines, the designer must:

1. Select DRAW LINE, using either the HORIZONTAL or VERTICAL modifiers and any others that are appropriate.

2. Digitize the beginning point of the line.

3. Digitize a location that indicates the direction and length of the line.

A horizontal line runs parallel to the X axis. In Figure 5–37, a horizontal line was created using *DRAW LINE HORIZONTAL* and two digitized points. The first point established the starting point, and the second established the *direction* and length. If the line's length is given, however, the first point establishes the starting point, and the second establishes only the direction, as in Figure 5–38.

The vertical line is parallel to the Y axis. In Figure 5–39, *DRAW LINE VERTICAL* was selected and two points digitized. The first point established the starting point, and the second point established the direction and distance.

Figure 5–34
Creating a line by free
digitizing.

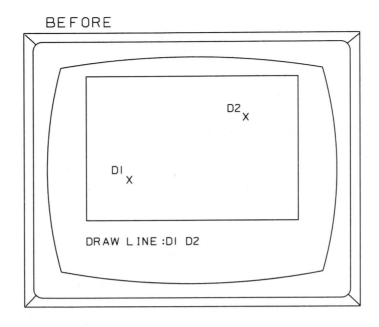

BEFORE

DRAW LINE :DI D2

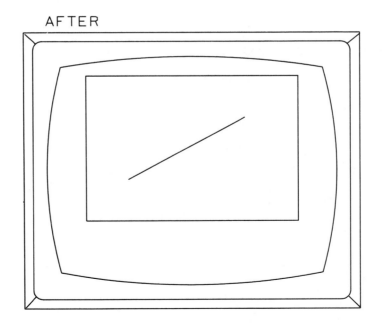

AFTER

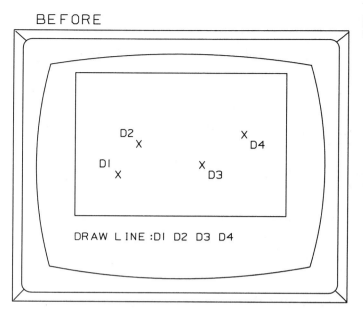

BEFORE

DRAW LINE :DI D2 D3 D4

Figure 5–35
Creating multiple lines.

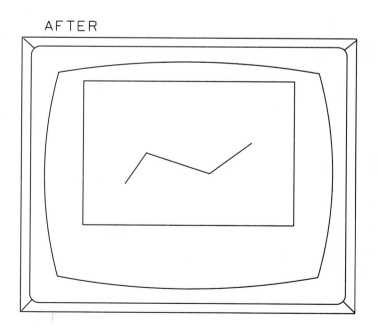

AFTER

Figure 5–36
Creating lines.

BEFORE

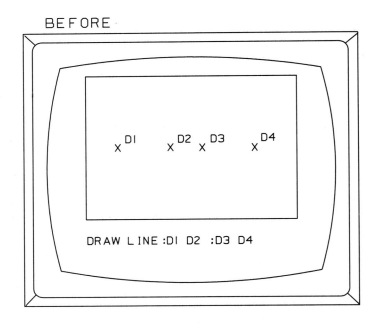

AFTER

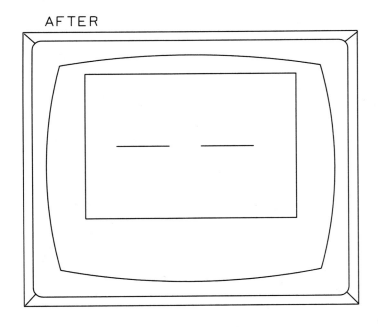

BEFORE

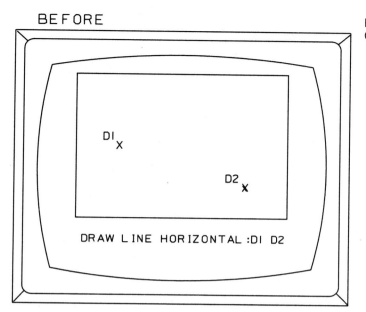

DRAW LINE HORIZONTAL :DI D2

AFTER

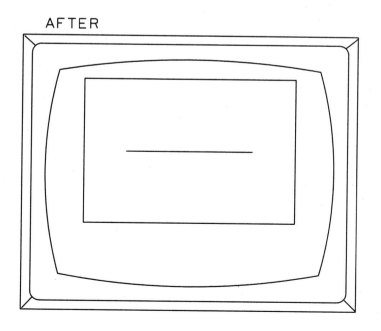

Figure 5–37
Creating a horizontal line.

Figure 5–38
Creating a horizontal line
using the length modifier.

BEFORE

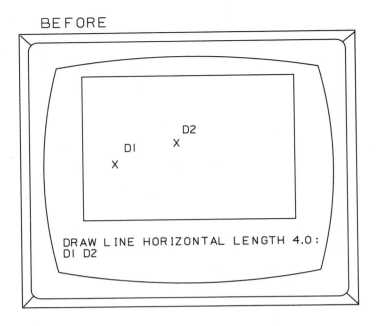

AFTER

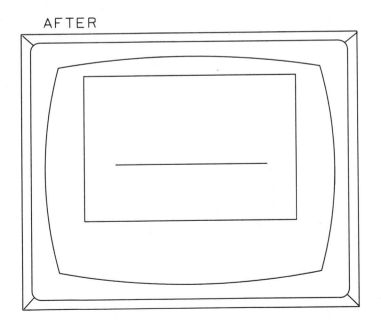

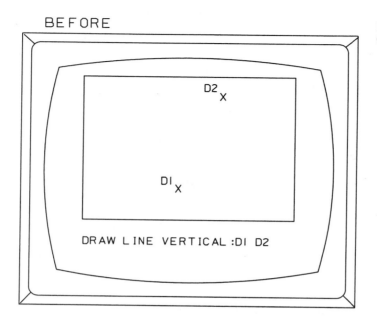

BEFORE

DRAW LINE VERTICAL :DI D2

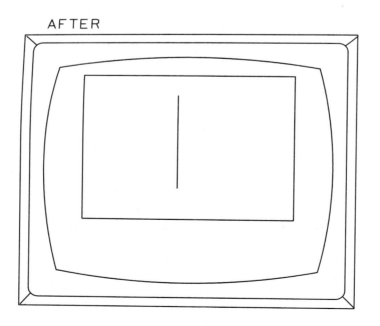

AFTER

Figure 5–39
Creating a vertical line.

Creating Lines at an Angle

To create lines at any specified angle, the designer must:

1. Select DRAW LINE ANGLE, including the number of degrees (if the default is not used) and any other modifiers.

2. Digitize the existing line.

3. Digitize the start point of the line.

4. Digitize a location that indicates the length of the line.

5. Repeat Steps 3 and 4 for each line to be inserted.

In Figure 5–40, a line has been created at 45 degrees to an existing line by *DRAW LINE ANGLE* along with three digitized points. The first point identified the existing line from which the angle would be measured, the second established the starting point, and the third established the endpoint and the length.

Creating Parallel Lines

To create a line parallel to a given line, the designer must:

1. Select DRAW LINE PARALLEL with the appropriate modifiers and enter a value to specify the distance between the existing line and new line.

2. Digitize the existing line.

3. Digitize the beginning position of the new line. (If a distance value is not used, this location would also determine the distance between the existing line and the new line.)

4. Digitize a location that indicates the direction and length of the line.

5. Repeat Steps 3 and 4 for each line to be inserted.

In Figure 5–41, a line has been created that is parallel to an existing line by *DRAW LINE PARALLEL* and three digitized points. D1 identified the existing line, D2 established the *starting point* and *distance* from the referenced line, and D3 established the *endpoint* of the new line.

When the distance between the two lines is given in the instruction, four points must be digitized, as Figure 5–42 illustrates. Here *DRAW LINE PARALLEL* was selected and a distance of 3 inches was specified. The first of the four points (D1) identified the existing reference line; D2 established the *side* that the new line would be on; D3 established the *beginning point*; and D4 established the *endpoint*.

In Figure 5–43, both distance (2.0) the length (3.5) were given in the instruction. The first of four digitized points (D1) identified the reference line,

BEFORE

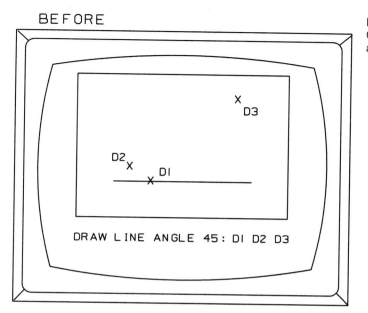

DRAW LINE ANGLE 45: DI D2 D3

AFTER

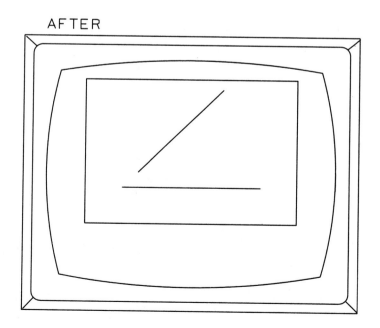

Figure 5–40
Creating a line at an
angle to an existing line.

Figure 5–41
Creating a line parallel to
an existing line.

BEFORE

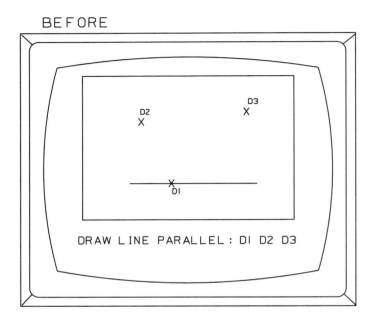

AFTER

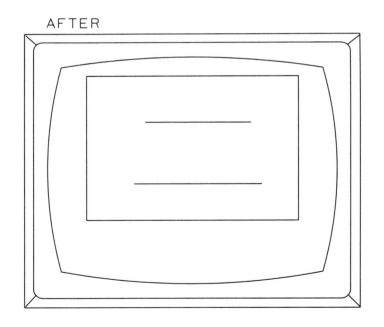

BEFORE

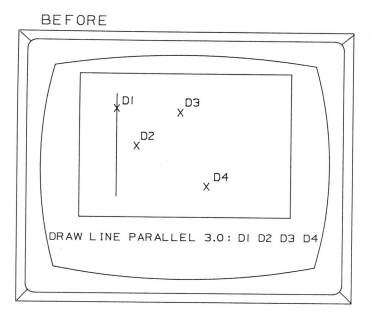

AFTER

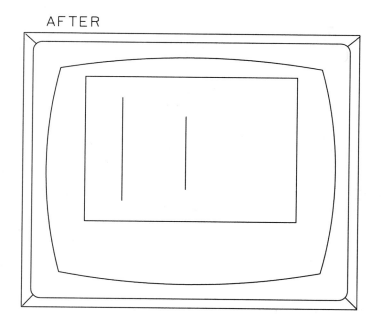

Figure 5–42
Creating parallel lines.

Figure 5–43
Creating a parallel line
giving the distance and
the length.

BEFORE

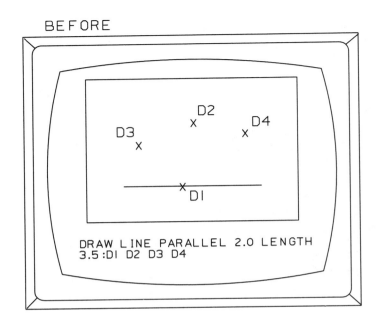

DRAW LINE PARALLEL 2.0 LENGTH
3.5 :DI D2 D3 D4

AFTER

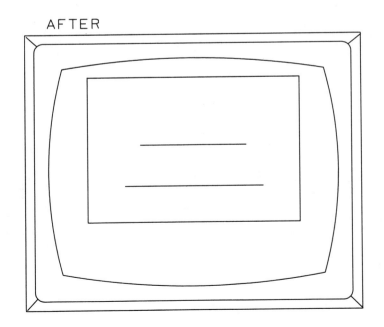

D2 established the side, D3 established the starting point, and D4 established the *direction*.

Creating Perpendicular Lines

To create a line perpendicular to a given line, the designer must:

1. Select DRAW LINE PERPENDICULAR and the desired modifiers.

2. Digitize the existing reference line.

3. Digitize the beginning position of the new line.

4. Digitize a location that indicates the direction and length of the new line.

5. Repeat Steps 3 and 4 for each line created.

In Figure 5–44, DRAW LINE PERPENDICULAR was selected and three points were digitized. The first point (D1) identified the existing reference line; the second (D2) established the starting point. The third (D3) established direction and end point.

When the length is given, Figure 5–45, the third digitize provides the direction, not the endpoint.

Creating Tangent Lines

To create a line tangent to an arc or circle, the designer must:

1. Select DRAW LINE TANGENT TO.

2. Digitize the two items to which the line is tangent, one of which must be an arc or circle.

In Figure 5–46, DRAW LINE TANGENT TO was selected and two items were digitized. D1 identified the first item and D2 the second. The line was then drawn tangent to the two circles. Since two tangency positions are possible for each circle, the digitizer must be *near* the point of tangency.

In Figure 5–47, a line was constructed tangent to an existing circle and connected to the *end* of an existing line. The use of an isolation option such as END helps in adding new geometry to existing geometry.

Inserting Lines by Isolation Options

As mentioned previously, isolation options can be very useful in adding a new item to an existing one. Figure 5–48 illustrates how a line is created between two lines and attached to their endpoints using the END isolation option.

Figure 5–44
Creating a line perpen-
dicular to an existing line.

BEFORE

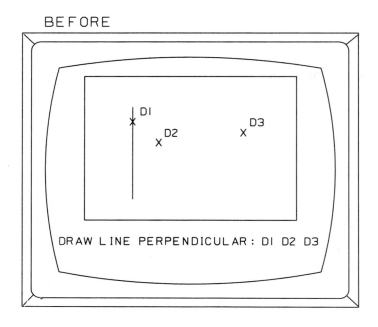

DRAW LINE PERPENDICULAR: DI D2 D3

AFTER

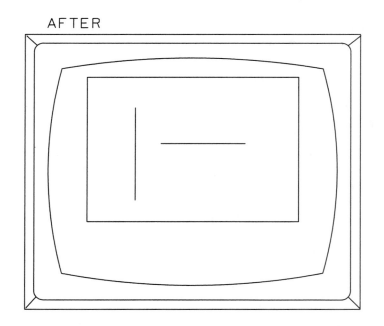

BEFORE

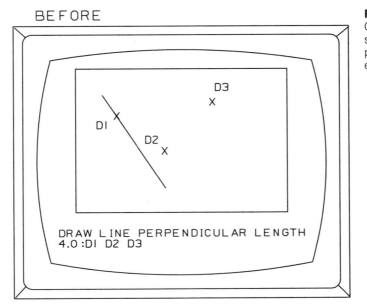

AFTER

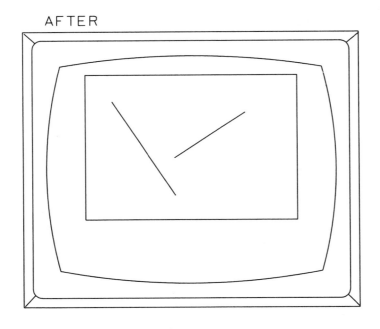

Figure 5–45
Creating a line with a
specified length and
perpendicular to an
existing line.

Figure 5–46
Creating a tangent line.

BEFORE

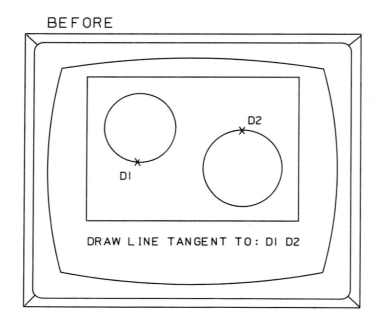

DRAW LINE TANGENT TO: DI D2

AFTER

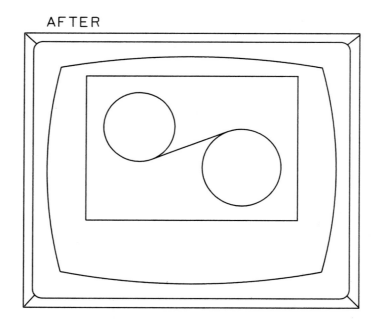

BEFORE

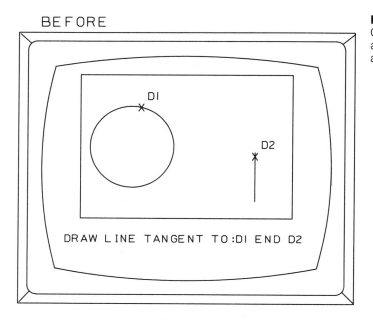

DRAW LINE TANGENT TO:DI END D2

Figure 5–47
Creating a line tangent to
a circle and at the end of
an existing line.

AFTER

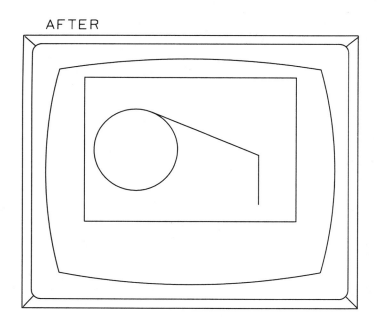

Figure 5–48
Creating a line between two existing lines using the end mask.

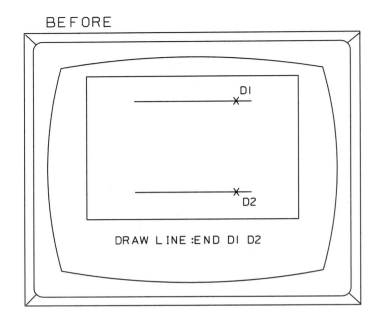

BEFORE

DI
D2

DRAW LINE :END DI D2

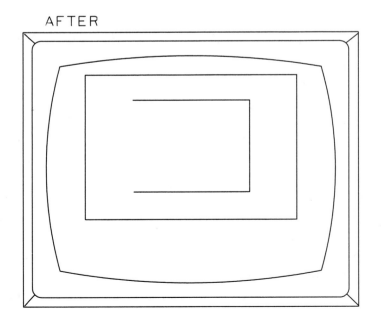

AFTER

Figure 5–49 shows how the designer is able to draw a line from the end of an existing line to a particular location by turning off the END option and isolating the last position with LOCATION and then IX5.

In Figure 5–50, the ORIGIN option is used to create a line from the midpoint (origin) of the line to the center of the circle (origin).

Adding a Line Using VersaCAD

The following section shows how the instruction for creating a line works in the popular two-dimensional system, VersaCAD. To begin, the ADD menu is chosen from the main menu by selecting [A] or placing the cursor over [ADD] and pressing the stylus.

The ADD menu enables the designer to create, on the CRT, the basic items that make up a drawing. A complete list of options the designer will need to create these basic objects using the ADD menu are shown on the CRT:

ADD

Line

Rectangle

Polygon

Circle

Ellipse

Arc

Symbol

Bezier (French curve)

Point

Dimension

Text

Guides

Sketch

Quit

Help

Figure 5–49
Creating a line using masks.

BEFORE

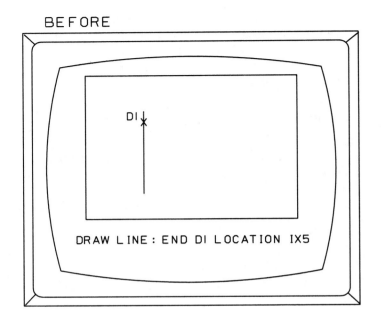

DRAW LINE: END DI LOCATION IX5

AFTER

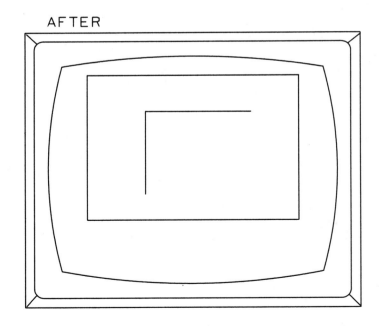

BEFORE

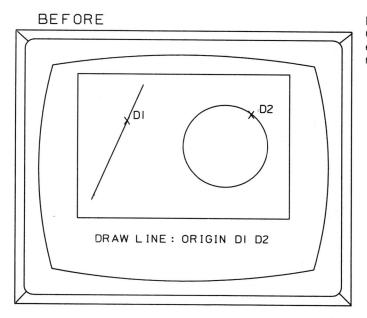

DRAW LINE: ORIGIN DI D2

AFTER

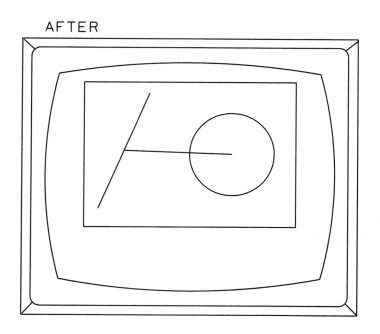

Figure 5–50
Creating a line between existing entities using masks.

A line is defined by two points:

1.   The first endpoint of the line.

2.   The second endpoint of the line.

To draw a line, the designer must place the cursor at the first endpoint, digitize the position with the stylus or keyboard, then move the cursor to the second endpoint. If the Object Tracking feature is turned on, a flashing rubberband line will appear from the first endpoint to the cursor position. When the designer is satisfied with the length and rotation of the line, he or she accepts the second endpoint and the line becomes fixed to indicate that the computer has accepted the information.

As the designer continues to move the cursor, another line will appear from the second endpoint of the previously created line to the present cursor location. This process will continue until the ADD menu is restored by pressing [Q] or the line is detached from the endpoint by pressing [D] (see Options below).

The options available during the creation of a line are:

Arrow [A]:	Places an arrowhead at the second endpoint of the line. Press [A] again to remove the arrowhead.
Template [T]:	Causes the line to become a template line. Press [T] again to turn off the template option.
Marker [M]:	Displays a marker at the center of the line. Press [M] again to remove the marker.
X-axis lock [X]:	Holds the line along the horizontal axis (0 or 180 degrees rotation).
Y-axis lock [Y]:	Holds the line along the vertical axis (90 or 270 degrees rotation).
FREE [F]:	Releases the X or Y option, returning to the normal, unlocked mode.
Rotate [R]:	Rotates the line counterclockwise with each keypress by the increment defined in the UNITS menu or with the UPDATE function key.
Detach [D]:	Detaches the current line from the last endpoint entered, which allows the designer to start a new line anywhere on the CRT.
Single [S]:	Allows the designer to draw a single line at a time (similar to Detach).
Erase [E]:	Erases the last endpoint entered, which allows the repositioning of the line. By repeatedly pressing [E] the designer can erase endpoints in the reverse order of their creation.
Quit [Q]:	Allows the designer to quit adding lines and return to the ADD menu.

Circles

The start and endpoint of a circle are at the *right, three o'clock* position, and its origin is at the center. With the exception of circles created with three digitized circumference points, the circumference of the circle begins and ends at three o'clock.

DRAW CIRCLE will create circles in several ways, depending on the type of information available to the designer. Some of the modifiers that can be used to create circles include:

RADIUS (R *n*)	Specifies the radius of the circle. The designer can provide the value or allow the system to provide it.
DIAMETER (D *n*)	Specifies the diameter of the circle. The designer can provide the value or allow the system to provide it.
TANGENT TO	Creates a circle tangent to another geometrical item.
ARC	Creates a circle from an arc.

It is important to use only one modifier at a time.

Creating Circles from Three Points on the Circumference

To create a circle from three points on the circumference, the designer must:

1. Select DRAW CIRCLE.

2. Digitize three points on the circle's circumference. The circle is created after the third point is digitized.

3. Repeat Step 2 for each additional circle.

The circle in Figure 5–51 was created by DRAW CIRCLE and three digitized points (D1, D2, and D3) on the circumference.

Letting the System Calculate the Diameter

To create a circle when the system must calculate the diameter, the designer must:

1. Select DRAW CIRCLE DIAMETER.

2. Digitize two opposite points on the circle's circumference. The circle is created after the second point is digitized.

3. Repeat Step 2 for each additional circle.

Figure 5–51
Creating a three point circle.

BEFORE

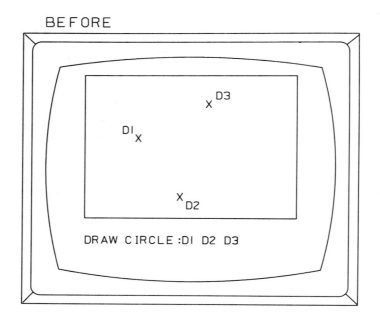

DRAW CIRCLE :DI D2 D3

AFTER

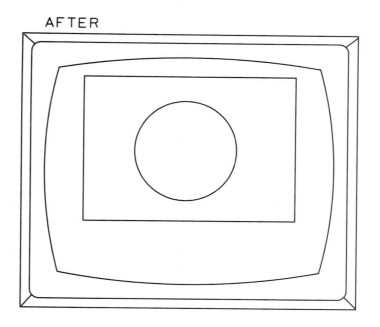

The system calculates the diameter from the distance between the two locations digitized.

The circle in Figure 5–52 was created by DRAW CIRCLE DIAMETER and two digitized points (D1 and D2), which established opposite points (the diameter) on the circle's circumference.

Letting the System Calculate the Radius

To create a circle when the system must calculate the radius, the designer must:

1. Select DRAW CIRCLE RADIUS.

2. Digitize the circle's center.

3. Digitize a point on the circle's circumference. The system calculates the radius from the two locations digitized.

4. Repeat Steps 2 and 3 for each additional circle.

The circle in Figure 5–53 was created by DRAW CIRCLE RADIUS along with two digitized locations. D1 established the circle's center and D2 a point on the circumference.

Specifying a Diameter or Radius

To create a circle with specified diameter or radius, the designer must:

1. Select DRAW CIRCLE.

2. Enter D or R and value.

3. Digitize the circle's center.

4. Repeat Step 3 for each additional circle.

As Figure 5–54 shows, only one digitized point is required for inserting a circle when the diameter or the radius value is given.

Creating a Circle Tangent to Another Circle

The circle in Figure 5–55 was created by DRAW CIRCLE TANGENT TO. D1 established the circle's center (origin), and D2 identified the circle (or arc) to which the new circle is tangent. The system used the distance from the origin (D1) to the circumference of the existing referenced circle to calculate the new circle's radius.

BEFORE

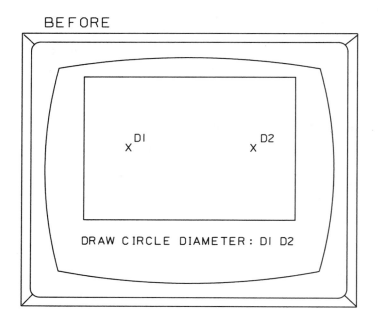

AFTER

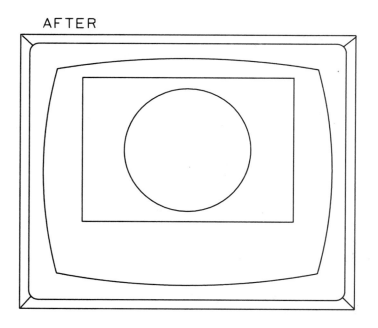

BEFORE

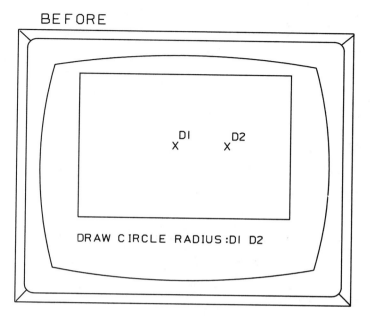

DRAW CIRCLE RADIUS:DI D2

Figure 5–53
Creating a circle by
digitizing a radius.

AFTER

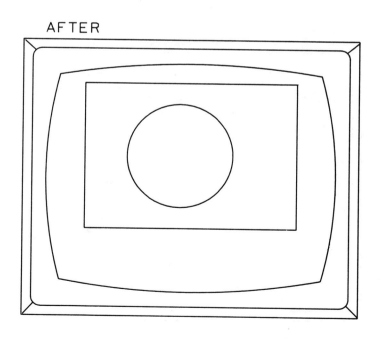

Figure 5–54
Creating a circle by
specifying the radius
value.

BEFORE

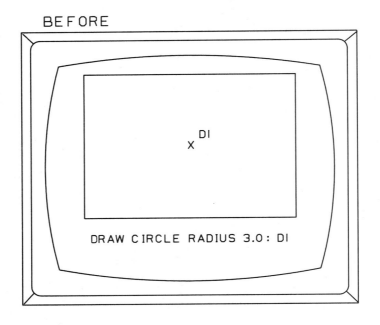

DRAW CIRCLE RADIUS 3.0: DI

AFTER

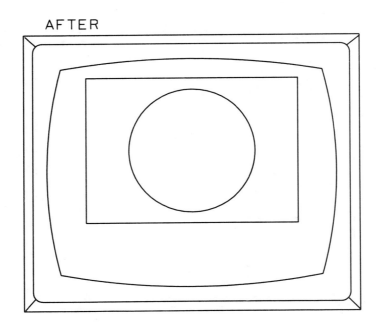

BEFORE

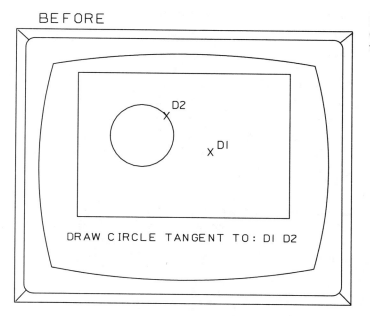

DRAW CIRCLE TANGENT TO: DI D2

AFTER

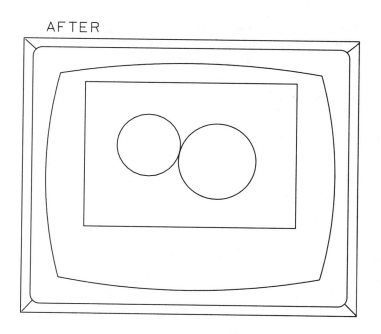

Figure 5–55
Creating a circle tangent
to an existing circle.

Adding a Circle Using AutoCAD

The following section shows how one system (AutoCAD) creates circles using CIRCLE.

Center and Radius   This method allows the designer to enter the circle's center point and radius. It is the default method, as indicated by the prompts:

    Command: CIRCLE   3P/2P/<Center point>   5.5

    Diameter/<Radius>:   3

Center and Diameter   If the designer prefers to specify the diameter, he or she selects the D modifier in response to the "Diameter/ <Radius>:" prompt. AutoCAD will then ask for the diameter. For instance, the following sequence creates the same circle as the previous one:

    Command: CIRCLE   3P/2P/<Center point>   5.5

    Diameter/<Radius>:   D

    Diameter: 6

Three-point Circles   On this system, the designer can also create a circle by entering three points on its circumference. To do this, the designer responds with "3P" to the "3P/2P/<Center point>": prompt. For example:

    Command: CIRCLE   3P/2P/<Center point>:   3P

    First point: 6.5

    Second point: 7.4

    Third point: 6.3

Two-point Circles   Alternatively, if the designer responds to the "3P/2P/< Center point>:" prompt with "2P," AutoCAD will specify the circle by the two endpoints of its diameter. For instance, the following sequence draws the same circle as the previous one:

    Command: CIRCLE   3P/2P/<Center point>:   2P

    First point: 6.5

    Second point on diameter: 6.3

Arcs

An arc is a partial circle. There are five basic ways to create an arc using DRAW ARC:

1. Specify the start point, a point on the arc's path, and the endpoint. The system creates the arc in the direction the points were digitized.

2. Let the system calculate the diameter but specify the start and the endpoints. The system creates a 180-degree arc.

3. Let the system calculate the radius but specify the arc's center, the start point, and ending angle.

4. Specify the diameter or radius, along with the arc's center, beginning angle, and ending angle.

5. Specify the diameter or radius, as well as the arc's center, and use the modifiers to specify the beginning and ending angles.

Specifying Three Points along the Arc

To create an arc in which three points are to be specified, the designer must:

1. Select DRAW ARC.

2. Digitize the start point, a point on the arc's path, and the endpoint. The system creates the arc after the endpoint is specified.

3. Repeat Step 2 for each arc to be inserted. The system will insert one that passes through the digitized points.

The arc in Figure 5–56 was created by DRAW ARC along with three digitized points. D1 established the arc's starting point, D2 is a point on the arc, and D3 established the endpoint. Note that the direction of digitizing (counterclockwise) determines the direction of the arc.

Letting the System Calculate the Radius or Diameter

To create an arc when the system must calculate the radius or diameter, the designer must:

1. Select DRAW ARC RADIUS.

2. Digitize the arc center, start point, and ending angle. The system creates the arc after the ending angle is specified and inserts an arc in a counter-

Figure 5–56
Creating an arc through
three digitized points.

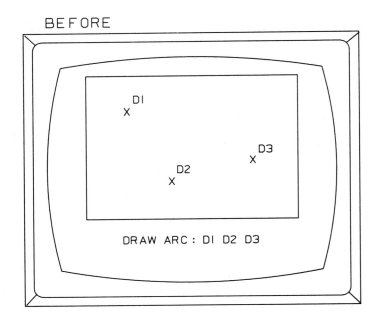

BEFORE

DRAW ARC: DI D2 D3

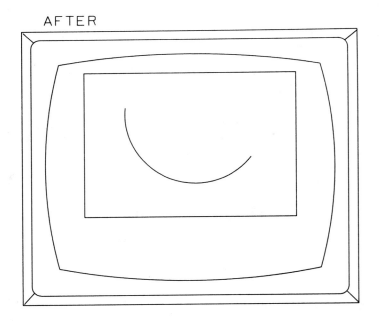

AFTER

counterclockwise direction. It calculates the radius from the arc center and start point.

3. Repeat Step 2 for each additional arc.

The arc in Figure 5–57 was created by DRAW ARC RADIUS along with three digitized points. D1 is the arc's center (origin), D2 is the starting point, and D3 is the endpoint.

In Figure 5–58, an arc connecting two lines was constructed by using DRAW ARC DIAMETER and the digitizes. D1 and D2 identified the two lines. The END isolation option was utilized to lock the arc onto the line's ends. The system created a half circle arc. This capability is useful in constructing slots.

Using Radius or Diameter Value to Create Arcs

To create an arc using a radius or diameter value, the designer must:

1. Select DRAW ARC.

2. Select DIAMETER or RADIUS and a value.

3. Select START ANGLE and END ANGLE and a degree value.

4. Digitize the arc center. The system creates the arc.

5. Repeat Step 4 for each additional arc.

In Figure 5–59, only one digitized point was necessary since the instruction included the RADIUS (2), START ANGLE (90), and END ANGLE (360). The system created an arc with a 2-inch radius, starting at 90 degrees (twelve o'clock position) and ending at 360 degrees (three o'clock position). D1 established the arc's center.

An option available on some systems will convert an existing arc into a circle, as Figure 5–60 shows. In this example, DRAW CIRCLE ARC changed the arc to a circle (with the same center point and radius value).

Creating an ARC using AutoCAD

The following section shows how one two-dimensional system (AutoCAD) creates arcs using the ARC command. There are eight different methods of specifying an arc on this system:

1. Specifying three points on the arc, the default method.

2. Specifying start point, center, end point.

3. Specifying start point, center, included angle.

Figure 5–57
Creating an arc by
digitizing the center,
radius, and endpoint.

BEFORE

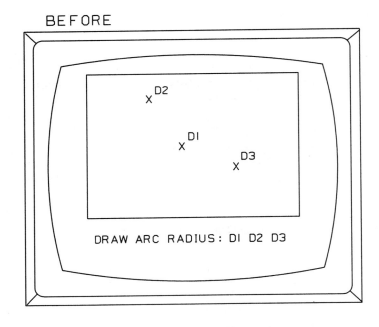

DRAW ARC RADIUS: DI D2 D3

AFTER

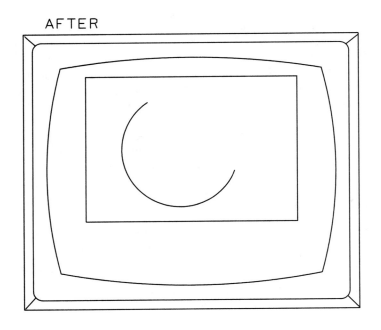

BEFORE

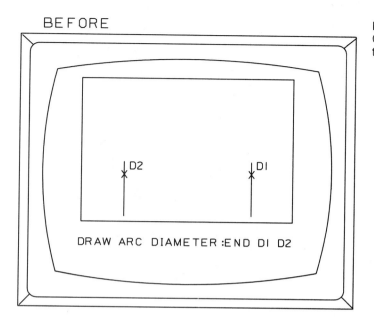

DRAW ARC DIAMETER :END DI D2

Figure 5–58
Creating an arc between
two lines.

AFTER

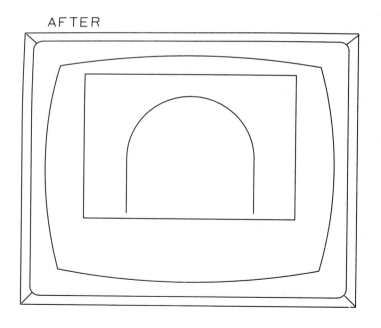

Figure 5–59
Creating an arc by giving
the radius value, starting
angle, and ending angle.

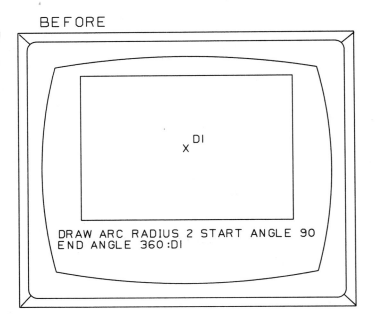

BEFORE

DRAW ARC RADIUS 2 START ANGLE 90
END ANGLE 360 :DI

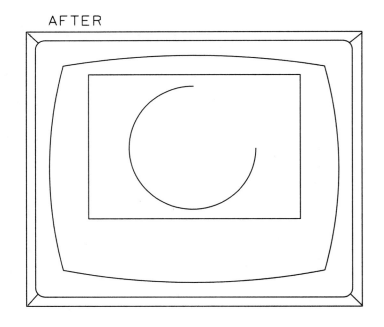

AFTER

BEFORE

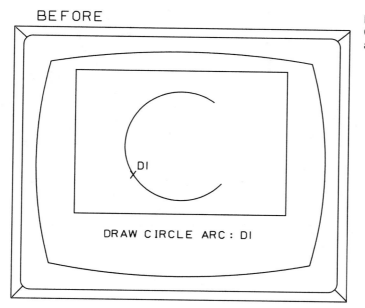

DRAW CIRCLE ARC: DI

Figure 5–60
Changing a circle into an
arc.

AFTER

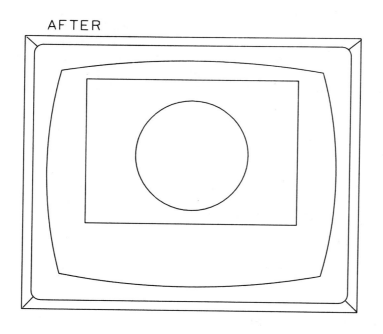

161

4. Specifying start point, center, length of chord.

5. Specifying start point, end point, radius.

6. Specifying start point, end point, included angle.

7. Specifying start point, end point, starting direction.

8. Continuing previous line or arc.

In this list, "center" refers to the center point of the circle of which the arc is a part.

With the exception of the default method, which is similar to the "3P" method of specifying a circle, the other arc specification methods require the designer to type a letter followed by a space or RETURN. The ARC option letters are:

A — Angle included

C — Center

D — Starting direction

E — End point

L — Length of chord

R — Radius

Prompts indicate which options are available at each step. Each method is discussed separately below. If the ADE-2 package is available, the designer can enter DRAG when prompted for the last parameter of each method to specify it dynamically on the CRT.

Three-point Arcs   This is the default method of arc specification and is similar to the "3P" method of specifying a circle. *The first and third points are the arc endpoints.* For example:

Command: ARC Center/<Start point>: 7,4

Center/End/<Second point>: 6,5

End point: 6,3

A three-point arc may be specified from either direction. The last point is the endpoint used to attach a continuation line or arc.

Start, Center, End   This method causes an arc to be created counterclockwise from the start to the end, with a specified centerpoint.

Command: ARC Center/<Start point>: 2,1

Center/End/<Second point>: C

Center: 1,1

Angle/Length of chord/<End point>: 1,2.3

As illustrated in this example, the endpoint specified is used only to determine the angle at which the arc ends; the arc does not necessarily pass through this point. The arc's radius is determined by the start and centerpoint.

It is sometimes convenient to give the centerpoint first. For instance, the center, radius, start angle, and end angle can be specified by relative coordinates, as in:

Command: ARC Center/<Start point> C

Center: 1,1

Start point: @ < 0

Angle/Length of chord/<End point>: @ < 90

This creates the same arc as in the previous example. As is commonly the case, a relative coordinate for the endpoint is based on the center, even though the start was entered late.

Start, Center, Included Angle This method creates an arc spanned by the specified center and start point. Ordinarily, the arc is drawn counterclockwise from the start point; however, if the specified angle is negative, the arc is drawn clockwise. For example:

Command: ARC Center/<Start point>: 2,1

Center/End/<Second point>: C

Center: 1,1

Angle/Length of chord/<End point>: A

Included angle: 90 or −90 or −270

Fillet

A fillet is an *arc* that is tangent to existing geometrical items, including *points*, *lines*, *circles*, and *arcs*. On most systems, digitizing should be *counterclockwise*.

A fillet is created by DRAW FILLET and the appropriate modifiers and values.

The modifiers available for diameter and radius, for the fillet itself, and for trimming are displayed below:

D *n*	(Diameter) Specifies the diameter of the fillet.
R *n*	(Radius) Specifies the radius of the fillet.

Fillet Modifiers

ARC	Creates the fillet as an arc. This is the default.
CIR	(Circle) Creates the fillet as a circle.

Trimming Modifiers

NOTRIM	Retains the original length of the items digitized.
TRIM	Shortens the items digitized to their point of intersection with the fillet. This is the default.

Creating a Fillet

To create a fillet, the designer must:

1. Select DRAW FILLET and the appropriate modifiers.

2. Digitize the two items to which the fillet will be tangent. The system creates the fillet. If two lines are digitized, they cannot be parallel.

3. Repeat Step 2 for each additional fillet.

The system creates an arc tangent to each of the two pairs of items and trims each to its point of intersection with the fillet.

In Figure 5–61, DRAW FILLET and two digitized points create a curve tangent to the two digitized lines. A fillet with a specified size is created by entering the diameter or radius value, as in Figure 5–62.

Figure 5–63 shows that the designer put multiple fillets on the drawing by continuing to digitize items. The items referenced need not be touching. The system trims and completes each filleted corner.

BEFORE

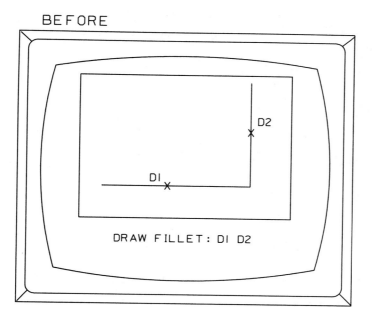

DRAW FILLET: DI D2

Figure 5–61
Creating a fillet between
two lines.

AFTER

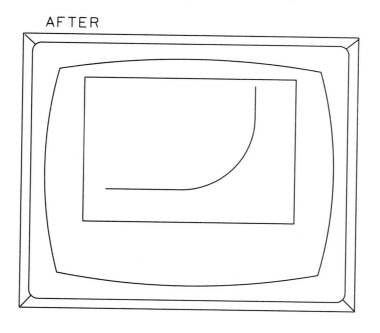

Figure 5–62
Drawing a fillet with a specified radius.

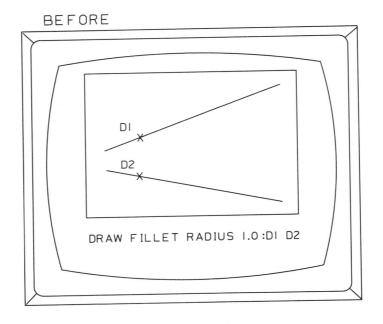

BEFORE

DRAW FILLET RADIUS 1.0 :DI D2

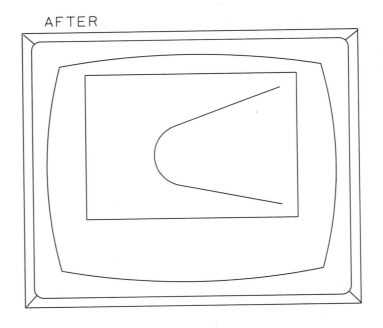

AFTER

BEFORE

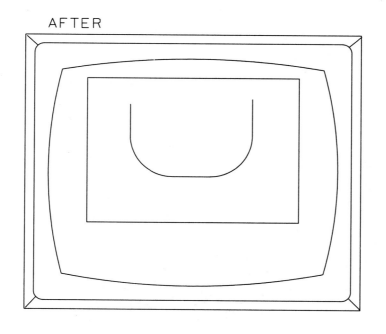

AFTER

Figure 5–63
Creating fillets.

Creating Fillets with AutoCAD

The following section shows how one two-dimensional system (AutoCAD) creates fillets, by using the FILLET command. FILLET connects two lines by means of a smoothly fitted arc of a specified radius and adjusts the lengths of the lines so that they end exactly on the arc.

    Command: FILLET

    Polyline/Radius/<Select two lines>: (Point to two lines)

    By default, FILLET expects two lines to be selected. After digitizing the two lines, do not press RETURN. FILLET knows that only two points will be selected.

    The radius to be used for fillets is remembered as part of the drawing file. The initial fillet radius for a new drawing is defined by the drawing defaults. To change the fillet radius, reply ''R'' to the prompt:

    Command: FILLET

    Polyline/Radius/<Select two lines>: R

    Enter fillet radius: (value)

    The radius can be entered numerically, or the desired radius can be selected by designating two points. AutoCAD will set the radius equal to the distance between those points.

    FILLET extends the two selected lines, if necessary, until they intersect. The lines are then trimmed and the fillet arc created. A fillet radius of zero can be used to adjust two lines so that they end precisely at the same point. If both lines are on the same drawing layer, the fillet is placed on that layer. If the lines are on different layers, the fillet is placed on the current layer. If no intersection point is found within the drawing limits (and the limits check is ON), the instruction is rejected.

    Command: FILLET

    Polyline/Radius/<Select two lines>: (Point to the two lines)

Chamfer

A chamfer is a bevel formed by an *angular* line connecting two intersecting *lines*. It is created by DRAW CHAMFER and the appropriate modifiers and values. Some of the modifiers that can be used to create chamfers include:

ANGLE	Angle with first line digitized (default = 45 degrees)
LENGTH A	Distance from intersection to chamfer along first line chosen (default = .5)
LENGTH B	Same as LENGTH A except that it refers to the second line chosen (do not use with ANGLE)
TRIM	Trim line extensions (default)
−TRIM	(Minus trim) leave line extensions

Creating Chamfers

The chamfer capability *bevels* the corner of a part. It can be created with specific lengths and angles, much like a fillet.

In Figure 5–64, DRAW CHAMFER was used on all corners of the rectangle along with the system default for angle (45 degrees) and size. In Figure 5–65, the angle and length modifiers were used to create chamfers.

In Figure 5–66, only the modifier was used. In this last case, D1 and D2 identified the existing lines. D3 established the starting point of the chamfer and the line from which the angle was taken.

Creating a Chamfer Using AutoCAD

The following section shows how one two-dimensional system (AutoCAD) creates chamfers, using CHAMFER to trim two intersecting lines a specified distance from the intersection and connect the trimmed ends with a new line segment. The CHAMFER operation is similar to that of FILLET.

Command: CHAMFER

Polyline/Distances/<Select first line>: (Point to one line)

Select second line: (Point to intersecting line)

By default, CHAMFER expects two lines to be selected. After digitizing the two lines, do not press RETURN. CHAMFER knows that only two points will be selected.

The distance at which lines are to be trimmed from their intersection point during chamfering is remembered as part of the drawing file. The initial chamfer distance for a new drawing is determined by the drawing defaults. To change the chamfer distance, reply "D" to the prompt.

Command: CHAMFER

Polyline/Distance/<Select first line>: (value)

Enter first chamfer distance <default>: (value)

Enter second chamfer distance <default>: (value)

Figure 5–64
Creating chamfers.

BEFORE

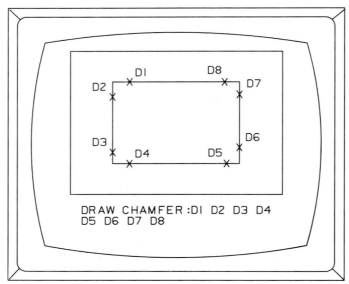

DRAW CHAMFER :DI D2 D3 D4
D5 D6 D7 D8

AFTER

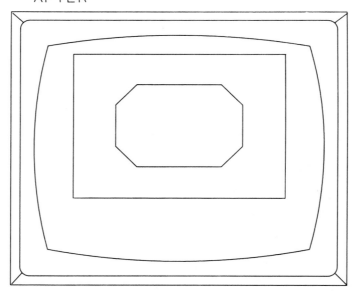

BEFORE

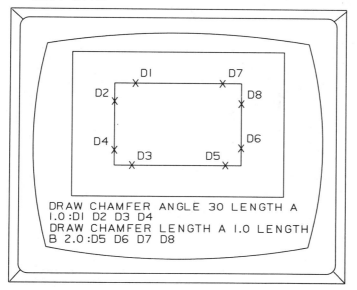

DRAW CHAMFER ANGLE 30 LENGTH A
1.0 :D1 D2 D3 D4
DRAW CHAMFER LENGTH A 1.0 LENGTH
B 2.0 :D5 D6 D7 D8

AFTER

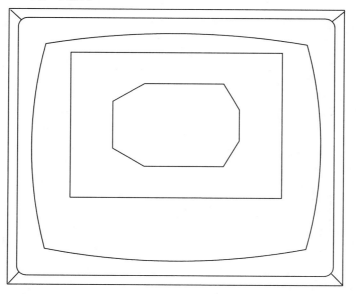

Figure 5–65
Creating chamfers with
specified angles and
lengths.

Figure 5–66
Creating a chamfer with a
specified angle.

BEFORE

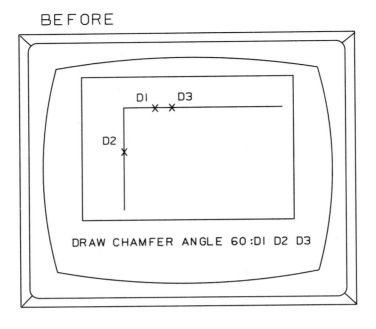

AFTER

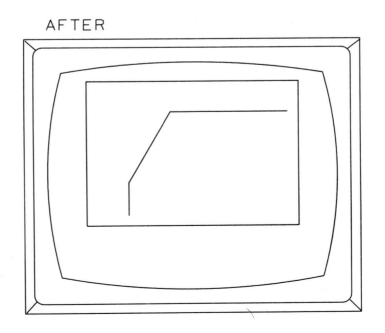

Each distance can be entered numerically, or the desired distance can be selected by designating two points. AutoCAD will measure the distance between those points and use that value. The default for the first distance is the most recent chamfer distance specified. The default for the second distance is whatever was chosen for the first distance.

CHAMFER extends lines, if necessary, until they intersect. It then trims the first line by the first distance, trims the second line by the second distance, and connects the trimmed ends with a straight line. If the first and second distances are both zero, the two lines are trimmed so that they end precisely at the same point.

If both lines are on the same drawing layer, the chamfer is placed on that layer. If the lines are on different layers, the chamfer is placed on the current layer. If no intersection point is found within the drawing limits (and the limits check is ON), the instruction is rejected.

The following instruction sequence sets the first and second chamfer distances to 0.5 and 0.25 respectively and then chamfers two lines.

Command: CHAMFER

Polyline/Distance/<Select first line>: D

Enter first chamfer distance <0.0>: 0.5

Enter second chamfer distance <0.5>: 0.25

Command: RETURN (to cause command repetition)

Polyline/Distance/<Select first line>: (Point to first line)

Splines

A spline is the CADD equivalent of a drafter's *french curve*. The designer creates a spline by selecting DRAW SPLINE and digitizing two or more points. A spline can be inserted either *through* or *between* specific points.

In Figure 5–67, the spline was created by digitizing five locations. The system generated a smooth curve through each point.

Rectangles

To create a rectangle, the designer merely selects DRAW RECTANGLE, then supplies the diagonal corners either alone or with the modifier WIDTH. The rectangle in Figure 5–68 was defined by selecting DRAW RECTANGLE and then digitizing its diagonal corners D1 and D2.

Figure 5–69 illustrates a rectangle created with the diagonal corners *and* WIDTH. In this case, the first digitized point established one corner and the second the direction and height of the rectangle.

Figure 5–67
Creating a spline.

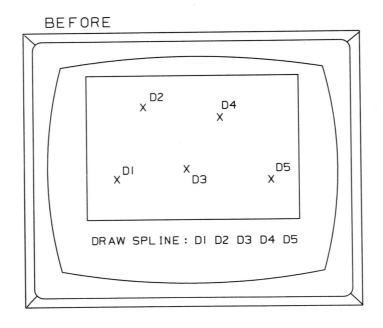

BEFORE

DRAW SPLINE : DI D2 D3 D4 D5

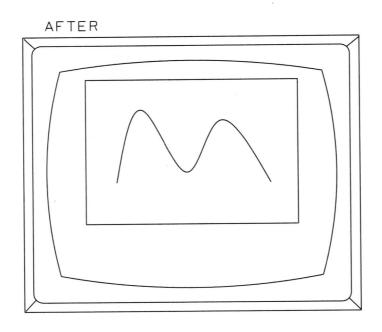

AFTER

BEFORE

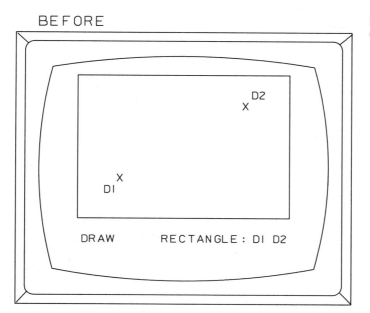

AFTER

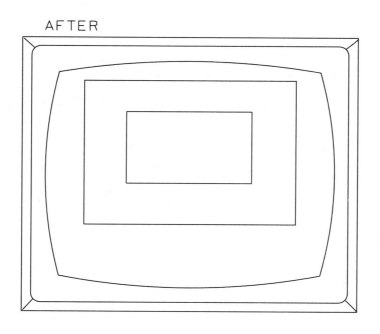

Figure 5–68
Creating a rectangle.

Figure 5–69
Creating a rectangle with
a specified width.

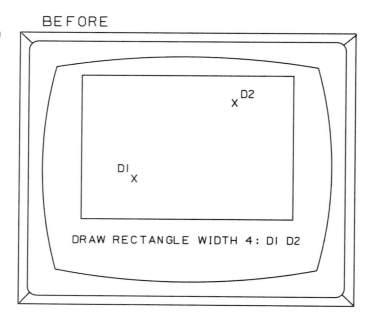

BEFORE

D2

DI

DRAW RECTANGLE WIDTH 4: DI D2

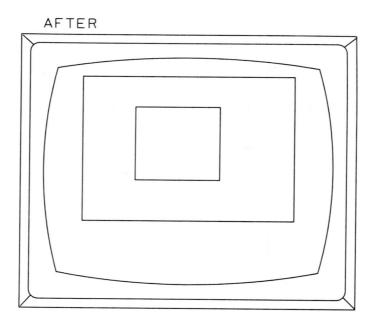

AFTER

Adding a Rectangle With VersaCAD

The following section shows how one two-dimensional system (VersaCAD) inserts rectangles. The RECTANGLE option is selected from the ADD menu by pressing [R] or placing the cursor over [Rectangle] and pressing the stylus. A rectangle is defined by two points:

1. One corner of the rectangle.

2. The opposite corner of the rectangle.

On this system the designer creates the rectangle by placing the cursor at the first corner, digitizing the position with the stylus or keyboard, then moving the cursor to the opposite corner. If Object Tracking is on, the computer will repeatedly draw a rectangle.

When the rectangle's size and proportions are satisfactory, the designer digitizes the second corner. The rectangle will then become fixed, indicating that the computer has accepted the input.

The options available for creating a rectangle are:

Template [T]	Causes the rectangle to become a template rectangle.
Marker [M]	Displays a marker at the center of the rectangle.
X–AXIS [X]	Locks the rectangle to an X–Y rotation. This is the normal or default mode of the program.
Rotate [R]	Rotates the rectangle counterclockwise with each keypress by the increment set up in the UNITS menu or with the UPDATE function key.

Ellipse

An ellipse is an elongated circle. Mathematically, it is defined as a cone sliced by a plane and is therefore sometimes referred to as a *conic*. The designer can use DRAW ELLIPSE with the appropriate modifiers to create an ellipse in three different ways:

1. By digitizing two existing lines as axes.

2. By digitizing two existing lines as foci.

3. By specifying the lengths of the horizontal and vertical axes.

The modifiers available for these tasks are listed below:

Axis/Focus Modifiers

AXIS	Specifies that two existing lines will be digitized as axes for the ellipse. This is the default.
FOCUS	Specifies that two existing lines will be digitized as foci of the ellipse.

Major/Minor Axis Modifiers

MAJOR AXIS	Specifies the length of the horizontal axis.
MINOR AXIS	Specifies the length of the vertical axis.

Layering Modifier

LAY *n*	(Layer) Places the ellipse on a designer-specified layer, rather than on the active layer.

Figure 5–70 illustrates four variations of the ELLIPSE command. The first ellipse is placed at the specified location (D1) using default values for its size. The second defines a major axis of 2 inches and a minor axis of 1 inch at a 30-degree angle. The third defines an ellipse with a major axis of 3 inches and a minor axis of 1 inch. The last creates an ellipse with a major axis of 2 inches and a minor axis of 1 inch. The beginning angle (A) for the ellipse is at 90 degrees (twelve o'clock position), and the ending angle (B) is at 330 degrees.

Figure 5–70
Creating ellipses.

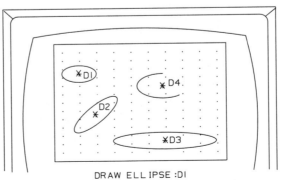

```
              DRAW ELL IPSE :DI
     DRAW ELL IPSE MAJOR 2 MINOR I ROTATE 30 :D2
          DRAW ELL IPSE MAJOR 3 MINOR I :D3
DRAW ELL IPSE MAJOR 2 MINOR I.3 ANGLEA 90 ANGLEB 330 :D4
```

Adding an Ellipse Using VersaCAD

The following section shows how one two-dimensional system (VersaCAD) inserts an ellipse. The ELLIPSE option is selected from the ADD menu by pressing [E] or placing the cursor over [Ellipse] and pressing the stylus. On this system an ellipse may be defined in two different ways: by *three axes* and by a *center point and two axes*.

To create an ellipse with the *three-axes* method, the designer must place the cursor at *one endpoint of the minor axis* and digitize the position, then move the cursor to the *other endpoint of the minor axis* and digitize it. If Object Tracking is on, the computer will repeatedly draw an ellipse the major axis of which is located at the position of the cursor.

To create an ellipse using a *center point and two axes*, the designer must first press [C] on the keyboard, then place the cursor at the *center* of the ellipse and digitize the location. Next, he or she moves the cursor to *one endpoint of the major and minor axes* and digitizes the point. If Object Tracking is on, the computer will repeatedly draw the ellipse.

The options available for creating an ellipse on VersaCAD are:

Template [T]	Causes the ellipse to become a template ellipse. Press [T] again to turn off the template option.
Marker [M]	Shows a marker at the center of the ellipse. Press [M] again to remove the marker.
X-axis lock [X]	Holds the rotation of the ellipse to zero degrees (major axis parallel to the X [horizontal] axis).
Y-axis lock [Y]	Holds the rotation of the ellipse to 90 degrees (major axis parallel to the Y [vertical] axis).
FREE [F]	Release the X or Y option, returning to the normal, unlocked state.
Rotate [R]	Rotates the ellipse counterclockwise with each keypress by the increment set up in the UNITS menu or with the UPDATE function key.

Strings

A string consists of two or more continuous line segments, which the system considers a *single item*. It therefore takes up less space in the database than multiple line segments. Once a string has been created, its individual line segments cannot be separated. The width and justification of the string can be specified on some systems. The WIDTH modifier is helpful if the designer needs to make a thick borderline or indicate piping.

To create a string, the designer must:

Figure 5–71
Creating a string.

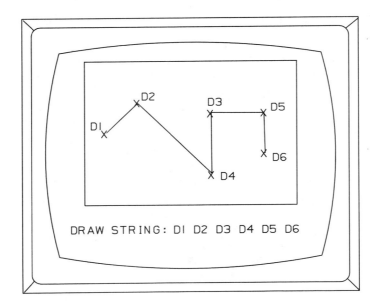

1. Select DRAW STRING and the appropriate modifiers.

2. Digitize the start point of the first line segment.

3. Digitize the endpoints of each connected line segment.

Figure 5–71 illustrates how six digitized points were used to create a string with five line segments.

STRING creates a single string from one or more lines, arcs, and strings. This capability is useful when a series of items must be used as a unit, such as the lines that make up a border.

Creating a Part

Figure 5–72 (A through K) shows how a sample part is created with POINT, LINE, CIRCLE, FILLET and CHAMFER.

In this example, a point was created at the origin (X0,Y0), (A and B). A series of lines was created using coordinates for the perimeter of the part (C and D). Fillets with two different radius values were then drawn (E and F) and a 56-degree chamfer was construction (G and H). That step completed the outside perimeter of the part. Three points were then entered as center marks for circles/holes (I and J). To complete the project, circles were drawn by isolating the existing points (K and L).

This part is dimensioned step by step at the end of Chapter 10.

BEFORE

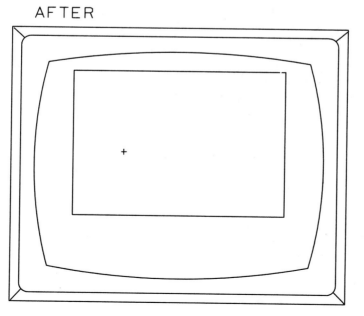

DRAW POINT: XOYOZO

AFTER

Figure 5–72
This figure is a series of drawings showing the step-by-step creation of a part.
(A) Creating a reference point at the origin of the part.

(B) Point is shown.

Figure 5–72 cont.
(C) Creating the outline of
the part with lines.

BEFORE

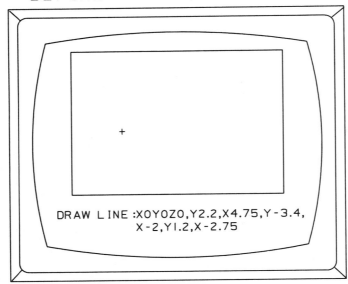

DRAW LINE :X0Y0Z0,Y2.2,X4.75,Y-3.4,
X-2,YI.2,X-2.75

(D) Lines are shown.

AFTER

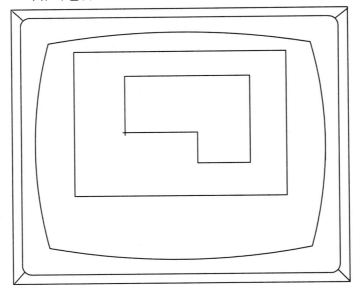

BEFORE

(E) Filleting the corners.

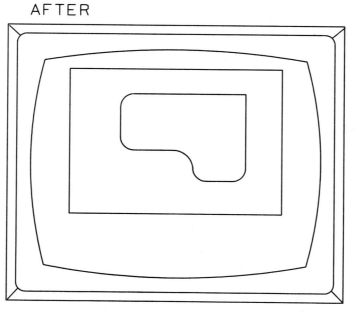

DRAW FILLET RADIUS .5: DI-D8
DRAW FILLET RADIUS .75: D9 DIO

AFTER

(F) Fillets shown.

Figure 5–72 cont.
(G) Chamfering a corner.

BEFORE

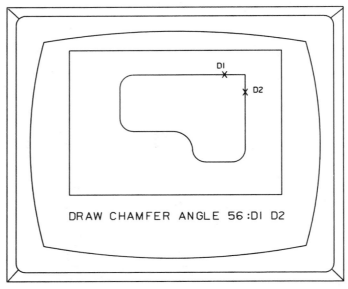

DRAW CHAMFER ANGLE 56 :DI D2

(H) Chamfer shown.

AFTER

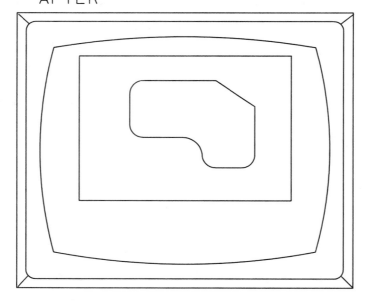

BEFORE

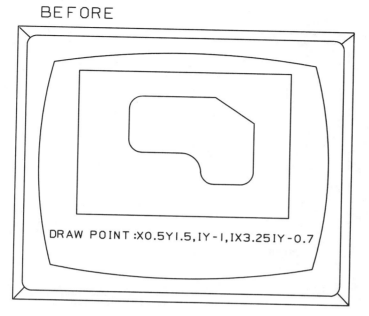

DRAW POINT :X0.5Y1.5,IY-1,IX3.25IY-0.7

(I) Creating points as circle reference center marks.

AFTER

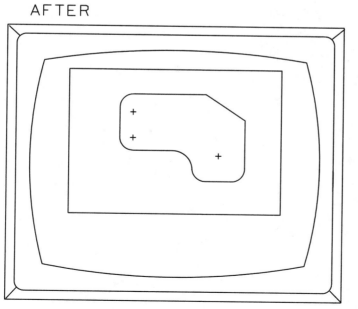

(J) Points shown.

Figure 5–72 cont.
(K) Creating circles
(holes).

BEFORE

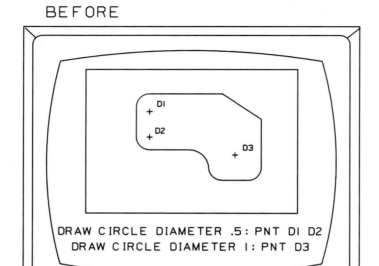

DRAW CIRCLE DIAMETER .5: PNT DI D2
DRAW CIRCLE DIAMETER I: PNT D3

(L) Showing the circles.
Part is finished.

AFTER

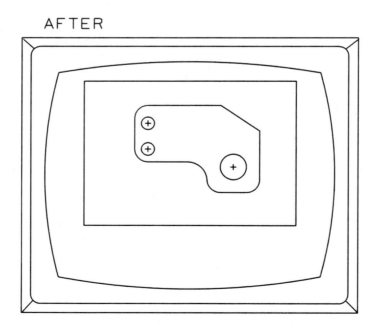

Filing and Exiting

Filing upon Exit

The designer has three options when filing a drawing upon exit:

- Renaming the drawing
- Filing the drawing under its original name
- Packing the database

A drawing should be renamed if the designer wishes to save revisions and design alternatives quickly and easily. This allows an old version of a drawing to be saved under its original name and a revised version under a new name.

A drawing should be filed under its original name if the designer wishes to update the drawing file with revisions when the old version of the file is being replaced.

Every time a drawing is filed, some systems pack the database, that is, the system reorganizes the information and fills in any empty spaces created from deletions or edits. The database should be packed if a significant amount of editing has been done or if the system's processing time seems unusually slow.

Updating without Exiting

When it is desirable to save changes periodically without exiting the drawing level—thereby protecting the work from possible power failures, editing errors, and other disasters—the designer can use SAVE:

    Command: SAVE File name: (name)

SAVE puts the current drawing on disk, but remains on the drawing level for further geometry creation or editing.

If a file name is specified and a drawing with that name already exists, most systems print the following message:

    A drawing with this name already exists.

        Do you want to replace it? <N>

Enter "Y" to override the information in the drawing file; enter "N" or a null response to cancel SAVE, leaving the file unchanged.

Directory Access

It is sometimes useful to list a disk directory without exiting the drawing level. The *FILES* command allows the designer to list, delete, rename, and copy files from within the drawing level.

Command: FILES

As a typical example, the File Utility Menu for AutoCAD displays the options listed below:

File Utility Menu

0.   Exit File Utility Menu

1.   List drawing files

2.   List user-specified files

3.   Delete files

4.   Rename files

5.   Copy file

Enter Selection

Selection 1 from the File Utility Menu searches for and lists the names of AutoCAD drawing files. If the disk contains many drawing files, the entire list may not fit on the CRT at once. If this situation occurs, the list is shown one page at a time.

File Utility Menu Selection 3 allows the designer to delete specified files. This can be very handy if disk space is running out, because the deletion of unneeded files can make extra room.

GLOSSARY

ABSOLUTE COORDINATES   The values of the X, Y, or Z coordinates with respect to the origin of the coordinate system.

ALPHANUMERIC   Consisting of letters, numbers, and/or characters.

ATTRIBUTE   A non-graphic characteristic of a part item.

AXIS   (1) One of the reference lines of a coordinate system, usually labelled X, Y, or Z. (2) A straight line around which a geometric figure rotates.

CARTESIAN COORDINATES   The distance of a point from any of three intersecting perpendicular planes; X, Y, Z coordinates.

CATALOG   The directory of files contained in storage.

CHARACTER   (1) A letter, number, or other symbol used to represent data. Symbols include the letters A through Z, numbers 0 through 9, punctuation marks, logical symbols, relational operators, and any other single symbol that may be interpreted by computer languages; a character is represented as a byte in the computer.

CHARACTER (2) Any letter, number, or graphic symbol.

COMMAND A verb or verb-noun combination specifying an action to be performed.

CONFIGURATION The arrangement of hardware, software, and peripherals that composes a computer system.

CONFIGURATION FILE The file that contains information on the relationships between the parts of a system and on the system defaults.

COORDINATE DIMENSIONING A system of dimensioning in which points are defined as being a specified distance and direction from a reference point.

CROSSHAIRS A horizontal line intersected by a vertical line to indicate a point on the display.

CURSOR (1) A special character, such as a small cross, on the screen that follows every movement of the stylus, light pen, or joystick.

CURSOR (2) The visual tracking symbol on the screen that allows the user to select items or define locations where the next action will occur. In microCADDS, it can be moved by using the stylus or the arrow keys on the keyboard.

DATA BASE An organized collection of standard parts libraries, completed designs, documentation, and computer programs.

DATABASE A comprehensive collection of information with a predetermined structure. Consists of the results of all user input and the relationship between various subdivisions of the data.

DATA TABLET A graphical input device consisting of a board area capable of monitoring the position of a pen-shaped stylus.

DEFAULT The predetermined value of a parameter that is automatically supplied by the system whenever that value is not specified by the user.

DIGITIZE (1) To convert lines and shapes into digital form. (2) To specify a coordinate location or entity by using an electronic pen.

DIGITIZERS A table or tablet on which the designer moves a puck or stylus to selected points and enters coordinates for lines and shapes by pressing down the input button on the puck or stylus.

DISPLAY ELEMENTS Points, line segments, and characters that are used to describe an object on the display.

DISPLAY MENU A display option that allows an operator to select the next action by indicating one or more choices with an input device.

DRAWING A file that contains a representation of a part design within the CAD/CAM system, including all associated geometry, mathematics, and textual information.

FIGURE A symbol or a part, which may contain other figures, attributes, and associations.

FILE (1) A name set of data on magnetic disk or tape. (2) To transfer the contents of working storage to permanent storage. (3) A collection of related information stored on the system and having a unique file name and an extension. The major types of files in microCADDS are drawings, execute files, key files, and configuration files.

FILLET   (1) A rounded corner or arc that blends two intersecting curves, lines, or surfaces. (2) An arc inserted in the angle formed by two intersecting curves or lines.

FINITE ELEMENTS   The subdivision of a complex structure into small pieces.

FONT   (1) The pattern of a line that differentiates it from other lines, such as dot, dash, dot-dash. (2) The specific typeface of letters and numbers.

FUNCTION KEY   An area on the digitizing tablet or a key on a box or terminal that is used to enter a command.

FUNCTION KEYBOARD   (1) The 10 keys labelled F1 through F10 on the IBM PC AT or XT keyboard that are preprogrammed to execute various commands. (2) A part of the workstation that contains a number of function keys.

FUNCTION MENU   The display or list of commands that the designer can use to perform a task.

GETDATA   The portion of a system instruction that follows the colon. It contains coordinate information and may contain data commands, references, and/or item masks.

GRAPHIC PRIMITIVES   Simple geometric shapes such as lines, circles, cones, cylinders, ellipses, and rectangles that can be used to construct more complex shapes.

GRAPHICS   Pictorial data such as points, lines, and shapes.

GRAPHICS TABLET   A surface through which coordinate points can be transmitted with a cursor or stylus. Another term for a digitizing tablet.

GRID   A matrix of uniformly spaced points displayed on the screen for approximately locating and digitizing a position or placing symbols in the creation of a schematic.

HIDDEN LINES   Line segments that would ordinarily be hidden from view in a three-dimensional display of a solid object because they are behind other items in the display.

INPUT   To enter data or a program into the system.

INPUT DEVICE   Devices such as graphic tablets or keyboards that allow the user to input data into the CAD system.

INQUIRY   A request for information from the computer.

INSERT   To enter items, figures, or information into a design that is on the display.

ITEM   A fundamental building block that a designer uses to represent a product (e.g., arc, circle, line, text, point, line, figure, nodal line).

ITEM MASK   A modifier that focuses the action of a command on one or more specific types of items.

KEY FILE   A file that associates specific commands with specific areas of a tablet menu. A key file can be edited by the user.

KEYBOARD   A device that resembles a typewriter and is used to enter instructions or coordinates into the computer.

LIGHT PEN   A penlike device used in conjunction with a vector-refresh screen that identifies displayed elements from the light sources on the screen.

LOAD   To enter data into computer memory for later processing on the system.

LOG ON   To follow the procedure by which a user begins a workstation session.

LOG OFF   To follow the procedure by which a user ends a workstation session. Also referred to as LOG OUT.

MENU   A listing, either on the screen or on a tablet, of command options that can be selected without entering instructions.

MODIFIER   The variable portion of a command that alters the effect of the command.

NUMERIC KEYPAD   A calculator-type numeric input device that is generally part of the keyboard.

ORIGIN   (1) The point from which an entity is derived. (2) The intersection of coordinate axes.

ORTHOGRAPHIC   The method of making a layout, drawing, or map in which the projecting lines are perpendicular to the plane of the drawing or map.

OUTPUT   The end result of a process or series of processes.

PART   The product or component of the part being designed or manufactured.

POINT   An element that represents a single X, Y, Z coordinate.

POLAR COORDINATES   The two numbers that locate a point by (1) its radial distance from the origin and (2) the angle a line through this point makes with the X-axis.

PROMPT   A message or symbol appearing on the screen that informs the user of a procedural error, incorrect input to the program being executed, or the next expected action.

REFERENCE   A portion of the command line that refers to existing geometry such as END, INTERSECTION OF, and ORIGIN>.

REPAINT   Redraw a display image on a CRT to reflect its updated status.

RUBBERBANDING   A technique for displaying a straight line with one end fixed and the other end attached to the movable cursor.

SCALE   To enlarge or shrink an image without changing its shape.

SCREEN COORDINATES   The X, Y, and Z axes to which the screen refers, unless model coordinates are specified. The X coordinate is always horizontal with respect to the CRT screen, the Y coordinate is vertical, and the Z coordinate extends infinitely out from the screen.

SPLINE   A smooth curve between a sequence of points in one place.

STYLUS   A hand-held object that provides coordinate input to the display device.

STRING   A sequence of characters such as a word or sentence.

STRING   (1) For text, a sequence of characters, words, or symbols. (2) For graphics, interconnected items that behave as one.

TABLET   An input device that a designer can use to digitize coordinate data or enter commands into a CADD system by means of a stylus or puck. Also called a digitizing pad.

TABLET   An electronic device that conveys data or commands to the system when touched by an electronic pen.

TEXT   Letters, numbers, and special characters.

THUMB WHEELS   A CADD input device that uses a manually controlled vertical wheel for locating a coordinate on the Y axis and a horizontal wheel for locating a coordinate on the X axis.

TRACKING   Moving a cursor across the surface of the screen with a light pen, stylus, or puck.

TRACKING SYMBOL (CURSOR)   A symbol such as a cross, dot, angle, or square used for indicating the position of a stylus.

TREE   A method of file storage structured with a top level and one or more sublevels, which in turn may contain additional sublevels.

TUTORIAL   A message that is displayed to show the user how to perform a task.

UP   A term used to denote that the computer is working properly.

QUIZ

True or False

1. The TRIM function will lengthen as well as shorten geometry.

2. Grids can be two-dimensional or three-dimensional.

3. Drawing units and grid units must always be the same.

4. After a grid has been selected, it must be echoed and repainted in order to be shown.

5. When the grid is activated, all digitized points will snap to the grid points.

6. Menus can be tailored to perform multiple functions.

7. The angle for polar coordinates is measured clockwise.

8. Display fonts and plotting fonts are the same.

Fill in the Blank

9. Drawing a line requires _____ digitized points.

10. Screen menus are usually displayed along the _____ and _____ of the CRT.

11. A string is a series of _____ segments.

12. _____ are specific variables in the work environment of the CADD system.

13. The _____ defines the tablet area use.

14. To move the _____ across the screen, move the _____ on the digitizer tablet.

15. The drawing units must be selected _____ _____ the drawing.

16. When a line is drawn tangent to a circle, the digitized position on the circle must be _____ the _____.

Answer the Following

17. Describe the process of selecting and displaying an X .5 and Y 1.5 spacing.

18. Explain the four standard ways of inputting functions and digitizing.

19. Give a short definition of the following geometric items: point, line, arc, circle, and spline.

20. Describe four methods of creating circles.

21. Describe the three types of coordinate input.

22. What is a menu on the CRT and how is it used?

23. What is a key file and how is one created?

24. Explain two ways of creating a line parallel to an existing line.

Problems

25. Draw the two views of the Torque Wrench (Figure 5–73). Do not dimension until completing Chapter 10.

26. Draw the Upper Link Arm (Figure 5–74). Do not dimension until completing Chapter 10.

27. Draw the Spanner Ring (Figure 5–75) and dimension after completing Chapter 10.

28. Draw the Polarizer Bracket (Figure 5–76) and dimension after completing Chapter 10.

29. Draw the Ring (Figure 5–77). Do not dimension until completing Chapter 10.

30. Draw the side view and the unfolded view of the Spring Clip (Figure 5–78). Do not dimension until completing Chapter 10.

31. Draw the three views CRT holder (Figure 5–79) and dimension after completing Chapter 10.

Figure 5–73

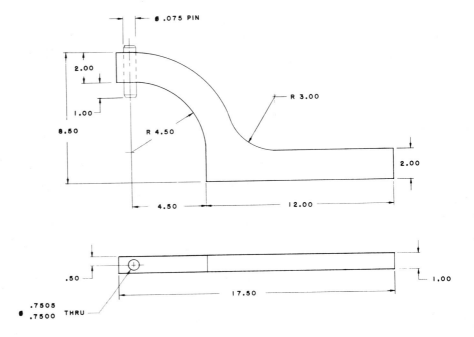

Figure 5–74

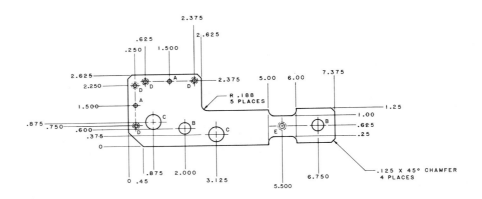

.25 ALY ALUM ANODIZE BLACK

HOLE	DESCRIPTION	QTY
A	∅ .125 THRU	2
B	∅ .375 THRU	2
C	∅ .50 THRU	2
D	∅ .149 THRU ∅ .281 X .073 DP FS	4
E	8-32 UNC-2B	1

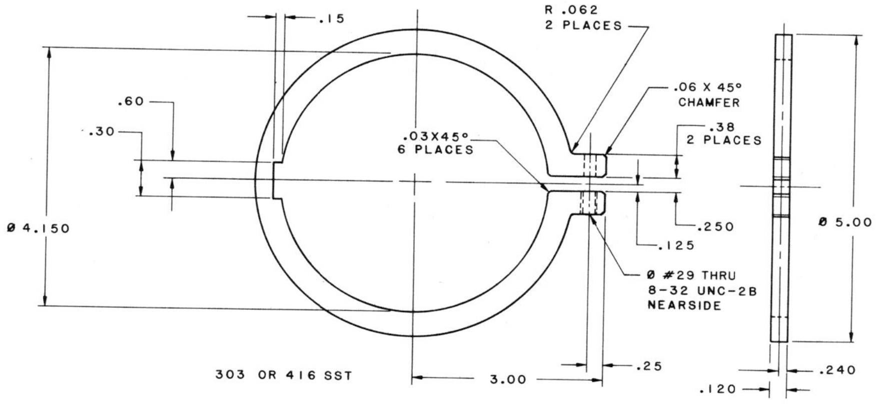

Figure 5–75

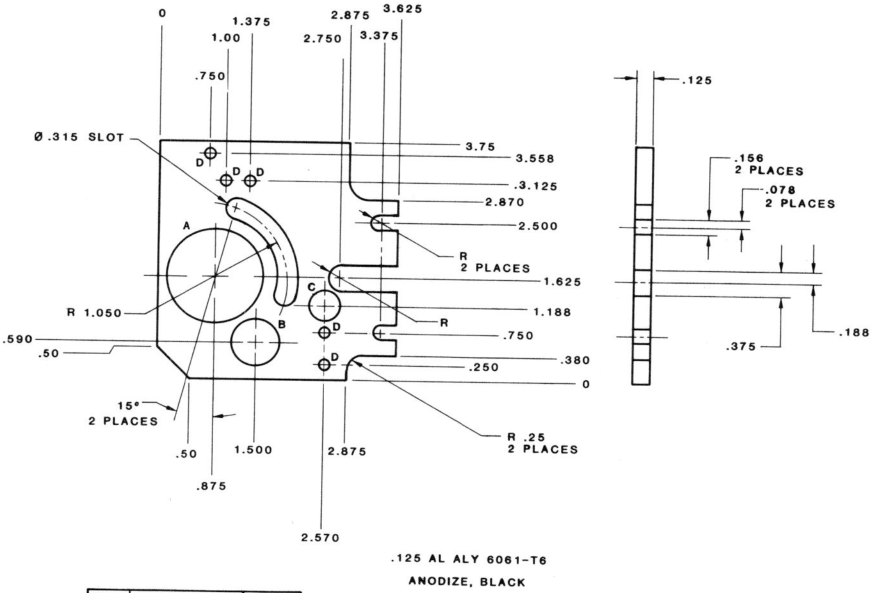

.15

R .062
2 PLACES

.06 X 45°
CHAMFER

.60

.30

.03X45°
6 PLACES

.38
2 PLACES

Ø 4.150

.250

.125

Ø 5.00

Ø #29 THRU
8–32 UNC–2B
NEARSIDE

303 OR 416 SST

3.00

.25

.240

.120

Figure 5–76

0   1.375   2.875   3.625
   1.00   2.750   3.375

.750

Ø .315 SLOT

.125

D

D   D

3.75   3.558

.156
2 PLACES

.078
2 PLACES

.3125

2.870

2.500

A

R
2 PLACES

1.625

R 1.050

C

1.188

.590

B

D

R

.750

.188

.50

D

.380

.375

.250

0

15°
2 PLACES

.50   1.500   2.875

R .25
2 PLACES

.875

2.570

.125 AL ALY 6061–T6
ANODIZE, BLACK

HOLE	DESCRIPTION	QTY
A	Ø 1.552	1
B	Ø .688	1
C	Ø .500	1
D	Ø .149	5

195

Figure 5–77

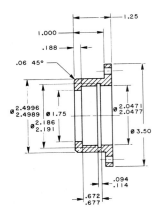

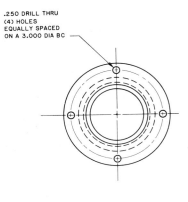

.250 DRILL THRU
(4) HOLES
EQUALLY SPACED
ON A 3.000 DIA BC

Figure 5–78

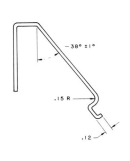

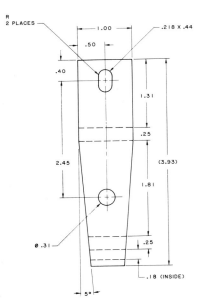

NOTES:

1. USE .010/.020 BEND RADIUS
   EXCEPT WHERE NOTED

2. ALL BENDS TO BE 90°
   EXCEPT WHERE NOTED

3. AFTER FABRICATION HEAT
   TREAT TO CONDITION 1050

Figure 5–79

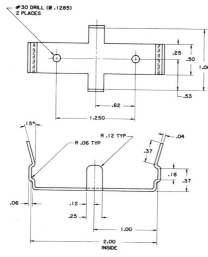

NOTES:

1. HEAT TREAT TO CONDITION R.H. 950
   (REF. JORGENSEN STEEL BOOK)
   HEAT CONDITION "A" MATERIAL
   TO 1750° F FOR 10 MIN. COOL TO 100° F AND HOLD FOR 8 HOURS
   HEAT TO 950° F AND HOLD FOR 1 HOUR. COOL IN AIR TO ROOM TEMP.

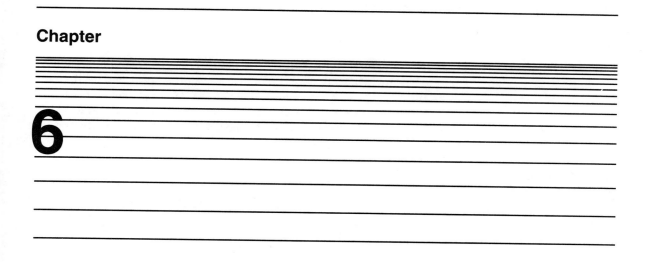

6

Modifying the Geometry

Objectives

After completing this chapter the reader will be able to:

- Discuss the manipulation of views of a drawing on the CRT.

- Edit geometry using TRIM, DIVIDE, STRETCH, and DELETE.

- Manipulate views using ZOOM and PAN.

- Explain how MIRROR, ROTATE, MOVE, and COPY can expedite the design process.

- Discuss the various options provided by the TRIM capability.

Introduction

This chapter covers four basic capabilities of a typical CADD system:

View Modification (ZOOM, PAN, AND SAVE VIEW)

Geometry Removal (DELETE, ERASE, AND BLANK)

Geometry Altering (TRIM, DIVIDE, AND STRETCH)

Modifying Geometry (ROTATE, MIRROR, MOVE, and COPY)

These capabilities are some of the more advanced techniques the designer will learn. They are very useful in the design process and can reduce design time significantly. The discussion in this chapter of these capabilities is of a general nature. Some of the discussions may not apply to the CADD system that the reader is using, but each system has similar capabilities.

View Manipulation

View manipulation includes the ability to ZOOM, PAN (SCROLL), and SAVE views of the design as shown on the CRT. The ability to enlarge or shrink the displayed view of the design is provided by ZOOM functions. The functions that enable the designer or drafter to move the display to a different part of the design are called PAN or SCROLL. The ability to save a particular view and then to recall it is referred to as SAVE view. Each of these three functions increases the designer's or drafter's efficiency and improves drawing precision. Although these capabilities only modify the display, they are covered in this chapter because they are frequently used in conjunction with DELETE, ERASE, BLANK, ROTATE, MIRROR, and MOVE.

Zoom

The **ZOOM** capability increases and decreases the size of the view of the design CRT without affecting the information in the database. Zoom can be used to enlarge or reduce a section of a drawing, or see an entire drawing on the CRT.

The design (Figure 6–1) can be zoomed in or out to magnify or shrink the displayed view of the part or drawing. When the view is *zoomed out*, the designer can see a large portion of the geometry; *zoom in* will enlarge a small portion of the drawing and show more of its details. The designer can zoom in to draw intricate parts of the drawing with exacting detail and then zoom out to look at the finished drawing. One system, AutoCAD, has a zoom ratio of about ten trillion to one, more than adequate for most applications.

The CRT is used as a **window** through which the designer can look at all or part of his or her drawing. Keep in mind that coordinates refer to fixed locations in the drawing, not to the physical location on the CRT. This means that the absolute size of a part always remains constant. Only the size on the CRT changes. Similarly, the designer can pan across the drawing in any direction without changing its magnification.

The ZOOM capability is like the zoom lens on a camera. It lets the designer increase or decrease the apparent size of items he or she is viewing, although the actual size of the items remains constant. As the apparent size of objects is increased a smaller area of the drawing is viewed in greater detail. Decreasing the apparent size allows the designer to view a larger area.

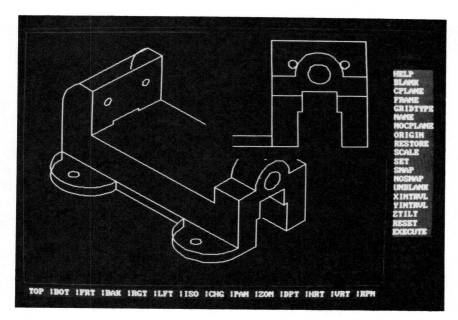

Figure 6–1
Part displayed in pictorial and partial frontal view. (Courtesy Tasvir)

ZOOM has several options, each offers a different way to specify the magnification and the portion of the drawing to be shown on the CRT.

The simplest type of ZOOM option lets the designer enter a view magnification factor. A magnification factor of 1 shows the entire drawing (the full view). If any other number is entered, the magnification is computed relative to the full view. For instance, if a value of 3 is entered, each object appears three times as large as it does in the full view (Figure 6–2). A value of .25 will show each object at one-fourth its current size on the CRT (Figure 6–3).

ZOOM does not change the spatial relationship of the parts on the drawing. Thus, when the magnification increased, parts near the edge of the CRT may be off the screen. On the other hand, when the magnification is de-

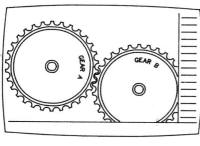

Before

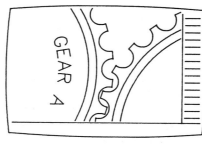

After ZOOM 3X

Figure 6–2
ZOOM used to enlarge the drawing 3 times. (Courtesy AUTODESK, Inc.)

Figure 6–3
ZOOM used to reduce
the drawing to 25% of the
full view. (Courtesy
AUTODESK, Inc.)

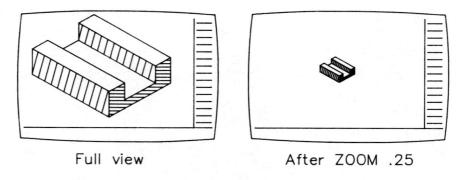

Full view   After ZOOM .25

creased, parts off the screen may become visible on the CRT. In Figure 6–4, the part was zoomed to two times its original size.

The ZOOM ALL option changes the view so that all of the drawing can be seen on the CRT.

The ZOOM WINDOW option allows the designer to specify the area of the drawing he or she wishes to see by framing the area in a rectangular window. The center of the window becomes the new center of the CRT and the drawing inside the window is enlarged or reduced to fill the CRT. The opposite corners of the window can be entered by keying in coordinates or with the electronic pen/puck. In Figure 6–5, the ZOOM WINDOW option was used and the corners of the window were digitized (D1, D2). This process was repeated in Figure 6–6 to show how the option can be used to keep zooming in on a specific area of the drawing. A typical system uses a screen or tablet menu (Figure 6–7) to initiate zoom and pan (scroll) options.

The three views of the piping isometric in Figure 6–8 show how ZOOM is used to enlarge an area of the drawing.

Pan

The **PAN** capability lets the designer look at a different portion of the drawing, without changing the magnification. The designer is able to see portions of the drawing that were off the CRT. This capability can be best visualized by imagining that the drawing is being seen through the display window, and that the drawing can be slid left, right, up, and down, without moving the window.

Of course, the designer must specify what direction to move the drawing, and how far to move it. This information is called the *displacement*. A single coordinate pair can be entered, indicating the relative displacement of the drawing with respect to the CRT, or two points can be designated, in which case the system computes the displacement from the first point to the second. For instance, either of the following specifications would shift the

BEFORE

Figure 6–4
ZOOM 2 times.

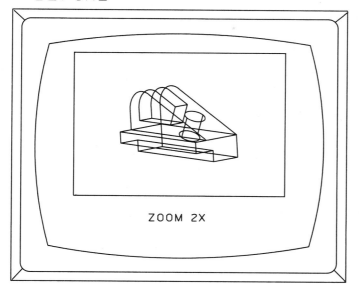

ZOOM 2X

AFTER

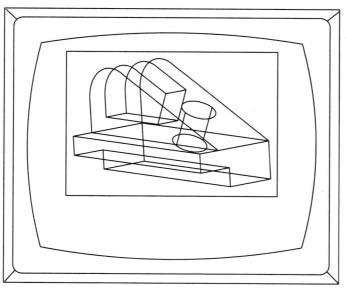

BEFORE

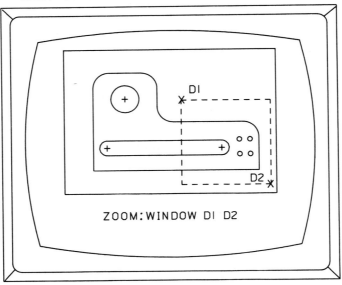

AFTER

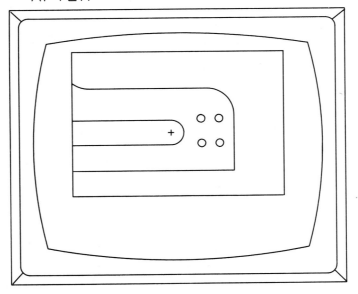

BEFORE

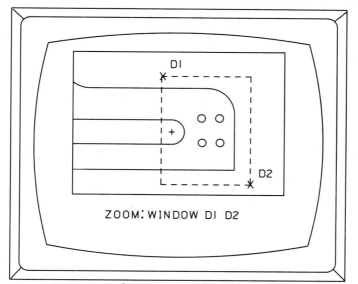

Figure 6–6
ZOOM WINDOW.

AFTER

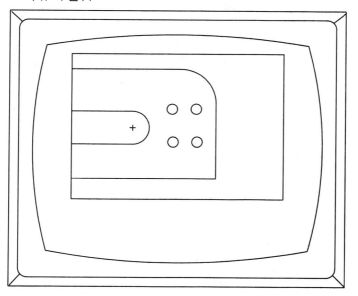

Figure 6–7
Menu area for SCROLL
and ZOOM.

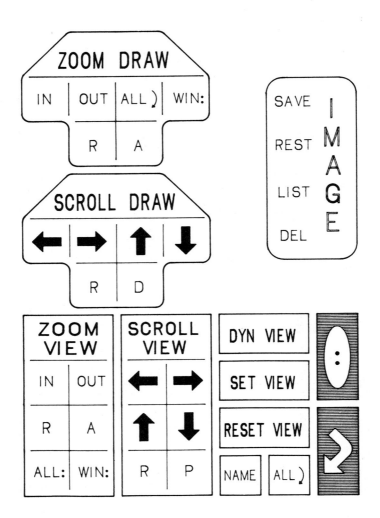

portion of the drawing shown on the CRT five units to the left and three units down (Figure 6–9):

    PAN   Displacement: −5, −3

    PAN   Displacement: 7, 7
             Second point: 2, 4

    PAN also allows the location at which the drawing will be at the center of the CRT to be redefined. The viewing scale stays the same. This capability is helpful if the designer needs to work on a part that is not completely in view. There are two ways to change the center of the CRT: digitize the new

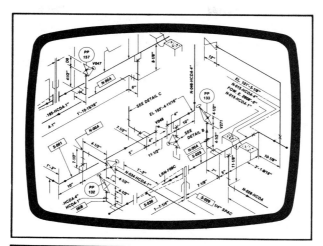

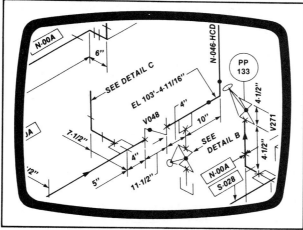

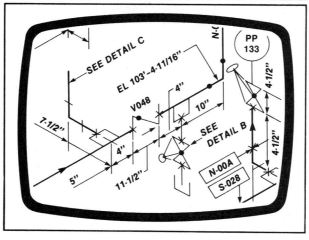

Figure 6–8
Zooming a piping isometric. (Courtesy Calma Company, a wholly-owned subsidiary of General Electric Company, U.S.A.)

center or digitize two points to specify the direction and displacement. Two locations are digitized to specify the direction and displacement of the move. The system drags the view of the drawing from the first point toward the second. It moves the view by the distance between the two locations (Figure 6–10).

Save View

Saving a particular view of the drawing provides a quick method for returning to that view later. Recalling a saved view will show that view on the CRT.

SAVE VIEW files the view currently on the CRT. A view has a specific scale and orientation. A view is similar to a snapshot of the CRT. When it is recalled, the orientation, position, and zoom factor appear as they did when the view was saved.

Views are helpful when working on a complex drawing. The designer zooms in on smaller areas and saves them as unique views.

Figure 6–9
PAN (SCROLL).
(Courtesy AUTODESK,
Inc.)

Before
PAN

After
PAN

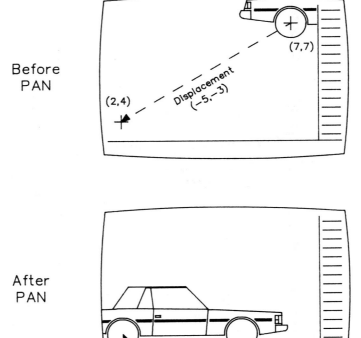

BEFORE

AFTER

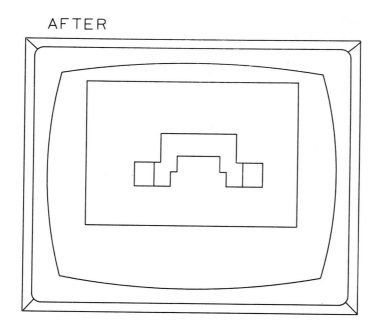

Figure 6–10
Scrolling a drawing.

Revising Geometry

Once the basic design has been created, *geometry revision* capabilities can be used to refine and alter the design. The designer does not need to create a finished part the first time. CADD programs allow the designer to explore different options and revise the drawing quickly and easily. The drawing can be revised by *deleting, trimming, dividing,* or *stretching* the geometry.

DELETING. DELETE is used to correct construction errors and to remove unwanted geometry.

TRIMMING. TRIM lengthens or shortens lines, arcs, circles, and splines.

DIVIDING. DIVIDE is similar to trim, but does not remove any of the original geometry. Divide puts a break in a line or an arc (or another type of geometry) at a specified position.

STRETCHING. STRETCH moves one end of a line or an arc (or other type of geometry) while keeping the other end fixed.

Geometry Removal and Editing

DELETE removes one or more selected lines or arcs (or other types of geometry) from the drawing and the database. Some systems use the term ERASE instead of DELETE. DELETE ALL removes all of the geometry and associated properties from the drawing and the database. It also deletes all previously saved views of the drawing. This capability is used only if the designer wants to start over on the drawing. Since DELETE ALL is permanent, the system will usually ask for confirmation before it processes the request, such as, "DO YOU REALLY WANT TO DELETE EVERYTHING?."

BLANK is similar to DELETE in that the geometry is removed from all views but it remains in the database. To restore the visibility of the geometry that is blanked, the system allows the designer to unblank the geometry. In Figure 6–11 two lines were deleted using the DELETE capability by digitizing each line (D1, D2). A new line was then added to complete the new design (D3, D4).

In order to ensure that the system selects the proper geometry to be deleted, reference the geometry with the type: POINT, LINE, ARC, CIRCLE, etc.; this will ensure that only the referenced geometry is deleted.

To delete multiple lines or arcs (or any type of geometry) at one time the WINDOW option can be used (Figure 6–12). Here, the WINDOW option was used to identify and then delete the three circles.

BEFORE

Figure 6–11
Deleting a line.

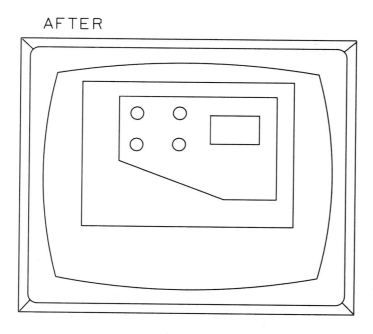

```
DELETE (ERASE):DI D2
DRAW LINE :END D3 D4
```

AFTER

Figure 6–12
DELETE WINDOW.

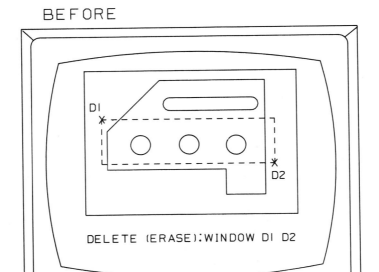

DELETE (ERASE):WINDOW DI D2

AFTER

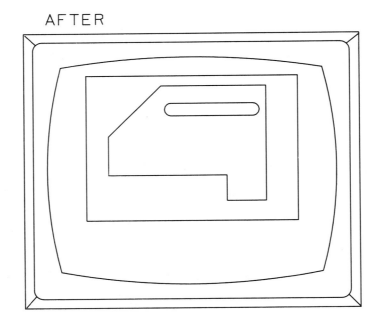

Refresh or Repaint

The REFRESH or **REPAINT** capability allows the designer to revise and re-draw the currently displayed view. REPAINT and REFRESH are also used to revise a drawing after geometry is deleted or erased. Many systems have an automatic refresh/repaint capability which is activated after deleting geometry.

Trim

TRIM shortens or extends the end point of an arc or a line. An arc or a line can be trimmed in one of two ways:

- Digitize the location to which the line or arc will be trimmed.

- Specify a new length.

The designer can also use TRIM to trim an arc or a line to its intersection with another arc or line (or other piece of geometry). TRIM has many options and uses in CADD drafting and design.

The most common use of TRIM is to shorten an existing line or arc. In Figure 6–13, the option TRIM LINE was used and the line to be trimmed was digitized (D1). The new location for the endpoint of the line was then digitized (D2). The line was shortened to the new endpoint.

Using the same option, the line could also have been extended (Figure 6–14). Here, the first digitize (D1) identified the line to be trimmed and the second digitize (D2) established the new endpoint. Since D2 was positioned beyond the line's original endpoint, the line was extended to that position.

An arc or line can also be extended to a new location by referencing existing geometry. In Figure 6–15, the line to be extended was identified first (D1) then the second line digitized (D2). The AFTER illustration shows the lines as the same length. The END reference was used in this situation.

A line can be trimmed by giving it a new length. In Figure 6–16, the line was extended to 6.5 inches by using TRIM. The line was identified by digitizing (D1) near the end to be extended. If a length smaller than the original line was entered into the command, the line could have been shortened using TRIM.

To trim a line at its intersection with another line or arc, both must be digitized as in Figure 6–17. Here, the original line was digitized (D1) and the intersecting line was identified (D2). The AFTER illustration shows the original line ending at the intersection of the two lines. Figure 6–18 shows the same option, but since the original line does not cross the referenced line, it was extended to the intersection point.

Figure 6–13
Trimming a line.

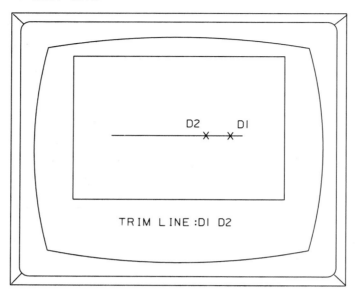

BEFORE

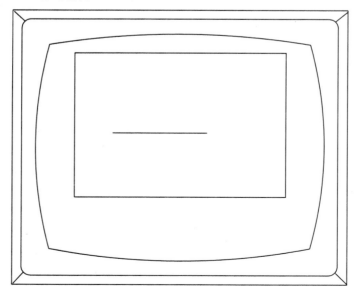

AFTER

BEFORE

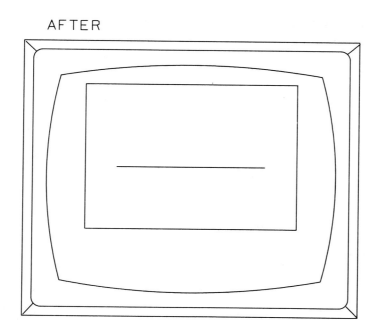

Figure 6–14
Extending a line using TRIM.

TRIM LINE :DI D2

AFTER

Figure 6–15
Trimming a line to the
END of an existing line.

BEFORE

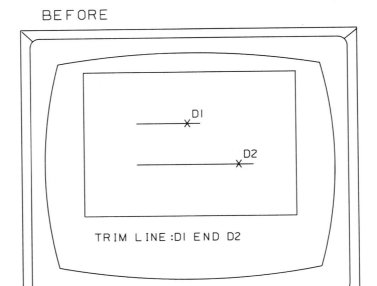

AFTER

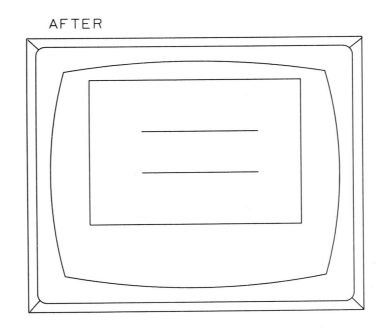

BEFORE

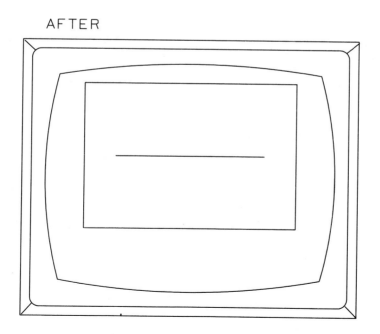

TRIM LINE LENGTH 6.5:DI

AFTER

Figure 6–16
Trimming a line to a
specified length.

Figure 6–17
Trimming a line to the
intersection of an existing
line.

BEFORE

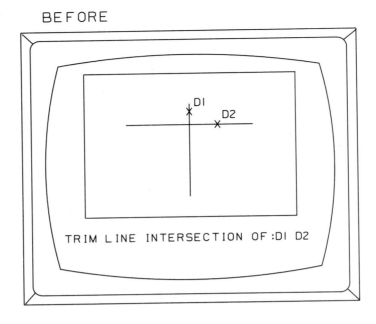

AFTER

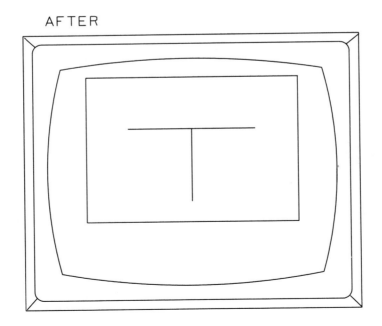

BEFORE

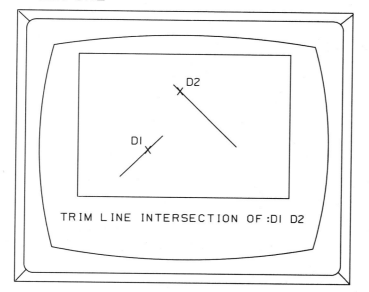

TRIM LINE INTERSECTION OF :DI D2

Figure 6–18
Trimming a line using
INTERSECTION OF.

AFTER

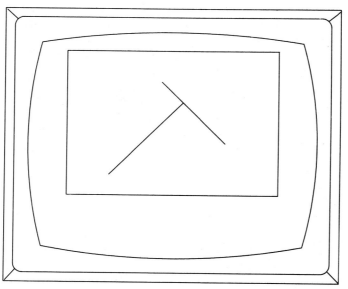

Another similar example (Figure 6–19) shows the line to be changed, extended to two intersecting lines. D1 identifies the line to be trimmed; D2 and D3 identify the intersecting lines.

In Figure 6–20, a circle is trimmed by digitizing it (D1), then identifying *two* new endpoints. D2 and D3 establish the length of the arc in a counterclockwise direction as shown in the AFTER illustration. Arcs can be trimmed (shortened or lengthened) in the same way as circles (Figure 6–21).

Arcs and lines can also have sections removed. This capability allows the removal of a section from the original arc or line. Figure 6–22 shows an example of this procedure. The circle is identified by the first digitize (D1). The next four digitized positions locate the endpoints of the removed sections.

Another way of removing sections from an existing circle is shown in Figure 6–23. Here, the gap in the circle is defined by digitizing the two intersecting lines.

Combining *intersection* and *dividing*, as shown in Figure 6–24, removes two sections from the circle. Figures 6–25 and 6–26 show examples of divide and intersection options as applied to lines.

Divide

Dividing makes a single piece of geometry into several pieces that can be revised, manipulated, or deleted individually. Dividing an arc or line (or other piece of geometry) does not change its appearance. When the designer divides an arc or line, he or she either indicates the division points, lets the system calculate a specified number of equal divisions, or divides an arc or line at the intersection of two existing arcs or lines.

DIVIDE is illustrated in Figure 6–27. The first digitize (D1) identified the circle to be divided; the subsequent digitizes establish division points. In Figure 6–27, the CHANGE APPEARANCE option shows how the circle is now four separate arcs. The solid and dashed arcs visually identify the arc segments. Any piece of geometry can be divided using this capability.

Stretch

The **STRETCH** capability is used with the WINDOW option. The window identifies the geometry to be moved. Any lines or arcs that cross the window (are not completely within the window area) will be stretched to a new position. The 3rd and 4th digitizes establish a *vector*. The starting position (D3) and the direction and distance (D4) define the vector. Incremental coordinates could also be used for this distance.

In Figure 6–28, STRETCH is illustrated. D1 and D2 determined the window position. D3 was used to establish the starting point of the vector and

BEFORE

Figure 6–19
Trimming a line.

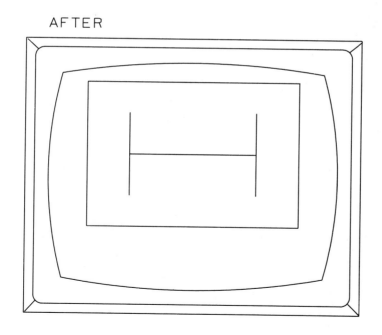

TRIM LINE INTERSECTION OF :DI D2 D3

AFTER

Figure 6–20
Trimming a circle.

BEFORE

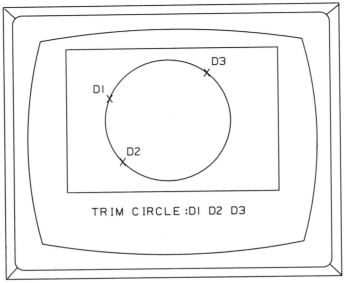

TRIM CIRCLE :DI D2 D3

AFTER

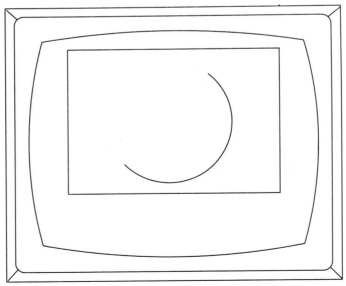

BEFORE

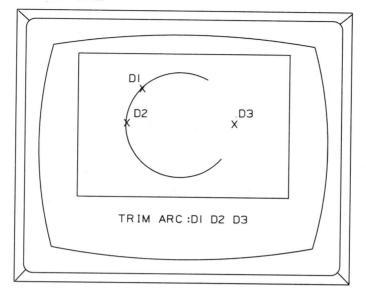

TRIM ARC :DI D2 D3

Figure 6–21
Trimming an arc.

AFTER

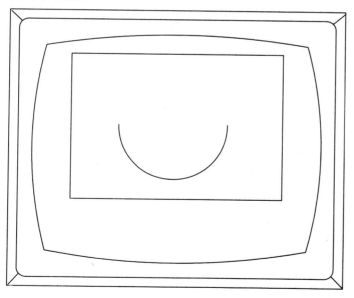

Figure 6–22
Using the TRIM command to take out a section of a circle.

BEFORE

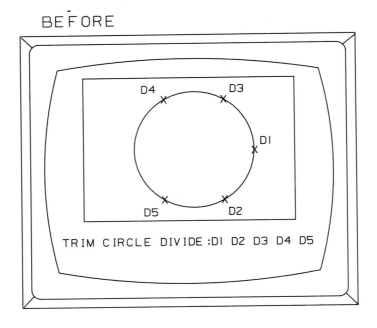

TRIM CIRCLE DIVIDE :DI D2 D3 D4 D5

AFTER

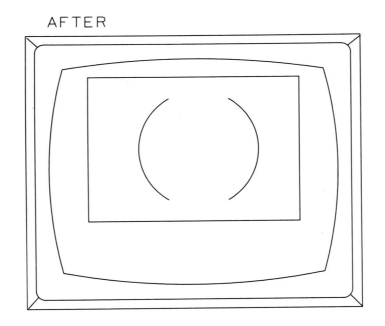

BEFORE

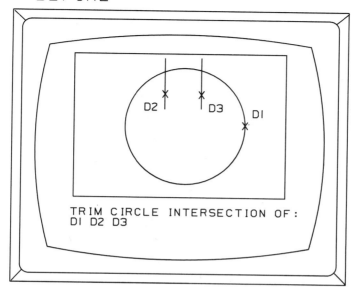

TRIM CIRCLE INTERSECTION OF:
DI D2 D3

AFTER

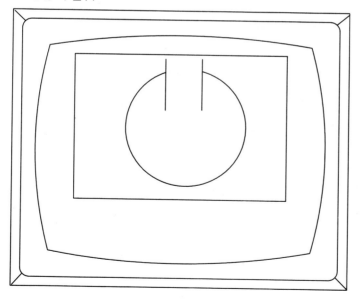

Figure 6–23
Trimming a circle at the
intersection of two lines.

Figure 6–24
Trimming and dividing a circle.

BEFORE

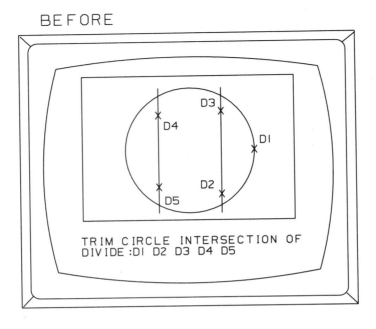

AFTER

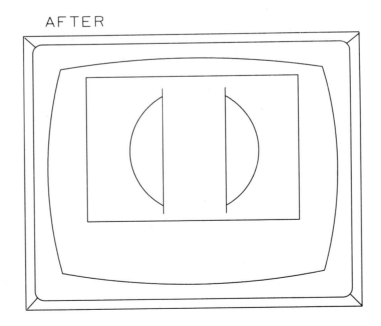

BEFORE

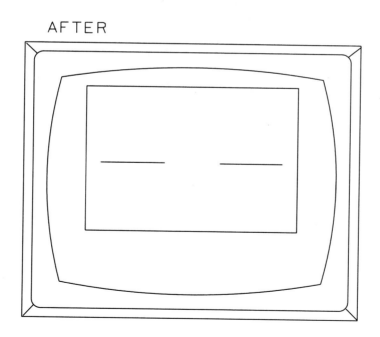

Figure 6–25
Trimming a line and
removing a section.

AFTER

Figure 6–26
Trimming and dividing a
line at the intersection of
a line.

BEFORE

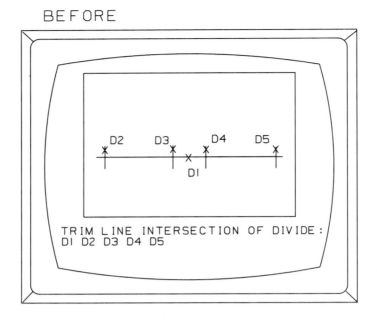

AFTER

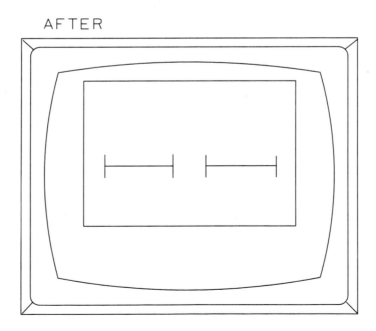

BEFORE

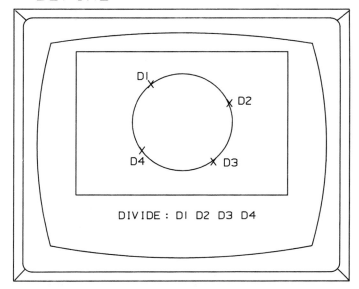

Figure 6–27
Dividing a circle and
changing the appear-
ance of the circle.

DIVIDE : DI D2 D3 D4

AFTER

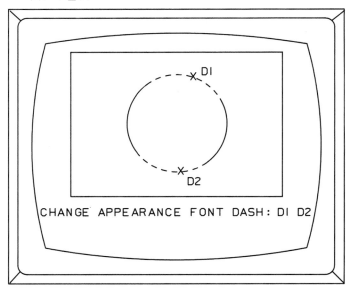

CHANGE APPEARANCE FONT DASH : DI D2

229

Figure 6–28
Using STRETCH.

BEFORE

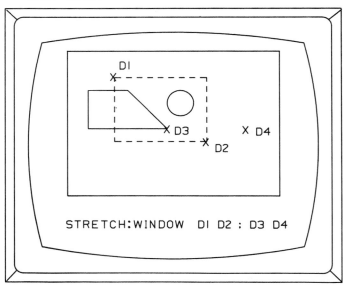

STRETCH:WINDOW DI D2 : D3 D4

AFTER

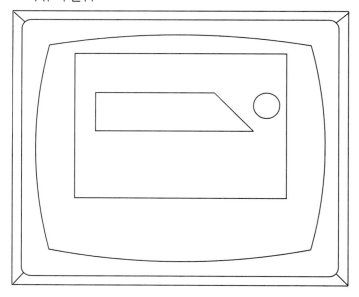

D4 its endpoint. It is easier and more accurate to establish the vector using a position referenced to existing geometry (D3). The AFTER illustration shows the part stretched to its new position. The circle was moved but not altered since it was entirely within the window.

Figure 6–29 shows another example of this capability. The part was stretched to a new position by windowing the right side. Since the slot end was completely within the window area, it was not altered. Therefore, the slot appears distorted in the AFTER illustration.

Modifying Geometry with Move, Mirror, and Rotate

CADD systems allow the designer to use existing geometry to create additional geometry by moving, mirroring, and rotating a copy of the existing geometry. The system assigns the copy and properties associated with the original geometry.

Copying and *moving* allow the designer to copy geometry and insert it in one or more locations on the current drawing. This capability is used to repeat parts on the same drawing (Figure 6–30).

Copying and *mirroring* allow the designer to mirror a copy of the geometry about an axis to construct additional geometry. This capability is used to construct the remaining half of a symmetrical part.

Copying and *rotating* allow the designer to rotate geometry about a point on a plane or an axis. Geometry can be constructed by rotating a copy of some geometry several times around a radial origin.

Copying geometry saves a great deal of construction time. These capabilities should be used as early and as often as possible in the design process.

Move

MOVE allows the designer to reposition geometry from its present location on a drawing to a new location. First, the geometry to be moved is identified, then a vector is defined to indicate how far and in what direction the geometry is to be moved. This is done designating two points, the move-from point, and then the move-to point, or by entering a *displacement*. The displacement indicated by the vector applies to all of the selected geometry.

Figure 6–30 shows an example of using the MOVE COPY option to repeat the multiple copies of the simple cell. This option eliminated a considerable amount of work.

MOVE without the COPY option is shown in Figure 6–31. The geometry to be moved was identified using a window, but digitizing each part of the geometry individually is also possible. D3 and D4 are the beginning and ending points of the displacement vector. Since the copy option was not used, the selected geometry is simply moved to its new position.

Figure 6–29
Stretching geometry.

BEFORE

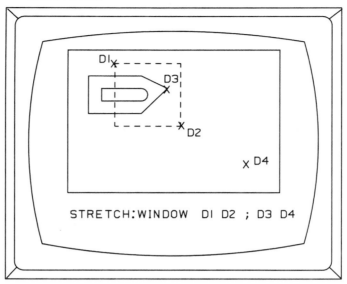

STRETCH:WINDOW DI D2 ; D3 D4

AFTER

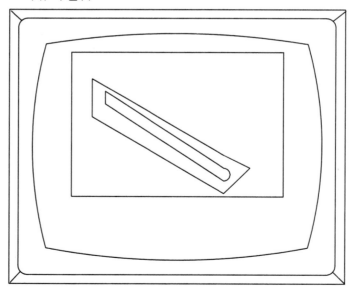

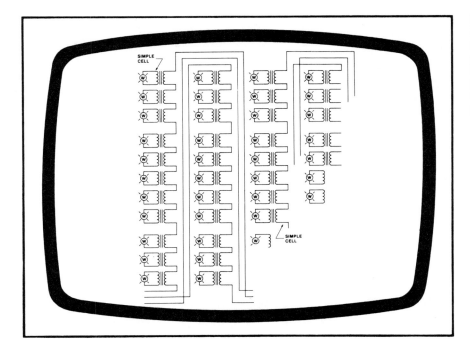

Figure 6–30
Cell diagram created using MOVE COPY. (Courtesy Calma Company, a wholly-owned subsidiary of General Electric Company, U.S.A.)

Figure 6–32 shows how to make multiple copies of a part using the MOVE COPY option. The geometry to be moved and copied is identified and given the new positions by digitizing.

Mirror

Some systems refer to mirroring as IMAGING. Regardless of the terminology, **MIRROR** provides a quick method to create a mirror image of an existing design. In Figure 6–33, the flow diagram was drawn using the mirror copy option.

In Figure 6–34, MIRROR was used to create a mirror image of the part. The geometry to be mirrored was identified by using a window and the mirror *axis* was established by digitizing positions D3 and D4. The part was completely mirrored about axis D3-D4 and the original geometry removed since the COPY option was not used.

A symmetrical two-dimensional part is created by identifying the geometry to be mirrored and using the part's center line as the mirror axis (Figure 6–35). Three-dimensional parts can also be mirrored.

In Figure 6–36, the part has been mirrored and copied at an angle instead of about a vertical or horizontal axis.

BEFORE

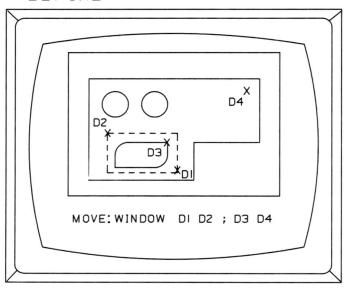

MOVE: WINDOW DI D2 ; D3 D4

AFTER

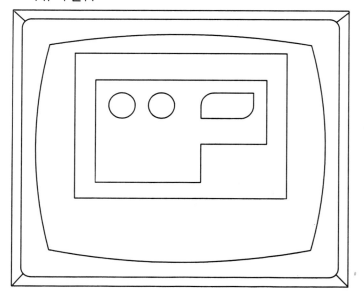

BEFORE

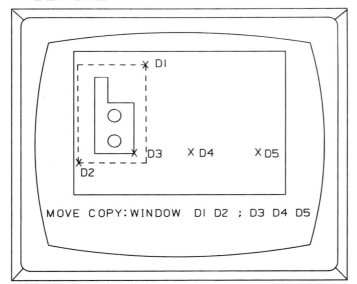

AFTER

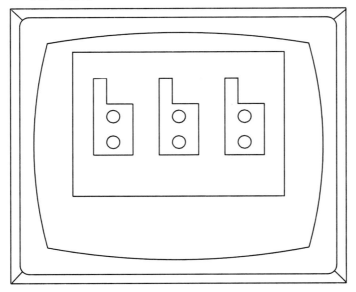

Figure 6–32
Moving and copying
geometry.

Figure 6–33
Piping flow diagram
created with MIRROR
COPY.

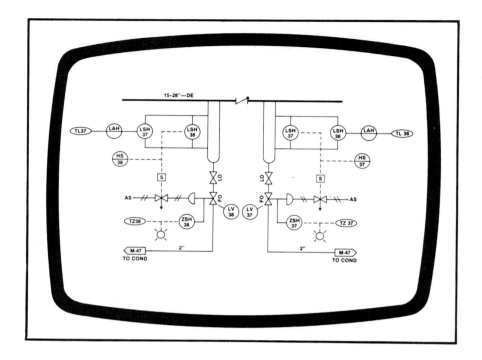

Rotate

ROTATE moves geometry about a specified *axis of rotation*. Figure 6–37 shows examples of ROTATE with and without the COPY option.

ROTATE is similar to MOVE and MIRROR in that the geometry to be rotated is identified first and then the axis of rotation given. In Figure 6–38, ROTATE without the COPY option was used. The *angle of rotation* was specified as 45 degrees. The geometry to be rotated was then identified by a window (D1 and D2). The center of the circle (D3) was selected as the axis of rotation by referencing the circle's **origin**. The part was then rotated at a 45 degree angle about the center of the circle.

ROTATE is very useful in creating *bolt circles* as in Figure 6–39. Here, the small circle (hole) was rotated and copied about the center of the large circle eleven times at an angle of 30 degrees for each copy. Twelve circles spaced at 30 degrees was the end result.

Offset

OFFSET allows the creation of lines, arcs, circles, or splines spaced a specific distance from existing geometry.

BEFORE

Figure 6–34
Mirroring geometry.

MIRROR : WINDOW DI D2 ; D3 D4

AFTER

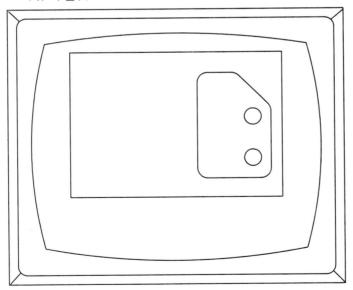

Figure 6–35
Mirroring and copying
geometry.

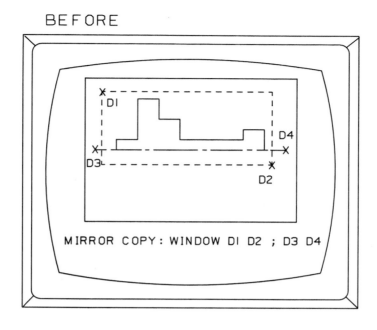

BEFORE

MIRROR COPY: WINDOW DI D2 ; D3 D4

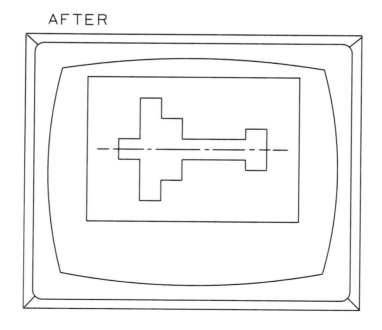

AFTER

BEFORE

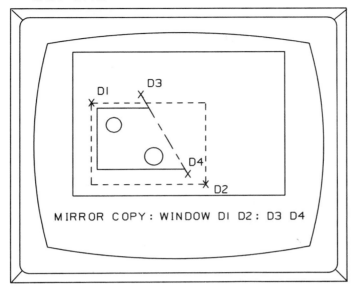

MIRROR COPY: WINDOW DI D2: D3 D4

AFTER

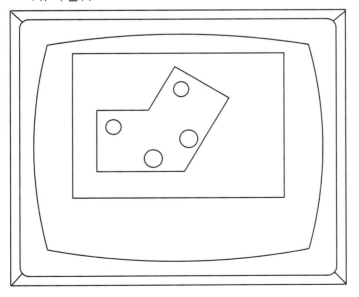

Figure 6–36
Mirroring at an angle.

Figure 6–37
ROTATE and COPY.
(Reprinted with permission from Computervision Corporation, Bedford, Massachusetts)

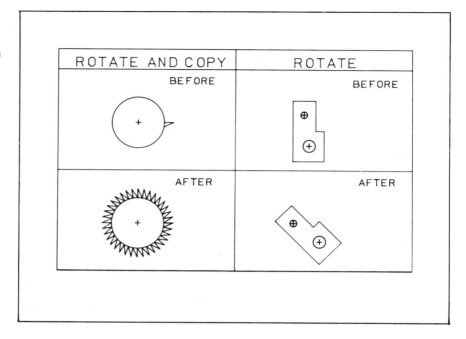

In Figure 6–40, an offset of .25 inches was required. The controlling geometry was digitized (D1, D2, D3) and then the side where the offset was to be constructed was digitized (D4). The AFTER illustration shows the original geometry and the offset geometry exactly .25 inches away. Since the inside and outside radii would be different at the bend, OFFSET is excellent for creating geometry for bends with a specific thickness of material.

Group

GROUP allows the designer to manipulate any collection of objects and symbols as a single object. The collection is identified in a variety of ways such as all objects stored on one or more levels, objects with certain line styles, text sizes, geometry within a window, or digitized geometry. Once the working group has been established, the objects remain together as a group until cleared out (ungrouped).

A group is specified by identifying the geometry to be grouped (Figure 6–41). In this example, the geometry on the left was grouped using a window to show how a group can be manipulated. The second illustration shows the ROTATE GROUP ANGLE option. The AFTER illustration shows the whole group rotated.

BEFORE

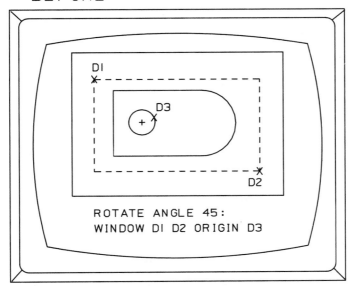

ROTATE ANGLE 45:
WINDOW DI D2 ORIGIN D3

AFTER

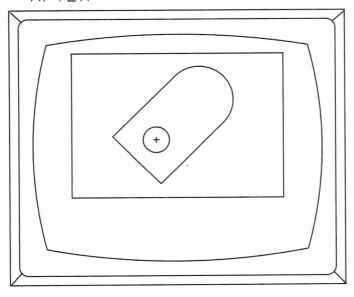

Figure 6–38
Rotating geometry.

Figure 6–39
Rotating and copying
geometry.

BEFORE

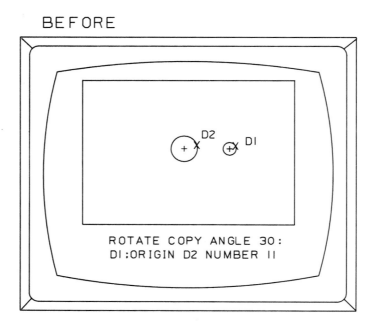

AFTER

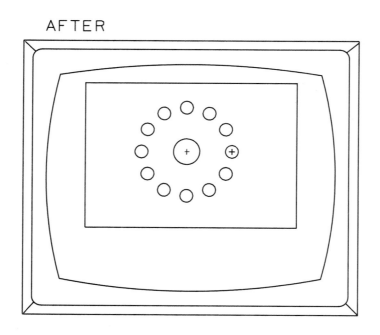

BEFORE

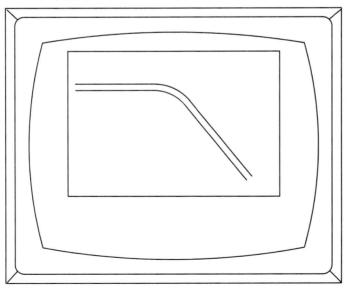

DRAW OFFSET DISTANCE .25:
DI D2 D3 : D4

AFTER

Figure 6–40
Drawing and offset.

243

BEFORE

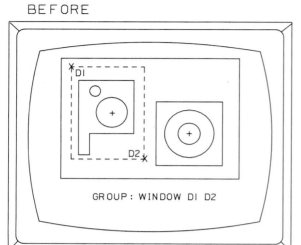

GROUP: WINDOW D1 D2

BEFORE

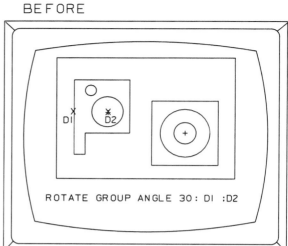

ROTATE GROUP ANGLE 30: D1 :D2

AFTER

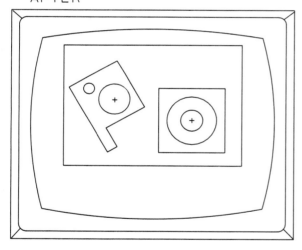

Figure 6–41
Grouping and rotating
geometry.

Conclusion

There are other geometry modification capabilities available on CADD systems. The ones presented here vary on different systems. Other variations, options, and capabilities may be peculiar to the reader's system and, therefore, outside the scope of this text.

GLOSSARY

COPY   To reproduce a design in a different location on the CRT or to duplicate a file and its contents.

DEFAULT   The predetermined value of a parameter that is automatically supplied by the system whenever that value is not specified by the designer.

DELETE   To erase information from the computer's memory or from storage.

DISPLAY SPACE   The usable area of the CRT surface that includes all addressable points.

EDIT   To change, add, or delete data.

FULL FRAME   A view of the design scaled to maximize use of the viewing surface of the CRT.

LOOP   A sequence of instructions that is executed repeatedly in the computer until stopped by the designer or some predetermined condition.

MACRO   A combination of commands executed as a single command.

MIRROR   In computer graphics, the reflection of displayed geometry with respect to a specific straight line or plane, synonymous with *flip* or *reflect*.

NESTING   Embedding data in levels of other data so that certain routines or data can be executed or accessed continuously, in loops.

ORIGIN   An X, Y, or X, Y, Z coordinate from which all geometry is referenced.

OVERLAY   To position one or more drawings on top of another and view them simultaneously on the CRT.

PAINT   To fill in a bounded figure on a display using a combination of repetitive patterns or line fonts.

PAN   To scroll the view of an object on the CRT.

PROMPT   A message or symbol appearing on the CRT that informs the designer of a procedural error, incorrect input to the program being executed, or the next expected action.

QUEUE   A waiting list of tasks to be performed or messages to be transmitted.

REFLECT   Same as *mirror*.

REPAINT   Redraw a view of the design on a CRT to reflect its updated status.

REPLICATE   To generate an exact copy of a design on the CRT at any location or scale desired.

RESTORE   To return a design to its original configuration after *editing* or *modification*.

ROTATE   To turn a view of the design about an axis through a predefined angle.

SCALE   To enlarge or shrink view on the CRT without changing its shape.

SCISSOR   To trim a drawing in the database so that it can be viewed on a CRT.

SCROLL   To automatically roll up on a CRT, as on a spool, a message or drawing too large to be shown all at once.

SELECTIVE ERASE   The deletion of portions of a design without repainting the entire view.

STRETCH   To automatically extend or retract selected geometry a specific distance in any direction.

TRANSLATE To move geometry from one position to another.

UPDATING Changing a drawing by adding, modifying, or deleting geometry.

VIEW The retrievable representation on the CRT of an object or part.

WINDOW A portion or view of a design that is framed on the CRT.

WINDOWING Proportionally enlarging a figure or portion of a figure so it fills the CRT or window.

ZOOM The successive enlargement or shrinking of a portion of the drawing on the CRT.

QUIZ

True or False

1. The ZOOM capability increases and decreases the size of a part on the drawing.

2. ZOOM does not change the spatial relationship of the parts on the drawing.

3. The PAN capability lets the designer look at a different portion of the drawing without changing the magnification.

4. Saving a particular view of the drawing provides a quick method for changing the scale.

5. TRIM lengthens or shortens lines, arcs, circles, and splines.

6. DELETE ALL only removes all of the text from the drawing.

7. DELETE and BLANK are the same capability.

8. GROUP allows the designer to manipulate any collection of objects and symbols as a single object.

Fill in the Blank

9. A _____ factor of 1 shows the entire drawing.

10. The _____ _____ option changes the view so that all of the drawing can be seen on the CRT.

11. The direction and distance a drawing is moved by PAN is called the _____.

12. Recalling a saved _____ will show that _____ on the CRT.

13. _____ _____ removes all of the geometry and associated properties from the drawing and database.

14. _____ shortens or extends the end point of an arc or a line.

15. The _____ option is very helpful in creating symmetrical parts.

16. The _____ option is very useful in creating bolt circles.

Answer the Following

17. Discuss how a designer might manipulate a drawing on the CADD system to look at a small area not shown on the CRT.

18. Explain the difference between DELETE and BLANK.

19. What is the difference in results between MOVE and MOVE COPY?

20. Discuss how to delete a segment from a circle using TRIM.

21. How does the location of the window determine the effect of STRETCH on the geometry?

22. Discuss how a designer might create a 32-teeth gear using ROTATE COPY.

23. How does the zoom and pan capability of a CADD system help in the design process?

24. How are MOVE, ROTATE, and MIRROR similar in capability and in use?

Problems

25. Draw the Panel Mounting Plate (Figure 6–42). Use the capabilities introduced in this chapter. Do not dimension until after completing Chapter 10.

26. Draw the two views of the Cap (Figure 6–43). Do not dimension or section until completing Chapter 10. Use ROTATE COPY to insert the holes.

27. Draw the Slide Plate (Figure 6–44) and mirror the part to create a left-handed finished part. Do not dimension until completing Chapter 10.

28. Draw the Swivel Plate (Figure 6–45) by creating one-half of the part and then using MIRROR COPY. Do not dimension until completing Chapter 10.

29. Draw the Slide Holder (Figure 6–46) and dimension after completing Chapter 10.

Figure 6–42

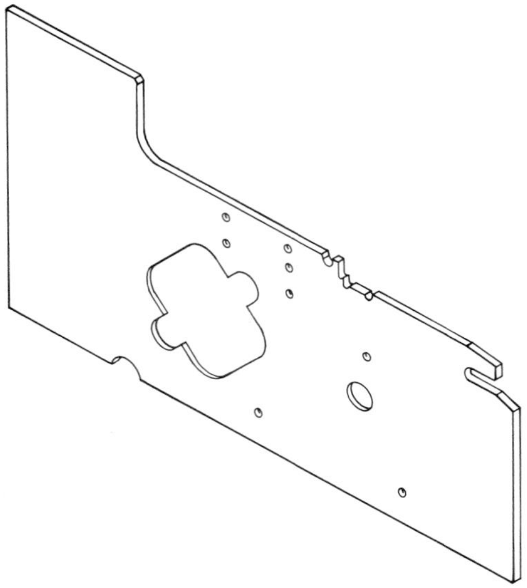

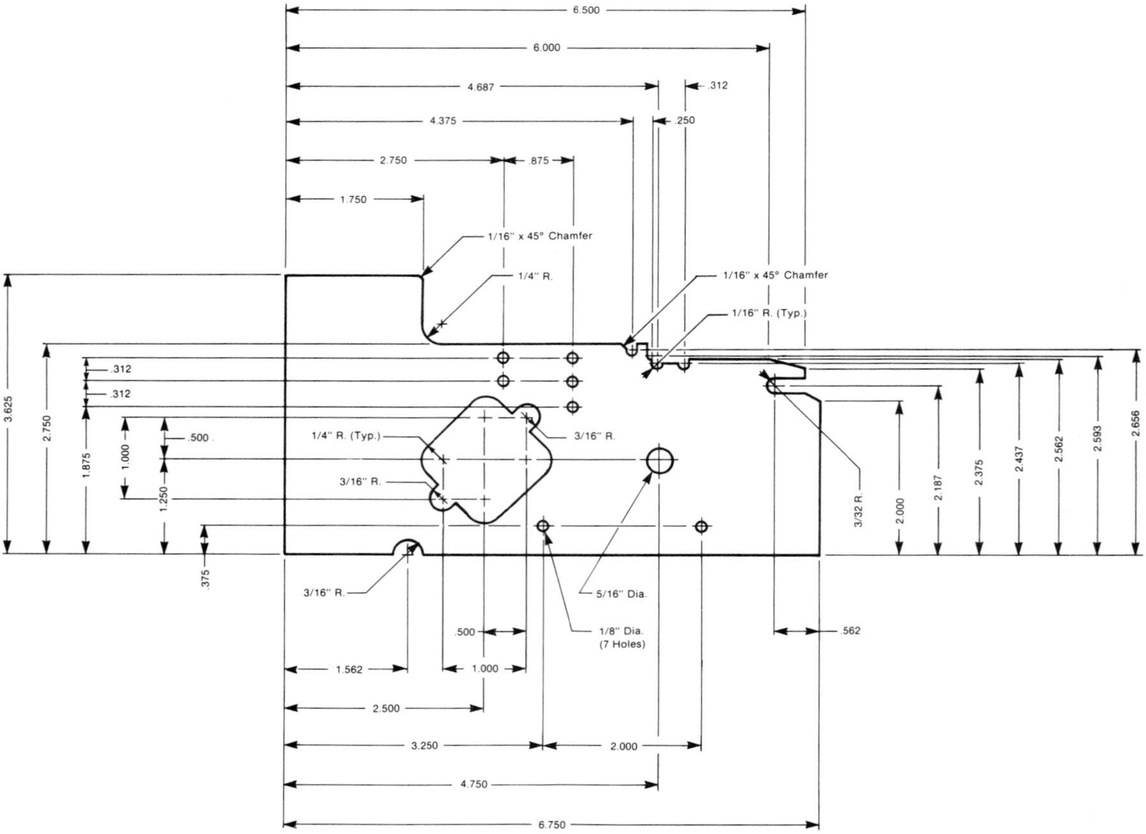

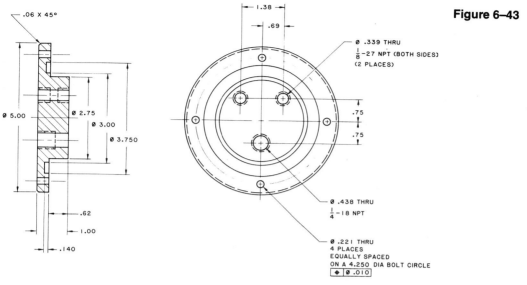

Figure 6–43

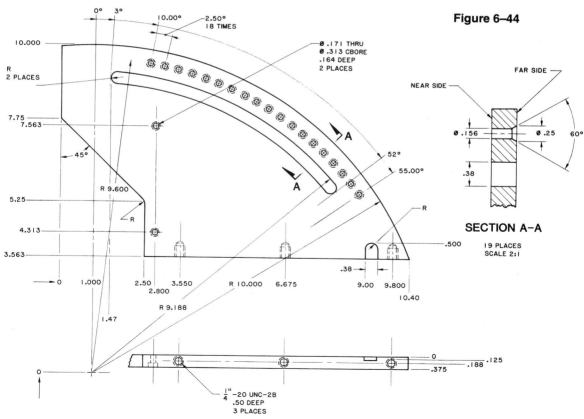

Figure 6–44

Figure 6–45

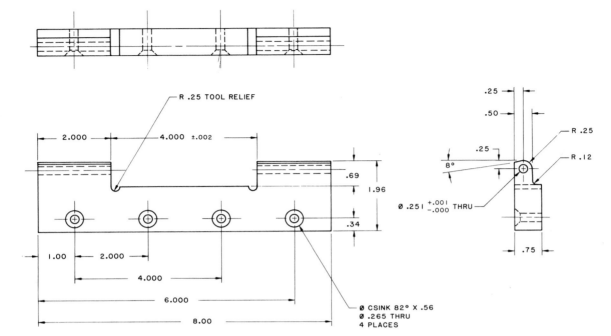

R .25 TOOL RELIEF

2.000
4.000 ±.002
.69
1.96
.34
1.00
2.000
4.000
6.000
8.00

.25
.50
.25
8°
R .25
R .12
Ø .251 +.001 −.000 THRU
.75

Ø CSINK 82° X .56
Ø .265 THRU
4 PLACES

Figure 6–46

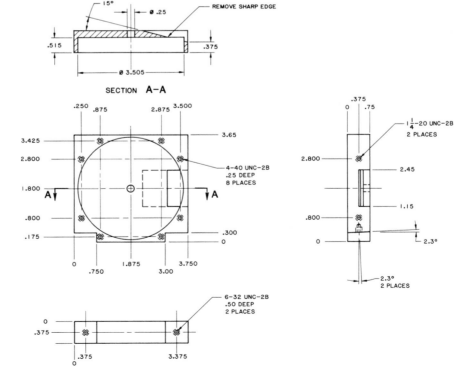

15°
Ø .25
REMOVE SHARP EDGE
.515
.375
Ø 3.505

SECTION A–A

.250   .875   2.875 3.500
3.425   3.65
2.800
                             4-40 UNC-2B
                             .25 DEEP
1.800 A   A   8 PLACES
.800
.175   .300
       0   0
       0   .750 1.875 3.00 3.750

.375
0   .75
1¼-20 UNC-2B
2 PLACES
2.800   2.45
.800   1.15
0   2.3°
2.3°
2 PLACES

6-32 UNC-2B
.50 DEEP
2 PLACES
0
.375
.375   3.375
0

Chapter

7

Special Functions

Objectives

Upon completion of this chapter the reader will be able to:

- Verify specific geometry that makes up the drawing.

- Use on-line documentation to get information and help directly from the system.

- Measure angles, distances, and calculate areas for a part.

- Use the LIST capability to get information from the system.

- Discuss layering and color discrimination and how they are used in drafting and design with a CADD system.

- Understand how to make two-dimensional views of a part look more realistic.

Introduction

Special functions include capabilities to verify, list, measure, count, and request information from the system. Also included within this category is the capability to display and organize geometry efficiently with colors, discrimination and layer options. Lastly, *three-dimensional simulation* techniques (isometric, oblique, 2¹/₂ dimensional, and for surfaces) are overviewed, as are basic three-dimensional surface and solids capabilities.

The functions discussed in this chapter are those that manipulate existing geometry. With the exception of an overview of three-dimensional surface capabilities, no new geometry is added. In addition, the existing geometry is used to provide additional information.

On-Line Documentation

Most CADD systems have an *on-line documentation* facility. This documentation is available to the designer on the system and is therefore considered *on-line* (Figure 7–1). The designer doesn't have to leave his or her workstation to consult a manual. Instead, the proper prompt is entered and the system gives the information requested. In Figure 7–2 the system's response to the HELP request provided the options to FILLET and the default values. DRAW FILLET ?: listed the options: TRIM, NO TRIM, TRIM A, TRIM B, RADIUS (with a .5 inch default), DIAMETER (with a 1.00 inch default), CIRCLE, and THREE ENTITIES.

The on-line documentation available to the designer gives explanations of how to use a capability. The documentation will answer many types of questions about a capability. At the most generalized level, the designer can

Figure 7–1
CRT with menu with HELP shown on right side of CRT. (Courtesy Tasvir Corp.)

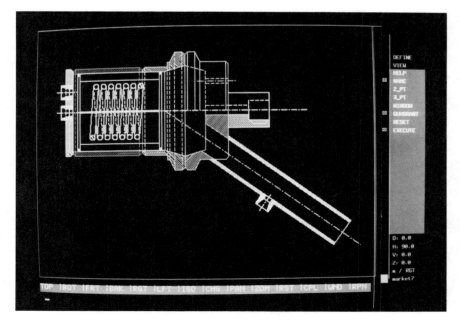

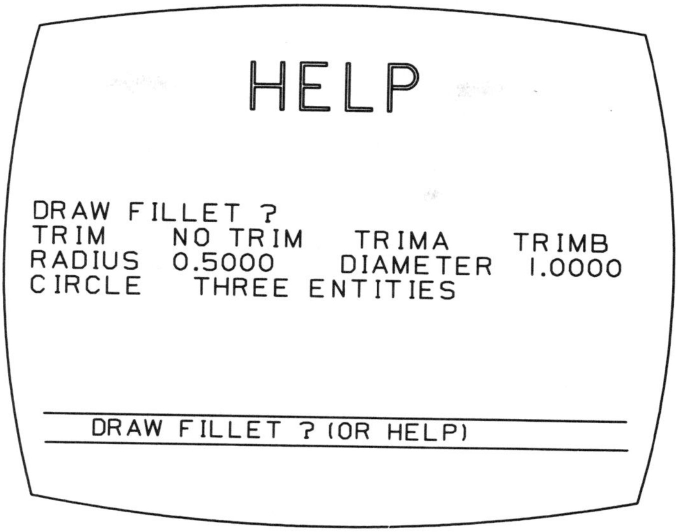

Figure 7–2
Getting help from the
system.

get a list of all the primary capabilities. The designer may also get a list of all primary capabilities starting with a specific letter. The system also displays a list of all legal second-level capabilities that can be used with a specific first-level capability. The system can show a list of all options that can be used with a particular combination of capabilities.

Because some capabilities will include numerous options for versatility, the on-line documentation is tailored for easy referencing. The documentation provides a series of multiple choices for the options. The system will guide the designer through these options, showing only the applicable choices. For instance, if a particular option is chosen, only the additional options that can be used with it will be shown. Finally, the system will show brief descriptions of how a particular capability can be used including its function, the proper syntax needed and which options are valid to use within that capability. Some systems refer to this capability as the HELP. See the box on page 254 for an example of Computervision's on-line documentation.

Getting Analysis Information

As a part is created, the current defaults, such as color or depth, may need to be determined. The geometry entered may need to be verified. Prompting the system for this information is called **verification**. The following capabilities are available on most systems:

- *Displaying Defaults*. The LIST and HELP capabilities are used to show the current color, layer, and depth.

INSERT POINT !

PURPOSE: To insert a Point entity
VALID MODES: MODEL, DRAWING
BASIC SYNTAX: INSERT POINT <modifiers>: loc d...d
MODIFIERS: ON, PROJ, CPLANE
SPECIAL NOTES:
INS POINT ON: ent <1> loc <2> <2> ... :ent <1> loc <2> ...
<1>—SELECT CURVE (LINES, CIRCLES, ARCS, FILLETS, PARABOLAS,
                  ELLIPSES, HYPERBOLAS, SPLINES AND
                  B-SPLINES ONLY)
                  AND SURFACE (TABCYL, RULSUR, SREV)
<2>—SPECIFY POSITION WHICH IS DROPPED PERPENDICULAR
     ONTO THE SELECTED CURVE <1> OR SURFACE <2>

INS POINT PROJ: ent <1> end <2> <3> :loc <4> ...
<1>—IDENTIFIES A SURFACE
<2> <3>—SPECIFIES A VECTOR
<4>—IDENTIFIES THE POINT TO BE PROJECTED TO THE SURFACE

INSERT FILLET !

PURPOSE: To insert a fillet between two or three entities
VALID MODES: Valid in both model and drawing mode
COMMAND SYNTAX: #n#INSERT FILLET (modifiers):
    Model ent d1d2[d3]

The third entity [d3] is digitized only if the three (THRENT) modifier is used. Otherwise, two entities are digitized.

CAUTION: For line entities, always digitize in a counterclockwise order so that the fillet is inserted from one entity counterclockwise to the next one. Otherwise, the major portion of each line will be trimmed off instead of the short segments extending beyond the fillet.

MODIFIERS:

TRIM: Trim the two entities after fillet is created, default

−TRIM: Don't trim the two entities

TRIMA: Trim the first digitized entry only

TRIMB: For two entity fillet, trim the second digitized entry; for three entity fillet, trim the third digitized entry

RADIUS X: The value of X specifies the diameter of fillet; default is
            X = .5 inches

DIAMETER X (DIAM X):   The value of X specifies the diameter of fillet; default
                       is X = 1.0 inches

CIRCLE (CIR):   If this modifier is specified, a circle is created instead of an arc

THREE (THRENT):   Indicates three entity fillet; three entities must be
                  digitized

- *Verifying.* Any part of the geometry can be verified to find out its characteristics such as color, layer, and coordinate location. Often the designer needs to know the length or origin of some geometry to enter additional geometry relative to it. The coordinate information in the verification varies with the type of geometry. If a line is verified, the system shows the coordinate locations of the end points and the length. An arc or circle verification shows the coordinate location of the center and the radius.

- *Counting Portions of the Geometry and Views.* After the system counts the number of lines, arcs, circles, or splines in the drawing, it lists them by type. The system also counts the number of designer-defined views and determines the size of the drawing.

- *Measuring.* The distance between portions of the geometry, the angle between lines, and the area of polygons can be measured by the system using the MEASURE and CALCULATE capabilities.

Verify The system will verify any item of geometry in the database. In general, the size, type, and location of the geometry are given along with the color, layer, and any other type of identifying information attached to the specific type of geometry.

If the designer is unsure of the geometry that make up a figure, he or she can verify it. The system verifies each individual item of geometry that is part of the figure.

Figure 7–3 shows how VERIFY was used to verify the length of a line. The system showed the *type* of geometry, coordination *location*, *length*, and *layer* of the line.

In Figure 7–4, the circle was verified, providing the type of geometry, coordinate location of its center, radius, circumference, and layer.

Count The COUNT capability is used to determine how many unique figures and/or figure copies are in a drawing. The system totals the number of individual types of geometry (Figure 7–5). COUNT provides statistical information on the drawing currently shown on the CRT. The following list is an example of some of the statistics provided:

- Types of geometry and the number of each type

- Number of designer-defined views

- Number of extents

- Number of erased items of geometry

- Size of the part

- Numbers assigned to designer-defined views

Figure 7–3
Verifying a line.

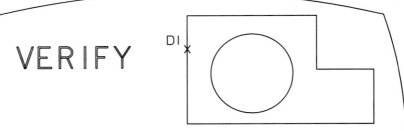

VERIFY

VERIFY ENTITY:DI

LINE = ENTITY TYPE
DRAW: COORDINATE OUTPUT
. XI = 7.85302   YI = I4.I2368   ZI = 0.0
. X2 = 7.85302   Y2 = 9.205487   Z2 = 0.0
. LENGTH = 4.9I8I92

LAYER = 0

Figure 7–4
Verifying a circle.

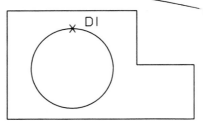

VERIFY

VERIFY ENTITY:DI

CIRCLE = ENTITY TYPE
DRAW: COORDINATE OUTPUT
. X = I2.788II   Y = II.4962I   Z = 0.0
. RADIUS = I.800203
. START ANGLE = 0.0   END ANGLE = 360.0
. CIRCUMFERENCE: II.3II

LAYER = 0

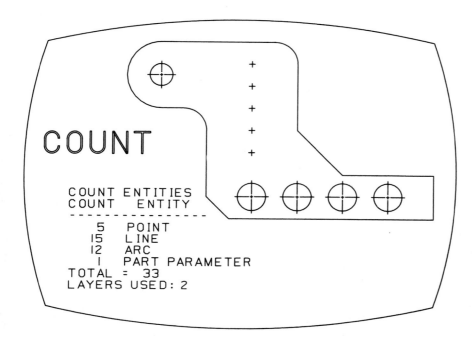

Figure 7–5
Using COUNT.

The following is an example of the output from COUNT:

LINE: 45
ARC: 12
POINT: 10
XHATCH: 1
DISPLAY: 2
VIEW: 1
EXTENT: 2
FIG-IL: 2
FIGURES: 3
FIGURE SUB-ITEMS: 17
ERASED ITEMS: 8
TOTAL ITEMS: 103
MASTER INDEX BLOCK = 245 PART DATA FILE
VIEWS: 7
DISPLAYS: 20 30

Measure   This capability permits the designer to measure the distance and angle between two designated points and shows that distance on the CRT. MEASURE also provides the capability to determine the area defined by a series of points.

MEASURE ANGLE calculates the inner and outer angles formed by two existing lines (Figure 7–6).

To measure an angle formed by two lines, digitize the two lines that form the angle. The system shows the angle values. The process is repeated

Figure 7–6
Measuring the angle
between two lines.

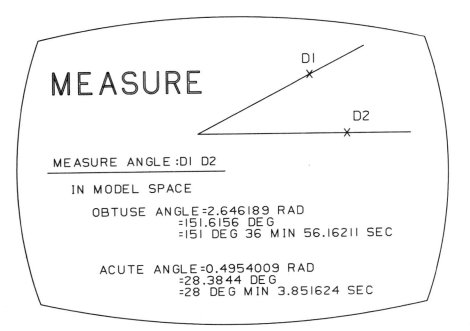

```
MEASURE                          DI
                                  x
                                        D2
                                        x

MEASURE ANGLE :DI D2

    IN MODEL SPACE

        OBTUSE ANGLE =2.646189 RAD
                    =151.6156 DEG
                    =151 DEG 36 MIN 56.16211 SEC


        ACUTE ANGLE =0.4954009 RAD
                    =28.3844 DEG
                    =28 DEG MIN 3.851624 SEC
```

for each angle to be measured. The system shows the number of degrees in each angle.

MEASURE DISTANCE calculates the distance between two locations (Figure 7–7). The distance between the line and the arc's center was measured.

CALCULATE AREA calculates the area inside a defined boundary. The shape can either be closed or open. The area to be calculated is defined by digitizing the boundary geometry. The system traces the boundary lines as they are digitized (Figure 7–8) and gives the area measurement.

List   LIST provides *graphic* and *non-graphic* information. Information can be related to a part or drawing. As an example, LIST EXTENTS shows the current boundaries of the screen and the screen scale. The system specifies the screen's minimum and maximum X, Y values. LIST FILES shows the names of files in the directory. The system can list all the files or a collection of specific files.

The parameters that can be queried vary from system to system, but most of the systems offer a basic list of options similar to those shown below.

LIST PART lists information on a part

LIST DRAWING lists selected status information on specified drawings (Figure 7–9)

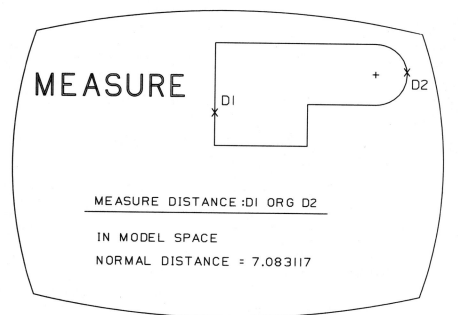

Figure 7–7
Measuring the distance between two points.

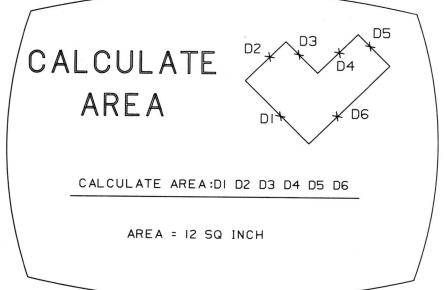

Figure 7–8
Calculating the area of a part.

LIST VIEW lists status of views (Figure 7–9)

LIST CPL lists the construction planes

LIST IMAGE provides information on specified saved views

LIST LAYER lists layers

LIST LAYER DISCRIMINATION lists layers assigned to different font types

LIST PARAMETERS lists current designer-defined parameters

LIST TEXT lists selected text parameters (Figure 7–10)

LIST DIMENSION lists current dimension parameters

LIST APPEARANCE lists status of the selected font parameters, including font name, weight, and value

Geometry Appearance

Most CADD systems provide capabilities to control the *appearance*, *discrimination*, and *sorting* of geometry. The following capabilities illustrate this facility:

Figure 7–9
Using LIST to access information.

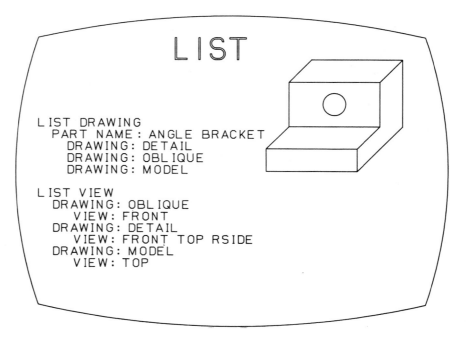

Figure 7–10
Listing text parameters.

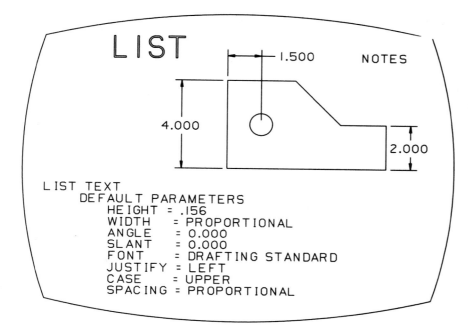

Drawing Appearance Control   The visual appearance of geometry can be controlled through the selection of certain physical characteristics. Commonly used line fonts (or line types) are available. Geometry appearance can also be controlled by specifying the *weight*, *intervals* and *width* of the line. Any item of the geometry can be changed to a particular font. A variety of line fonts are available from which to choose.

Geometry Discrimination   CADD systems have different ways to show that an item of the geometry has been identified by the designer. The geometry may change from solid lines to dashed lines or may flash when selected. All of these appearance controls for identification can be determined by the designer.

Layer Separation   Layering is used to separate groups or types of geometry. Each part created on the CADD system has multiple layers. Any one of these layers can be viewed separately and have a specific type of geometry or information contained on it. Layers are like transparent sheets, e.g., acetate, on which the designer places specific types of geometry (or information). Any number of these layers can be shown at one time. For example, all text can be placed on one layer, all bolt holes on another layer, and all the bolts on the third layer. Any combination of these layers can be displayed at one time. In addition, the designer can automatically define specific geometry types to be placed on specific layers (Figure 7–11).

Color Separation Layers, geometry, or information such as dimensions or notes can all be given a specific color.

Layers

Some CADD programs provide multiple layers on which to place geometry and text. Layers are like sheets of drawing mylar. Information can be created and then viewed on an individual sheet. One sheet can be placed on top of another to view the information on all the sheets simultaneously. The layers allow the designer to separate different types of information such as geometry and text (Figure 7–11). This information can then be viewed or plotted separately.

Geometry can be placed on the drawing on one or more drawing layers. It may be helpful to think of layers as transparent overlays, although layers

Figure 7–11
Layers.

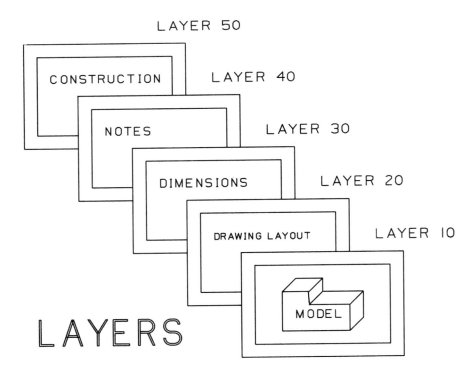

are not limited to such uses. With layers, associated components of a drawing can be grouped. A layer (or a set of layers) can contain the geometry related to a particular aspect of the drawing. The visibility, color, and line type of all this geometry can be controlled globally.

The same drawing limits, coordinate system, and zoom factor apply to all layers on a drawing. Layers are always perfectly registered with one another; a designated point on one layer aligns precisely with the same point on every other layer.

Many systems have no limit to the number of layers on a drawing, nor is the number of entities per layer restricted in any way. A name can be given to each layer, and any combination of layers can be shown. Layers and their properties are part of the drawing, and they are saved in the drawing database.

Working on a layer is similar to working on any *one* of a stack of *transparent overlays*. Layers are numbered. Layers allow part geometry, notes, and dimensions to be placed on different layers. Although work is possible only on the *selected* layer, any combination of layers may be viewed. It is possible to put lines, fonts, and colors on specific layers to aid in discrimination.

The LAYER capability can have many options. The following options are a sample of some typical examples:

SELECT LAYERn = select the active/construction working layer (Figure 7–12 (A))

ECH LAY ALL = all layers visible (default)

n = number of layer or layers to be visible (Figure 7–12 (B))

ADD or INCLUDEn = include new layers in present list (Figure 7–12 (C))

SUBTRACT or EXCLUDEn = exclude these layers from present list

DRAW = limits echoing to drawing geometry

LIST LAYER ALL = shows which layers are active and echoed (default)

ACT = shows which layer is active

MODEL or DRAW = list model or drawing layers

CHANGE LAYERn = change digitized geometry to layer n

Most companies develop a standard layering scheme, with designated layers for construction lines, dimensions, and so on. Table 7–1 shows one possible layering scheme.

Figure 7–12
(A) Selecting and
echoing layers.

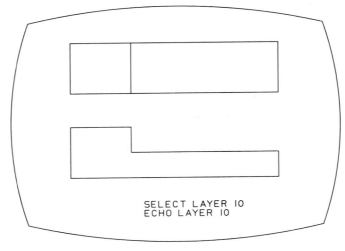

(B) Selecting and
echoing layers (con-
tinued).

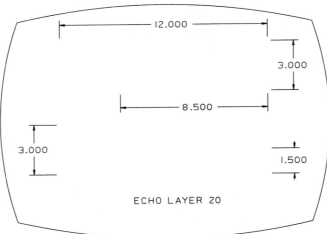

(C) Selecting and
echoing layers (con-
tinued).

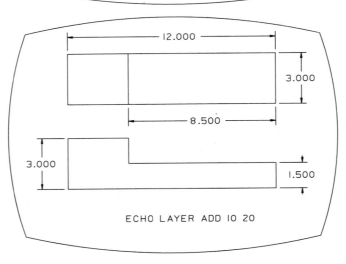

A standard layering scheme makes it easy to keep track of where different information resides. Layering can be used to temporarily sort graphic information. For example, the designer can use layers to separate geometry in a congested area of his or her drawing. When unnecessary information, such as text and dimensions, is not shown, processing takes less time. Placing geometry on one layer and dimensions on another allows the designer to view a drawing with or without dimensions. Figure 7–11 shows layering where the model is on layer 10, drawing border format on layer 20, dimensioning on layer 30, notes on layer 40, and construction aids on layer 50.

SELECT LAYER defines the layer on which the system places new geometry (Figure 7–12 (A)). This layer is referred to as the active layer. The active layer cannot be removed from the display. ECHO LAYER shows the specific layers that are requested (Figure 7–12 (B)).

Changing the Layer of the Geometry

CHANGE LAYER is used to change the layer of existing geometry by digitizing the geometry to be changed to a different layer. The system places the geometry on the newly specified layer.

In Figure 7–12 (A), layer 10 was selected as the active construction layer for the parts geometry. ECHO LAYER defines layer 10 as the only layer shown. In Figure 7–12 (B), only layer 20 is shown and, in Figure 7–12 (C), both layers 10 and 20 are echoed. Layer 20 was used for dimensions. Figure 7–13 shows a portion of a menu dedicated to layer capabilities.

Table 7–1

Layering Scheme

Layer No.	Contents
0	Layer Index/Table of Contents
1–50	Construction Geometry and Drawing Formats (contains all construction geometry used in the design of the part(s), e.g., lines, points, and arcs, etc., and the different types of drawing formats)
51–100	Manufacturing (contains manufacturing information, e.g. NC and tool path information, jigs, fixtures, and tooling)
101–145	Dimensions, Text, Labels, and Layers per View (contains all dimension information, text, and labels)
146–175	Illustrations (contains technical illustrations using the part(s) as its source)
176–200	Analysis (Engineering), FEM, and Physical Properties (contain different kinds of analytical information concerning the part's structure, contents, and properties)
201–254	Construction Aids and Miscellaneous Information (contains construction geometry which help design and dimension a part, as well as any miscellaneous information connected with the part design

Figure 7–13
Menu area for using
layering capabilities.

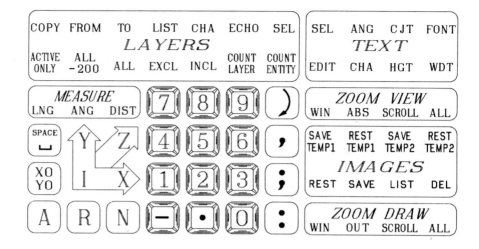

Color

A color can be associated with each drawing layer. The designated color selects the actual color in which geometry is drawn on the CRT. Using this property, the designer can draw attention to important details on the drawing, highlight recent changes, or visually indicate the relationship among items in the geometry.

Most CADD systems provide a palette of multiple colors. Colors make it easy to identify and distinguish between different kinds of information on the drawing. A particular color can be associated with a specific layer. SELECT COLOR is used to determine the default color of new geometry.

A sample of colors and their identifying numbers for a typical system is shown below.

1 Red

2 Green

3 Blue

4 Yellow

5 Cyan

6 Magenta

7 Grey

8 Dark Grey

9 Light Red

10 Light Green

11 Light Blue

12 Light Yellow

13 Light Cyan

14 Light Magenta

15 White

A part can be built using a layering and color scheme that defines individual layers for basic construction, dimensions, labels, and construction lines. Each layer is then given a different color (Table 7–2).

Discrimination of Geometry

The discriminate feature provides the *temporary* identification of the geometry shown on the CRT. It can be used for specific *geometry* or *layers*. The discrimination can be done in either *monochrome* or *color*. Colors and fonts can be selected either by a *specific name* or a *corresponding number*.

Each drawing layer or portion of geometry can have an associated linetype. A linetype is a repeating pattern of dashes, dots, and blank spaces. Each linetype has a name and a definition that stipulates the particular dash–dot sequence and the relative lengths of the dashes and blank spaces. Most systems provide a library of standard linetypes or the designer can create his or her own linetype patterns. If the CRT is monochrome, dashed and dotted linetypes can be used instead of color to differentiate one layer from another. In some drafting disciplines, conventions have been established that give specific meanings to particular dash–dot patterns. The default linetype for all newly created layers is a solid line.

Figure 7–14 shows the technique used to select a linetype other than a solid line. SELECT LINE FONT was used along with the font type—DASH. A 3-inch circle and a line were then drawn. Since the dash font was selected, the circle and line are shown as dashed lines.

To change an existing linetype from one type to another, CHANGE LINE FONT is used. In Figure 7–15, the existing lines were solid. The CHANGE LINE FONT TO DASH was used and the lines to be changed were digitized. In Figure 7–16, the existing dashed lines were changed to solid.

Table 7–2

Layer	Color	Use
1	4	Model geometry
10	6	Dimensions
20	8	Labels
30	10	Construction lines

Figure 7–14
Selecting a different font than the default.

BEFORE

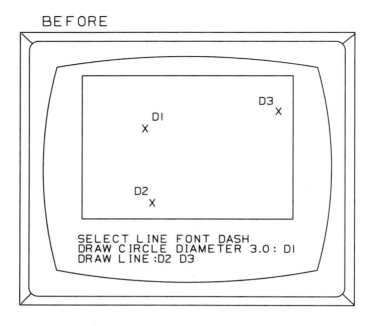

```
SELECT LINE FONT DASH
DRAW CIRCLE DIAMETER 3.0: DI
DRAW LINE :D2 D3
```

AFTER

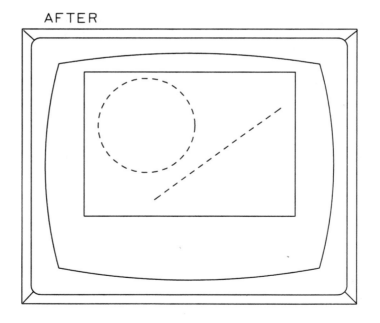

BEFORE

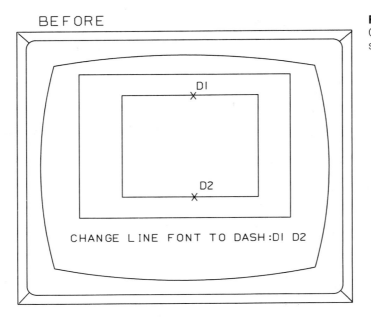

CHANGE LINE FONT TO DASH:DI D2

AFTER

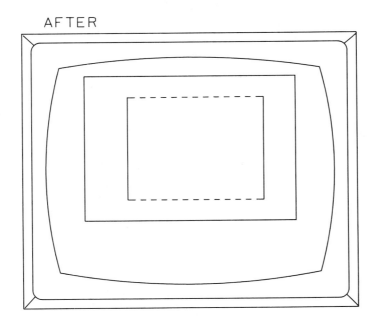

Figure 7–15
Changing a line font from
solid to dash.

Figure 7–16
Changing a line font from
dash to solid.

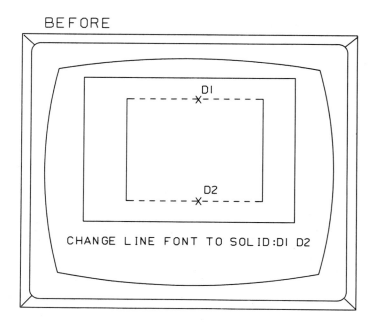

BEFORE

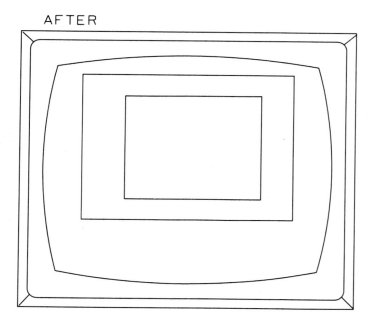

AFTER

True Three-Dimensional and Simulated Three-Dimensional

The designer seated at a CADD CRT gets no more feeling of three-dimensional definition from a single view on the CRT than he or she would from a drawing on paper. However, the designer can better visualize the three-dimensional part when he or she sees features in the view that indicate depth, even if it is indicated in an artificial way. Creating drawings with *perspective*, *isometric*, or *oblique* views help to indicate depth to the designer.

The **perspective** capability is different from parallel orthographic projection in that it uses depth information. Here, the size of the part is scaled in proportion to its distance from the viewer. The perspective projection of the part shown in Figure 7–17 demonstrates this scaling.

SELECT PERSPECTIVE temporarily distorts the part so that it can be viewed in perspective. This option is limited to three-dimensional systems with modeling capabilities. Some systems automatically set the perspective parameters to give the part a certain amount of distortion. The location of the station point can be specified or the default can be used. The default location assumes that the part is in the center of the CRT. The distance between the station point and the picture plane can also be specified.

Two-dimensional pictures can be made to look more realistic with **isometric** views of three-dimensional objects such as the cube shown in Figure 7–18. Figure 7–19 and Figure 7–20 show a three-dimensional part in an isometric view. *Oblique* views are also used to create illustrations that simulate the third dimension (Figure 7–21).

While perspective, isometric, and oblique views are useful in depicting three-dimensional objects more realistically in a two-dimensional view, many CADD systems offer the capability to use solid models. Here, the illusion of depth can be added through the use of color and shading. This technique is covered in more detail in Chapter 9.

PROJECT sweeps one or more entities through space in the direction of the axis you specify. The system generates connecting lines between the geometry and the resulting projection. Geometry can be projected along any arbitrary axis. An item is specified by projecting its current location and the location to which it is to be projected.

A three-dimensional part is created or an existing three-dimensional part is given additional depth by projecting it along the Z axis. A negative Z value extends the item into the screen while a positive Z value projects it out of the screen. Figure 7–22 shows a simulated isometric projection in 2 1/2 dimensions.

To specify a depth value relative to the model, an incremental value is entered, for example, IZn. In Figure 7–23, the part was projected at a distance of 3 inches in the positive Z direction. The pictorial view shows how the part was given depth.

In Figure 7–24, a hole was entered onto the inclined surface of the three-dimensional part. The HOLE capability is similar to PROJECT. This capability is discussed in more detail in Chapter 9.

Figure 7–17
Three-dimensional model displayed in perspective.

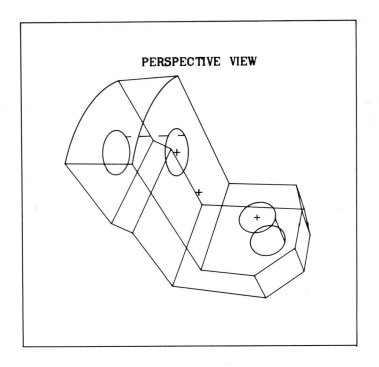

PERSPECTIVE VIEW

Figure 7–18
Isometric projection, simulated three-dimensional.

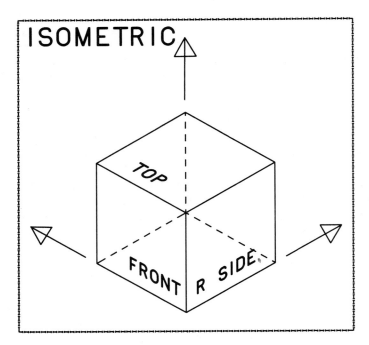

ISOMETRIC

TOP

FRONT   R SIDE

Figure 7–19
Designer creating a
three-dimensional part.
(Courtesy Tasvir Corp.)

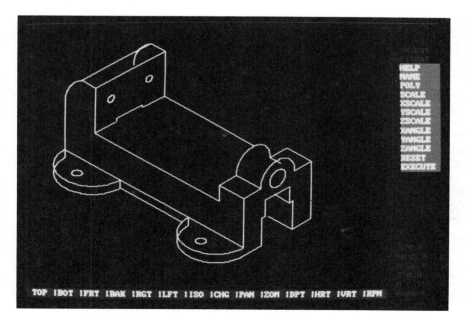

Figure 7–20
Three-dimensional part
shown in isometric
projection. (Courtesy
Tasvir Corp.)

Figure 7–21
Oblique projection,
simulated three-dimen-
sional.

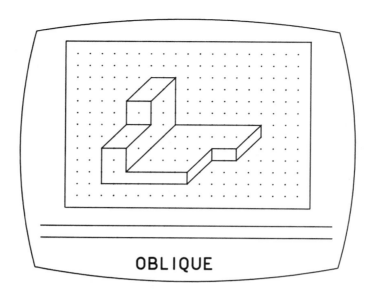

OBLIQUE

Figure 7–22
Cam assembly three-
dimensional simulated
visualization drawing
produced by Gary Wells,
Autodesk, Inc. (Courtesy
Autodesk, Inc.)

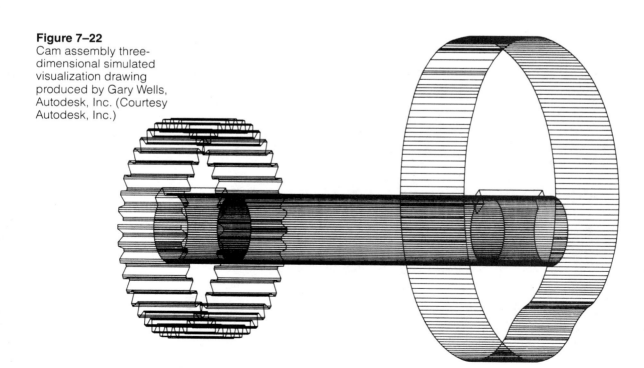

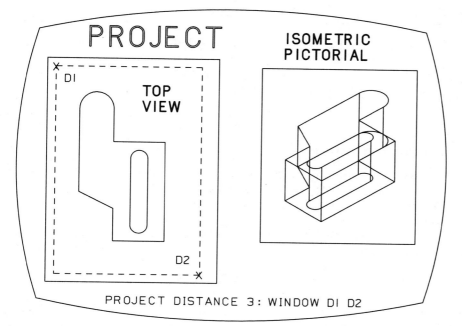

Figure 7–23
Projecting the third dimension of a part.

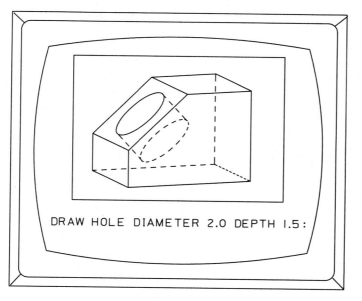

Figure 7–24
Inserting a hole in a three-dimensional part.

Three-Dimensional Surfaces

A *surface* depicts the face of an object, whether that face is flat, cylindrical, spherical, or sculptured. It defines the contour of the geometry between the edges of a part, providing a "skin" for wire-frame models created with lines, arcs, and other curves. A surface reveals the contours between the edges of a wireframe model (see Chapter 9 for more information).

Constructing Surfaces

This section introduces the creation of surfaces. It covers making a surface from the curve profile, putting surfaces on a wireframe model, and specifying the mesh density. Figure 7–25 shows a menu for three-dimensional surface construction.

A swept surface is called a *surface of revolution* and a projected surface is called a *tabulated cylinder*. Both types can be created by a profile using one or more curves or lines.

A surface of revolution is three-dimensional and can be generated when a piece of geometry is spun about an axis of rotation. The generating geometry can be a line (Figure 7–26), conic, circle, arc (Figure 7–27), or spline (Figure 7–28). This can only be accomplished with a three-dimensional system, since it is a three-dimensional capability.

The system makes the surface of revolution using information provided about the distance for the sweep, the axis, and the origin. Figure 7–26 shows a surface of revolution. Specify the distance, in degrees, using ANGLE or let the distance default to 360 degrees. The value can be any positive or negative number. Positive numbers sweep clockwise; negative numbers sweep counterclockwise.

The *axis of rotation* is the angle at which the system holds the profile during the sweep. VECTOR is used to digitize an axis of rotation. If using the default, the profile is held parallel to the Z axis. The axis of rotation is indicated by digitizing twice. It often helps to use construction geometry to get the correct angle. Two-and-one-half dimensional systems allow for the projection of geometry in one direction only (refer to Chapter 9 on Modeling).

A *ruled surface* is another example of a three-dimensional surface. The system draws straight lines between two separate lines or curves, thereby creating the surface. The system draws the first line between the ends of the curves that are digitized. If adjacent ends are digitized, the surface is twisted.

The system makes a ruled surface by drawing straight lines between two curves or lines. The surface in Figure 7–29 is twisted because opposite ends were digitized first.

At the same time a surface is created, a MESH density can be specified. The mesh density is specified by entering values that correspond to the two

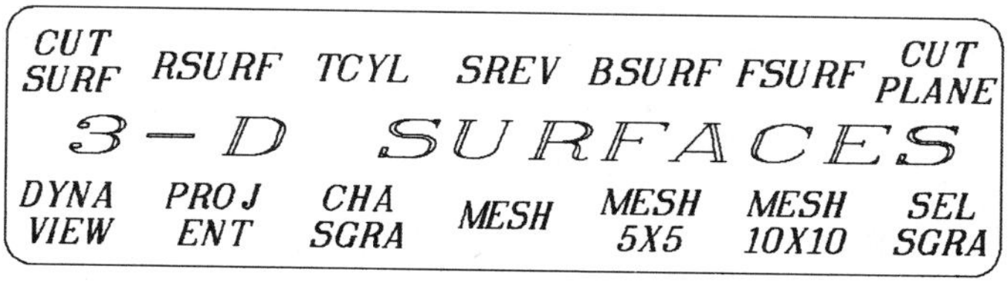

CUT SURF
RSURF
TCYL
SREV
BSURF
FSURF
CUT PLANE
3-D SURFACES
DYNA VIEW
PROJ ENT
CHA SGRA
MESH
MESH 5X5
MESH 10X10
SEL SGRA

Figure 7–25
Menu area for inputting three-dimensional surface commands.

directions of the mesh. In Figure 7–29, a 4 × 6 mesh was put on the surface. Meshes are for viewing purposes only. If a mesh density isn't specified, a mesh won't be seen, but the surface is there nonetheless.

Z-Clipping

Another special function aid available to the designer is the **Z-clipping** capability. Z-clipping allows the designer to easily define a section (or sections) of a three-dimensional model. This enhances visual clarification of the model, especially if the model is very complex. Z-clipping enables the designer to clip the model at any defined location along the Z axis. This capability is very useful for construction purposes in dense areas of geometry or can be used for viewing clearance checks and interference fits.

SURFACE OF REVOLUTION
D3
D1
D2
TOP VIEW
ISOMETRIC PICTORIAL
DRAW SURFACE OF REVOLUTION:
D1 : D2 D3

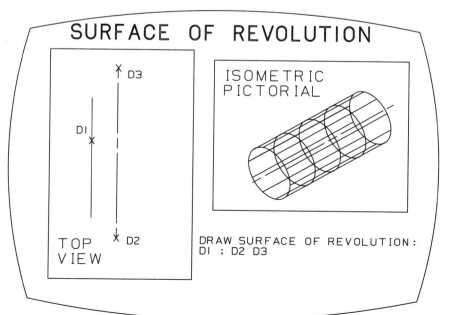

Figure 7–26
Generating a cylinder surface of revolution.

Figure 7–27
Generating a sphere
surface of revolution.

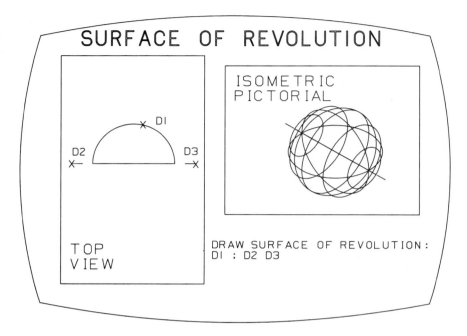

Figure 7–28
Generating a surface of
revolution using a spline.

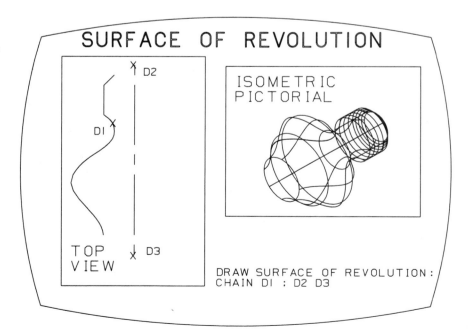

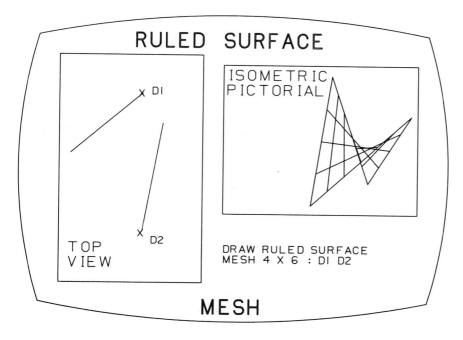

Figure 7–29
Generating a ruled surface.

Figure 7–30 illustrates this Z-clipping feature. The figure shows a top view of a part's geometry as well as an isometric auxiliary view. The top view is very dense. The pictorial view shows a clearer display of the part. The Z-clipping feature allows the designer to section this part's geometry for a clearer picture. Figure 7–30 (right) illustrates the Z-clipping feature. The geometry on the right has four levels identified to be clipped. A small section at the top of the geometry is clipped just above and below the arrow labeled Level 1.

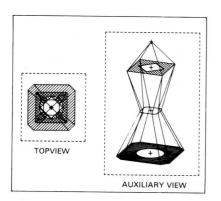

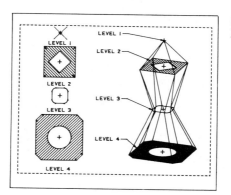

Figure 7–30
Z-clipping.

INSERT PART copies the geometry and associated properties stored in another drawing into the current drawing.

This command is used to avoid recreating geometry that already exists in a different drawing. After inserting a part, individual items can be altered. Figure 7–31 is an assembly created from the individual parts shown in Figures 7–32 and 7–33. Figure 7–32 is the base and was used as the control part. The top plate part was inserted into the base part as shown.

When inserting a part, the designer can usually specify one or more of the following:

- *Location* of the part's point of origin

- *Orientation* of the part inserted

- *Angle* (relative to the X axis or a vector defined)

- *Layering* scheme for the part's geometry

- *Scale* along all three axes or a specific axis

- Whether to *group* the part's individual geometries

Figure 7–31
Assembly created by inserting figures and parts.

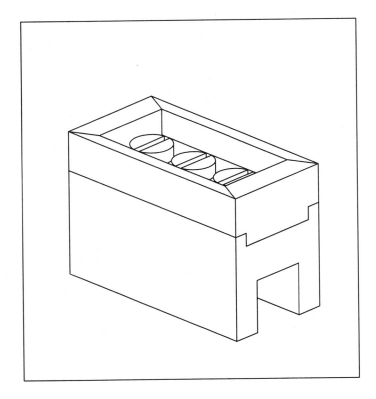

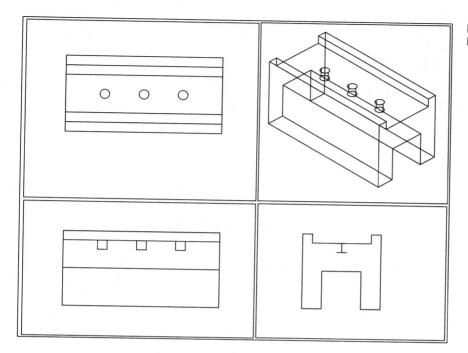

Figure 7–32
Base part of assembly.

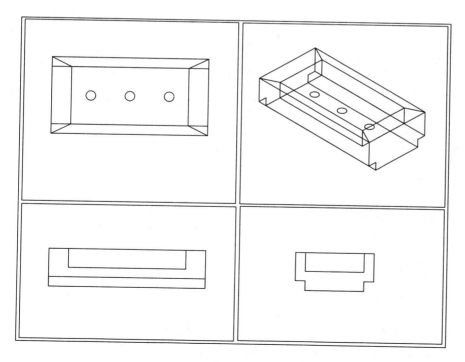

Figure 7–33
Slide plate part of
assembly shown in
Figure 7–32.

If the designer doesn't need to work with a part's individual pieces of geometry, insert the part as a *figure* (Figure 7–34). See the following section for more information.

When inserting one part into another, geometry in the inserted part can be modified. To bring standard parts which may require modification into an assembly, insert a part into a model (refer to Chapter 9 for a discussion on models and modeling).

Library Parts

Library parts which require modification in the new drawing are inserted as parts (Figure 7–34). Parts that do not require modification should be grouped and inserted as figures. INSERT FIGURE inserts one or more copies of a part into the current drawing as a figure. The system considers a figure to be a single piece of geometry. Individual pieces of geometry that make up the figure cannot be manipulated. However, if the original part is changed at a later time, the system can automatically update the corresponding figures. For more information on library parts, see Chapter 8 on Symbols.

When inserting a figure, specify one or more of the following:

Figure 7–34
Bolt part inserted as a figure in Figure 7–32.

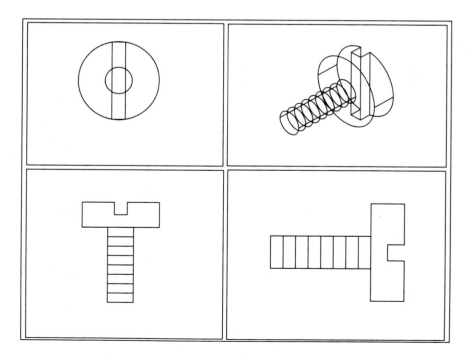

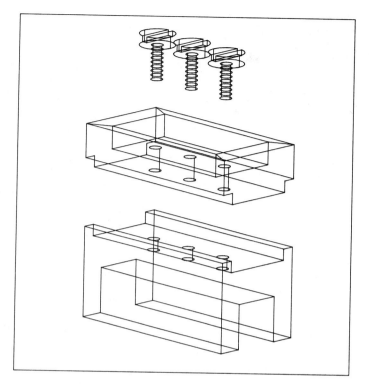

Figure 7–35
Exploded view of
assembly shown in
Figure 7–32.

- Location of the figure's point of origin
- View of the figure where it is to be inserted
- Angle (relative to the X axis or a vector)
- Layering scheme of the geometry in the first copy
- Scale along all axes or a specific axis

 Regardless of the number of copies inserted, the system only counts the individual items of geometry that make up the figure once. As a result, multiple copies of a figure require less space in the database than multiple copies of a part. In Figure 7–31, three bolts (Figure 7–34) were inserted in the assembly as figures. An exploded assembly is shown in Figure 7–35.

GLOSSARY

ASSOCIATIVITY The linking of parts, components, or elements with their
 attributes or with other geometry.

ATTRIBUTE   A nongraphic characteristic of a part, component, or element; for example: length, diameter, name, volume, use, and creation date.

BENCHMARK   A set of standards used in testing a software or hardware product or system from which a measurement can be made. Benchmarks are often run on a system to verify that it performs according to specifications.

CUT PLANE   A plane intersected with a three-dimensional object to derive a sectional view.

DEDICATED   Assigned to a single function, such as a workstation used exclusively for engineering calculations.

DEFAULT   The predetermined value of a parameter that is automatically supplied by the system whenever that value is not specified by the user.

DELETE   To erase information from the computer's memory or from storage.

DELIMITER   A space, slash, asterisk, etc., that separates data within a continuous string.

DIGITIZE   To convert lines and shapes into digital form.

DIGITIZER   A table or tablet on which the designer moves a puck or stylus to selected points and enters coordinates for lines and shapes by pressing down the input button on the puck or stylus.

DISPLAY GROUP   A collection of geometry that can be manipulated as a unit and that may be further combined to form larger groups.

DYNAMIC MOVEMENT   The ability to zoom, scroll, and rotate the view on the CRT interactively.

FAMILY OF PARTS   A collection of previously designed parts with similar geometric characteristics but differing in physical measurement.

FINITE ELEMENT MODELING (FEM)   The creation of a mathematical model by breaking the part to be modeled into component shapes such as rectangles, triangles, or wedges.

FUNCTION KEY   An area on the digitizing tablet or a key on a box or terminal that is used to enter a command.

FUNCTION MENU   The display or list of commands that the user can use to perform a task.

ISOMETRIC   A drawing in which the object is drawn from an oblique view so that the object appears as a solid object.

LAYER   A logical concept used to distinguish individual group(s) of data within a given drawing. It may be thought of as a series of transparencies (overlayed) in any order, yet having no depth.

LAYER DISCRIMINATION   The selective assignment of colors to a layer, or the highlighting of geometry to distinguish between data on different layers shown on a CRT.

MACRO   A combination of commands executed as a single command.

MODEL   An accurate three-dimensional representation of a part, assembly, or plant designed on a CADD system and stored in the database.

MODEL COORDINATE SYSTEM   The X, Y, and Z axes to which a model refers. The coordinate location that defines the model remains the same, regardless of the angle from which the model is viewed.

ORTHOGONAL VIEW   A perspective view that assumes an infinite vanishing point. All vertical lines appear to be parallel to each other, and all horizontal lines appear to be parallel to each other.

OVERLAY   To position one or more drawings on top of another and view them simultaneously on the CRT.

PERSPECTIVE   A method of representing a three-dimensional object as it would appear to the eye. This assumes a vanishing point and shows parallel lines at an angle relative to this point.

SECTION   To cut an object with an intersecting plane, then request generation and display of the total intersection geometry on a display surface.

TUTORIAL   A message that is shown on the CRT to show the designer how to perform a task.

UTILITY PROGRAM   A specific system software program such as a diagnostic program, a plot program, or a sort program.

VECTOR   A quantity that has magnitude and direction.

VERIFICATION   The message feedback to a display device acknowledging that an input was detected, e.g., the brightening of a display element selected by a light pen.

VIEW PORT   A user-selected viewing area on the CRT which frames the contents of a window.

WINDOWING   Proportionally enlarging a figure or portion of a figure so it fills the screen or view port.

Z-CLIPPING   The ability to specify depth parameter for a three-dimensional drawing such that all geometry above or below the specified depth(s) become invisible. No change is made to the database of the part or drawing. Useful in viewing cluttered or complex part geometry.

ZOOM   The successive enlargement or shrinking of a view on the CRT.

QUIZ

True or False

1.   Prompting the system for analysis information is called verification.

2.   COUNT provides statistical information on any drawing in the database.

3.   Layers, geometry, or information can all be given a specific color.

4.   Working on a layer is similar to working on any one of a stack of transparent overlays.

5.   A label is a repeating pattern of dashes, dots, and blank spaces.

6.   The designer can better visualize a three-dimensional part when there is some indication of depth.

7. Z-clipping allows the designer to define a section of a two-dimensional model.

8. Most systems can measure the area of a polygon.

Fill in the Blank

9. The on-line _____ available to the designer gives explanations of how to use a capability.

10. The _____ and _____ capabilities are used to show the current color, layer, and depth.

11. _____ provide the capability to determine the area defined by a series of points.

12. LIST provides _____ and _____ information.

13. The _____ of geometry can be controlled through the selection of certain physical characteristics.

14. _____ are like sheets of drawing mylar.

15. A _____ is a repeating pattern of dashes, dots and blank spaces.

16. Creating drawings with _____, _____, or _____ views help to indicate depth to the designer.

Answer the Following

17. Discuss how a designer might find out how to use a capability if there is no manual available.

18. Discuss three uses for layering.

19. Explain how a designer can find the area of a shape.

20. Discuss how line types are used.

21. Discuss how a designer can draw a three-dimensional part to make it more realistic.

22. What is a surface of revolution?

23. How is a mesh defined and what is its purpose?

24. What is the difference between inserting parts and inserting figures?

Problems

25. Draw the Cap (Figure 7–36). If a three-dimensional system is available, use either SURFACE OF REVOLUTION or SOLID OF REVOLUTION to

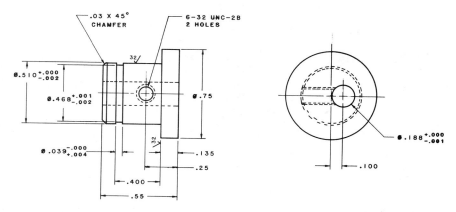

Figure 7–36

create the cylinders. If a two-dimensional system is used, draw all views individually. Do not dimension until Chapter 10 is completed.

26. Draw the Pedestal (Figure 7–37) using the same instructions as Problem 25.

27. Draw the Base Mounting (Figure 7–38) in isometric or oblique simulated projection if a two-dimensional system is available. If a three-dimensional system is used, create the part as a three-dimensional model and plot. Do not dimension.

28. Create the Pad Mounting part (Figure 7–39) as a three-dimensional model and dimension after completing Chapter 10. If a two-dimensional system is used, draw each view individually.

Figure 7–37

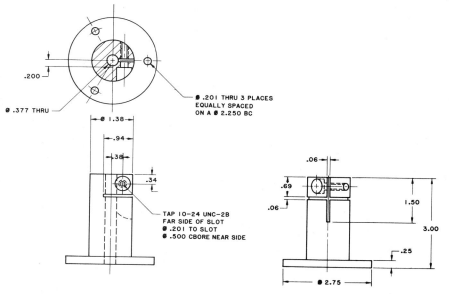

Figure 7-38

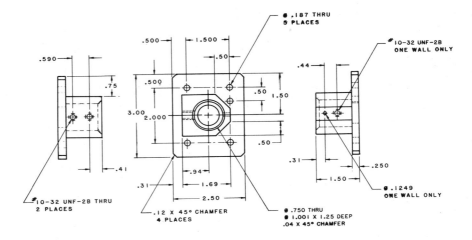

.187 THRU
5 PLACES

#10-32 UNF-2B
ONE WALL ONLY

.590

.75

.500   1.500

.50

.500

.50

1.50

3.00   2.000

.50

.44

.41

#10-32 UNF-2B THRU
2 PLACES

.31

.94

1.69

2.50

.12 X 45° CHAMFER
4 PLACES

.750 THRU
1.001 X 1.25 DEEP
.04 X 45° CHAMFER

.31

.250

1.50

.1249
ONE WALL ONLY

6061-T6 ALUM ALY BLACK ANODIZE

Figure 7-39

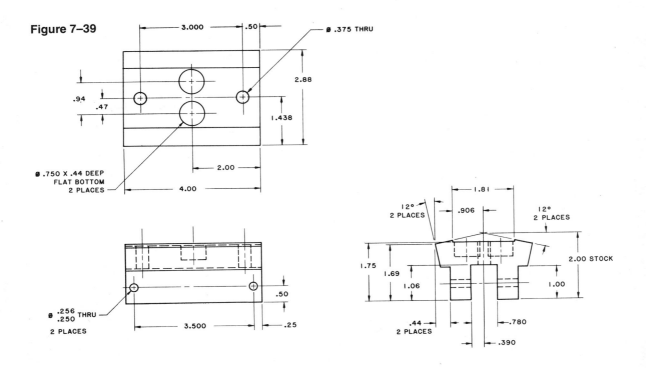

3.000   .50

.375 THRU

2.88

.94

.47

1.438

2.00

.750 X .44 DEEP
FLAT BOTTOM
2 PLACES

4.00

.256 THRU
.250
2 PLACES

.50

3.500   .25

1.81

12°
2 PLACES

.906

12°
2 PLACES

2.00 STOCK

1.75

1.69

1.06

1.00

.44
2 PLACES

.780

.390

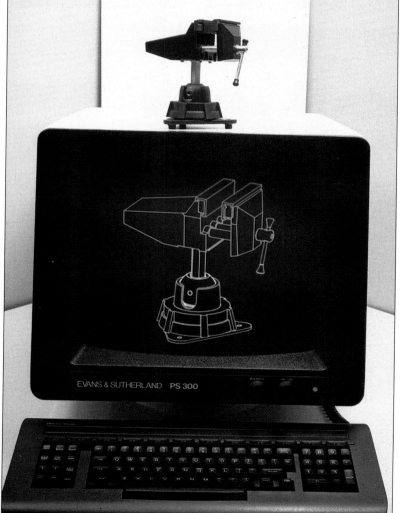

Plate 1
IBM-X5081 Display showing a solid model assembly.
(Courtesy International Business Machines Corp.)

Plate 2
Exploded view of vise assembly.
(Courtesy Evans & Sutherland)

Plate 3
Vise assembly shown on the display.
(Courtesy Evans & Sutherland)

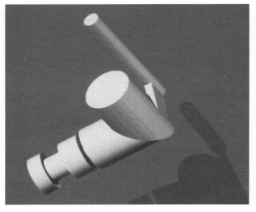

Plate 4
Three-dimensional model of mechanical part.
(Courtesy Evans & Sutherland)

Plate 5
Wireframe model of car.
(Courtesy Megatek Corp.)

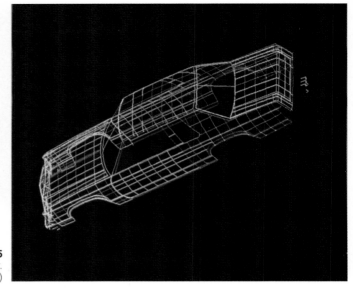

Plate 6
Solid model of mechanical part.
(Courtesy Evans & Sutherland)

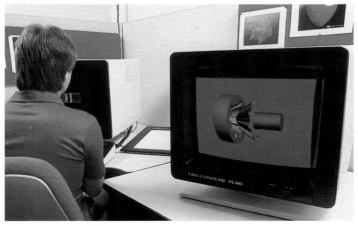

Plate 7
Solid model of mechanical assembly.
(Courtesy Evans & Sutherland)

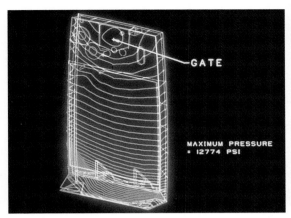

Plate 8
Wireframe model of mold part undergoing analysis.
(Courtesy Calma Co., a wholly owned subsidiary of
General Electric Co., U.S.A.)

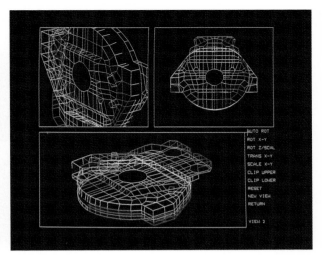

Plate 9
Three views of a three-dimensional wireframe model of a
flywheel undergoing stress analysis. (Courtesy Megatek Corp.)

Plate 10
Smooth solid model of a wine glass with
shading and highlights. (Courtesy
Megatek Corp.)

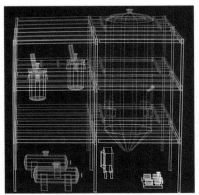

Plate 12
Three-dimensional wireframe model of a
process plant design. (Courtesy Evans &
Sutherland)

Plate 11
Three-dimensional section of mountain.
(Courtesy Megatek Corp.)

KASARMA GORGE
Pindus Mountains, GREECE

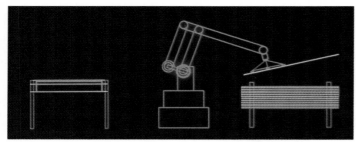

Plate 13

Sideview of robot work cell, designed using Calma's ROBOT-SIM computer-aided design software. Conveyor (left), indexing pallet (right), and robot (center) are drawn from the robot library. Other robot and work cell components, such as the end effector (shown in green), may be added using three-dimensional Design, Drafting and Manufacturing core mechanical software, integrated with the ROBOT-SIM package. (Courtesy Calma Co., a wholly owned subsidiary of General Electric Co., U.S.A.)

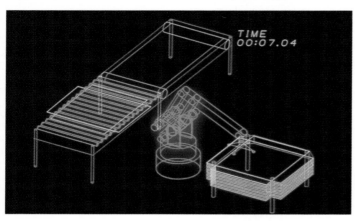

Plate 14

During robot simulation, work cell cycle time is displayed on screen at the computer-aided design station. Throughout the simulation, ROBOT-SIM software allows the operator to check work cell design elements such as interferences in the motion of the robot or end effector with other work cell components. (Courtesy Calma Co., a wholly owned subsidiary of General Electric Co., U.S.A.)

Plate 15

This work cell was modeled using Calma's ROBOT-SIM software package. The P5 robot, and its later generations, are in wide use in welding, assembly, machine loading, and many other manufacturing operations worldwide. (Courtesy Calma Co., a wholly owned subsidiary of General Electric Co., U.S.A.)

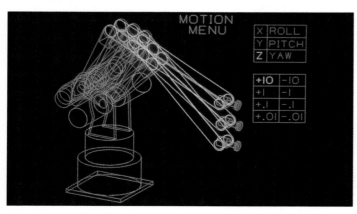

Plate 16

Using the motion menu feature of Calma's ROBOT-SIM software, a work cell designer can analyze and simulate robot movement within its factory floor environment. This screen view shows superimposed robot images obtained from motion simulation. (Courtesy Calma Co., a wholly owned subsidiary of General Electric Co., U.S.A.)

Chapter

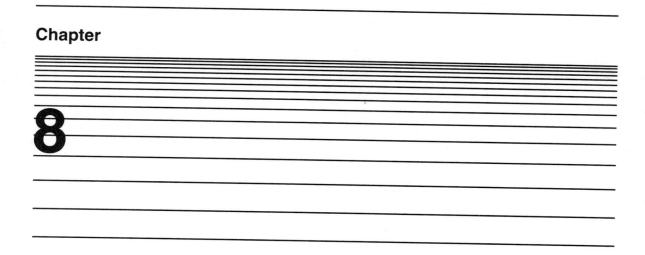

8

Symbols, Diagrams, and Data Retrieval

Objectives

After completing this chapter the reader will be able to:

- Create a symbol.

- Create and use a symbol library.

- Discuss the use of diagrams.

- Understand the use of attributes.

- Explain the use of symbols on drawings.

- Use the retrieval of attributes for reports.

Introduction

A **symbol** is a graphic representation of standard parts or items used repeatedly by the designer. Using traditional drafting methods, a template would be used to draw common features such as bolts. With CADD, these common features are drawn once and stored in memory. Once stored in memory, these symbols can be recalled, scaled, rotated, or mirrored.

When symbols are created, information about the part can be included. This information can then be used later to create bills of material or do calculations.

Symbols

Symbols are geometry items grouped together in a two-dimensional construction. Symbols may include other symbols. Symbols are used in schematics, charts, flow diagrams, and other types of pictorial representation (Figure 8–1).

Basic definitions and concepts essential to understanding symbols are presented first. The creation, definition, modification and updating, and usage of symbols are then discussed.

Basic Concepts and Definitions

Symbol Base—This is the collection of all geometry and character data constituting a symbol. This data is the same for all ''instances'' of the symbol base.

Symbol Instance—The placement of a previously created symbol onto a drawing is called a symbol instance. The instance refers to the symbol base for its graphic and connect node data. The instance utilizes origin, rotation angle, scale, and mirror parameters.

Figure 8–1
Schematic diagram.
(Courtesy EG & G)

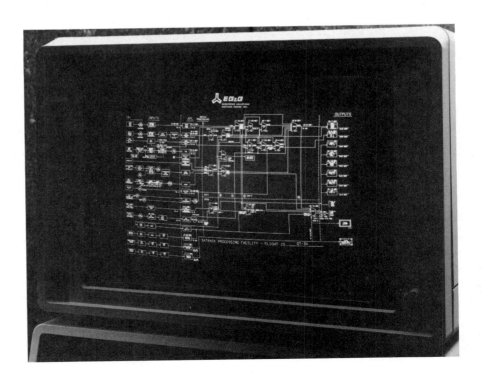

Base Text — This is a general note which becomes part of a symbol base. The text remains the same for all instances of the symbol and cannot be changed unless the symbol base is redefined.

Instance Text — This is a general note which is related to a particular symbol instance. Instance text can be moved or edited as any general note, but it cannot be deleted unless the instance is deleted. When moved, it moves independent of the symbol instance.

Connect Node — This is a defined location on a symbol instance at which an interconnect can be attached. The connect nodes are established at the time the symbol base is created.

Symbol Library — The collection of stored symbols is called the **symbol library** (Figure 8–2). Combinations of symbols nested together can be used to create new symbols. However, when a symbol is incorporated into another symbol, it loses its identity or link to its symbol base.

There should be two types of symbol libraries — a *system library* and a *user library*. The system library should be created for multiple use and should be protected from unauthorized change. The user library is created by each individual designer for his or her own use or for use by a small group. The user library is local only.

Creating and Defining Symbols — Forming a symbol base involves creating the geometry of the symbol, defining its base and instance text, and storing the symbol for future use.

Symbol Graphics — Symbols are created using all of the available construction instructions. The connect nodes of a symbol must be created along with the other geometry. The nodes are created as permanent points.

Base and Instance Text — Base and instance text are added to the symbol in the same manner as a general note.

Storing the Symbol — After the symbol geometry has been constructed and text properly assigned, the symbol can be stored as a symbol base. The symbol origin must be specified when the symbol is stored. The symbol origin is used as the reference point for future placement of the symbol.

Modifying Symbols — A symbol can be altered by recalling the symbol geometry library, making the desired changes, and restoring the symbol. A modified symbol can be stored with its old name, thereby replacing the old symbol base, or stored under a new symbol name, creating a new symbol. The latter method is an easy way of forming a new symbol similar to an existing one.

Updating Symbols — A new version of a symbol can be used to replace its old version on any drawing on which it appears by executing an "update symbol" instruction. The old symbol is automatically updated to its new version at every location at which it appears on the selected drawing. All other drawings on which the old version appears are left unaltered.

Placing and Annotating Symbols — Each placement or instance of the symbol is oriented and placed according to the selected parameter — origin, rotation angle, scale, and mirror.

Figure 8–2
Electrical symbol library.
(Courtesy Interactive
Computer Systems)

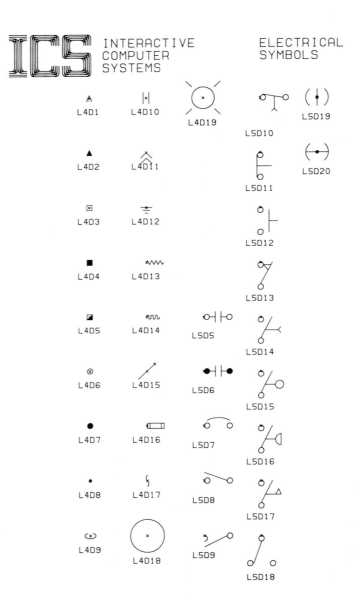

Interconnecting Symbols — Interconnect is used to connect symbol instances. The connect nodes are the points of connection for symbols. When interconnects cross each other, the system should automatically break one of the interconnects at the intersection. When a symbol is placed on an existing interconnect, the interconnect should be automatically broken around the symbol. Conversely, if a symbol is removed, the system will automatically reconnect the interconnect.

Libraries are easy to make and are a great aid to productivity. Symbols are the CADD designer's equivalent of a manual drafter's template.

Creating a Symbol Library

The following is an example of how to create a symbol library using VersaCAD:

Step 1: Create symbols one at a time and save each as a separate two-dimensional drawing. (Remember, a symbol is nothing more than a drawing placed in a symbol library.) Give the drawings any name such as A1 or A2 to help keep them organized (Figure 8–2).

It is recommended that the library is built on a formatted blank floppy diskette to provide a permanent "original" that can be stored as a backup and to ensure enough room for the library.

Step 2: Select the Make option from the LIBRARY menu, and when the program asks, give the library a name (such as LIB1 or ELEC). VersaCAD ADVANCED then builds the library framework on the disk (although this library grid is still empty).

Step 3: Select the Action option from the LIBRARY menu, and when the program asks, type in the name just assigned the new library. This makes the new library into the current library.

Step 4: Select the Symbol option from the LIBRARY menu and then the Add sub-option. For each drawing that will be made into a symbol, type in the drawing name and then the "cell" or square number it will occupy in the 10 × 10 library grid. As symbols are added, periodically use the List sub-option under Symbol to see which drawings have been put into which cells. When all of the symbols are added (all the cells do not need to be filled), Quit back to the LIBRARY menu.

Step 5: Select the Overlay option from the LIBRARY menu. The program will draw a 10 × 10 grid on the display screen and place the symbols created in Step 4. When the overlay drawing is complete, Quit from the LIBRARY menu and select Plotter from the OUTPUT menu. The plot spec called OVERLAY has already been created for the designer; use it to plot the 10 × 10 grid on paper (Figure 8–3) to be placed on the digitizer tablet. The library is now completed.

Step 6: To use the newly created symbols in a drawing, place the plotted overlay (Figures 8–4, 8–5, and 8–6) on the digitizer and select Boundary from the LIBRARY menu. The program will ask for the lower left and upper right corners of the overlay to be specified.

Step 7: Clear the overlay out of the workfile with FILER/New and the symbols are ready to be placed in a drawing. Select the Symbol option from the ADD menu and pick the symbol from the digitized overlay. It will appear on the screen, ready to be placed wherever desired. Figures 8–7 and 8–8 show examples of the use of symbols.

Figure 8–3
10 × 10 grid for symbol library. (Courtesy T&W System, Inc.)

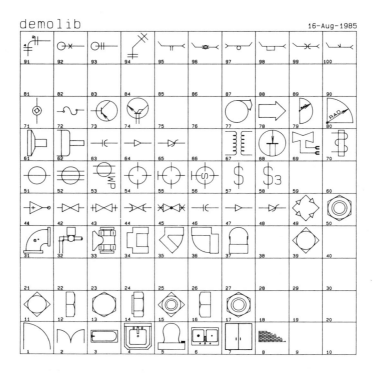

Select the Active Library (VersaCAD)

The Active option is selected from the LIBRARY menu by pressing [A] or placing the cursor over [Active] and pressing the stylus. It allows changes to the library from which symbols are currently being retrieved (with ADD/Symbol).

While creating a drawing, symbols can only be taken from one library at a time. This is known as the "active" library. When this option is selected, the program will remind the designer of the name of the currently active library and ask for the name of the new library (up to 8 characters). Type in the name and press [Enter].

Symbol Operations (VersaCAD)

The Symbol option is selected from the LIBRARY menu by pressing [S] or placing the cursor over [Symbol] and pressing the stylus. It allows the manipulation of the individual symbols stored in a library. When this option is selected, a complete list of manipulations which can be made to symbols in a library is shown.

Add a Symbol to the Library (VersaCAD)

The ADD option allows a symbol to be added to the current symbol library. For two-dimensional systems, each symbol that is added to the library is

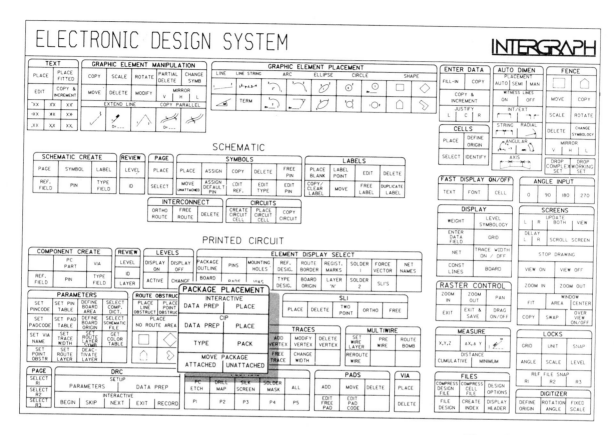

Figure 8–4
Symbol library overlay.
(Courtesy Intergraph)

nothing more than a two-dimensional drawing previously created and saved to disk in the normal manner. It may be as simple or complicated as needed. Adding a symbol to a library basically amounts to copying the symbol from the two-dimensional drawing file into the library (Figure 8–9). Once added to the library, the original file containing the symbol may be deleted without affecting the copy in the symbol library.

Diagrams

Diagrams include such things as electronic circuit schematics (Figures 8–10 and 8–11), piping and instrumentation diagrams, and specialized diagrams such as welding symbols.

In general, the creation of a diagram on a CADD system is not much different from preparing the diagram manually on a drafting board. The big

Figure 8–5
Symbol library overlay.
(Courtesy Bausch &
Lomb)

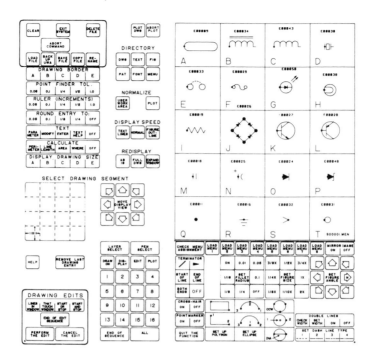

difference, if using a CADD system, is the capability to instantly recall all the needed schematic symbols and place them wherever desired.

A typical example of the use of diagrams is in electronic circuit design (Figure 8–8). A schematic diagram provides a means of capturing, concisely and accurately, all the data required to describe a particular circuit. As such, it forms an essential basis for any electronic design project and is used throughout the design process from development, through printed circuit board layout, to inclusion in service handbooks.

Diagram symbols and interconnects can be edited by using the standard editing capabilities of the CADD system. Symbols can be moved or reoriented if necessary. Symbol instance text can also be added, deleted, or modified. In addition, basic symbols themselves can be modified and redefined directly if desired. Interconnects can be added, rerouted, or deleted as required. If two interconnects cross but are not intended to be electrically connected, a semicircular bridge can be added to one of the crossing interconnects. An interconnect may also be broken, if desired, without affecting its electrical continuity.

Data Retrieval

Most of the CADD systems available provide the capability to extract the data from the drawing to automatically generate a **bill of materials** (Figure

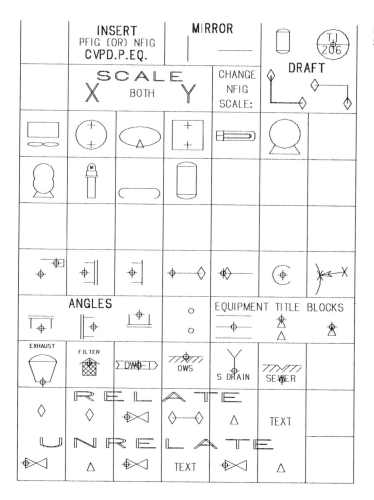

Figure 8–6
Symbol library overlay.

8–12) or other associated reports (Figure 8–13). Information such as part number, material, vendor, and cost are entered into the system when the part is placed on a drawing. The information can then be tallied and a report generated by the system.

Some CADD systems provide programs to make use of this nongraphic data to perform design functions — electronic circuit board design programs are a good example. Though many of these programs are dedicated to a particular design function, many systems have a general capability that can be adapted to a variety of design tasks, including numerical control part programming, interior design, landscape design, and others.

Figure 8–7
Example of symbol
usage. (courtesy Calma
Company, a wholly-
owned subsidiary of
General Electric Com-
pany, U.S.A.)

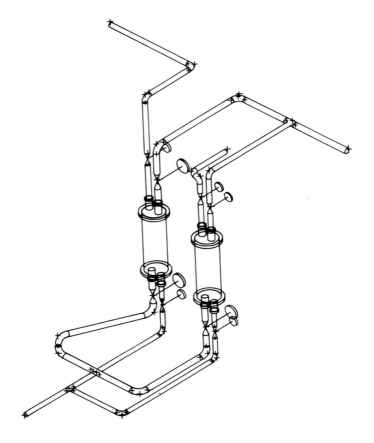

Figure 8–8
Example of symbol
usage.

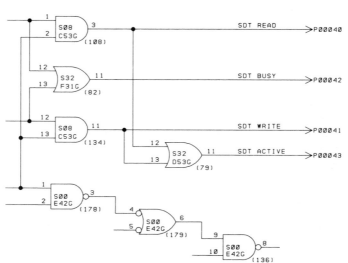

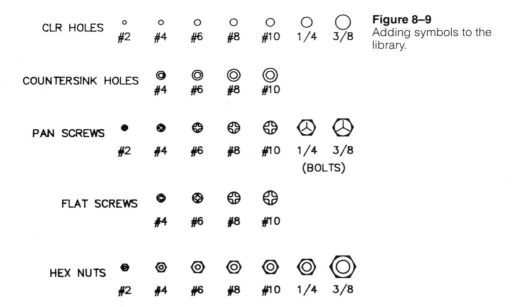

CLR HOLES   #2   #4   #6   #8   #10   1/4   3/8

COUNTERSINK HOLES   #4   #6   #8   #10

PAN SCREWS   #2   #4   #6   #8   #10   1/4   3/8 (BOLTS)

FLAT SCREWS   #4   #6   #8   #10

HEX NUTS   #2   #4   #6   #8   #10   1/4   3/8

Figure 8–9
Adding symbols to the library.

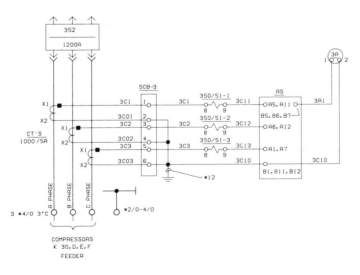

Figure 8–10
Electronic circuit schematic.

Figure 8–11
Electronic circuit
schematic.

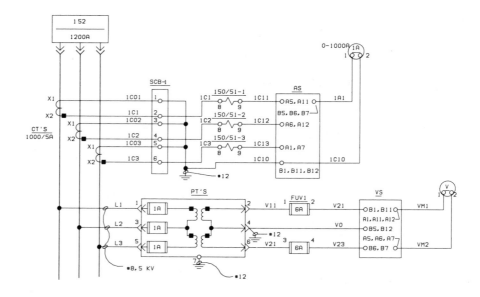

Attributes

Some programs, such as AutoCAD, use attributes. **Attributes** are special drawing entities that contain text. The designer can later collect them into a disk file for processing by an application such as a bill of materials program.

Attributes can also be invisible. An invisible Attribute is not displayed or plotted (Figure 8–14); however, information about it is stored in the drawing file and can be used for processing.

Here is a simple example of Attribute usage. Suppose an office manager or a facility planner wants to place several desks in an office drawing. Each desk is assigned to an individual employee, and the employee's name needs to be drawn inside or adjacent to his or her desk. Also, when the drawing is

Figure 8–12
Bill of Materials.
(Courtesy Calma
Company, a wholly-
owned subsidiary of
General Electric Com-
pany, U.S.A.)

```
PRELIMINARY BOM REPORT  ---  6-12-81,  9:32:32  --- PAGE #1
DRAWING:

LINE                    COMP    QTY    STOCK#
CW-27-24"-A6A           CRED     1     CREDWEAA010-3024
CW-27-24"-A6A           ELR9     4     ELR9WEAA010-24
CW-27-24"-A6A           ELR9           ELR9WEAA010-24
CW-27-24"-A6A           ELR9           ELR9WEAA010-24
CW-27-24"-A6A           ELR9           ELR9WEAA010-30
CW-27-24"-A6A           GATV     1     GATVRFAD150-24
CW-27-24"-A6A           RTEE     1     RTEEWEAA010-3018
CW-27-24"-A6A           STEE     1     STEEWEAA010-24
CW-27-24"-A6A           WNFF     2     WNFFPAABO10-24
CW-27-24"-A6A           WNFF           WNFFPAABO10-24
CW-28-18"-A6A           ELR9     1     ELR9WEAA010-18
```

Figure 8–13
From-to report. (Courtesy
Calma Company, a
wholly-owned subsidiary
of General Electric
Company, U.S.A.)

```
LINE                            FROM                         TO                      PIPE
CW-26-24"-A6A                   A12                          B10                     33'-4"
- - - - - - - - - - - - - - - - - - - - - - - - - - - - - - - - - - - - - - - - - - - - - - - - - - - - - - - - -
     SPEC                       COMP                         STK#
     24"-A6A                     PIPE: 7'-0"
     24"-A6A                     ELR9                                                 ELR9WEAA010-24
     24"-A6A                     WNFF                                                 WNFFPAAB010-24
     24"-A6A                     GASKET                                               GASKFFAG150-24
     24"-A6A                     GATV                                                 GATVRFAD150-24
     24"-A6A                     GASKET                                               GASKFFAG150-24
     24"-A6A                     WNFF                                                 WNFFPAAB010-24
     24"-A6A                     PIPE: 8'-6"
     24"-A6A                     STEE                         STEEWEAA010-24
     24"-A6A                     ELR9                         ELR9WEAA010-24
     24"-A6A                     PIPE: 2'-0"
     24"-A6A                     ELR9                                                 ELR9WEAA010-24
     24"-A6A                     CRED                                                 CREDWEAA010-3024
     30"-A6A                     RTEE                                                 RTEEWEAA010-3018
     30"-A6A                     PIPE: 12'-7"
     30"-A6A                     ELR9                         ELR9WEAA010-30
     30"-A6A                     PIPE: 3'-3"


LINE                            FROM                         TO                      PIPE
CW-27-24"-A6A                   CW-26-24"-A6A                D05                     13'-8  3/16"
- - - - - - - - - - - - - - - - - - - - - - - - - - - - - - - - - - - - - - - - - - - - - - - - - - - - - - - - -
     SPEC                       COMP                         STK#
     24"-A6A                     PIPE: 13'-8  3/16"


LINE                            FROM                         TO                      PIPE
CW-28-18"-A6A                   CW-26-24"-A6A                C07                     17'-0  1/2"
- - - - - - - - - - - - - - - - - - - - - - - - - - - - - - - - - - - - - - - - - - - - - - - - - - - - - - - - -
     SPEC                       COMP                         STK#
     18"-A6A                     PIPE: 6'-1  1/2"
     18"-A6A                     ELR9                         ELR9WEAA010-18
     18"-A6A                     PIPE: 10'-11"
```

complete, a list of all the desks in the office, showing their locations and occupants, should be made. To accomplish this, first draw one desk. Then use
ATTDEF to create an Attribute Definition with a tag of "EMPLOYEE" and
prompt of "Employee name." If some of the desks in the office are currently
unassigned, provide a default value of "CLERK" for this Attribute. When
ATTDEF is complete, the word "EMPLOYEE" is drawn at the position and
size specified inside or adjacent to the desk drawing.

Next, use BLOCK to create a Block called DESK, selecting both the desk
drawing and the Attribute Definition by means of a window. Both are deleted
from the drawings as the Block is defined. Later, when the Block named
DESK is inserted, AutoCAD prompts for an insertion point, X- and Y-scale
factors, and a rotation angle. Then it displays:

Enter Attribute values

followed by the prompt:

Employee name <CLERK>:

Figure 8–14
Nongraphical attributes.
(Courtesy Calma
company, a wholly-owned
subsidiary of General
Electric Company, U.S.A.)

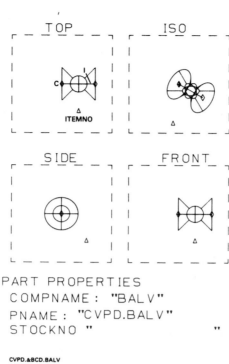

BALL VALVE

PART PROPERTIES
COMPNAME: "BALV"
PNAME: "CVPD.BALV"
STOCKNO "   "

CVPD.&BCD.BALV
5-2-81 19:43:12

1I*
2ISHAPE = CYL,L = T1,D1 = T2
3ISHAPE = CONE,D1 = T3,D2 = 0,L = .5*T4-T1
4I*
5ISHAPE = CONE,D1 = 0,D2 = T3,L = .5*T4-T1
6ISHAPE = CYL,L = T1,D1 = T2
7I*
8ICLEARANCE
9ISHAPE = CYL,DI = T2,L = T4

Suppose the response is to enter RETURN to accept the value. Then AutoCAD draws a copy of the desk, and in the place where the word "EMPLOYEE" appeared when the Attribute was defined, "CLERK" is drawn. If Jim Smith's desk should be drawn, insert the DESK Block again, but this time enter "Jim Smith" in response to the "Employee name" prompt.

Later ATTEXT (ATTribute EXTract) can be invoked to create a file whose entries contain Block names, X/Y coordinates, and Attribute values, as shown below:

DESK	110.0	250.0	CLERK
DESK	150.0	300.0	Jim Smith

ATTEXT allows the inclusion of other information as well, such as the scale and rotation of the Block; it also allows a different format for the file to be specified.

Expanding on the previous example, suppose additional information associated with each desk is wanted. The employee's department and telephone extension could be easily added by means of Attribute Definitions similar to that for the employee's name. For facility planning and cost estimation, the color, manufacturer, model number, and price of each desk need to be known. Attributes could be defined to hold these pieces of information as well. Make some of them invisible. Now, every time a DESK is inserted, AutoCAD prompts for all these Attributes and draws the visible ones.

The drawing could now be used to produce extract files for various purposes. For office management, extract the locations, occupants, departments, and telephone extensions of all the desks, as in:

DESK	150.0	300.0	Jane Doe	Accounting	402
DESK	200.0	320.0	Jim Smith	Sales	511
DESK	220.0	320.0	Carol White	Sales	512

For facility planning, extract a different set of Attributes (such as location, color, manufacturer, model number, and price) from the same drawing, as in:

DESK	150.0	300.0	walnut	Acme Mfg.	14–1550W	179.9
DESK	200.0	320.0	walnut	Acme Mfg.	14–1550W	179.95
DESK	220.0	320.0	beige	Acme Mfg.	14–1550B	159.95

Summary

The real power of the CADD system becomes apparent when designers have accumulated a library of standard symbols. Third-party software vendors offer many such packages, but designers may create their own libraries. As the symbol library grows, the drawing process becomes more efficient; standard symbols can be inserted rather than drawn from scratch.

A good example of this process is in electrical design where elementary diagrams are initially prepared in order to design the electrical circuit. All electrical circuits are intended to operate in a specific way. To build these electrical circuits, it is to the designer's advantage to develop their concepts by recording them as simply as possibly. This makes design and understanding as easy and uncomplicated as it can be. The diagrams are used to relate understanding of system operations, to develop wiring data, and to make a reference for circuit operation. Such diagrams are often invaluable for troubleshooting because they are much less complicated than the complete wiring diagrams.

Graphic symbols are used on elementary diagrams as a short-hand method of showing the devices and other elements of the circuit. If attributes are attached to the standard symbols, data can be extracted to link a wide range of NC/CNC equipment, including drilling machines, board profilers, automatic component insertion machines, and automatic test equipment (ATE).

To complete the design cycle, the system can also provide design documentation with engineers' reports and full parts listings.

GLOSSARY

ATTRIBUTES A nongraphic characteristic of a part, component, or element; for example: length, diameter, name, volume, use, and creation data.

BILL OF MATERIALS (BOM) A listing of all the subassemblies, parts, materials, and quantities required to manufacture an assembly or to build a plant.

COMPONENT A subassembly or part that goes into higher-level assemblies.

CONNECT NODE An attachment point for lines, text, or symbols.

COPY To reproduce a design in a different location on the CRT or to duplicate a file and its contents.

DATABASE An organized collection of standard parts libraries, completed designs, documentation, and computer programs.

DATA TABLET A graphical input device consisting of a board area capable of monitoring the position of a pen shaped stylus.

DEFAULT The predetermined value of a parameter that is automatically supplied by the system whenever that value is not specified by the user.

DOCUMENTATION The general description, user's manual, and maintenance manual necessary to operate and maintain the system.

FIGURE A symbol or a part which may contain other figures, attributes, and associations.

FLOWCHART A graphical representation of the solution of a problem in which symbols are used to represent operations, data flow, and equipment.

INQUIRY A request for information from the computer.

LAYER A logical concept used to distinguish subdividual group(s) of data within a given drawing. It may be thought of as a series of transparencies overlayed in any order, yet having no depth.

LAYER DISCRIMINATION The selective assignment of colors to a layer or the highlighting of entities to distinguish data on different layers displayed on a CRT.

LIBRARY A collection of symbols, components, shapes, or parts stored in the CADD database as templates for future design work on the system.

OVERLAY To position one or more drawings on top of another and view them simultaneously on the CRT.

PROPERTIES Nongraphic items which may be associated. Properties in electrical design may include component name and identification, color, wire size, pin number, lug type, and signal values.

REPLICATE To generate an exact copy of a design on the CRT at any location or scale desired.

ROUTING Placing the interconnects between components on a printed circuit board or integrated circuit.

RUBBERBANDING A technique for displaying a straight line with one end fixed and the other end attached to the moveable cursor.

SCALE   To enlarge or shrink an image without changing its shape.

STYLUS   A hand-held object that provides coordinate input to the CRT.

SYMBOL   A set of primitive geometry items. Lines, points, arcs, circles, and text that are grouped together as a unit. Symbols may be combined or nested to form larger symbols or drawings.

TABLET   An input device that a designer can use to digitize coordinate data or enter instructions into a CADD system by means of a stylus or puck, also called a *digitizing pad*.

TEMPLATE   A commonly used component or part that serves as a design aid and can be subsequently traced instead of redrawn whenever needed. The CADD equivalent of a designer's template is a symbol in the symbol library.

QUIZ

True or False

1. Once stored in memory, symbols cannot be recalled.

2. The placement of a previously created symbol onto a drawing is called a symbol instance.

3. The collection of stored symbols is called the symbol base.

4. Interconnects are straight lines that connect the symbols on a diagram.

5. Some systems can automatically generate a bill of materials.

6. Attributes are special geometry items that contain text.

7. Once a symbol has been placed on a diagram it cannot be moved or reoriented.

8. A symbol is a graphical representation of standard parts.

Fill in the Blank

9. When _____ are created, _____ about the part can be included.

10. _____ may include other _____.

11. The placement of a previously created symbol onto a drawing is called a _____.

12. The symbol _____ must be specified when the symbol is _____.

13. _____ include such things as electronic circuit schematics.

14. Symbol _____ text can be added, deleted, or modified on a drawing.

15. An invisible attribute is not _____ or _____.

16. If attributes are attached to the standard symbols, _____ can be _____.

Answer the Following

17. Discuss the difference between symbol base and symbol instance.

18. What is a connect mode and how is it used?

19. Explain how a symbol library is created.

20. Explain how a symbol library can increase efficiency in the drawing task.

21. Discuss how diagram symbols with interconnects can be edited.

22. Explain how attributes are used to create a list of desks in an office.

23. Discuss why diagrams are used in electrical design.

24. Discuss some of the uses for a capability to retrieve attributes.

Problems

25. Lay out the flowchart shown in the sketch for the DATA ANALYZER (Figure 8–15).

26. Create a symbol library and draw the schematic diagram for the VOLT-AGE REGULATOR (Figure 8–16).

27. Use the symbol library created in Problem 26 and add any needed symbols to draw the schematic diagram of the SAMPLE AND HOLD AMPLIFIER (Figure 8–17).

28. Create a symbol library and draw the piping spool shown in Figure 8–18.

29. Use the symbol library created in Problem 28 and add any needed symbols to draw the piping spool shown in Figure 8–19.

30. Create a symbol library and draw the piping diagram shown in Figure 8–20.

31. Use the symbol library created in Problem 30 and add any needed symbols to draw the piping diagram shown in Figure 8–21. Use the sizes of the valves as attributes and create a list showing the total quantity of each size of valve.

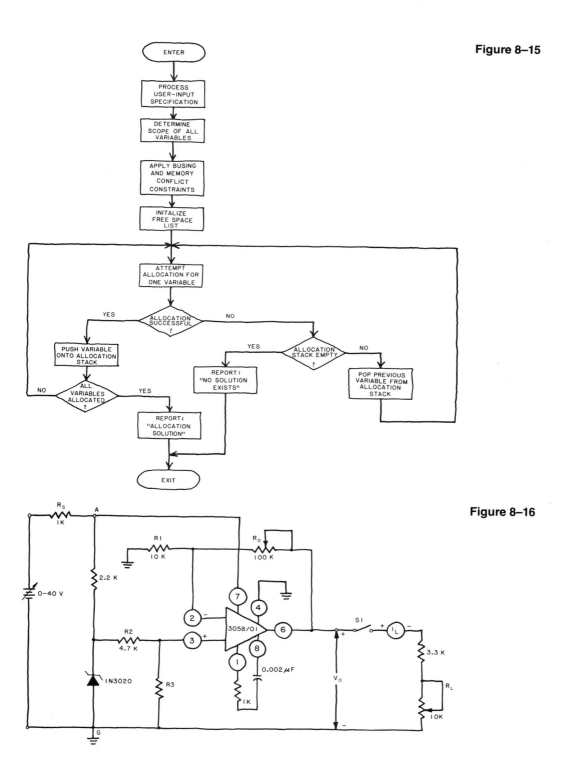

Figure 8–15

Figure 8–16

Figure 8–17

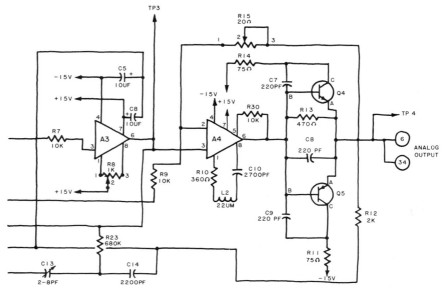

Figure 8–18

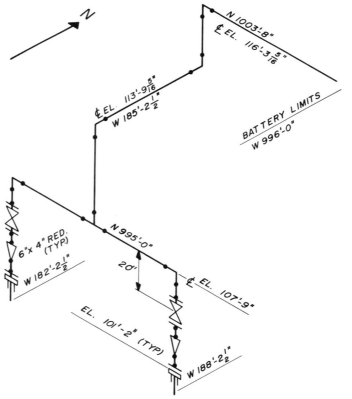

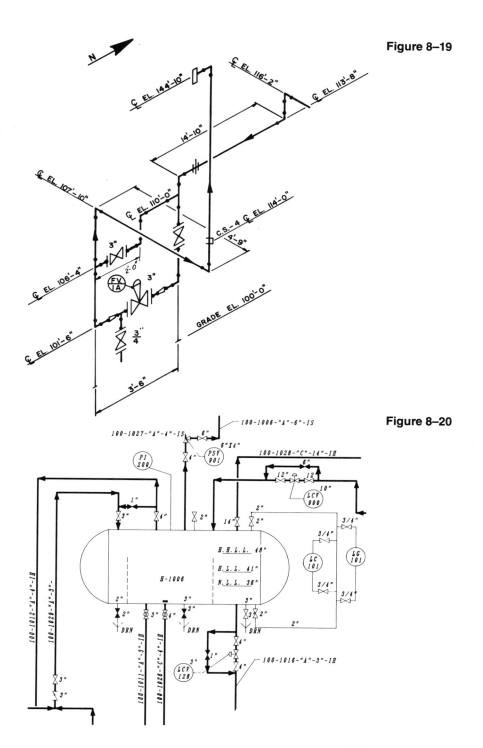

Figure 8–19

Figure 8–20

Figure 8–21

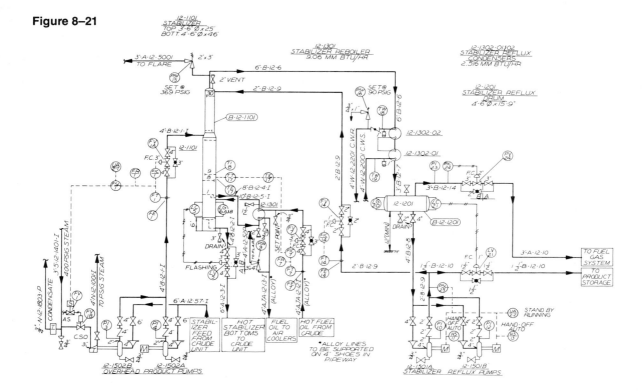

Chapter

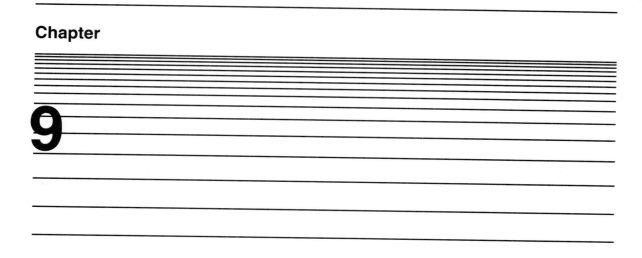

9

·Modeling

Objectives

Upon completion of this chapter the reader will be able to:

- List the three major types of CADD modeling.

- Provide examples of three-dimensional modeling applications in electronics; mechanical, architectural, and piping design; and mapping.

- Discuss the differences and uses of wireframe, surface, and solid models.

- Describe the use of simulation software for NC programming and robotics.

- Explain the function and activities of the model and draw mode.

- Define the term *view* as it relates to the model and the drawing.

- Describe construction planes and how they aid the designer in creating a three-dimensional part.

- Give an overview of a typical finite element modeling package, including modeling and analysis.

Introduction

Design/Drafting

There are two distinct tasks that require a CADD system: *design* and *drafting*. Design is the process by which an object is conceptualized and then represented pictorially. Drafting is the process of representing the geometry for an object in two dimensions in accordance with standard procedures. This two-dimensional representation is done on paper in manual drafting and on the display device in CADD.

The designer can use a two-dimensional system to do design work by creating a part in orthographic projections or by using the system as a copying device to reproduce an existing drawing. The three-dimensional system can be used for design or drafting, but the drafting capability only exists as an add-on feature. Thus, it is correct to say that drafting is always two-dimensional even if the pictorial representation is isometric.

Model

The graphic representation of the object in a CADD system is called the **model**. This model is mathematically defined and stored in the computer's memory (Figure 9–1). There are various mathematical methods that are used to define this model. The three basic methods are wireframe, surfaces, and solids.

In addition to the geometric model, the design also includes other attributes such as material, weight, volume, function, and color. The model of the mechanical assembly shown in Plate 1 gives an example of a three-dimensional solid model in color. The model can also be used to functionally "test" the design before it is built. An example of this type of test is a kinematic study of linking mechanisms.

Two-Dimensional/Three-Dimensional

Designers and engineers think in three dimensions and then they try to show the concept in two-dimensional views. So designing with a three-dimensional system is a much more natural way to conceptualize the creation of the model of an object. The three-dimensional model is the starting point for engineering analysis, drafting, and manufacturing (Figure 9–2).

A three-dimensional system makes it easier to check the spatial relationship between parts in an assembly (Figure 9–3). The assembly can be rotated to view it from any angle to easily examine the spatial relationship. With a two-dimensional system, complex projections are required to achieve the same results. Since the three-dimensional system can view an object from any angle, isometric and perspective views can be created with little extra effort. The vise shown in Figures 9–3 and 9–4, and in Plates 2 and 3, was designed on a three-dimensional CADD system. Figure D shows the wireframe model of the vise assembly. Three-dimensional systems with surface or solid modeling capabilities allow realistic rendering of objects by a shading process (see Plate 4). Since the model in the three-dimensional sys-

Figure 9–1
Designer is using a light
pen to design in three
dimensions on the CRT.
(Courtesy Lockheed-
California Co.)

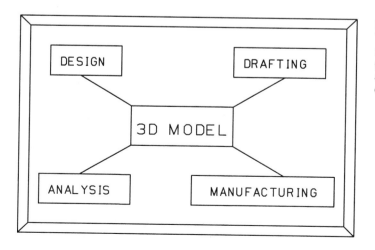

Figure 9–2
The three-dimensional
model supports all
groups involved in the
activities that create and
develop products.

Figure 9–3
Three-dimensional design of a vise showing the assembly with hidden lines removed and the menu on the CRT along the right side and the top. (Courtesy Evans and Sutherland)

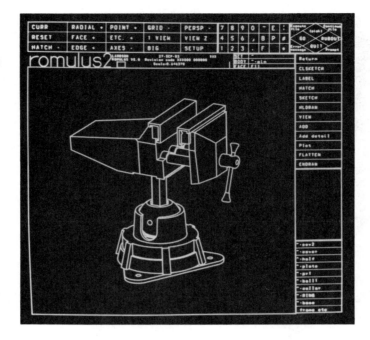

tem has an interior as well as an exterior, volumes and mass properties of objects can be easily calculated. Hidden lines are removed automatically (as in the mechanical design shown in Figure 9–5) and blending contours between intersecting surfaces are easily created. Three-dimensional models can produce output for multi-axis numerical control machines and, thus, diminish the need for dimensioned drawings for manufacturing. NC tool paths can be simulated on the part model before the piece even gets to the machine shop (Figure 9–6).

Model Types

Wireframe Models

As the name signifies, a **wireframe** model is one in which the objects are represented by interconnected edges only, as in Plate 5, which shows a wireframe model of an automobile. These edges may be lines, arcs, or **splines**. Most CADD systems with two-dimensional drafting capabilities may be used to create two-dimensional wireframe models which can be used for numerical control or drawings. Three-dimensional models, however, provide better modeling capability than the two-dimensional systems. Three-dimensional modeling capabilities are grouped into three basic categories: *three-dimensional wireframe models*, an extension of two-dimensional wireframe; *three-dimensional surface models*; and *solid models*.

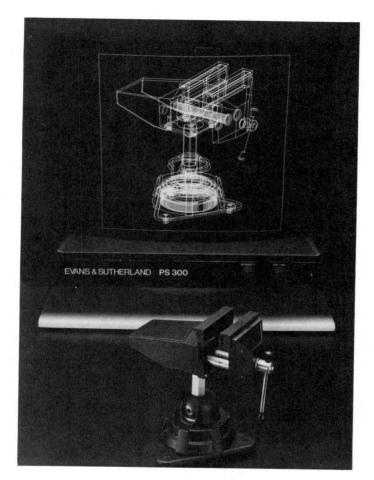

Figure 9–4
Wireframe model shown
on the CRT with the
actual product in front of
the station. (Courtesy
Evans and Sutherland)

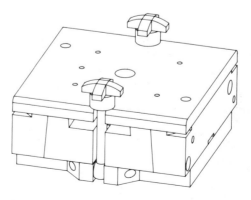

Figure 9–5
A three-dimensional
mechanical design with
hidden lines removed.
(Reprinted with permis-
sion from Computervision
Corporation, Bedford,
Massachusetts)

Figure 9–6
A variety of NC tool paths can be created using three-dimensional NC programming software packages. The illustration above shows pocketing and profiling tool paths. (Reprinted wiht permission from Computervision Corporation, Bedford, Massachusetts)

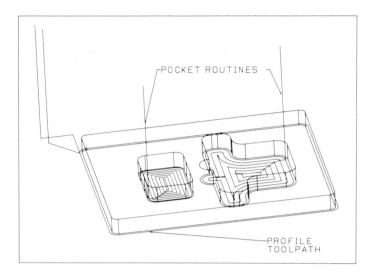

Three-dimensional wireframe models use the same basic elements as the two-dimensional model but with extension to add the Z-coordinates: three-dimensional points (X, Y, Z); straight lines between points; circular arcs on a plane; and splines fitted to a series of points. The visualization and ease of use is much better for the three-dimensional wireframe model than the two-dimensional wireframe model.

A wireframe model (Figure 9–7) uses a network of interconnected lines (or wires) to represent the edges of the physical objects being modeled. Wireframes are relatively simple to create and provide a convenient geometric definition for many engineering applications. Since wireframe modeling closely emulates the process of making drawings, it supports a large class of two-dimensional design tasks that lend themselves to being solved on a flat sheet of paper.

Figure 9–7
Finite element model of a bottle. (Courtesy Megatek Corp.)

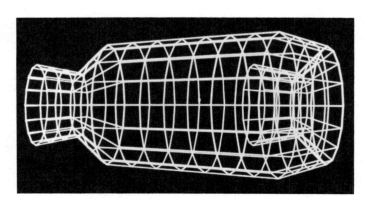

These applications include engineering drafting, 2 and 2 $\frac{1}{2}$-axis NC programming, and area-property computation. But wireframe modeling has some severe limitations. Blended, curved, or nonplanar surfaces are not readily represented. Furthermore, overlapping lines can make complex three-dimensional objects appear confusing and often ambiguous to the eye.

Surface Models

Three-dimensional surface models are constructed by stretching a transparent membrane over the wireframe model. These membranes then become the faces to the model. These faces may be simple surfaces such as planes, cylinders, and spheres, or they may be more complex such as ruled surfaces, extrusions, and rotations of spline curves and sculpted surfaces.

Three-dimensional surface models can be used to represent shapes that are difficult to construct with wireframes. Examples of these shapes are: styled surfaces, such as the outer skins of automobiles and airplanes; and function surfaces, such as turbine blades and gears.

With surface models, the boundary faces of an object are represented within the computer by various surface types. The model is easily edited by stretching, scaling, repositioning, or erasing portions of the surface. Plate 6 shows a surface model with shading.

Hybrid Models

Most of the three-dimensional modeling systems on the market are a combination of wireframe and surface modeling. The addition of the surfaces eliminates some of the deficiencies of the wireframe model, namely, the model can be unambiguous and complete. Although the surface modeler provides many of the capabilities lacking in wireframe modelers, surface modelers are more expensive and more difficult to use than wireframe modelers.

Solid Models

The major requirement of a solid modeler is to be able to construct an unambiguous representation of parts or assemblies (see Plate 7). Constructive solid geometry (CSG) and boundary representation (b-rep) are the two popular methods used to create a solid model. With CSG, an object is represented by a treelike data structure that describes how the object is built up from simpler objects. Boolean operators (union, difference, and intersection) are used to combine the simpler objects. At the base of the tree are primitives such as cubes, spheres, and cones which make up the foundation of this building process. Boundary representation is a list of the surfaces, or boundaries of an object. For a cube, a b-rep is a list of the six square faces.

Very few of the current solid modeling systems rely exclusively on CSG because of the amount of time required to generate the display of the object.

With b-rep, the edges of the object are drawn, and a solid image can be displayed in a short time. The biggest advantage of systems containing both CSG and b-rep is that if representation is CSG, a b-rep can be developed from it, whereas the reverse is not true. It is also fairly easy to convert the CSG information into other types of representations to generate finite element meshes and several other applications.

The CSG representation is easier to use and allows faster construction of relatively simple objects with the primitive solids. However, the b-rep allows the use of existing wireframe and surface models to create the solid model. This is an advantage especially if the solid modeler is used with an existing CADD system. In a few years, the type of representation used will become less important.

In the near future, a solid model will form the master representation of a part in contrast to the current practice of using the engineering drawing as the master representation. The main output of a design/drafting office will be a solid model of the part together with all the associated information that is contained on the engineering drawing and the provision engineering drawings will be a secondary function. In particular, the drawings, if required, will be generated from the model. The combination of a solid model and the necessary tolerance and associated technical data will be called the **product model**. Functions downstream of the design office will take the product model as their primary input. They will extract data from the model using query functions and may also produce secondary models for their own purposes.

Solid models represent the mass and surface boundary of the object in a complete, unambiguous form. The model database contains enough information to define whether a point is inside. This is a typical "solids test" to determine whether or not a computer representation of an object is a solid model.

The interference of various parts of an assembly can be readily checked. NC cutting operations and tool paths are more easily verified. Color-shaded images may be produced as well as line drawings with hidden lines removed.

Applications

The three-dimensional part model supports all engineering design and manufacturing groups associated with the **design-through-manufacturing cycle** (Figure 9–8).

Manufacturing Simulation

The stock material, machine workplace, tools, and fixtures are all modeled with solids; the numerical control program is then fed to a simulated machining process (Figure 9–6). The program will then check that the part was cut

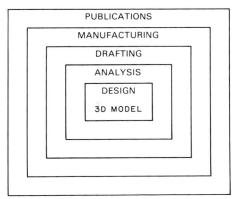

Figure 9–8
One common database supports all groups associated with the design-through-manufacturing cycle. (Reprinted with permission from Computervision Corporation, Bedford, Massachusetts)

properly and also check tool conditions. In an enhanced version of this program, the numerical control program is automatically generated from the geometric description of the part that is included in the solid model.

Assembly Analysis

The entire assembly is checked for interference between the various parts. The analysis considers not only nominal geometry but also is able to model the tolerances to see if the assembly will always fit together within the specified clearances.

Mechanism Analysis

The analysis uses the volumetric relationship of the parts to do kinematic analysis. The analysis not only considers static loads but will also use dynamic loading conditions. Plate 8 shows analysis of a mold design and maximum pressure limitations.

Mesh Generation

Finite element analysis of solid models is much easier due to the automatic generation of the mesh used for the analysis. The generator will create a mesh of solid elements that can be interactively adjusted by the designer after it has been generated. Plate 9 shows three views of a flywheel model with a mesh generated for analysis.

Automatic Drawings

Fully dimensioned drawings are automatically created from the solid model rather than creating a special two-dimensional picture. The dimension and tolerance information is carried with the model.

Illustrations

Illustrations include line drawings, shaded images, and color renditions of parts and assemblies. Solid modeling systems are an excellent way to produce low-cost, accurate, good-looking illustrations. The model of the wine glass shown in Plate 10 is an excellent example of modeling used for illustration. Consequently, illustrations will be used much more frequently for: visualization of parts for design reviews; pictorial instructions for assembly and processing; proposals and presentations for new products; and manuals for installation, maintenance, and operation.

Application Areas for Modeling

Three-dimensional modeling has a variety of uses in all major engineering fields, including mechanical design analysis and manufacturing.

Mapping

Civil engineering mapping and geological studies, Plate 11, also are available on CADD systems. These features include site selection, site preparation, digital terrain modeling, and earthwork calculations.

Piping and Plant Design

Designs for process and power plant construction can be created as a true three-dimensional model on the system (see Plate 12). The three-dimensional modeling allows for revisions, graphics manipulations, and analyses such as piping interference checks to pinpoint interferences between plant components early in the design cycle, hidden line removal to enhance the visual representation of the model, and pipeline from-to reports. These capabilities allow the designer to recognize and rectify potential plant problems early in the design phase, eliminating costly and time-consuming construction delays.

Plant design CADD programs permit the extraction of a wide range of drawings and reports directly from the database, including flow diagrams, isometrics, spools, pipe fabrication, pipe supports, plan, elevation, and section drawings, solid views, from-to lists, bills-of-material, and formatted lists.

Robotics

A CADD robotics package is a computer-aided design and manufacturing (CAD/CAM) tool for robotic simulation and robot work cell design (see Plates 13 and 14). Robot simulators are three-dimensional models of robot workcells (Figure 9–9).

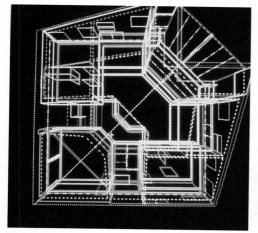

Plate 17

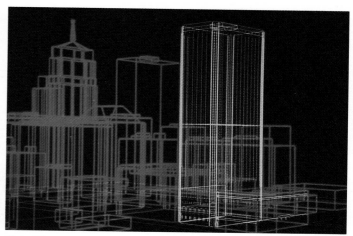

Plate 19

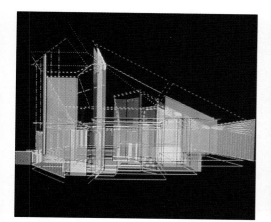

Plate 18

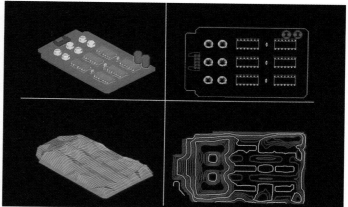

Plate 20

Plate 17
Plan view of an architectural model. (Courtesy McDonnell Douglas Information Systems Group.)

Plate 18
Three-dimensional wireframe of an architectural project. (Courtesy McDonnell Douglas Information Systems Group.)

Plate 19
Wireframe model of city with new architectural project highlighted. (Courtesy Evans & Sutherland)

Plate 20
Three-dimensional model of a printed circuit board undergoing heat analysis. (Courtesy Intergraph Corp.)

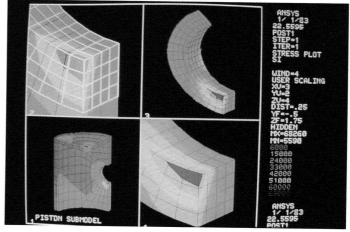

Plate 21
Stress analysis using a three-dimensional modeler. (Courtesy Megatek Corp.)

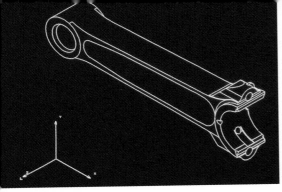

Plate 22
ICEM Solid Modeler automatically creates wireframe model from the solid geometry of connecting rod. Hidden line removal is also automatic, and resultant drawing can be used in drafting application without reformatting data. (Courtesy Control Data Corp.)

Plate 23
ICEM Engineering Data Library provides the design engineer with comprehensive, automatic, and security controlled progression of product documentation. (Courtesy Control Data Corp.)

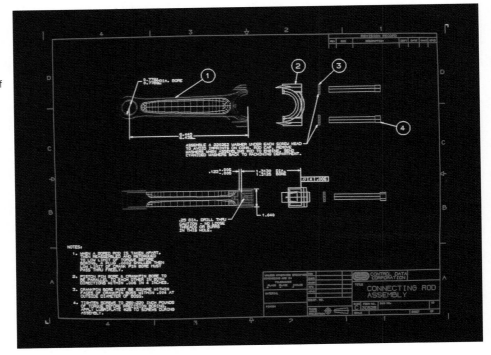

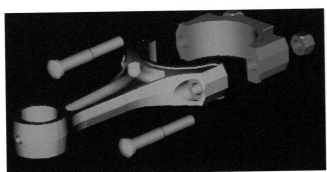

Plate 24
Once the geometric model is created, ICEM Solid Modeler can be used to explode the connecting rod into component parts, rotate it for viewing from different angles, create a cross section, and check for interference with related parts. (Courtesy of Control Data Corp.)

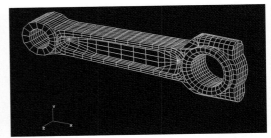

Plate 25
ICEM utilizes Control Data's UNISTRUC II system or Patran-O for automatic mesh generation of finite element models used for analysis. ICEM can build finite element models of up to 20,000 nodes or elements, with larger projects analyzed by segmenting model into blocks. Resultant model can be rotated, sectioned, or viewed from different angles. (Courtesy Control Data Corp.)

Plate 26

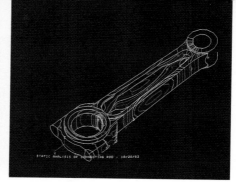

Plate 28

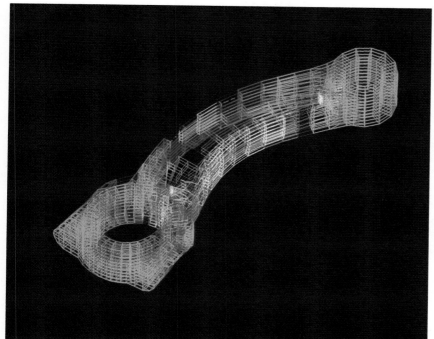

Plate 27

Plate 26
ICEM provides the design engineer with a variety of mesh patterns and color schemes to depict a particular analysis. Bricklike mesh of this connecting rod displays gradations of stress measured at the centroid of each element. (Courtesy Control Data Corp.)

Plate 27
Magnified deformation depicts same stress data for connecting rod in motion. (Courtesy Control Data Corp.)

Plate 28
Colored iso lines display uniform stress contours. (Courtesy Control Data Corp.)

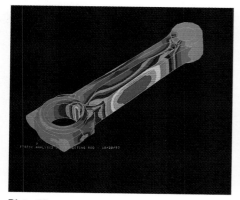

Plate 29
Color regions indicate ranges of stress displacements. (Courtesy Control Data Corp.)

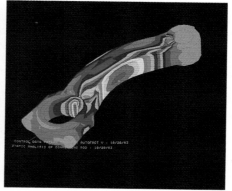

Plate 30
Color regions are contoured to accurately display stress of connection rod in motion. (Courtesy Control Data Corp.)

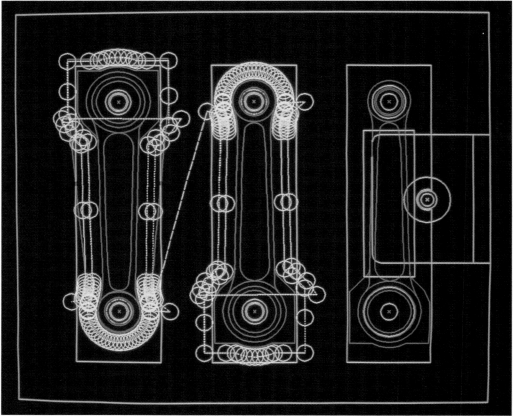

Plate 31
Design engineers can preview cutter paths with ICEM and automatically input needed changes to insure the most accurate and precise paths before machining the actual part. This shortens many time-consuming processes in manually readjusting cutter paths to obtain optimum cutter path design. (Courtesy Control Data Corp.)

Plate 32
ICEM numerical control capability allows generation of control tapes directly from design geometry. NC output is used for machining the actual part. (Courtesy Control Data Corp.)

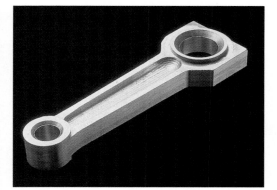

Plate 33
ICEM assists design engineers in creating numerical control machining for complex surfaces of dies, molds, and finished parts. ICEM NC features point-to-point construction, pocketing, profiling, 3-axis machining, 5-axis swarf cutting, dynamic tool path display, and lace and nonlace cutting. (Courtesy Control Data Corp.)

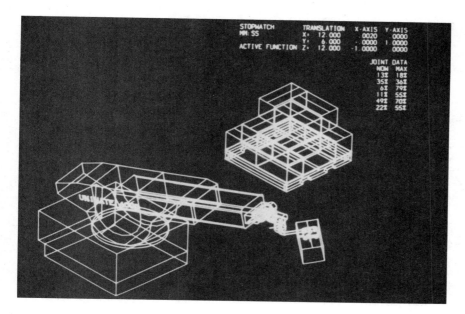

STOPWATCH   TRANSLATION   X-AXIS   Y-AXIS
MM: SS   X: 12.000   .0020   .0000
    Y: 6.000   .0000   1.0000
ACTIVE FUNCTION   Z: 12.000   -1.0000   .0000

JOINT DATA
NOW   MAX
13%   18%
35%   36%
6%   79%
11%   55%
49%   70%
22%   55%

Figure 9–9
CADD simulation of a
robot work cell. (Courtesy
Evans and Sutherland)

With a robot-simulator software capability, a designer on a CADD system can design a factory workcell, simulate a robot's movements and performance in the cell, and then modify both the robot's movements and the surrounding machinery for optimal efficiency. All of this can be accomplished without employing a single piece of robotic hardware. Plates 13 through 16 show robots programmed with a CADD system.

Robot workcells consist of the robot itself, robot end effectors, or hands, part orienters, the part being operated upon, fixtures, and the surrounding equipment with which the robot interacts. Using a robot-simulator package, automation engineers can consult libraries of robots and equipment to design a workcell and simulate actual robot motion within the cell (see Plate 16). From the simulation, an engineer can accurately determine the workcell cycle time and check for interferences in the motion of the robot with other workcell components.

Robots are widely used in the automotive, aerospace, and other manufacturing industries in the United States and overseas. According to industry estimates, 60 to 80 percent of the time required for total robot cell implementation is devoted to the design and layout of the workcell. By using a robot-simulator for the design and layout, designers can significantly reduce the time needed for workcell implementation.

Architectural/Structural

Three-dimensional modeling is also used in the construction industry to model architectural design (see Plates 17, 18, and 19).

Electronics

Printed circuit boards can also be modeled, analyzed, and tested as shown in Plate 20.

Two Operational Modes

CADD systems with three-dimensional capabilities have been designed so that the way the system is used is as natural as possible. This includes recognizing the different thought processes used and normally associated with design and drafting. Two operational modes normally exist: the *model mode* (for designing a part and generating NC data) and the *drawing mode*, for creating detail drawings of the part (Figure 9–10). Operations performed in the *model mode* create model descriptions and model geometry of the parts designed. The database that is created in this mode for a particular part model is distinct and separate from all other models.

The *drawing mode* is used to create drawing representations of the model by modifying or editing the model's geometry to change its visual appearance. The drawing mode uses the model's database solely for pictorial information representing the model's geometry but does not alter the model's database in any way. All models created in the model mode are usually "protected" from drawing mode activity.

The model mode is used to create a representation of a real-world three-dimensional object. When a designer is in the model mode, he or she is creating an actual three-dimensional layout of model geometry. A designer can also create two-dimensional representations of three-dimensional objects or just two-dimensional design geometry. When a detailer or drafter is in the drawing mode, he or she accesses the model database to create two-dimensional drawings using the model's database. Detail drawings with dimen-

Figure 9–10
The model and draw modes.

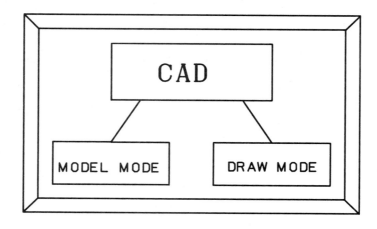

sions, text, and notes are created in the drawing mode. Drawing items can also be inserted in the drawing mode and are separate from model items. One way of seeing this concept more clearly is to imagine the model being created within a transparent three-dimensional box where the model's geometry physically exists in three-dimensional space. In contrast, a drawing created from the model in the drawing mode shows the model's projections on the sides of the box. Figure 9–11 illustrates these concepts and the difference between them.

When the drawing mode is used to edit the visual appearance of the model, the changes that are made are only pictorial. This is similar to air brushing a photograph. This is in contrast to the model mode where the changes are to the model and are reflected in all views. Changes in the drawing mode allow the detailer to manipulate the model for drafting purposes. For example, solid lines could be made into dashed lines to show that they are hidden or to indicate where a hole might be located. Lines can be temporarily erased for visual clarity or to prevent certain lines from being plotted (as hard copy) twice if they are normally seen one behind the other in a particular view. In this way the model's database retains its integrity while different views of the model are altered as needed for detailing purposes.

A large number of drawings can be created in the *drawing mode* and associated with a specific model (Figure 9–12). These drawings can be created at any size. It is important to realize that a drawing is a collection of views which depict the part. A view shows the part at a particular orientation (e.g., TOP, FRONT, RIGHT). Three-dimensional CADD provides the capability to define any number of views for a drawing. These views can be scaled at any display size. Additionally, a view will be defined by a border or frame whose size can also be defined by the operator.

The following example will illustrate this concept. An assembly is composed of three different parts. All three parts make up the model. Five drawings are created and associated to this model.

Model Mode Space   **Drawing Mode Space**

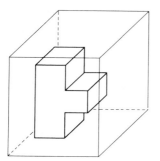
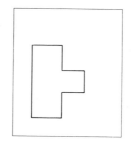

Figure 9–11
The model space is a real three-dimensional space, the drawing mode space is two-dimensional. (Reprinted with permission from Computervision Corporation, Bedford, Massachusetts)

Figure 9–12
Models and drawings—
the part contains a
three-dimensional model
and any number of
drawings associated with
it. Each drawing can
contain any number of
views with any scale
selected. (Reprinted with
permission from Com-
putervision Corporation,
Bedford, Massachusetts)

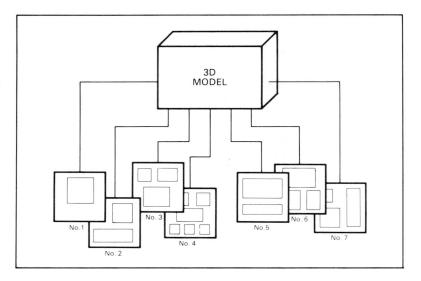

1. A design layout

2. A detail drawing for the first part

3. A detail drawing for the second part

4. A detail drawing for the third part

5. An assembly drawing

   Annotation can be added to the drawing to enhance its representation. Annotation includes dimensions, text, and graphic items. Drawing items— lines, points, arcs, circles—look the same as model items except that they are always associated with the drawing and never affect the model itself (and are never added to the model's database). The model's geometry is pictorially transferred to the drawing mode and the drafter can alter it, but only the appearance is altered. In addition, the transferred geometry can be manipulated in any number of ways. For example, it can be scaled larger or smaller in size, sectioned, manipulated into a particular view or set of views simultaneously. Geometry can be added (or deleted) for drawing purposes of presentation. The geometry of the model can be selectively hidden to represent normal viewing. Dimensional information, including notes and labels, can be added.

Model Space, Drawing Space, and Their Coordinate Systems

The model mode and the drafting mode have distinct spatial coordinate systems associated with them. Model space is the ***three-dimensional coordi-***

nate system in which model geometry is constructed. Model space is considered to be a real-world space existing in three directions or axes. Those axes are X (horizontal or left and right direction equating to width), Y (vertical or up and down direction equating to height) and Z (back and forth direction which moves in and out from the CRT equating to depth). The origin of all three axes is defined by the designer.

Drawing space is a ***two-dimensional coordinate system*** which is associated with the drawing mode. Drawing space is considered to be a flat two-dimensional coordinate system existing in two directions or axes. Those axes are X and Y. The *illusion* of depth, or replicating the Z axis, can be created using a two-dimensional coordinate system. Figure 9–13 illustrates the difference between model and drawing space and their associated coordinate systems. The origin or intersection of the X and Y axes is located at the lower left corner of the drawing.

Construction Planes

The concept and application of ***construction planes*** is another CADD feature which provides a real breakthrough for the designer. The use of construction planes makes the construction of model geometry an easier and faster process.

A construction plane is a planar surface which can be selected from the model's geometry. A construction plane can be predefined because it is associated to a specific view, e.g., for a FRONT view the construction plane is FRONT (Figure 9–14A). A designer can also define a construction plane from pre-existing geometry in any view that shows the model in three dimensions. This is called an auxiliary construction plane (Figure 9–14B). Think of an auxiliary construction plane as a secondary coordinate system. Once a

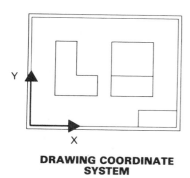

DRAWING COORDINATE SYSTEM

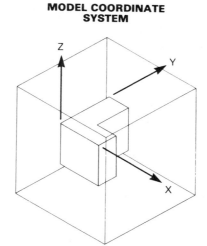

MODEL COORDINATE SYSTEM

Figure 9–13
Model and drawing coordinate systems. (Reprinted with permission from Computervision Corporation, Bedford, Massachusetts)

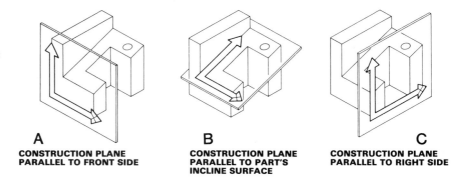

A
**CONSTRUCTION PLANE
PARALLEL TO FRONT SIDE**

B
**CONSTRUCTION PLANE
PARALLEL TO PART'S
INCLINE SURFACE**

C
**CONSTRUCTION PLANE
PARALLEL TO RIGHT SIDE**

construction plane is defined and activated, the following types of activities can take place:

- All digitizes are projected directly onto the construction plane.

- A coordinate system is set up when a construction plane is defined by the designer or drafter. The origin of the coordinate system is the same as the origin of the construction plane. Geometry can be created and/or located using this coordinate system; the coordinate system will be "local."

- Construction planes can be used to insert geometry or text, directly on the plane or parallel to it.

Construction planes serve as design aids. If multiple views are selected by the designer, each orthographic view will have an equivalent construction plane associated with it. For example, a right side view has a *construction plane* RIGHT, (Figure 9–14C), associated to it and a front view has a *construction plane* FRONT, (Figure 9–14A) associated with it. These types of construction planes allow geometry items to be directly projected onto them and facilitate a two-dimensional approach to model construction. Figure 9–15 shows a three-dimensional model and a variety of construction plane coordinate systems that could be established to construct the part.

The power of using construction planes may be seen in a three-dimensional approach to model construction. For example, if the designer were constructing model geometry using one view along with the dynamics capabilities, designer-defined construction planes would be useful. Assume that the model was displayed in some isometric auxiliary view. The drafter or designer wants to add some circles to one side or face of the model and that particular side is not directly parallel to the screen (CRT). Only the side or plane of the model to which the circles will be added would need to be defined. Once the side or construction plane is defined and selected, either use explicit coordinates or digitize the location of the circles and they are

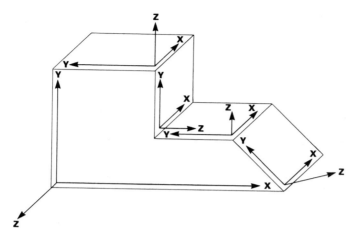

Figure 9–15
Designer defined construction planes and their associated local coordinate systems. (Reprinted with permission from Computervision Corporation, Bedford, Massachusetts)

added. The circles are not only added to that plane, but they are also displayed elliptically as they should be.

Views

Models or drawings are created on the system and shown on the CRT. The designer will be concerned with the way these images are shown and oriented. Capability to provide specific views of the model is provided to the designer. This capability facilitates the numerous ways in which models and drawings are visually presented. The capability provided is to establish **views**. A view could be defined as a window through which a model, or part of a model, can be seen.

Since views allow the designer to select ways of seeing designs or model geometry, a means to define the orientation of a design within a view is needed (e.g., a right view or a top view). To define the orientation of a model within a view, standard construction planes that have associated orientations connected to them are normally provided (Figure 9–16).

When the designer is in the model mode, he or she can select any number of views as the design is constructed. With the capability for rotation, scaling (zooming) and placement (scrolling), the designer could work in just one view in the model mode. If more than one view has been defined, any construction in one view will automatically and immediately be seen in all other views. The designer can also work between views by constructing items using existing geometry seen in one view and referencing geometry shown in another view.

The drawing mode uses this view definition capability to help create finished drawings. The drafter selects any number of views necessary to portray the model design. View definition is primarily used in the drawing mode

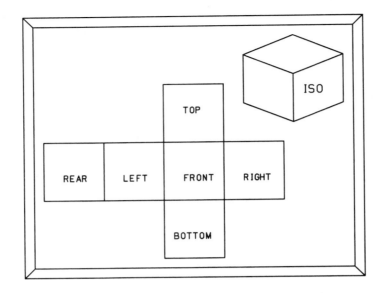

Figure 9–16
The six standard views
and an isometric
projection.

to enhance the visual appearance and presentation of the model design. Views can be placed by the drafter in any configuration for the drawing. The view's window frame can also be defined at any scale. Geometry items added to the drawing in a particular view are only associated with that view. These items are annotation and are not added to the model database.

Figure 9–17 illustrates the relationship between a model and a drawing in terms of views. The model shown in this figure is three-dimensional and is shown isometrically. Each view of the model can be seen as a window that frames an area of the model. All windows frame the model at specific orientations. This figure illustrates five different views of the model. After this model was constructed, the view defined for the drawing shown here automatically displays the geometry of the model. Each view displays the geometry at the selected view orientation. This figure also shows the five views of the model transferred to a drawing.

Three-Dimensional Command Capabilities

A variety of three-dimensional capabilities are available to the designer using three-dimensional CADD systems:

The ability to add depth (Figure 9–18A) quickly and easily gives three-dimensional depth to existing two-dimensional graphical entities. The designer identifies the two-dimensional geometry which will be made three-dimensional. Once the geometry is identified, it is projected along a specific vector to the depth selected. The depth selected can be positive or negative. The positive or negative value specifies the direction and depth the

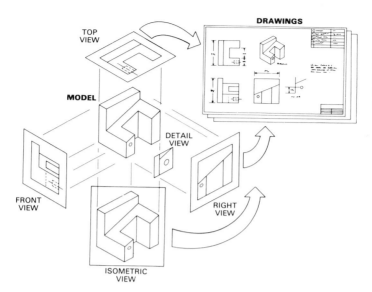

Figure 9–17
Models, views and drawings. (Reprinted with permission from Computervision Corporation, Bedford, Massachusetts)

geometry will be projected. Figure 9–18B illustrates the results of adding depth to three separate pieces of geometry.

The ability to add ruled surfaces (Figure 9–19) creates a three-dimensional surface between two selected pieces of geometry. The geometry items that can be selected are lines, arcs, circles, conics, and splines. Once two geometry items are selected, a surface is created between them. This capability is especially useful to the designer who wishes to locate the intersec-

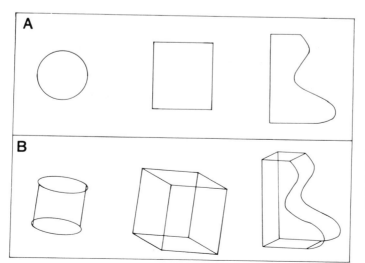

Figure 9–18
ADD DEPTH—Three pieces of geometry (top panel) are transformed into three-dimensional geometry by depth projection (bottom panel). The new three-dimensional geometry has been rotated for viewing purposes. (Reprinted with permission from Computervision Corporation, Bedford, Massachusetts)

Figure 9–19
Three-dimensional
geometry items.

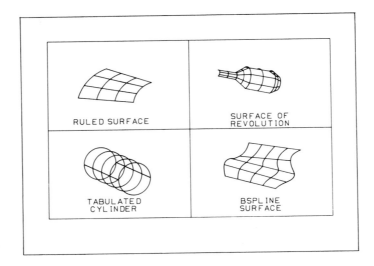

RULED SURFACE

SURFACE OF
REVOLUTION

TABULATED
CYLINDER

BSPLINE
SURFACE

tion of two pieces of geometry. For example, two pieces of three-dimensional geometry are to be joined at a particular side or face. By using the *ruled surface* capability on one of the faces, a three-dimensional surface is created between the frame of the selected sides of the geometry. The other piece of geometry is defined as the cutting plane. The **cutting plane** cuts through the *ruled surface* and the result is the generation of a b-spline on the surface which indicates the intersection.

Three-Dimensional Digitizing

Until recently, designers that use CADD have relied upon various two-dimensional input devices (two-dimensional graphics tablets with cursors, light pens, mice) to provide the X and Y coordinates of a point in two-dimensional space. The Z coordinate has either been entered through the keyboard or supplied through construction techniques in software to arrive at a three-dimensional model. With the introduction of three-dimensional digitizers (Figure 9–20) designers can interactively digitize any three-dimensional object, however irregular its surface, to create a *model* of it on their computer (Figure 9–20). A three-dimensional digitizer, together with appropriate software, allows CADD designers to input three-dimensional wireframe objects, and then manipulate, rotate, scale, duplicate, dimension, and plot them.

The applications for three-dimensional digitizers are widespread, ranging from interactive three-dimensional CADD, to contour analysis of any object, to medical applications, to field mapping of various information by fixing specific sensors to the tip of the three-dimensional digitizer's pointer. Three-dimensional digitizers can be used for:

Figure 9–20
The Space Table (TM) is a three-dimensional coordinate digitizer that plots and records X, Y, and Z coordinates of any point in space within the 16" x 14" tablet. Advanced Space Graphics (TM) 2.0 is a digitization package which when used with a personal computer acts as a stand-alone digitizing workstation. This software package allows the manipulation and transformation of wireframe drawings on the graphics monitor of a personal computer, including rotating, scaling, moving points or whole objects with the pointer, and dimensioning. (Courtesy Micro Control Systems, Inc.)

- Tracing irregular surfaces not previously able to be entered, such as curves, sculptured surfaces, user-defined surfaces. This capability is necessary in medical applications, reverse engineering of products, and "what if" modeling of objects prior to their final design and manufacturing.

- Tracing "nesting" patterns for three-dimensional products, such as plastics, which need to be cut from a single sheet, or molded products produced from other materials.

- Product packaging of irregular objects, or optimal packaging of many objects.

- Three-dimensional field mapping of such information as radiation, sound, and temperature by fixing specific sensors to the pointer's removable tip.

- Molecular modeling of complex three-dimensional molecules.

- Robotic training; interactive positioning of the Percepter's pointer to teach robot movement patterns.

- Inspection; testing of moving parts for fatigue.

- Classification of art objects or antiquities for archaeology (Figure 9–21).

A Typical Finite Element Modeling Package

To design an optimal structure or to determine the cause of failure after manufacture, design engineers commonly use computerized design and analysis methods. One such method, that is supported by a CADD system, is the *finite element* method. The finite element method is a versatile engineering tool that provides a mathematical simulation of the behavior of a complex structure. Using this method, the designer can determine the amount and location of stress in a structural design, without building a test prototype.

The finite element method consists of three basic components:

Figure 9–21
An archaeologist uses Micro Control System's Perceptor (TM) to construct the images of an artifact. The three-dimensional digitizer allows archaeologists to reconstruct vessel forms in three dimensions within minutes instead of days needed for manual drawings. (Courtesy Micro Control Systems, Inc.)

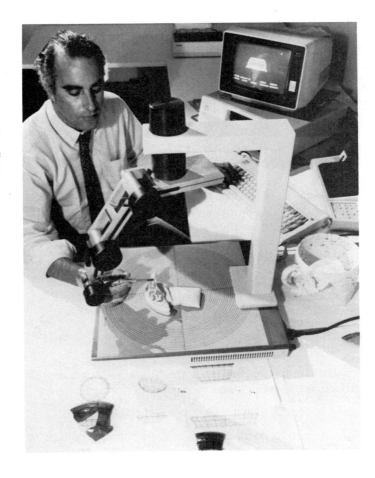

- Finite element modeling
- Finite element analysis
- Finite element analysis postprocessing

A typical finite element modeling (FEM) package allows the designer to create the model and prepare it for analysis, and then show the results of the analysis on the CRT. As an integral part of a CADD system, the FEM package takes full advantage of all graphics and dynamics features. It also uses part information (since the part design information already exists), thus reducing the likelihood of errors and speeding the entire analysis cycle. The FEM package normally uses the same Englishlike command language as used in all CADD applications. This makes learning and using the FEM package quick and easy.

Finite Element Modeling

The first component of the finite element method, **finite element modeling**, involves subdividing a structure into a network of simple elements that have easily definable characteristics. A mesh that is composed of associative grid points and elements is generated (Figure 9–22). The designer then interactively defines material properties, boundary conditions, and loads, such as forces/moments, pressures, and displacements applied to the structure. Since the FEM package is fully integrated into the CADD system and shares the same database, the designer can quickly develop error-free models either from a design in the database or an engineering drawing. Grid points and

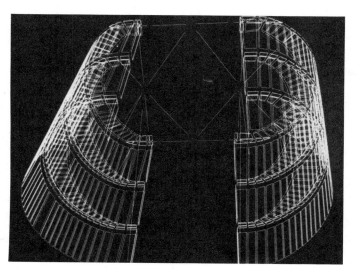

Figure 9–22
FEM design. (Courtesy Evans and Sutherland)

elements can be created either interactively or automatically, and verified immediately. This creates the complete finite element model. Plate 21 shows a finite element model and stress analysis data. Once the finite element model information is generated, the designer prepares it for analysis. Preparation is accomplished with one simple CADD command that creates a text file on the system. The text file contains model information ready to be sent to a mainframe computer for analysis.

CAD FEM Features

A CADD three-dimensional system offers the following finite element modeling capabilities.

- Standard set of two-dimensional and three-dimensional elements.
- User-defined elements.
- Automatic mesh generation of (1) beams and pipes, (2) plate and shell elements on all mechanical design surfaces and on Coon's patch surfaces, and (3) brick elements in three-dimensional volumes.
- Automatic numbering of grid points and elements (with an option for a designer-defined numbering scheme).
- Interactive insertion of initial conditions and loads including forces, moments, pressures, temperature gradients, and displacements.
- Editing and verification features, including associativity between grid points and elements, shrink elements, and blanking/unblanking of entity tags.
- Location, merging, and deletion of coincident nodes to form a contiguous mesh.
- User-defined tolerance for coincident node location.
- Creation of an editable text file containing formatted database information prepared for mainframe analysis.
- Formatting for NASTRAN, ANSYS, SAP, STRUDL, SUPERB, and similar finite element analysis programs.
- Creation of a neutral test file for in-house or other analysis programs.

Finite Element Analysis

Finite element analysis is the second part of the finite element method. It is generally a mainframe computer program which analyzes the information from the text file to determine the amount and location of stress on a structure (Figure 9–23).

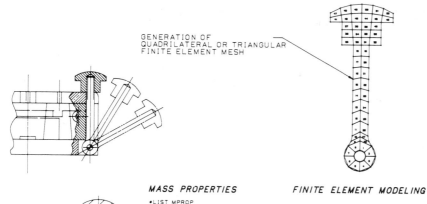

GENERATION OF
QUADRILATERAL OR TRIANGULAR
FINITE ELEMENT MESH

Figure 9–23
Design analysis includes generation of finite element models and calculating mass properties. (Reprinted with permission from Computervision Corporation, Bedford, Massachusetts)

CENTER OF MASS

MASS PROPERTIES   FINITE ELEMENT MODELING

```
•LIST MPROP
   ALL OUTPUT ARE IN VIEW I
   DENSITY: 0.40000    VOLUME: 0.42411   MASS: 0.16964
   FIRST MOMENTS
      MX: 0.00000      MY: 0.28976    MZ: 0.00000
   SECOND  MOMENTS
      0.00553        0.00000        0.00000
      0.00000        0.60909        0.00000
      0.00000        0.00000        0.00542
   CENTER OF MASS
      X: 0.00000     Y: 1.70805     Z: 0.00000
   MOMENTS OF INERTIA (AT CM)
      X-AXIS: 0.11959     Y-AXIS: 0.01095    Z-AXIS: 0.11969
```

Once the analysis is performed, numerical results are returned to the CADD system and the finite element analysis postprocessing phase begins. This involves reviewing the analysis results, determing structural problem areas, and modifying the design.

A FEM package adds extensive capabilities to postprocessing. Full advantage can be taken of all CADD display and manipulation capabilities such as view selection, zooming, rotation, and scrolling to dynamically review a true three-dimensional representation of the structure and the analysis results — for example, to see how much deformation there is and where it is (Plate 20). In this way, it is possible to quickly check the results and refine the design on the system. CADD analysis postprocessing capabilities include:

- Deformation plots due to static analysis. The results can be superimposed on the undeformed geometry. The results can be zoomed or rotated for better viewing.

- Dynamic display of deformations calculated from normal mode or transient analysis. Vector motion can be simulated and a structure's major dynamic characteristics can be determined graphically.

The FEM package is an integral part of a mechanical design system. Because all functions use the same database, there is a continuous flow of information during part development, analysis, and modification.

Developing a Construction Strategy

The basis for creating a part on a CADD system is the model, a three-dimensional representation of the part generated in the database. As the model is being constructed by the designer, it is shown on the CRT. During construction, the designer can rotate and turn the display of the model in any direction to allow additional geometry to be added from the best angle. For instance, if a hole is to be bored in the bottom of a part, the bottom can be turned to face the display. This technique, using dynamics during design, significantly affects preplanning. Figure 9–24 shows a brace plate that will be designed on a three-dimensional CADD system.

Identifying Geometric Features

Since a CADD part is constructed in three dimensions almost as if it were being sculpted in clay—one section developed first, and then another section added to it—one important decision during preplanning is to identify those sections of the part's geometry that will form the foundation for the construction. In some cases, where every dimension for building the part is supplied in the conceptual layout (Figure 9–25), this decision may be based on the designer's personal preference. In other cases, where dimension information is not supplied, the decision is critical.

Figure 9–24
Brace plate assembly.
(Reprinted with permission from Computervision Corporation, Bedford, Massachusetts)

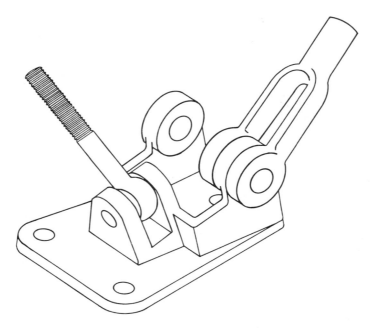

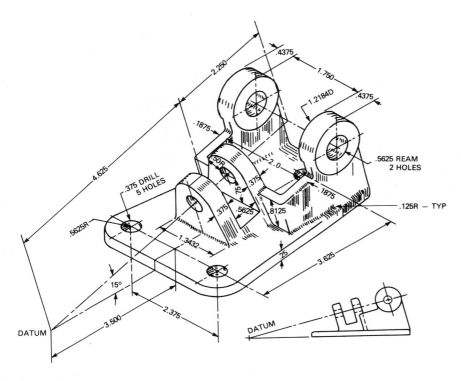

Figure 9–25
Brace Plate conceptual
design layout. (Reprinted
with permission from
Computervision Corpora-
tion, Bedford, Mas-
sachusetts)

In the conceptual design layout, the Brace Plate is shown as an assembly three-dimensional model. In Figure 9–25, notice that one of the most important dimensions is the 15-degree angle around which the entire forward
bracket area of the part is constructed. The side view shows this very clearly.
Many of the angular faces of the Brace Plate are not defined; they are projected directly from this 15-degree angle (Figure 9–25). Unless the geometry
directly related to this angle is created first, it would be very difficult, if not
impossible, to complete the Brace Plate. In addition, existing geometry will
be used once developed to help locate and place new geometry.

To reduce construction time and simplify the construction process, the
designer can take advantage of the symmetry within a part's geometry. If a
section of the part's geometry is symmetrical, it is unnecessary to use repetitious and redundant construction processes to create all reflections of
symmetry. Instead, a representative section of the geometry is created. The
remaining section(s) that completes the part is created by copying the representative section and mirroring it into the proper position.

The Brace Plate is symmetrical around a vertical plane that bisects the
bores of the forward bracket area or tabs. To make use of this fact, only half
of the symmetrical geometry will be created. It will then be mirrored across

Figure 9–26
Wireframe model of
brace plate. (Reprinted
with permission from
Computervision Corpora-
tion, Bedford, Mas-
sachusetts)

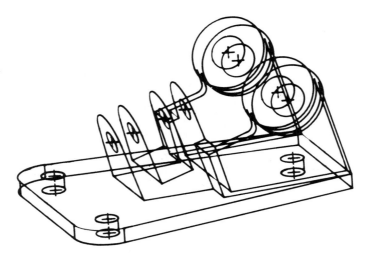

and over this hinge or axis of the part's geometry. Figure 9–26 shows the
wireframe three-dimensional model of the completed part.

GLOSSARY

ABSOLUTE COORDINATES   The values of the X, Y, or Z coordinates with
respect to the origin of the coordinate system.

CARTESIAN COORDINATES   The distance of a point from any of three
intersecting perpendicular planes; X, Y, Z coordinates.

COMPUTER NUMERICAL CONTROL (CNC)   Using a computer to store
numerical control instructions generated by a CADD system. CNC is the direct
control of the NC machine by computer — there is no punched tape required.

CONSTRUCTION PLANE   A predefined or designer-defined plane to which all
construction is either normal or parallel.

CRT   A computer display device, also called a monitor or cathode ray tube.

CUT PLANE   A plane that passes through a three-dimensional object to derive a
sectional view.

DESIGN AUTOMATION (DA)   Using a computer to automate portions of the
design process.

DYNAMIC MOVEMENT   The ability to zoom, scroll, and rotate the image on the
CRT interactively.

DYNAMIC ROTATION   When a geometry item or group is rotated continuously
at a fixed rate until stopped by the designer.

FINITE ELEMENT ANALYSIS (FEA)   The determination of the structural
integrity of a part by mathematical simulation of the part and the forces acting
on the part.

FINITE ELEMENTS   The subdivision of a complex structure into small pieces.

FINITE ELEMENT MODELING (FEM)   The creation of a mathematical model of a part for input to a finite element analysis program.

HIDDEN LINES   Line segments that would ordinarily be hidden from view in a three-dimensional view of a solid object because they are behind other items in the view.

KINEMATICS   A process for simulating the motion of mechanisms to study interference, acceleration, and forces.

MODELING   Constructing a mathematical or geometric model of a physical object or system for analysis.

NUMERICAL CONTROL (NC)   The control of machine tools, drafting machines, and plotters by punched paper or magnetic tape encoded with the proper information to cut a part or draw a figure.

ON-LINE   Equipment or devices in a system that are directly connected to and under the control of the system's computer.

ROBOTICS   The use of computer controlled robots to automate manufacturing processes such as welding, material handling, painting, and assembly.

ROTATE   To turn a view about an axis through a predefined angle.

SCROLL   To automatically roll up on a CRT, as on a spool, a message or drawing too large to be shown all at once.

SOLID MODEL   A complete and unambiguous mathematical representation of a part as a solid object.

SPLINE   A smooth curve between a sequence of points in space.

SURFACE OF REVOLUTION   Rotation of a curve around an axis through a specified angle.

SURFACE MACHINING   The ability to output 3-, 4-, and 5-axis NC toolpaths using three-dimensional surface definition capabilities (e.g., ruled surfaces, tabulated cylinders, and surfaces of revolution).

TOOL PATH   A trace of the movement of the tip of a numerical control cutting tool that is used to guide or control machining equipment.

WIREFRAME   A three-dimensional object shown on the CRT as a series of lines that represent the edges of its surfaces. The picture looks as if it were made from coat hangers.

QUIZ

True or False

1. There are normally two modes associated with CADD systems, modeling and drawing.

2. Wireframe models show the surfaces of a model as planes, cylinders, spheres, or ruled surfaces.

3. Solid models are created from primitives such as cubes, spheres, and cones.

4. In the draw mode, annotation will not affect the original three-dimensional model.

5. A designer on the CADD system can define any number of construction planes to aid in the design of a part.

6. The ruled surface capability allows the designer to add depth.

7. Tool paths can be simulated and verified using an NC software package.

8. Hidden line removal is used to enhance the visual representation of the model.

Fill in the Blank

9. A wireframe model represents an object by _____ only.

10. Three-dimensional modeling can be grouped into _____ , _____ , and _____ types.

11. The _____ mode is used for designing a part and generating NC data.

12. Detailed drawings with dimensions, text, and notes are created in the _____ mode.

13. The _____ of all three axes are defined by the operator.

14. _____ is a two-dimensional coordinate system associated with the drawing mode.

15. A _____ is a window through which a model or part of a model can be seen.

16. A coordinate system is set up when a _____ is defined by the designer.

Answer the Following

17. Explain the major elements of a FEM package.

18. Describe the ability to add depth.

19. Explain the uses and the creation of a construction plane and how it is related to a coordinate system.

20. What is the difference between a model space coordinate system and a drawing space coordinate system?

21. Why is it more efficient to design a part in the model mode?

22. What can a robot simulator software program typically do?

23. What is the design-through-manufacturing cycle and how is the three-dimensional model used in this sequence?

24. Describe the difference between the CGS and b-rep methods to create a solid model.

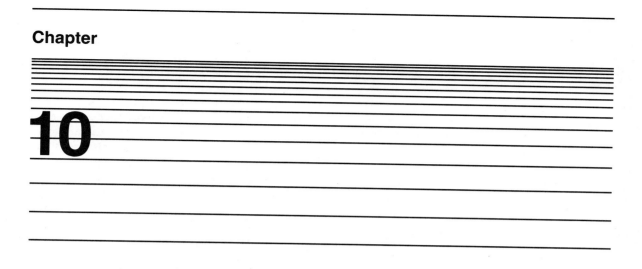

Chapter

10

Preparing the Drawing

Objectives

Upon completion of this chapter, the reader will be able to:

- Understand the difference between draw mode and model mode activity and how the availability of a three-dimensional system affects "drawing" preparation.

- Be able to effect line and text font parameter changes and selections.

- Describe in a general sense the step-by-step methods used to dimension a part using CADD dimensioning capabilities.

- Explain the practice of crosshatching and how it is accomplished using CADD.

- Create text using the various types of text justification and text character parameters available on most CADD systems.

- Show the variations of linear dimensioning and the other basic types of dimensioning associated with CADD dimensioning practices.

Introduction

Chapter 9 discussed the two different CADD operational modes available for three-dimensional systems—*model* and *drawing*—and concepts that relate to both. Chapter 9 also examined concepts and features specifically associated with the model mode. The *drawing mode* also has specific concepts and features uniquely associated with it. This chapter examines these concepts and features and how they are applied in *preparing the drawing*. Note that all of this chapter can be applied to both two- and three-dimensional systems. For two-dimensional systems the separation of design and detailing modes is not as important since the user creates the part and dimensions it according to traditional standard views that must be created individually as in manual drafting.

With a two-dimensional CADD system all parts are completed in the draw mode since the model mode is only available with systems that have three-dimensional capabilities. Therefore, the two-dimensional system relies on the construction of each view and the placing of dimensions and notes, all on the same "drawing." A three-dimensional system allows the use of the three-dimensional model database in the draw mode to "detail" the part without altering the model database. A multitude of "drawings" can be created using the same "model" database.

Regardless of which type of system is available, the drafter or designer must prepare the design to be used in the manufacturing sequence. This preparation usually means showing the design in standardized views and applying dimensioning procedures. Borders, title blocks, dimensions, notes, and drawing appearance modifications such as line font changes and crosshatching all fall within the preparation of drawing category.

Drawing Mode

The **drawing mode** is the operational mode a drafter or detailer uses to create detail drawings for a part. As discussed before, a part may be constructed by a design engineer in the model mode on a three-dimensional system or on a drawing for a two-dimensional system. The detailer uses this part and its associated geometry as the basis to create detail drawings (Figure 10–1). Any number and type of drawings can be created for a part regardless of which type of system is used.

Drawing Items and the Three-Dimensional System

Drawing items are geometry items that look just like model mode geometry and include points, lines, circles, arcs, and text. Chapter 5 discusses geometry creation. In addition, drawing items include dimensional characters, symbols, notes labels, crosshatching, and line appearance changes each existing in a two-dimensional space. Figure 10–2 illustrates this concept and shows the difference between model space and drawing space and their associated coordinate systems. As this figure illustrates, drawing space

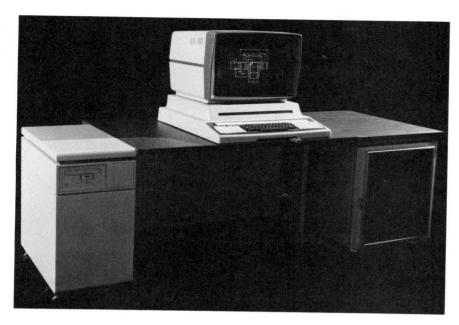

Figure 10–1
CAD/CAM system
showing a dimensioned
mechanical part.
(Courtesy Gerber
Systems Technology Inc.)

and drawing items can be seen to exist on a single flat plane just like a piece of paper, whereas model space is three-dimensional. This two-dimensional sheet of paper example demonstrates the concept of the natural aspect of a three-dimensional CADD system: a detailer is concerned with drawings which are two-dimensional; the designer is concerned with models which are three-dimensional.

Drawing items have no effect on the model's database since these pieces of geometry are totally independent from them. This geometry is primarily used to enhance a detail drawing for its final presentation. Enhancements may be for visual clarification of the three-dimensional model's two-dimensional representation or for purely aesthetic reasons. In addition, drawing items can be added as a detailing aid to assist in the dimensioning process.

As stated above, drawing items are added to enhance the appearance of the model (e.g., adding a dashed line to indicate it is hidden) but also include dimensional characteristics (dimensions, center lines, extension lines, and arrowheads) and text. This geometry is not affected by three-dimensional operations. This is a logical and natural limitation since there would be no reason to make dimensional information or drawing formats three-dimensional.

If the system is limited to two-dimensional geometry then all drawing items including the part representation and the dimensions will be two-dimensional and the above description will not apply.

Figure 10–2
Drawing mode and
model mode coordinate
systems. (Reprinted with
permission from Com-
putervision Corporation,
Bedford, Massachusetts)

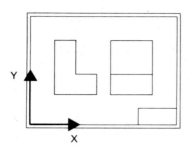

DRAWING COORDINATE
SYSTEM

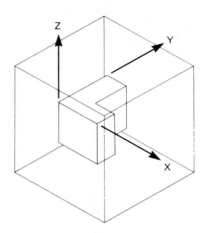

MODEL COORDINATE
SYSTEM

Three-Dimensional Systems and the Detailing Process

It might be helpful to give a general description of the transition from the model mode to the drawing mode at this time. Once the model design for a part has been completed in the model mode, the drafter's work begins. The drafter retrieves the completed part model and then defines a drawing (by name) to start his or her work. Any size drawing can be defined on the CADD system. Once a drawing size is determined, for example, a D-size or C-size, (Figure 10–3) the drafter then selects the types and numbers of views he or she wants to have defined to show the part. Any type of view can be defined — the six standard orthographic views as well as any number of auxiliary views. In addition, a number of views can be located on the drawing format; on most systems there is a limit on the number of views for each drawing. The scale of the geometry within a view can also be selected by the drafter. Each view that is defined will appear at the scale selected. Scale affects the viewed size of the model. This means that the visual appearance of the model is affected, not its actual size as it is represented in the model's database. For example, the drafter might select a scale of 2 which would increase the viewed size of the model. This scale factor might be used for visual clarification to make dimensioning easier. Another situation might have the drafter select a scale of .5 which would decrease the viewed size of the model. This scale factor might be used to allow a large assembly to be printed on a smaller sized drawing. Once the part has been retrieved and all views have been defined (and scaled), the part is automatically shown in the defined views in the orientations associated with the views. Since any number

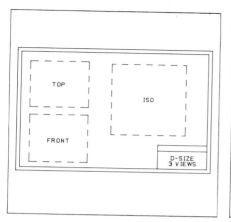 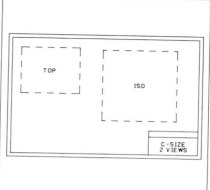

Figure 10–3
Form Parts—"D" size drawing format on left has three predetermined "views": top, front and isometric. The "C" size format on the left has only the top and isometric views predefined. (Reprinted with permission from Computervision Corporation, Bedford, Massachusetts)

of drawings can be produced for a part, this view definition procedure would occur for each drawing created.

A drafter will most likely have to prepare the model with its associated geometry for the detailing process. Preparation of this sort has to do with modifying the geometry of the part for detailing purposes. For example, geometry items in the model's geometry may have to be hidden. As discussed previously, erasing temporarily removes geometry for viewing purposes. In this drawing mode case, erasing of model geometry is used to visually enhance the drawing for its final presentation. Erasing does not affect the model's database; erasing only affects the appearance of the model's geometry.

The Two-Dimensional Detailing Process

The two-dimensional detailing process would be similar to the three-dimensional process if one takes the starting point as the point at which the part is to be dimensioned. Otherwise the two-dimensional process starts with the drawing of the part in the appropriate views, including sectioned views with crosshatching and auxiliary views, and then adding dimensions, notes, title block, and border. Note that a two-dimensional system is really a "detailing" system and is severely limited as a true design tool.

Form Parts

We have just discussed the transition that takes place from the model mode to the drawing mode and how a drafter would approach detailing for a two-dimensional and a three-dimensional system. We have also mentioned how a drafter selects a drawing format and the views he or she feels are necessary to present the part. Many CADD systems have features which help the drafter in regard to this formatting and view selection process. This feature will be referred to as *form parts*.

Form parts is a process by which a drafter can define a standard format for any size drawing. Any number of standard formats can be defined. These formats include the size of the drawing, border information, title block design, logo, metric or English standards, and text. In addition, any number and type of views can be associated with a specified format including the locations of the views on the drawing format when a three-dimensional system is available (Figure 10–3). A two-dimensional system may also have a form parts capability but it is limited to creating and recalling standard drawing formats, borders, and title blocks; in other words, it is two-dimensional. A three-dimensional system has the same two-dimensional capability but the drafter can also recall formats that have the views already defined. In this situation the drafter merely calls up an existing design created in the model mode and the system puts the model into the views defined by the format without the need to create or draw the views as with the two-dimensional system.

This form parts feature is quite useful to the drafter when company standard formats are used repeatedly. Instead of recreating a format each time a detail drawing is needed, the drafter simply retrieves the desired format that was predefined. The drafter would create a library of these formats which are retrieved when necessary. This feature saves the drafter much time. When a particular form part format is retrieved, the CADD system automatically displays the activated part model in all the views associated with the format (Figure 10–3). The transition from the model mode to the drawing mode, and consequently the detailing process, is made much faster. Scales can also be selected for each view.

Figure 10–4 shows the creation of a form part on a two-dimensional system. The border and the title block have been constructed using standard geometry commands. The form is then saved to be used later. On a system where form parts is not available, the drafter merely follows the steps shown in Figure 10–5. First the size of the drawing is decided (A, B, C, D, E). Then the border is drawn along with the title block using ANSI, company, or other standards. The part is then drawn with the views needed to describe the object. Lastly, the part is detailed by adding dimensions, notes, and title block information.

Drawing Appearance Modification

Whether a two-dimensional or three-dimensional system is used, the part must be shown according to standard drafting conventions. Lines represent-

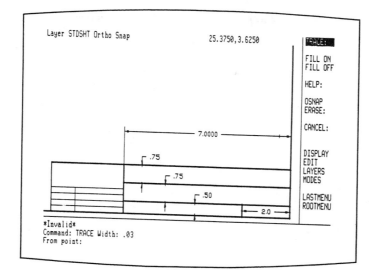

Figure 10–4
Title block and border created on a AutoCAD system and used for a Form Part. (Courtesy Autodesk Inc.)

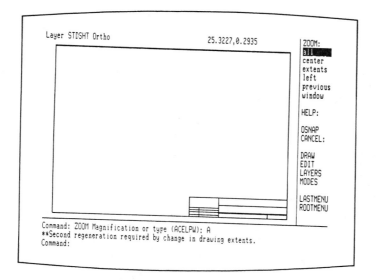

ing edges of the part that are hidden must be shown as dashed. Center lines must be added for all circles and round portions of the part. Sectioned drawings will require crosshatch patterns appropriately shown. These changes are called appearance modifications.

Line Fonts

Most systems have a variety of standard line fonts or styles available and provide the ability to create a number of user defined fonts. Solid lines for

Figure 10–5
Preparing the drawing—
determine the drawing
size, draw the border,
draw the title block,
construct the views,
dimension the part, and
add notes and title block
information.

DRAW BORDER

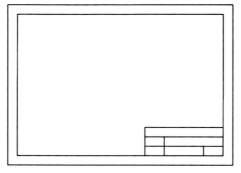

DRAW TITLE BLOCK

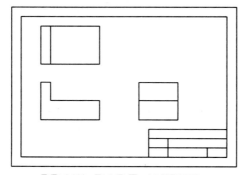

DRAW PART VIEWS

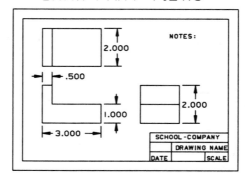

DIMENSION PART

object lines, dashed lines for hidden edges, center lines for holes and circular objects, and phantom lines are just a few of the available fonts.

Figure 10–6 shows a few line font variations that may be standard to a system. In addition to the style of line, most systems allow the line to be drawn with a variety of thicknesses. Lines can normally be selected from a CRT or a tablet menu as shown in Figure 10–7. Here the drafter could select

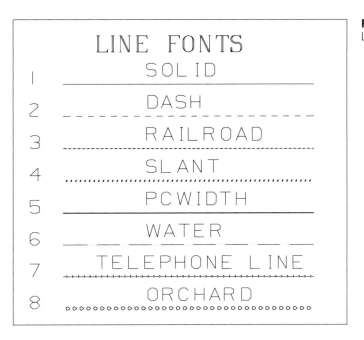

Figure 10–6
Line fonts.

a number of standard lines; select the weight, thickness, or interval; and change an existing line all from the menu.

Since most systems have a line default, usually solid, the drafter can *select* a different style that will remain the default until another is selected or the system is started up again.

The weight of a line could also be altered by the selection of a pen thickness during the plotting stage. Many systems allow the drafter to embed

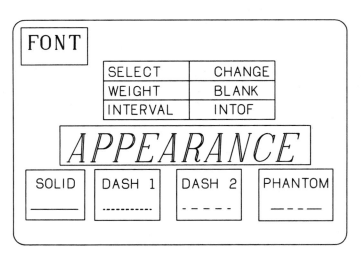

Figure 10–7
Line font menu.

plotting instructions such as pen selection directly in the part description. The drafter would select a particular **pen number** when a multiple plotter is available. Plots can be made with varying pen thicknesses and colors. When the system allows the instruction to be embedded in the part description, the choice of pen thickness is normally made before the item is drawn.

Changing an Existing Line Font

The most common type of line for most drawings is the solid line that represents a visible edge of a part. Because of this, the default font is usually a solid line. If the part was created in three-dimensional model space it will normally show all lines as solid. This model will need to be altered in appearance during the detailing stage. Figure 10–8 shows the model before and after the altering of the font style of three lines on the model. This work will take place in the **draw mode**; therefore the model database will remain unaltered. The appearance changes will affect the detail drawing, not the model. The model and the detail should always be put on separate "drawings." In Figure 10–8 the three lines that are hidden have been changed to dashed by using **CHANGE FONT**. With a two-dimensional system these lines would probably have been drawn with the line type selected as dashed. The dash font would have been selected before the lines were drawn.

Center Lines

Center lines can be added to the part by using **CENTER LINE** or by specifying the center line font. The system default center line is usually a straight line between two specified points. On some systems, the center line capability allows the drafter to draw center lines using modifiers such as **model**, which puts the center line into the part as model geometry where it will be shown in all views (this is limited to three-dimensional systems). The **angle** variation constructs a center line through a specified point at an angle. The **diameter** modifier constructs a circular center line defined by the center and the diameter as used with a bolt/hole circle. The **radius** variation uses the center and the radius instead of the diameter. Lastly, the **circle** modifier draws two perpendicular center lines through the center of the circle (Figure 10–9). This last variation is one of the most common. In Figure 10–9, center lines were added to the part by giving the instruction and specifying the circles.

A two-dimensional system may have the same type of capabilities or they may limit it to creating the center lines as a particular line font and drawing them using regular line drawing capabilities.

Crosshatching and Pattern Filling

In many drafting applications, it is common practice to fill an area with a pattern of some sort. The **pattern** can help differentiate between compo-

BEFORE

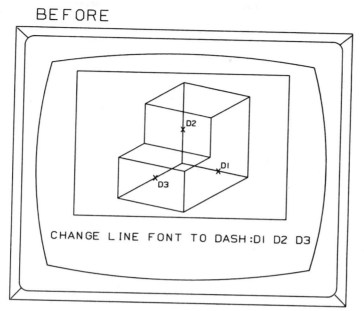

CHANGE LINE FONT TO DASH :DI D2 D3

Figure 10–8
Changing an existing
line's font from solid to
dashed (hidden).

AFTER

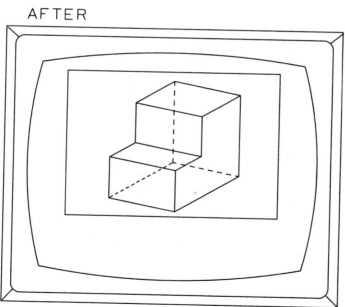

nents of a three-dimensional object, it can define an area of a part that has
been sectioned (Figure 10–10), or it can signify the material composing an
object (Figure 10–11). This process, called "crosshatching" or "pattern filling," can be accomplished using HATCH; it is referred to simply as "crosshatching." Hatching is a standard feature on most CADD software packages.

Figure 10–9
Creating center lines on
circles.

BEFORE

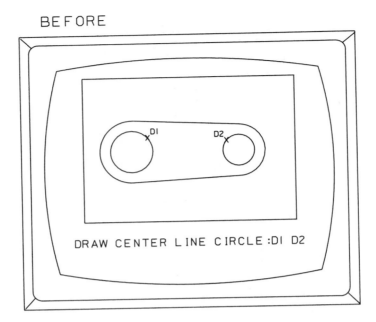

DRAW CENTER LINE CIRCLE :DI D2

AFTER

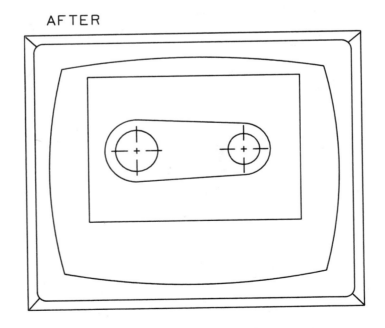

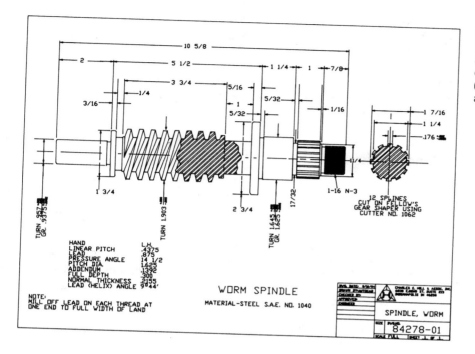

Figure 10–10
Worm spindle with cut away sections using crosshatch patterns. (Courtesy Charles Hill and Associates)

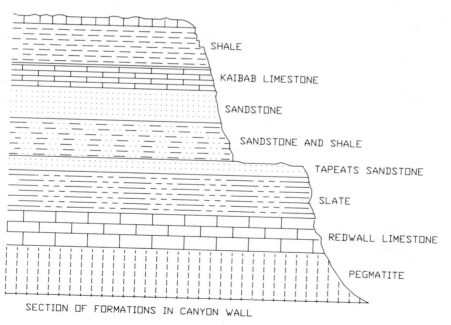

Figure 10–11
Section formations in canyon wall using crosshatch patterns to represent types of rock and mineral layers of stratification. (Courtesy Autodesk Inc.)

A variety of pattern *symbols* are provided on most systems. Patterns can be standard ANSI patterns or can be designer-defined symbols.

CADD systems are supplied with a library of standard hatch patterns. The designer can hatch with one of these standard patterns, with a custom pattern from his or her own file, or with a simple pattern defined when the instruction is given. A CRT or tablet menu will usually have a variety of hatch patterns available (Figure 10–12).

Hatch Patterns

Each hatch pattern is composed of one or more hatch lines or figures, at specified angles and spacing. The hatching may be continuous or broken into dots and dashes. The pattern is repeated or clipped, as necessary, to exactly fill the area being hatched.

Hatching generates the geometry for the chosen pattern and adds it to the drawing. Since a pattern may contain many lines, CADD systems normally group these lines together. Thus, if an area is hatched and the designer decides the hatching isn't right, he or she can just point to any line of it and select DELETE or ERASE to remove all of the hatching.

Figure 10–12
Typical crosshatch patterns.

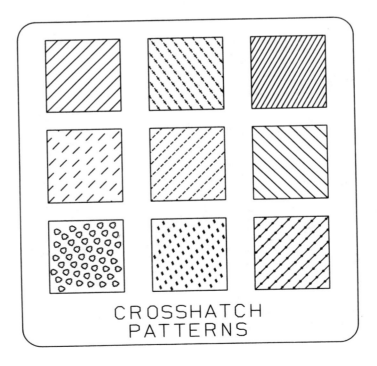

Defining the Boundary

Hatching fills in an area of the drawing enclosed by a boundary made up of lines, arcs, circles, splines, or other items. When hatching an area, the items that define the boundary must be selected. The geometry forming the hatching boundary should intersect; overhanging lines will produce incorrect hatching if the system requires that the end points of the lines meet. Some systems allow for lines to cross and some even hatch areas not completely enclosed by lines.

Consider a circle with a circle inside it (Figure 10–13). After the HATCH was selected, the outer circle was specified by digitizing. The drafter separated the identification portion of the instruction with a semicolon or another type of break and then digitized the inside circle. The resulting crosshatch filled a donut-shaped area on the part. Since the default values were used, the pattern was a series of lines with a predetermined angle and spacing.

The normal (default) style of hatching is illustrated in Figure 10–13. This style hatches inward starting at the area boundary, the first circle. If it encounters an internal intersection, it turns off hatching until another intersection is encountered.

Hatching a typical cross section of a part is shown in Figure 10–14. Here, HATCH is selected and the boundaries of the area to be crosshatched are successively indicated by digitizing each item.

Hatching patterns can be changed by specifying the angle of the hatching and the spacing as shown in Figure 10–15.

The CHAIN Capability

When the boundaries of the area to be crosshatched are composed of a multitude of intersecting items some systems provide a **CHAIN** capability. CHAIN ties all geometry items touching at their end points into a single unit. Therefore the area to be crosshatched is identified by selecting **CHAIN** and then digitizing one item of the CHAIN. The whole area defined by CHAIN is quickly crosshatched as in Figure 10–16.

Annotation

Annotation is the process of placing words and numbers (text) on a drawing (Figure 10–17). Add text to a drawing by means of **TEXT**. Text can be drawn with a variety of character patterns, or fonts, and can be stretched, compressed, obliqued, angled, slanted, thickened, or mirrored. A *text string* is one or more characters forming one unit or block. Each text string can be rotated and justified to fit the drawing's requirements. Text can be of any size.

Figure 10–13
Crosshatching an area
bounded by inside and
outside circles.

BEFORE

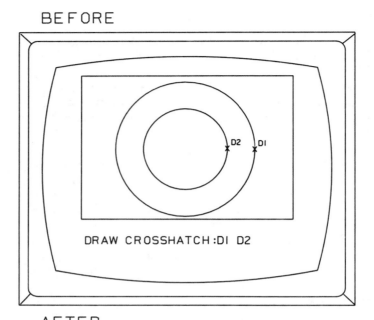

DRAW CROSSHATCH:DI D2

AFTER

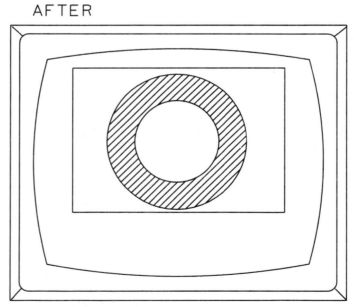

BEFORE

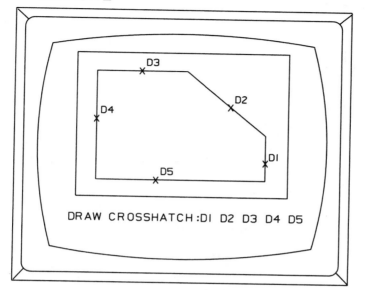

DRAW CROSSHATCH :DI D2 D3 D4 D5

AFTER

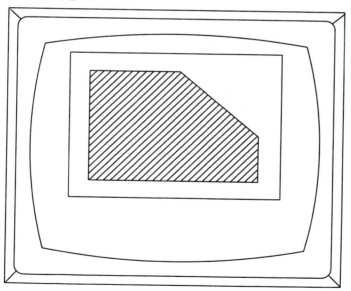

Figure 10–14
Defining areas of a part to
be pattern filled.

Figure 10–15
Altering the default angle
and spacing for a
crosshatch pattern.

BEFORE

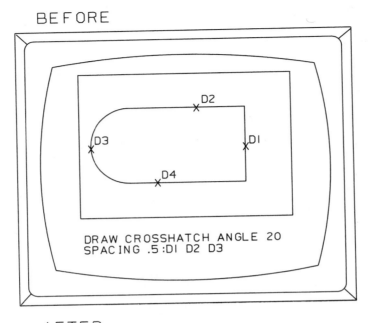

DRAW CROSSHATCH ANGLE 20
SPACING .5 :DI D2 D3

AFTER

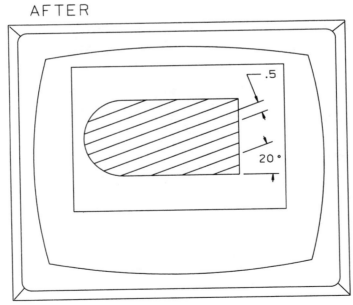

BEFORE

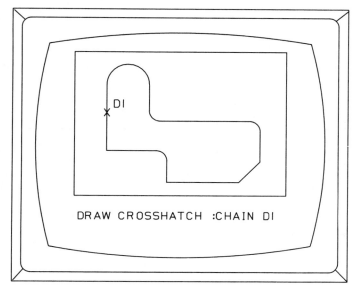

DRAW CROSSHATCH :CHAIN DI

AFTER

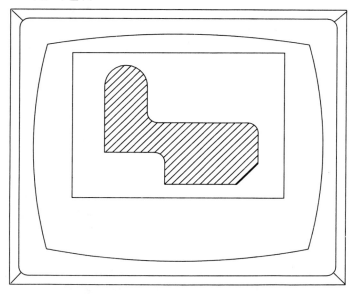

Figure 10–16
Crosshatching using the
chain command.

Figure 10–17
Organization chart,
drawn with AutoCAD
software by Peter
Barnett. (Courtesy
Autodesk Inc.)

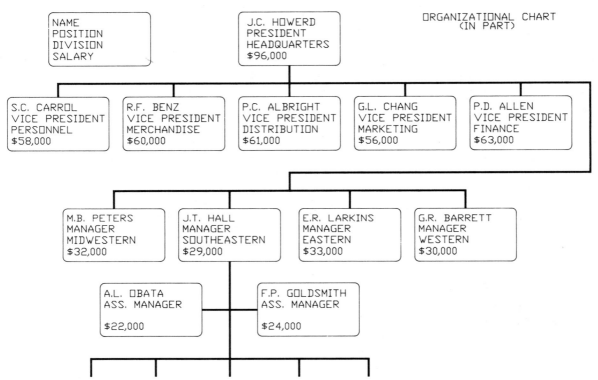

A text string can have just one text character or could be composed of many lines or paragraphs of text. Some systems allow text to be saved just like filing a part or drawing. The **text file** can then be recalled and reused on any drawing. This ability is particularly helpful when a company uses the same set of **notes** or instructions for a number of parts.

Text is **information**; it does not exist as a geometry item of the part unless of course the part is some form of lettering illustration such as a logo for a company. In general, text is information and is inserted in the draw mode since it is not to be part of the model database on a three-dimensional system. Since a two-dimensional system has only the draw mode, text like all other items on a two-dimensional drawing is information provided on the drawing.

Text Styles and Fonts

A **text font** defines the pattern used to draw text characters. Text can be drawn using any number of character fonts. Several such fonts are supplied with most CADD software; samples of each are shown in Figure 10–18.

Many systems have a variety of text fonts available on the CRT or tablet menu for quick and easy placement on the drawing. Figure 10–19 shows a menu that can be used for selecting a text font, changing the font style of an existing text string, and inserting text with variations of height, width, thickness, angle, slant, justification, layer, and mirrored locations.

Text Justification

Text is ordinarily *left justified* at the starting point specified (in Figure 10–17 all of the text strings are left justified). That is, the left end of the text baseline is placed at the starting point. *Right justified* text aligns the text with the right side as shown in Figure 10–20 where left, right, center, and aligned text samples are shown.

Before the text can be drawn, determine the desired text height, the rotation angle from the baseline, and the text string itself. A typical system may prompt for this information in the following manner.

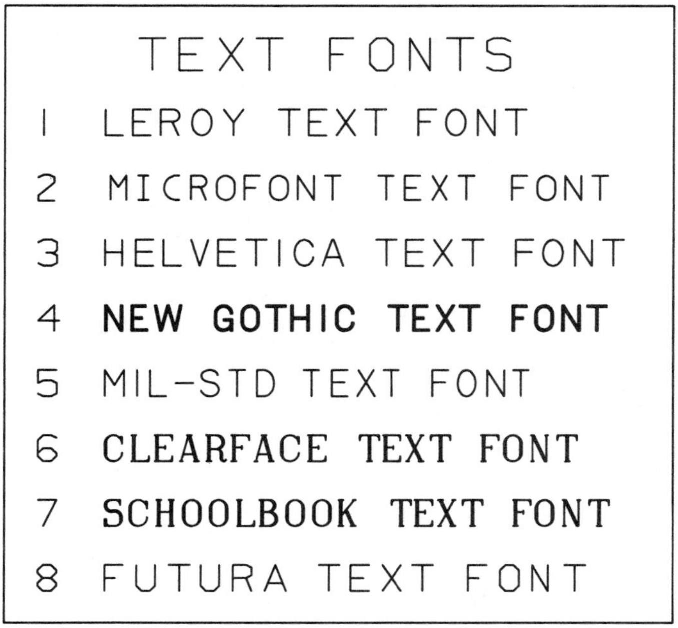

Figure 10–18
Text font examples.

Figure 10–19
Text font menu.

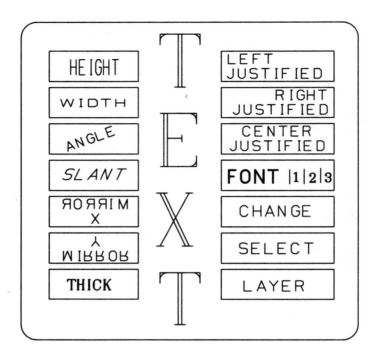

Figure 10–20
Justification options for text.

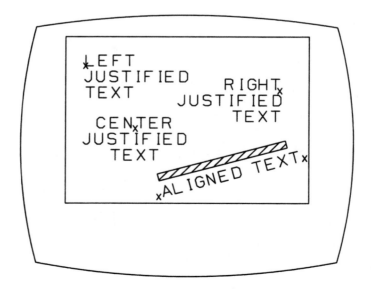

Height <default>:

Rotation angle <default>:

Text:

On many systems the default values have been set for standard text and the drafter can change the values before adding text to the drawing. The SELECT TEXT command normally affects all text including the parameters for the text characters used in dimensions.

The text height specifies how far above the baseline the capital letters extend, in drawing units. The default for most systems is upper case characters. Lower case lettering must be specified before inserting the text. Lower case characters have "descenders," which go below the baseline.

On some systems the height is specified by designating a point; the height will be the distance between this and the starting point. The height, width, slant, and angle can also be determined by the drafter. Figure 10–21 shows variations of these styles. Almost any style, size, and configuration of lettering is possible with a CADD system. Figure 10–22 shows some text examples that can be used for illustrations: mirrored, curved, block, and backwards.

The process for entering text on a drawing involves inputting the command and then digitizing the location of the required text. Multiple positions of the same text are added by simply digitizing more than one location for the string as in Figure 10–23, where "GUIDEPLATE" was placed at two positions.

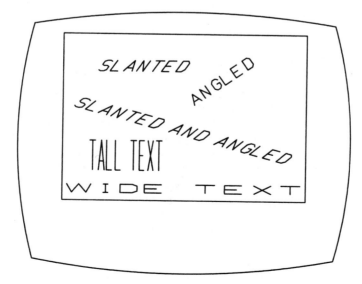

Figure 10–21
Slanted, angled, tall and wide lettering.

Figure 10–22
Mirrored, backwards,
and block lettering.

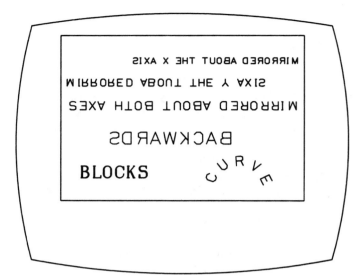

Introduction to Dimensioning

In most engineering applications, a precise drawing plotted to scale is not sufficient to convey the desired information; **annotations** must be added showing the lengths of objects or the distances or angles between objects. Figure 10–24 shows an example of a STAIR DETAIL for a house. The detail is completely dimensioned.

Dimensioning is the process of adding annotations to a drawing. The term *dimensioning* also refers to the annotations themselves. CADD systems provide four basic types of dimensioning: linear, angular, diameter, and radius. A simple example of each along with their variations is provided in this section. All systems have dimensioning capabilities. The instructions for dimensioning and the procedures for dimensioning will differ between systems. Note that all systems provide quick and easy creation of dimensions, but the drafter still needs to know why certain things are dimensioned and where to place the dimensions. CADD systems automate the process but the knowledge of ANSI or other standard dimensioning and tolerancing specifications must be mastered by the student along with learning how to create the dimensions on the system.

The detailer can select dimension options including decimal or fractional representation, English and/or metric units of measure, bilateral or unilateral tolerances, feature control symbols, and datum blocks.

Dimensions are easily created on a drawing by identifying (using the electronic pen) the two locations to be measured and dimensioned. A third location places the dimensioning text and associated values. The system au-

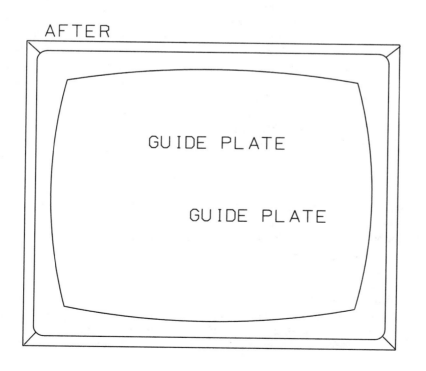

BEFORE

DI
×

D2
×

DRAW TEXT "GUIDE PLATE":DI D2

AFTER

GUIDE PLATE

GUIDE PLATE

Figure 10–23
Creating text on a
drawing.

Figure 10–24
Stair detail drawn by
Peter Barnett with an
AutoCAD system.
(Courtesy Autodesk, Inc.)

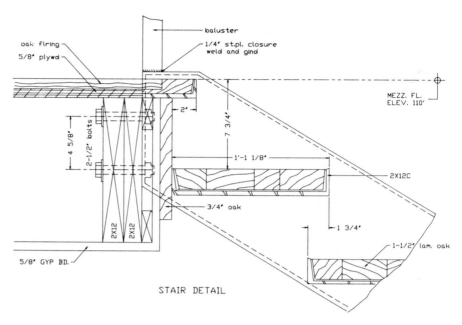

STAIR DETAIL

tomatically creates extension lines, dimension lines, leader lines, dimension arrowheads, and dimensioning text at the location indicated. Linear dimensions, parallel point-to-point (at an angle), diameter, radial, angular, and ordinate dimensioning (Figure 10–25) are available on most systems. A variety of arrowhead lengths and types can be selected (Figure 10–26). Dimension text, notes, and labels are easily created on detail drawings. The drafter can determine what type of text font to use including its height, width, slant, spacing, case, and justification. Labels have the same variety of characteristics that can be selected and include a leader line which is automatically created and attached to the associated label. The angle of the leader line can be defined by the drafter.

Dimensioning is a draw mode activity. Dimensions like text are information only; they do not exist as actual part geometry. Therefore all dimensions are two-dimensional. The same procedure is used when detailing a part generated on a two-dimensional as well as a three-dimensional system. Dimensions are not part of the model on a three-dimensional system.

Before proceeding with the details of dimensioning with CADD, an introduction to a few terms used throughout this discussion is necessary.

Dimension Line   This is a line with arrows at each end, drawn at the angle at which the dimension has been measured. The dimension text is situated along this line, sometimes dividing it into two lines. Usually, the dimension line is inside the measured area. Sometimes, however, it does not fit. In such

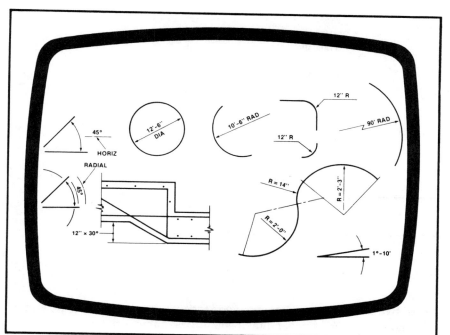

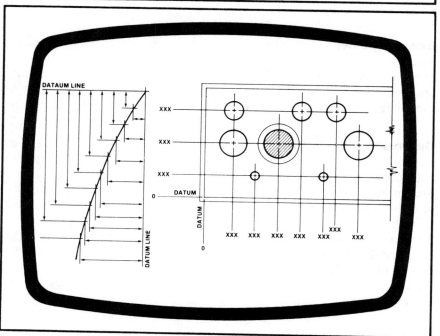

Figure 10–25
Variations in radial and angle dimensioning (top) and ordinate dimensioning (bottom). (Courtesy of Calma Company, a wholly-owned subsidiary of General Electric Company. U.S.A.)

Figure 10–26
Arrowhead variations.
(Reprinted with permission from Computervision Corporation, Bedford, Massachusetts)

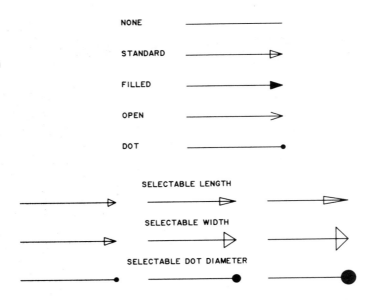

cases, two short lines are drawn outside the measured area, with the arrows pointing inward. For angular dimensioning, the dimension line is actually an arc.

Extension Lines   If the dimension line is drawn outside the object being measured, straight extension lines (called "witness lines" in some texts) are drawn from the object, perpendicular to the dimension line. Extension lines are used only in linear and angular dimensioning. Because they are sometimes superfluous, a means is provided to suppress one or both of them.

Dimension Text   This is a text string that usually specifies the actual measurement. Most CADD systems provide methods to use the measurement computed automatically by the system, supply different text, or suppress the text entirely. If the default text is used, instruct the system to append plus or minus tolerances to it automatically.

The text is created using the current text font. When using the default text, its format is governed by the default units selected before creating the part. The drafter can select "decimal degrees," "grads," "radians," or "degrees, minutes, and seconds" format for angular dimensions, and SI (metric), English units of "decimals," or "feet and inches" format for units of measurement.

Leaders   For some dimensioning and other annotations, the text may not fit comfortably next to the object it describes. In such cases, it is customary to place the text nearby and draw a leader line from the text to the object. For instance, when diameter or radius dimensioning is desired, but the arc or circle is too small for the dimension text to fit inside, a leader can be drawn from the text to the arc or circle.

Center Mark/Center Line A center mark is a small cross marking the center of a circle or arc. Center lines are broken lines crossing at the center and intersecting the circumference of the circle or arc at its quadrant points. A center mark and center lines are needed for all circular dimensions.

Layers The dimension line, extension lines, arrows, leaders, and dimension text are drawn as separate entities on the current layer. Thus, after a dimension has been drawn, it is possible to change the placement or content of the text. Many companies assign a particular layer for each activity; all ''design,'' construction, notes, and dimensioning may be on separate layers thereby making it easy for the drafters to locate information.

Dimensions and Scaling A drafter can change the viewing size of the part for dimensioning purposes. For example, if the part is increased in size for some reason (e.g., for visual clarification), dimensions created by the drafter will reflect the true size of the part and not the new viewing scale. In other words, the viewing size may be set at 2 to 1 but the dimensions will always be 1 to 1.

Dimensioning

When dimensioning a drawing, select **DIMENSION**. All systems provide CRT or tablet menus for quick and efficient dimensioning. Figure 10–27 shows a typical tablet menu with areas for selecting dimension parameters, changing existing dimensions, adding text, suppressing extension lines, altering the arrows' and leaders' style or location, and specifying the type of dimension and its tolerance. The right hand side of the menu is dedicated to geometric tolerancing feature control symbols.

The dimensioning instructions can be grouped into five categories:

1. Linear dimensioning
2. Angular dimensioning
3. Diameter dimensioning
4. Radius dimensioning
5. Labels

The capabilities in each category follow.

Figure 10–27
Dimensioning menu.

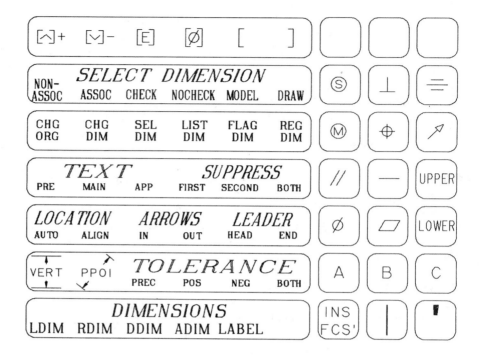

Linear Dimensioning

Horizontal. Creates a linear dimension with a horizontal dimension line (Figure 10–28). The drafter identifies the horizontal distance to be dimensioned with two digitizes and then places the dimension line and text with a third digitized location.

Vertical. Creates a linear dimension with a vertical dimension line (Figure 10–29).

Aligned. Creates a linear dimension with the dimension line parallel to the specified extension line origin points. This permits the alignment of the dimensioning notation (text) with the object.

Rotated (Point-to-Point). Creates a linear dimension with the dimension line drawn at a specified angle. An example of point-to-point dimensioning is provided later in the chapter.

Angular Dimensioning   Angular dimensioning creates an arc to show the angle between two nonparallel lines. The dimension can be either an inside angle or an outside angle. In Figure 10–30, examples of both inside (60 degrees) and outside (300 degrees) angular dimensioning are shown. For both types, the drafter inputs the command, identifies the two lines to be measured, and places the dimension with the third digitized location.

BEFORE

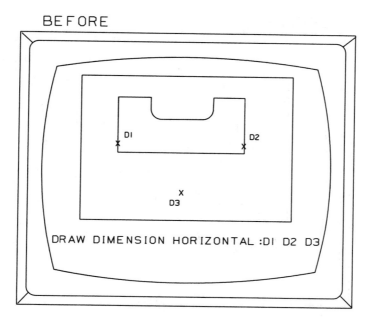

DRAW DIMENSION HORIZONTAL :DI D2 D3

AFTER

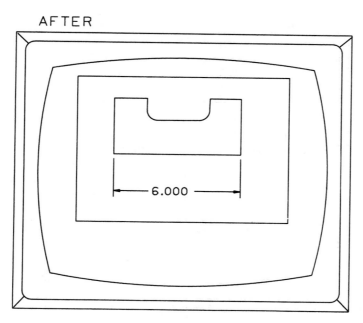

6.000

Figure 10–28
Placing a horizontal
dimension.

Figure 10–29
Placing a vertical
dimension.

BEFORE

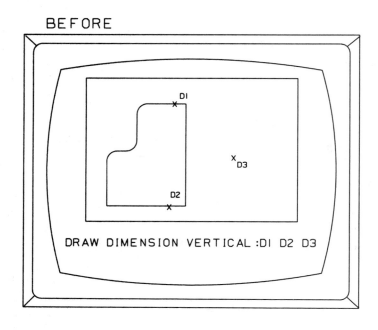

DRAW DIMENSION VERTICAL :DI D2 D3

AFTER

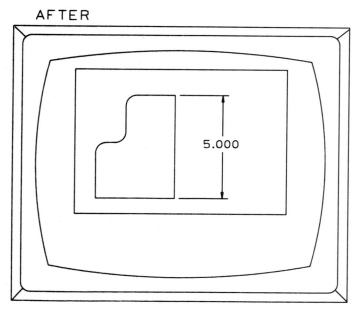

5.000

BEFORE

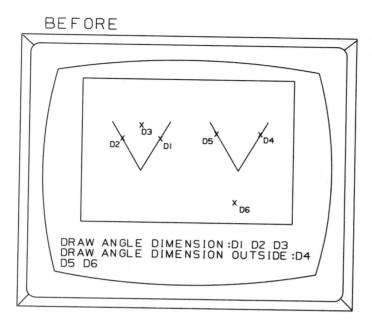

DRAW ANGLE DIMENSION:DI D2 D3
DRAW ANGLE DIMENSION OUTSIDE:D4
D5 D6

AFTER

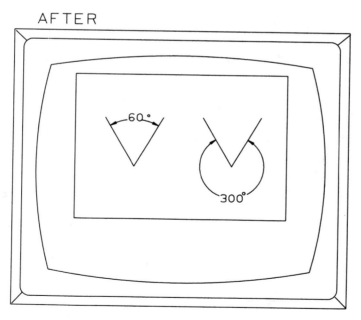

Figure 10–30
Placing angle dimen-
sions.

Figure 10–31
Placing radius and
diameter dimensions.

BEFORE

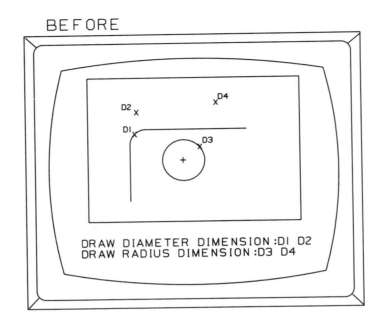

DRAW DIAMETER DIMENSION :DI D2
DRAW RADIUS DIMENSION :D3 D4

AFTER

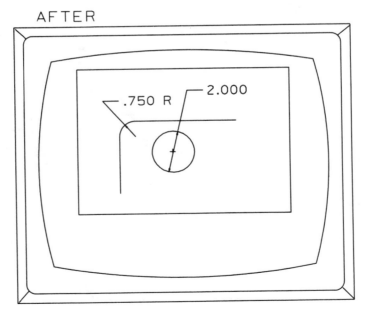

Diameter Dimensioning   When dimensioning the diameter of a circle or arc only two digitizes are required. After the command is input, the drafter identifies the circle or arc to be dimensioned and then places the dimension and the leader end with the second digitize (Figure 10–31).

Radius Dimensioning   Radius dimensioning is the same as diameter dimensioning, except that the system measures and then dimensions the radius of an arc or circle (Figure 10–31).

Dimension Standards

CADD systems permit the creation of linear, ordinate, angular, radial, and diameter dimensions which adhere to American National Standards Institute (ANSI) standards. On some systems, Japanese Industrial Standards (JIS) and the International Organization for Standardization (ISO) standards, which differ somewhat from the ANSI conventions, may be chosen. In brief, the differences between JIS, ISO, and ANSI standards are JIS and ISO standards require a solid dimension line as opposed to the ANSI standard which is a broken dimension line. Number and tolerance formats also differ. Symbols indicating a square end, diameter, or radius are prefixed to dimension values in the JIS and ISO method, whereas only radial dimensions are flagged for ANSI standard dimensions, and this symbol is unfixed. Adjoining arrowheads may be represented by a single dot for JIS and ISO standards.

Dimension Units

Any value for a dimension unit can be defined by the drafter to create dimensional information. The drafter can choose either metric or English standards. Both of these standards can have particular units specified for dimensions: inches, feet, yards, or miles for English; centimeters, millimeters, or kilometers for metric.

English or Metric Units   Some systems allow the automatic placement of English units on one layer and metric units on another. In addition, an option for dual dimensioning (to simultaneously dimension for English and metric values) may be available. The drafter dimensions the part once and the system automatically places the drafter-specified primary unit together with the secondary unit in one dimension. For example:

1.00		1.00
	or	
2.54		2.54 CM

Tolerance

Dimension tolerances can be specified. The system then can compute the tolerance stack-up of selected linear dimensions.

Dimension tolerances are plus or minus amounts that the system adds to the dimension text. The drafter can specify the plus and minus amounts; they may be equal or different. A typical mechanical design and drafting menu will have geometric control symbols available for dimensioning as shown in Figure 10–32. Feature control symbols and other items associated with geometric tolerancing (Figure 10–33) can be easily added to the drawing by picking the appropriate symbol and placing it by digitizing its location (Figure 10–34).

Limits The drafter can elect to have the tolerance values applied to the measurement. The default dimension text is then the resulting high and low limits rather than the nominal measurement with tolerances.

Tolerance can be represented as incremental, limit, or dash as shown below.

		+.01
Incremental	2.00	
		−.02
Limit	2.01	
	1.98	
Dash	2.01 − 1.98	

Associativity

Once a part is dimensioned, it is not unusual for design changes to take place. If the model has modifications, linear dimensions created by the draft-

Figure 10–32
Geometric tolerance menu.

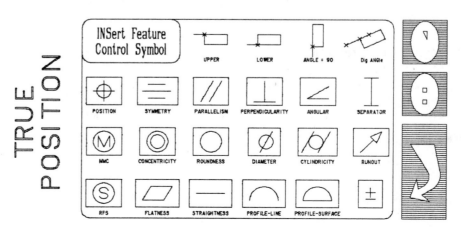

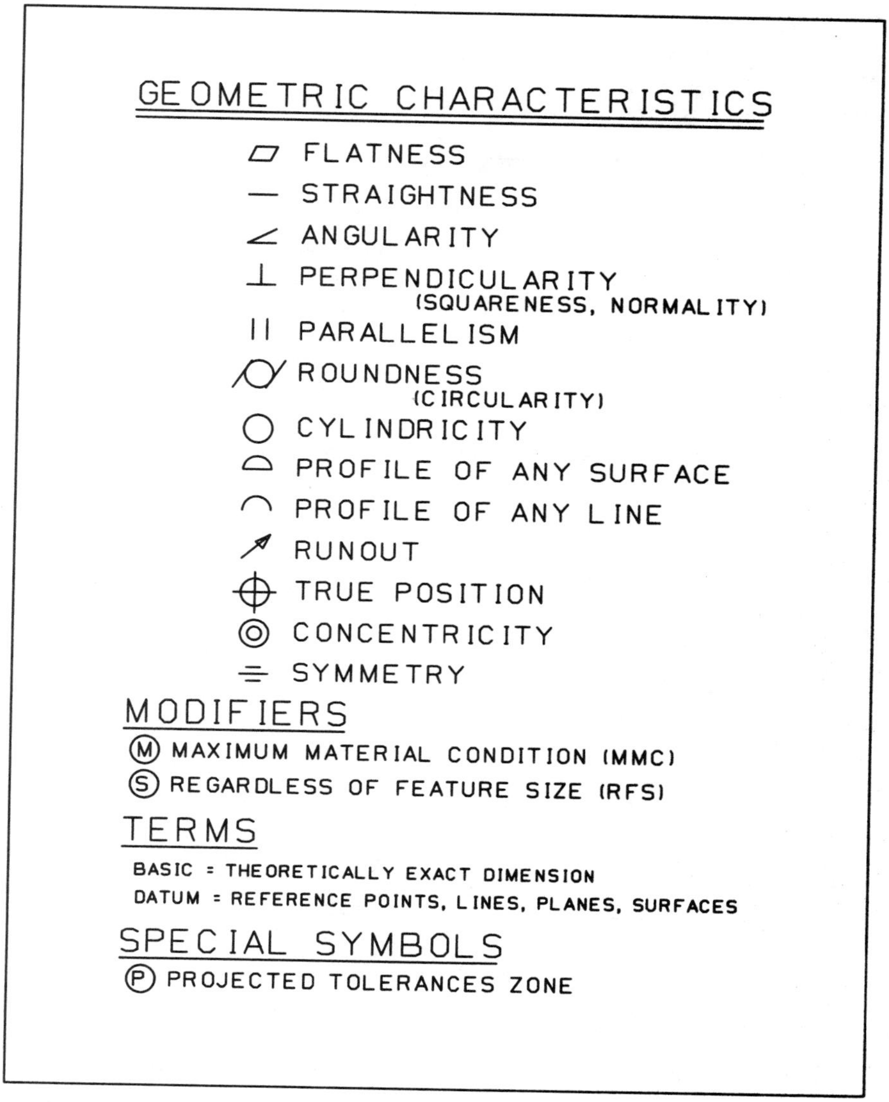

GEOMETRIC CHARACTERISTICS

⌑ FLATNESS

— STRAIGHTNESS

∠ ANGULARITY

⊥ PERPENDICULARITY
        (SQUARENESS, NORMALITY)

‖ PARALLELISM

⟋○ ROUNDNESS
        (CIRCULARITY)

○ CYLINDRICITY

⌒ PROFILE OF ANY SURFACE

⌒ PROFILE OF ANY LINE

⟋ RUNOUT

⊕ TRUE POSITION

◎ CONCENTRICITY

⹀ SYMMETRY

MODIFIERS

Ⓜ MAXIMUM MATERIAL CONDITION (MMC)

Ⓢ REGARDLESS OF FEATURE SIZE (RFS)

TERMS

BASIC = THEORETICALLY EXACT DIMENSION

DATUM = REFERENCE POINTS, LINES, PLANES, SURFACES

SPECIAL SYMBOLS

Ⓟ PROJECTED TOLERANCES ZONE

Figure 10–33
Geometric tolerancing symbols.

er will automatically be updated by the system to reflect those changes (Figure 10–35). The design on the left of the figure was the original dimensioned part. After design modifications to the part the dimensions were automatically updated by the system. This unique capability is not available on all systems.

DIMENSION ALL is available on some systems and is used when the part is to be dimensioned with the ordinate method. In this case, the drafter gives the command and identifies the two (X and Y) surfaces to be used as the control edges. Figure 10–25 (bottom) shows an example. Both associativ-

Figure 10–34
Placing feature control
symbols for geometric
tolerancing.

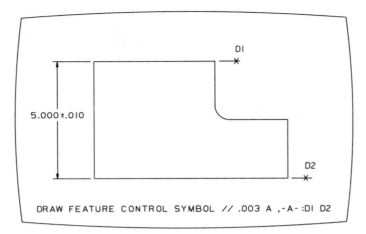

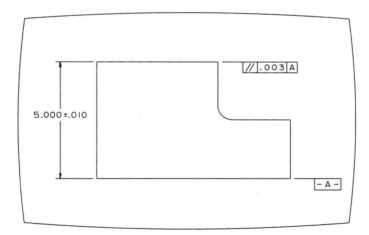

ity and DIMENSION ALL may still require alteration by the drafter for aesthetics. The drafter should never rely solely on the system, since the system can use incorrect dimensioning procedures. What is important is that the drafter know how to dimension using ANSI and other standards.

Preparing the Drawing: Two-Dimensional and Three-Dimensional Examples

Figures 10–36 through 10–44 show the step-by-step procedures used to detail the one-view drawing of the HOLD DOWN PLATE. The series starts with the part geometry already created (Figure 10–36). ZOOM WINDOW is

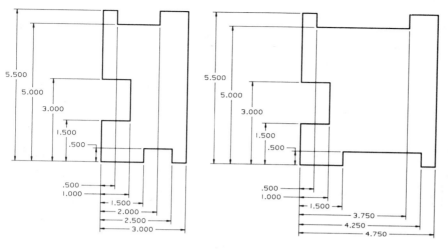

Figure 10–35
Associativity—The design on the left shows the original part geometry that was created and later dimensioned. The design on the right is the original part with design modifications made to it. The dimensions on the right were automatically updated when the modifications to the design were made. (Reprinted wiht permission from Computervision Corporation, Bedford, Massachusetts)

selected to show the portion of the part where a dimension is to be created. Figure 10–37 shows the before and after sequence for drawing a horizontal dimension on the lower portion of the piece. Not all of the parts dimensioning will be described in detail; only one example of each of the basic types will be shown.

A vertical dimension is created between the center of the hole and the bottom of the plate in Figure 10–38. Figure 10–39 shows an alternative to giving an angle dimension. Here a *"parallel"* or *"point to point"* dimension is created to measure the linear distance of the angled cut. ANGLE DIMEN-SION is used (Figure 10–40) to show the angle of the cut instead of using a point-to-point measurement. The diameter of the two small holes is dimensioned next (Figure 10–41). The large fillet is then dimensioned (Figure 10–42). Lastly the notes are added (Figure 10–43). Figure 10–44 shows the completed part with all dimensions on the drawing.

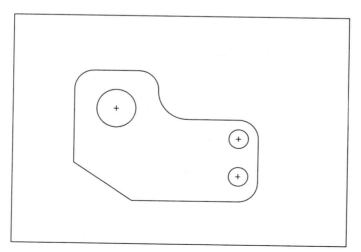

Figure 10–36
Single view drawing of the HOLD DOWN PLATE.

Figure 10–37
Placing a horizontal
dimension using the
zoom command to
enlarge the area to be
dimensioned and then
placing the dimension on
the HOLD DOWN PLATE.

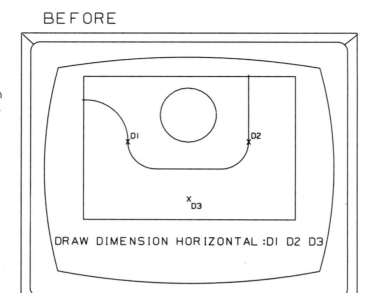

BEFORE

DRAW DIMENSION HORIZONTAL :DI D2 D3

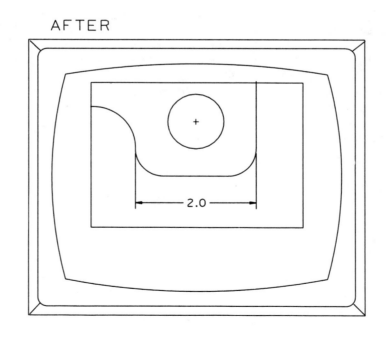

AFTER

BEFORE

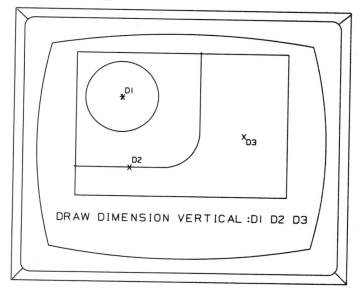

DRAW DIMENSION VERTICAL :DI D2 D3

AFTER

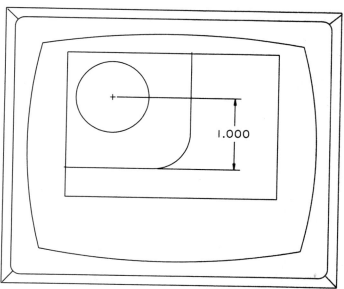

Figure 10–38
Dimensioning the vertical distance between the hole and the HOLD DOWN PLATE's lower edge.

Figure 10–39
Dimensioning the angled
cut of the HOLD DOWN
PLATE with point-to-point
linear dimensioning.

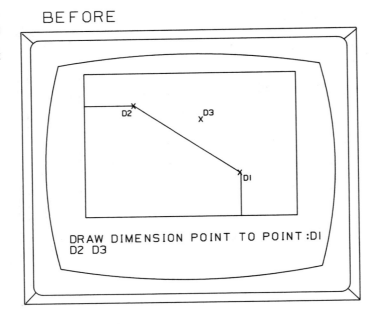

BEFORE

DRAW DIMENSION POINT TO POINT :DI
D2 D3

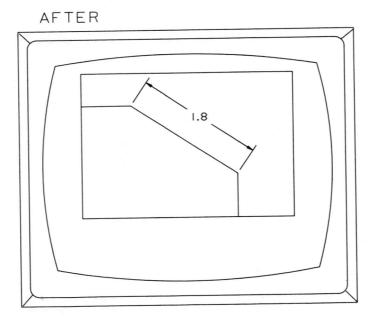

AFTER

BEFORE

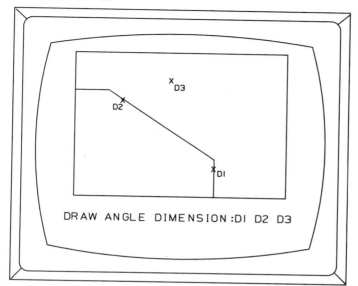

DRAW ANGLE DIMENSION :DI D2 D3

AFTER

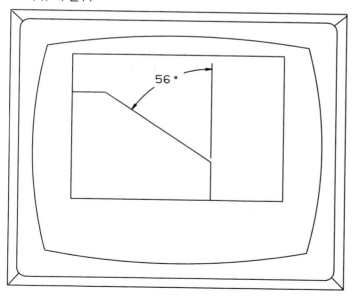

Figure 10–40
Dimensioning the angled
cut of the HOLD DOWN
PLATE using the angle
dimension.

Figure 10–41
Dimensioning the small
holes of the HOLD
DOWN PLATE.

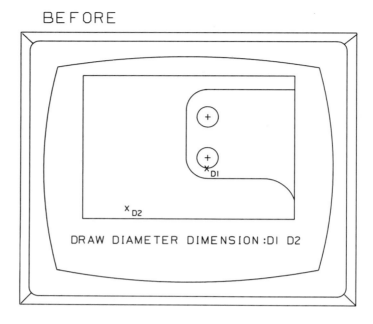

BEFORE

DRAW DIAMETER DIMENSION :DI D2

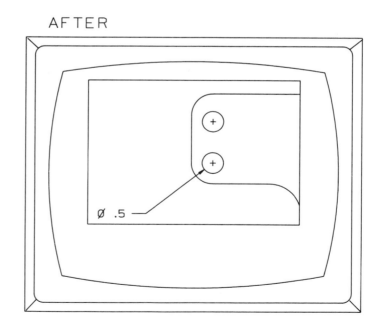

AFTER

Ø .5

BEFORE

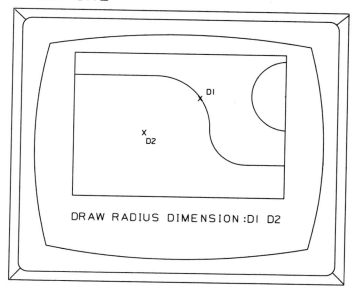

DRAW RADIUS DIMENSION :DI D2

Figure 10–42
Dimensioning the large radius of the HOLD DOWN PLATE.

AFTER

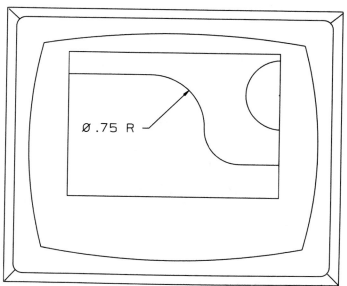

387

Figure 10–43
Placing the notes on the
HOLD DOWN PLATE.

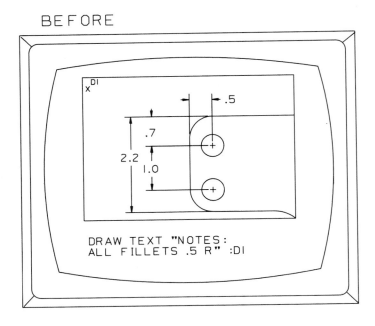

BEFORE

DRAW TEXT "NOTES:
ALL FILLETS .5 R" :DI

AFTER

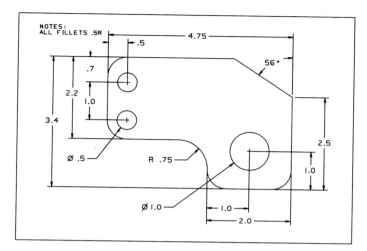

Figure 10–44
The completed detail of
the HOLD DOWN PLATE.

A three-dimensional system was used to create the BREAKER shown
as a three-dimensional finite element model in Figure 10–45. The drafter retrieves a **Form Part** drawing format from the part file and places the part in
it within predetermined views (Figure 10–46). The drafter then changes the
appearance of the model to conform to standard drafting conventions (e.g.,
the hidden lines are changed to dashed lines). Lastly the part is dimensioned
(Figure 10–47) using the same type of capabilities used in dimensioning two-
dimensional parts as shown in Figures 10–36 through 10–44.

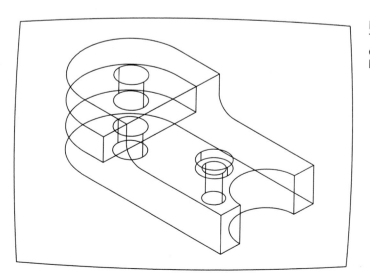

Figure 10–45
Three-dimensional finite
element model of the
BREAKER.

Figure 10–46
BREAKER placed in front
and top views with
border and title block
added to the "drawing."

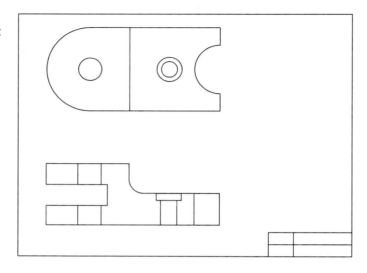

Figure 10–47
Completed detail of the
BREAKER.

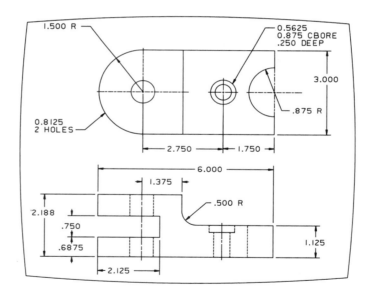

GLOSSARY

ANNOTATION The process of adding text, notes, or identification to a drawing, map, or diagram.

ANSI American National Standards Institute. An association formed by industry and the U.S. Government to produce and disseminate drafting and manufacturing standards.

ASSOCIATIVE DIMENSIONING   The means by which a CADD dimensioning program automatically updates the dimensions as the geometry changes.

ASSOCIATIVITY   The linking of parts, components, or elements with their attributes or with other geometric items.

AUTOMATIC DIMENSIONING   The CADD system computes the dimensions and automatically places dimensions, extension lines, and arrowheads where required.

BILL OF MATERIALS (BOM)   A listing of all the subassemblies, parts, materials, and quantities required to manufacture an assembly or to build a plant.

CARTESIAN COORDINATES   The distance of a point from any of three intersecting perpendicular planes; X, Y, Z coordinates.

COORDINATE DIMENSIONING   A system of dimensioning in which points are defined as being a specified distance and direction from a reference point.

CUT PLANE   A plane intersected with a three-dimensional object to derive a sectional view.

DATABASE   An organized collection of standard parts libraries, completed designs, documentation, and computer programs.

DEFAULT   The predetermined value of a parameter that is automatically supplied by the system whenever that value is not specified by the designer.

DELETE   To erase information from the computer's memory.

DESIGN FILE   The information in a CADD database which relates to a design project.

DETAIL DRAWINGS   The drawing of a single part with all the dimensions and annotations necessary to completely define the part for manufacturing and inspection.

EDIT   To change, add, or delete data.

FILLET   A rounded corner or arc that blends together two intersecting curves, lines, or surfaces.

FONT, LINE   Repetitive patterns used to make a line more easily recognized (e.g., a solid, dashed, or dotted line).

FONT, TEXT   An assortment of characters of a given size and style.

FORMAT   The specific arrangement of data for a list or report. A preprinted drawing border (i.e., title block and zones).

GRID   A matrix of uniformly spaced points displayed on the screen for approximately locating and digitizing a position or placing symbols in the creation of a schematic.

HIDDEN LINES   Line segments that would ordinarily be hidden from view in a three-dimensional view of a solid object because they are behind other items in the view.

LAYER   A logical concept used to distinguish subdividual group(s) of data within a given drawing. It may be thought of as a series of transparencies (overlayed) in any order, yet having no depth.

LAYOUT   A to-scale drawing of the physical components and the mechanical and electrical arrangement of a part, product, or plant.

MENU   A table of available commands, either on a digitizing tablet or on the CRT, that can be selected instead of using the keyboard.

MODEL   An accurate three-dimensional representation of a part, assembly, or plant designed on a CADD system and stored in the database.

MODELING   Constructing a mathematical or analytic model of a physical object or system for analysis.

ORIGIN   An X, Y or X, Y, Z coordinate from which all figures and entity locations are referenced.

ORTHOGRAPHIC   The method of making a layout, drawing, or map in which the projecting lines are perpendicular to the plane of the drawing or map.

SCALE   To enlarge or shrink an image without changing its shape.

SECTION   To cut an object with an intersecting plane, then show the total intersection geometry on the CRT.

SHAPE FILL   The automatic shading of an area on the CRT.

TEXT   Letters, numbers, and special characters.

TOLERANCE   The allowed variance from a given nominal dimension.

UPDATING   Changing a file by adding, modifying, or deleting information.

WORKING DRAWING   A detailed layout of a part with complete dimensions and notes.

QUIZ

True or False

1. The drawing mode is where the detailer "prepares the drawing" when a three-dimensional system is being used.

2. Dimensions, text, crosshatching, and feature control symbols are part of the parts model database.

3. A Form Part allows the detailer to recall a standard size drawing with predefined borders and title block.

4. A line font is a specific style of line used to represent a particular thing: piping, fencing, hidden lines, visible object lines, etc.

5. Center lines can be inserted only as model entities since they are an integral part of the object being represented.

6. A detailer can create only a limited variety of crosshatch patterns.

7. In order to insert a crosshatch pattern the boundary of the area to be hatched must be identified by digitizing the geometry items that surround it.

8. Annotation is the process of placing words, numbers, and lines on a drawing.

Fill in the Blank

9. Text is _____ and therefore does not exist as a geometry item of the part.

10. Most text is aligned along its _____ side. This is called _____ .

11. Default values for text fonts can be altered with _____ _____ .

12. _____ is the procedure of adding_____to a drawing.

13. With DIMENSION the designer can _____ either or both of the extension lines.

14. The ability of the system to update dimensions automatically by the system after design changes have been made is called_____.

15. _____ _____ will completely dimension the part using the ordinate system.

16. Many _____ can be created using the same part model database.

Answer the Following

17. Describe the differences between the model and the draw mode and what type of activity takes place in the draw mode. Be specific.

18. Describe the difference between the detailing process of a three-dimensional system and a two-dimensional system.

19. How can the Form Parts capability of a three-dimensional system save the detailer time?

20. Explain five modifier variations for inserting center lines.

21. What is a hatch pattern and when is it used? What is a designer-defined pattern?

22. What is a text string and how is it typically created on a drawing?

23. Explain the possible parameters that can be selected when creating text.

24. Name the four types of linear dimensions and describe the process of placing each on a part.

Problems

25. Draw the ANGLE BLOCK (Figure 10–48). Complete the front and side view showing the 25 diameter hole going through the part. Draw the

Figure 10–48

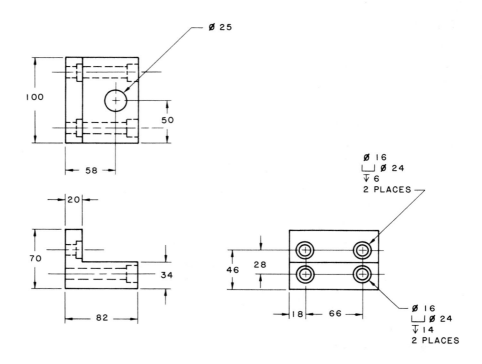

Figure 10–49

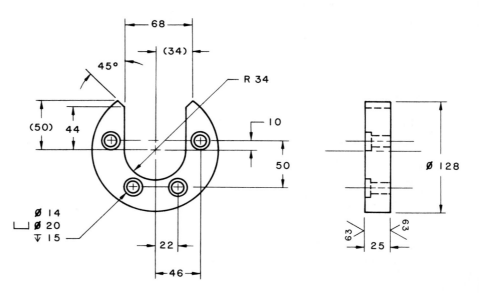

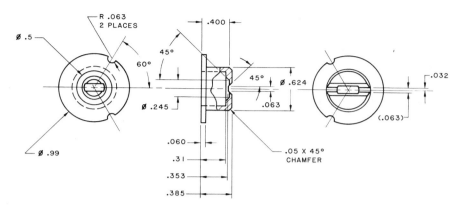

Figure 10–50

front view as a section passing through the 25 diameter hole. Dimension completely.

26. Draw the HOLDING PLATE (Figure 10–49) and dimension completely.

27. Draw the RETAINING RING (Figure 10–50) with a full section side view. Dimension completely.

28. Draw the RING SLEEVE as shown in Figure 10–51. Dimension completely.

29. Draw the ANGLE PLATE (Figure 10–52) and dimension completely.

30. Draw the Proto Draft Module CLAMP (Figure 10–53) and dimension completely. (Original part Courtesy South-Western Publishing Co.)

31. Draw the Proto Draft Module BASE ANGLE (Figure 10–54) and dimension completely. (Original part Courtesy South-Western Publishing Co.)

32. Draw the Proto Draft Module BREAKER (Figure 10–55) and dimension completely. (Original part Courtesy South-Western Publishing Co.)

33. Draw the Proto Draft Module POST REEL (Figure 10–56) and dimension completely. (Original part Courtesy South-Western Publishing Co.)

34. Draw the Proto Draft Module ANCHOR (Figure 10–57) and dimension completely. (Original part Courtesy South-Western Publishing Co.)

35. Draw the Proto Draft Module ANGLE FRAME (Figure 10–58) and dimension completely. (Original part Courtesy South-Western Publishing Co.)

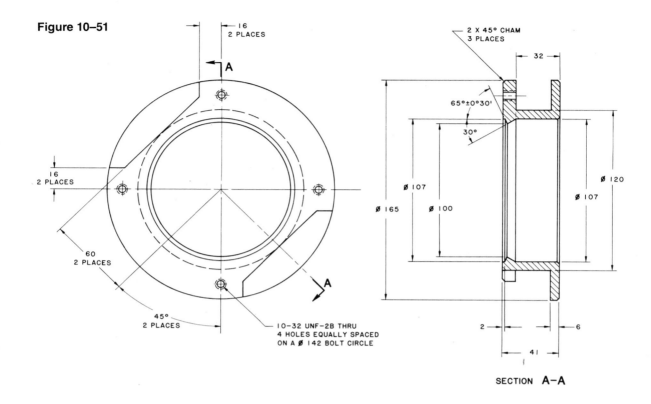

Figure 10–51

16
2 PLACES

A

16
2 PLACES

60
2 PLACES

45°
2 PLACES

10-32 UNF-2B THRU
4 HOLES EQUALLY SPACED
ON A Ø 142 BOLT CIRCLE

A

2 X 45° CHAM
3 PLACES

32

65°±0°30'

30°

Ø 107
Ø 165
Ø 100
Ø 120
Ø 107

2
6

41

SECTION A-A

Figure 10–52

.50

6.62

30°

1.00

1.00

(8.500)

9.75

(4.94)

(5.81)

4.250

Ø .375 THRU
3 HOLES

6.125

.50

13.486

(14.82)

(15.32)

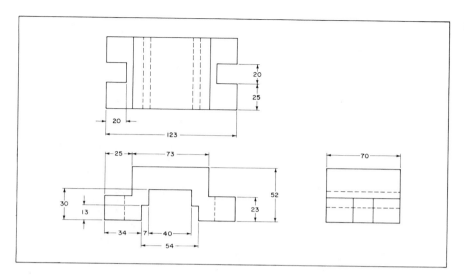

Figure 10–53

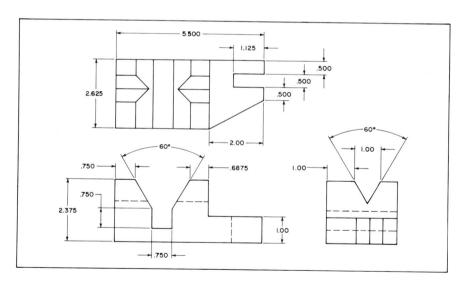

Figure 10–54

397

Figure 10–55

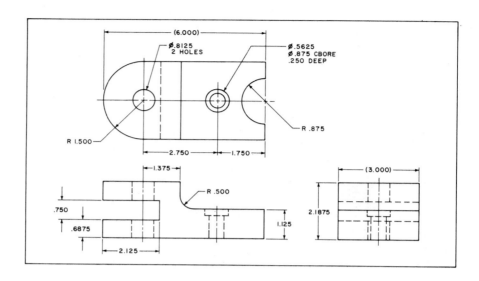

Figure 10–56

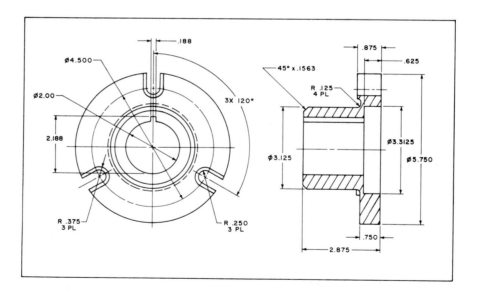

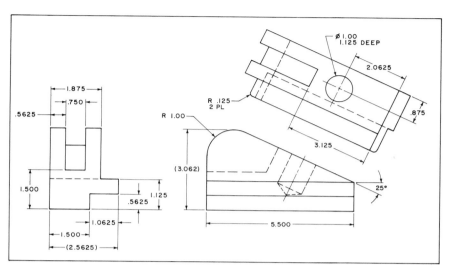

Figure 10–57

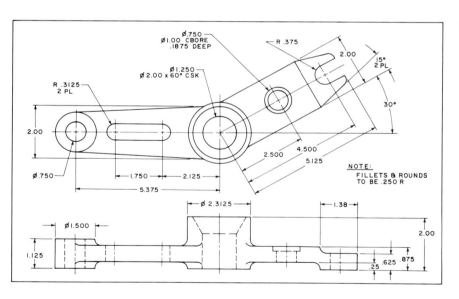

Figure 10–58

Chapter

Plotting and Archiving

Objectives

Upon completion of this chapter the reader will be able to:

- Plot a drawing.
- Explain the difference between check plots and final plots.
- Describe the uses and procedures for archiving.
- Define the plotting options available for most plotters.
- Understand the plotting procedure for a typical system.
- List and explain the various media available for archiving a drawing.

Introduction

Once a drawing or a part of a drawing is completed, either save it for safe-keeping or recreate the drawing on paper or plastic film by *plotting*.

The designer has a choice of making a reproduction (plotting) on paper at any time while making a drawing. For check prints or rough copies, electrostatic plotters (Figure 11–1) or thermal printers are used. For high quality output, pen plotters (Figure 11–2) are used on various drafting media such as Mylar, vellum, or paper.

When a drawing is no longer needed for a job or the designer doesn't need it immediately, the drawing can be saved safely; this filing process is called *archiving*.

Plotting

The designer can plot a hardcopy of the drawing at any stage in its development. Check plots can be produced while the drawing is in progress to check for positioning and dimensioning errors that might not be immediately apparent on the CRT. When the drawing is complete, the final plot is done to produce the finished drawing (Figure 11–3). **PLOT** makes a hardcopy of a drawing. The entire drawing or portion of it (Figure 11–4) can be plotted. The designer must specify the type and size of the plotter to be used. The designer has the option of specifying various plot characteristics, such as plotting scale and paper size.

Plotter Type and Size   Select the plotting menu to indicate the plotter type and paper size to be used. Any plotter that the CADD system supports can

Figure 11–1
Electrostatic plotter.
(Courtesy Versatec
Corp.)

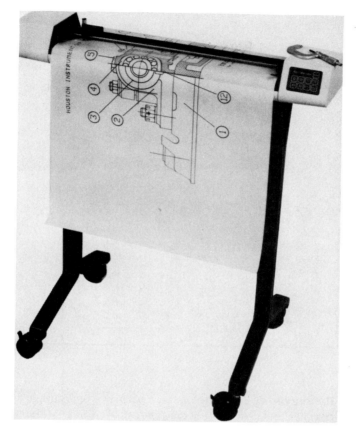

Figure 11–2
Pen plotter. (Courtesy Houston Instrument)

be used. See PLOT in the CADD system reference manual or on-line help on the CRT for a list of the supported plotters.

Plotting Options When plotting, specify the following:

- Automatic generation of borders
- Colors of entities
- Layering/pen scheme
- Portion of the paper to be used
- Scale
- Paper size
- Font style

Figure 11–3
Plotted drawing.
(Courtesy T&W Systems)

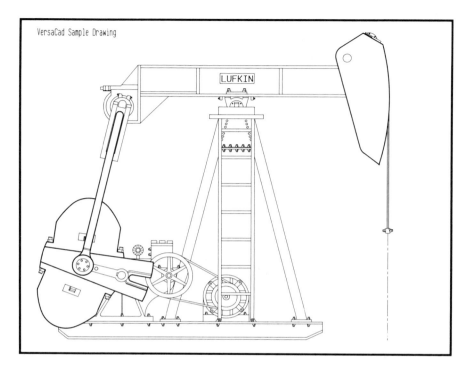

VersaCad Sample Drawing

Pen/Layering Scheme Many CADD systems supply a default pen scheme that assigns colors to specific pen slots in the plotter carousel. The default can be altered to:

- Reassign the pen/color assignments
- Assign pens to layers instead of colors

Plotter Definition When plotting, the system reads a file that contains information about the plotter. This file is stored along with the CADD part program and is accessible from the operating system but not from within the part file. Since the information contained in this file reflects the manufacturer's specifications for the plotters, most designers will never need to access it. Access the file to change:

- Plotter pen force—allows reduction or increase in the force for different types of pen point.
- Default pen speed—changes the pen speed for particular plots or changes the value here to be valid for all plots.

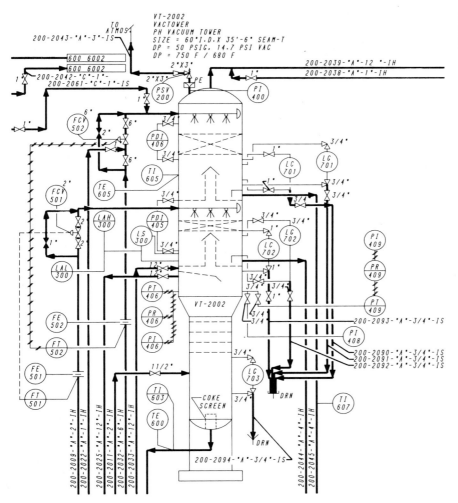

Figure 11-4
Portion of a plotted piping flow diagram.

- Paper size—adds nonstandard paper sizes to the existing standard sizes defined in the file.

Changing the Pen/Color Assignments Color is used to associate geometry items with pens of different widths. Many pen files can be created for different projects by saving the pen file under a different name and retaining the default pen file. Change the existing pen speed and enter varying speeds for different pen widths. If there is no value in the pen speed, the system defaults to the pen speed listed in the plotter file associated with the plotter.

Assigning Layers to Pens If pens are usually assigned to layers instead of colors, a default pen file that lists available layers should be made. The default pen file supplied with the system is for design organizations that assign pens according to color. The LAYER modifier must be used when plotting a drawing with a pen file that references layers instead of colors.

Plotting–An Example of Plotting a Drawing Using AutoCAD

Plot a drawing on either a pen plotter or an electrostatic plotter. Use whichever one seems more appropriate for a particular plot. Pen plotters are very accurate and many can plot on large paper sizes or in multiple colors. In general, electrostatic plotters have limited resolution and smaller paper sizes, and most produce monochrome output. Electrostatic plotters are usually faster than pen plotters.

In this chapter the terms plot and plotter are used in a generic sense, referring either to a pen plotter or an electrostatic plotter. When a distinction must be made, the type of device is indicated explicitly. The first thing to decide is which portion of the drawing to plot. When beginning a plot, the system may prompt for this information as follows:

Specify the part of the drawing to be plotted by entering:

Display, Extents, Limits, View, or Window <D>:

The response will specify a rectangular area of the drawing. The various options are described below. Each can be abbreviated to one letter. The option selected will be remembered and used as the default in the next plot. For the first plot, the default is D (for Display).

D (Display) The Display option requests a plot of the view that is currently shown on the CRT. When plotting a specified drawing, the Display option plots the view that was shown on the CRT just prior to the last SAVE of that drawing.

E (Extents) The plot will consist of that portion of the drawing which currently contains geometry.

L (Limits) The ''Limits'' option will plot the entire drawing area as defined by the drawing limits.

V (View) The View option is used to plot a view that was previously saved. This option is applicable only if the drawing contains named views. When this option is chosen, the system prompts:

View name:

Enter the name of the particular view to be plotted.

W (Window)   Using the Window option, plot any portion of the drawing by specifying a lower left corner and an upper right corner of the plot "window." The system prompts:

First point:

Second point:

The drawing is still on the CRT at this point and a pointing device can be used to designate the desired window if that area is totally visible on the CRT. If the area wanted is not on the CRT, enter the two requested points from the keyboard, in drawing units.

Once the portion of the drawing to be plotted has been chosen, the system will display the basic plot specifications and ask if any of them should be changed. For example:

Sizes are in Inches

Plotting area is 15.75 wide by 11.20 high (MAX size)

Plot origin is at (0.00,0.00)

Pen width is 0.010

Area fill will be adjusted for pen width

Plot will be scaled to fit available area

Do you want to change anything?<N>

These specifications were initially set when this plotter was attached to the system. The stored values can be used by responding "N" to the prompt or by pressing RETURN.

If the response is "Y" to the prompt, any or all of the basic plot specifications can be changed. But if the plotter supports multiple pens, hardware line types, or software-controlled pen speed, the specifications of these things can be modified. A list of the current values is displayed, as shown in Table 11–1.

Each layer of a drawing has a color associated with it. Each color may be plotted with a different plotter line type, pen, and pen speed. If the plotter supports multiple line types, the "Line types" display shows what patterns are available.

For plotters with software-selectable pen speeds, the fastest speed is normally used. A slower speed can be chosen on a pen-by-pen basis. This can be useful if, for example, there is one pen that skips if it is moved too fast.

A feature of some systems makes it possible to assign different pen numbers to different layer colors even for single-pen plotters. If this option is chosen when the plotter is attached, the system will pause each time a new pen is needed and prompt you to change the pen.

Table 11–1

Current values

Layer Color	Pen No.	Line Type	Pen Speed
1 (red)	1	0	38
2 (yellow)	2	0	38
3 (green)	3	0	38
4 (cyan)	4	0	38
5 (blue)	5	0	38
6 (magenta)	6	0	38
7 (white)	7	0	38
8	8	0	38

Line types	0 = Continuous line
	1 = ...
	2 = ...
	3 = --------------------
	4 = - - - - - - - - - - - - -

If the answer is "Y" to the question "Do you want to change any of these parameters?" the system will prompt:

Enter values. Blank = Next value, Cn = Color n, S = Show current values, X = Exit

Layer	Pen	Line	Pen
Color	No.	Type	Speed

(current values for this color)   (parameter to change)

The system begins by showing the pen number, line type, and pen speed currently assigned to color 1 and asks first for a new pen number. After a pen number is entered, the system asks for a line type and then a pen speed for color 1. It then proceeds to color 2 and goes through the same sequence of pen number, line type, and pen speed. At every step, the "parameter to change" prompt shows the current value; you can retain that value and proceed to the next parameter by pressing space or RETURN.

When the pen and line type are specified, the system will ask about the basic plot specification, such as "size units."

Most systems allow either inches or millimeters as the units to be used for all plot size specifications. When the following prompt appears:

Size units (Inches or Millimeters) <currents>:

enter "I" to give plot sizes in inches, or "M" to use millimeters. The current choice is shown in corner brackets; retain it by entering blank or RETURN. The next prompt is:

Plot origin in units <default X,Y>:

Table 11–2

Standard values for plotting size		
Size	Width	Height
A	10.50	8.00
B	16.00	10.00
C	21.00	16.00
D	33.00	21.00
E	43.00	33.00
MAX	44.72	35.31
USER	8.00	11.00

where "units" are "Inches" or "Millimeters." The plot normally begins in the lower left corner of the paper. Place the plot origin at another location on the paper by entering the plotter coordinates of the desired origin point, using the "size units" (inches or millimeters) that were selected above. For example, if inches were selected as the plot size units, entering "2.3" would set the plot origin to the point 2 inches to the right of and 3 inches above the position.

Next, the system lists the plotting sizes that the plotter can accommodate. If any of these sizes match a standard ANSI (if inches) or DIN (if millimeters) size, the mnemonic for that size is listed. Also included in the list is a special "MAX" size. This is the maximum size that the plotter can handle; it may be larger than the largest of the standard sizes. If the size has been set to something other than a standard size or MAX, that size will appear in the table with the label "USER" (Table 11–2).

Select one of the standard sizes from the list (or "MAX" or "USER" if shown) by typing in the mnemonic listed in the "Size" column. Alternatively, an explicit paper width and height can be entered separated by a comma (in inches or millimeters, whichever are the "size units"). For example:

Enter the Size or Width, Height (in Inches) <MAX>: *8.511*

A two-dimensional plot can be rotated 90 degrees on the paper. This will move the point that would have been at the lower left corner of the plot to the upper left corner, and the point that would have been at the upper left corner to the upper right corner.

The width of the pen tip to be used must be specified. This governs how much work must be done to "fill" a solid, trace, or wide line. During the plot specifications dialogue the system will prompt:

Pen width <default>:

Enter a new value in the size units previously specified (inches or millimeters). If retaining the default value is preferred, reply with a blank or RETURN.

Next, the system asks for the plot scale. The prompt is:

Specify scale by entering:
Plotted units = Drawing units or Fit or ? <default>:

where "units" are whatever was previously chosen for the size units (inches or millimeters). As indicated, there are three ways to respond. If "Fit" (or simply "F") is entered, the system will scale the plot so the view chosen (the portion of the drawing to be plotted) is made as large as possible for the specified paper size.

If an explicit scale for the plot is desired, tell the system how many drawing units are to be plotted per inch (or per millimeter) on the paper. Just enter the number of plotter units and the number of drawing units, separated by an equal sign ("="). For example:

Specify scale by entering:
Plotted Inches = Drawing units or Fit or ? <F>: *1 = 1*

would produce a plot at a scale of 1 drawing unit per inch on the plotter. Now suppose that drawing units represent kilometers and plotter size units are millimeters. Then:

Specify scale by entering:
Plotted Millimeters = Drawing units or Fit or ? <F>: *2.5 = 1*

would produce a plot in which 2.5 millimeters represented a kilometer.

If "feet and inches" mode has been selected for the drawing and inches selected as the plot size units, the plot scale can be entered in terms of feet and inches. For example, suppose a plot where one-quarter inch on the paper is equivalent to 1 foot needs to be produced. Enter:

1/4" = 1'

The part of the drawing you selected to plot won't always be fitted exactly to the plot area on the paper, specified by the plotting size.

1. If the scale specification was by "Fit," only one of the dimensions of the drawing area, horizontal or vertical, will be fitted to the corresponding dimension of the plot area. Blank space will be left along the top or right edge of the plot area unless the drawing area has the same shape as the plot area.

2. If an explicit plot scale is specified, the selected drawing area may map into an area either larger or smaller than the plot area. If larger, it will be truncated at the bounds of the plot area. If smaller, some space in the plot area will be left unused.

The current plot specifications are remembered in a special file. Whenever plot parameters are changed, the new values are stored so they don't have to be re-entered every time something is plotted.

When all the plot specifications are set satisfactorily, the system displays the message:

Effective plotting area: ww wide by hh high

where "ww" and "hh" are measurements in the current size units. It then pauses to permit paper and pens to be loaded into the plotter, prompting with "Position paper in plotter."

Press RETURN to continue or S to Stop for hardware setup.

If the response to this prompt is RETURN, the system will send a "reset" function to the plotter and begin plotting. Some plotters have additional features, such as selectable pen pressure and acceleration. It is usually possible to enter the desired values at the plotter's control panel.

Archiving

All of the information in the computer's memory is lost if the computer is turned off. Thus, using computers for design and drafting would not be a very productive tool to produce drawings if all the work were lost when the computer was turned off. Therefore, the drawings and any information processed by the computer must be permanently stored. Common methods for permanently storing information include magnetic tape, floppy and hard disks, and punch tape.

Magnetic tape is most commonly used on large computer systems to archive drawings. *Archiving* is the process of permanently storing a drawing or data on magnetic tape which is then stored in a safe place to prevent accidental loss due to fire or some other unexpected disaster.

Archiving is the technique used to store drawings or text. This is also the technique used when drawings or text must be retrieved for revisions or use. Archiving is like a bank account. Something must be put in the account to get anything out. One form is used to deposit funds, and another form to withdraw funds. To store drawings or text *archive out* from the user disk to an archive disk or tape; for retrieval, *archive in* from an archive disk or tape to the user disk.

Floppy disk and hard disk storage are the most common methods of storing information on workstation and PC-based CADD systems. Floppy disks are available in different sizes, and they can store in excess of 1 million bytes of information. Hard disks usually come in an airtight fixed cabinet, commonly called a Winchester disk drive, or in cartridge form, sometimes referred to as a disk pack. Storage capacities of hard disks greatly exceed those of floppy disks. Winchester disks have storage capacities in the range of 5 to 40 million bytes of information. See Chapter 2 for examples of disk drives and other storage related equipment.

Cartridge type disks have storage capacities of as much as 600 million bytes of information. Punched cards are not in great use today; however, the use of punched tape for memory storage is still a common method used to store programs for computer-controlled machines.

GLOSSARY

ARCHIVE   Placing infrequently used data in auxiliary storage.

AUXILIARY STORAGE   Storage devices other than the main memory, also called peripheral storage. For example, disk drives, magnetic tape.

BACKUP COPY   A copy of a file that is kept for (safe-keeping) reference in case the original file is destroyed.

COMPUTER OUTPUT MICROFILM (COM)   The image of a drawing plotted on 35mm film at a small scale by a beam of light, or microfilm containing computer-generated data. Also, to place computer-generated data on microfilm.

DIRECTORY   The location on the disk where the names of files and information about them are stored.

DISK   A circular plate of magnetic media on which information is stored.

DISK DRIVE   The device that reads data from or writes data on magnetic disks.

DISK STORAGE   The use of magnetic disks as a storage device.

DRUM PLOTTER   An electromechanical pen plotter that draws a picture on paper or film mounted on a drum using a combination of plotting head movement and drum rotation.

ELECTROSTATIC PLOTTER   Wire nibs, spaced 100 to 400 nibs per inch, that place dots where needed on a piece of paper to generate a drawing.

FILE   A name set of data on magnetic disk or tape. Also, to transfer the contents of working storage to permanent storage.

FILE MANAGEMENT SYSTEM   A software system that provides control of input, output, physical storage, and logical relationships for data files.

FLATBED PLOTTER   An electromechanical pen plotter that draws a picture on paper, glass, or film mounted on a flat table. The plotting head moves in both axial directions.

FORMAT   The specific arrangement of data for a list or report. A preprinted drawing border (i.e., title block and zones).

HARDCOPY   A copy, on paper, of what is shown on the screen, generated with an on-line printer or plotter.

MAGNETIC DISK   A flat circular plate with a magnetic surface on which data can be recorded and from which data can be read. The data can be randomly accessed.

MAGNETIC DRUM   A cylinder with a magnetic surface on which data can be recorded and from which data can be read.

MAGNETIC TAPE   A tape with a magnetic surface on which data can be recorded and from which data can be read. The data can only be sequentially accessed. The access speed is constrained by the location of the data on the tape, the speed of the tape drive, and the density of the data on the tape.

MAIN STORAGE   The general-purpose storage of a computer, program-addressable, from which instructions can be executed and from which data can be loaded directly into registers.

OUTPUT   The end result of a process or series of processes, such as artwork, hardcopy, reports, and drawings.

OUTPUT DEVICE   Hardware, such as a printer or plotter, used to produce a copy of the results of the computer's processing operations.

PEN PLOTTER   An electromechanical CADD output device that draws a picture on paper or film using a ballpoint pen or liquid ink.

PERIPHERALS   Devices connected to a computer such as tape drives, disks, workstations, and plotters.

PERMANENT STORAGE   The location, outside the central processing unit, where completed data is stored, such as a disk or tape.

PHOTOPLOTTER   A device used to generate artwork photographically for PC boards.

PLOT   Drawing by pen, pencil, or electrostatics of a design on paper film to create a drawing.

PLOTTER   An automated device used to produce accurate drawings. Plotters include electrostatic, photoplotter, and pen.

REPEATABILITY (OF A PLOTTER)   A measure of the hardware accuracy or the coincidence of successive retraces of a display element.

SATELLITE   A remote system, connected to a host system, that contains processors, memory, and mass storage to operate independently from the host.

SAVE   To transfer the data created at the workstation to a storage device.

WINDOW   A portion or view of a design that is framed by a view port.

WINDOWING   Proportionally enlarging a figure or portion of a figure so it fills the screen or view port.

QUIZ

True or False

1. Storing a drawing in a safe place for future use is called plotting.

2. The designer has the option of plotting the entire drawing or a portion of it.

3. Electrostatic plotters are usually faster than pen plotters.

4. For plotters with software-selectable pen speeds, the slowest speed is normally used.

5. Paper tape is most commonly used on large computer systems to archive drawings.

6. Floppy disk and hard disk storage are the most common methods of storing information on workstation and PC-based CADD systems.

7. Storage capacities of hard disks greatly exceed those of floppy disks.

8. Pen plotters have limited resolution and small paper sizes.

Fill in the Blank

9. The designer can plot a _____ of the drawing at any stage in its development.

10. When the drawing is complete, the _____ _____ is done to produce the finished drawing.

11. _____ is used to associate geometry with pens of different widths.

12. Each _____ of a drawing has a color associated with it.

13. Most systems allow the designer to choose either _____ or _____ as the units to be used for all plot size specifications.

14. _____ is the process of permanently storing a drawing in a safe place.

15. _____ disks usually come in an airtight fixed cabinet, commonly called a _____ disk drive.

16. Storage capacities of _____ disks greatly exceed those of _____ disks.

Answer the Following

17. Discuss when a designer would use an electrostatic plotter versus a pen plotter.

18. Discuss at least four of the plotting options that are available on most systems.

19. Explain how to plot a small portion of a drawing.

20. Discuss when to use a slower pen speed for the plotter.

21. Define archiving and when it is used.

22. Discuss the various types of disk drives.

23. How are different colors plotted with a one pen plotter?

24. Discuss how to choose an origin other than the lower left hand corner of the drawing for a plot.

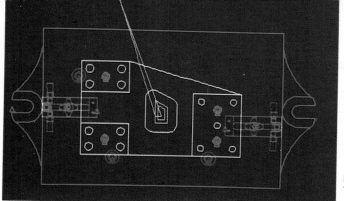

Plate 34
Tool fixture design using CADD software. (Courtesy Jergens Inc.)

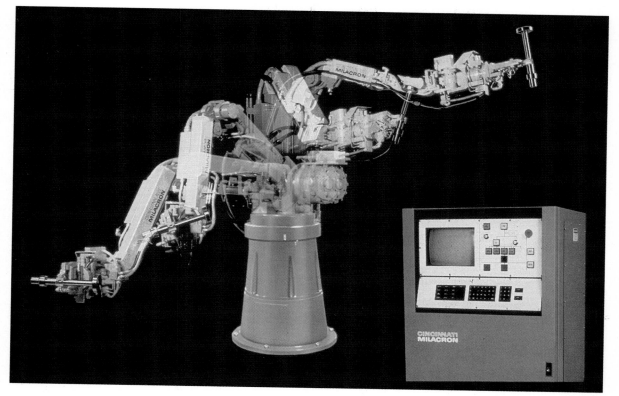

Plate 35
Industrial robot.
(Courtesy Cincinnati Milacron)

Plate 36
Control panel and arm of an industrial robot.
(Courtesy Cincinnati Milacron.)

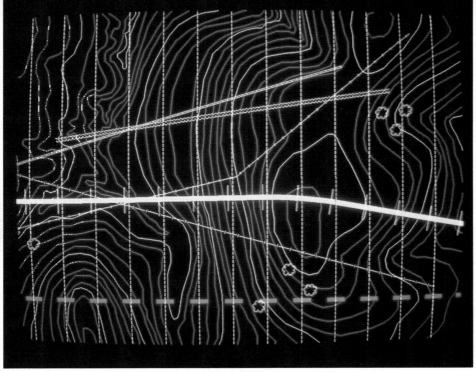

Plate 37
Data collected from field measurements or contour maps becomes the base map upon which the civil engineer can graphically experiment with alternative horizontal alignments. (Courtesy McDonnell Douglas Information Systems Group.)

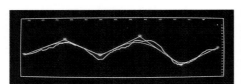

Plate 38
Existing ground profile information along this horizontal alignment is automatically generated. The engineer can add and graphically fine tune the proposed vertical control. (Courtesy McDonnell Douglas Information Systems Group.)

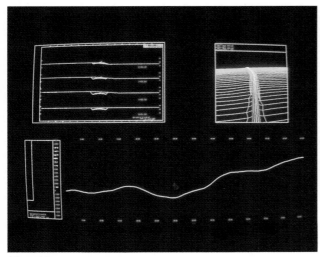

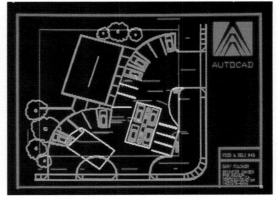

Plate 40
Site plan drawing produced by Gary Fulcher, Brighter Images, Lafayette, California, designed on AutoCAD. (Courtesy Autodesk, Inc.)

Plate 39
Define typical roadway cross-sections and the design is complete. Graphical options provide a variety of mechanisms for evaluation of this design, including cross-section plots, mass haul diagrams, perspectives, etc. (Courtesy McDonnell Douglas Information Systems Group.)

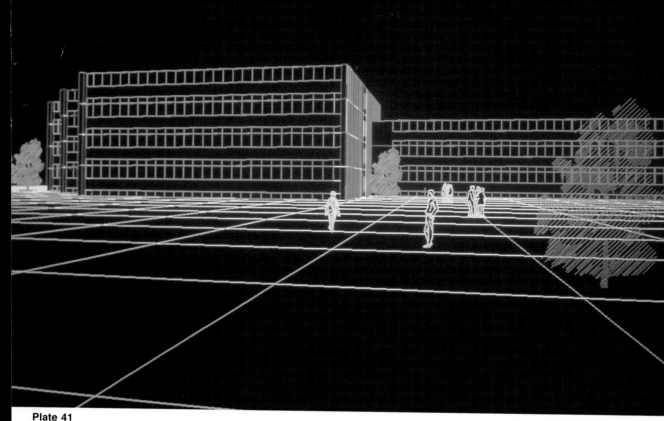

Plate 41
Perspective at the McDonnell Douglas ISG Campus in the Building Design Systems. (Courtesy McDonnell Douglas Information Systems Group.)

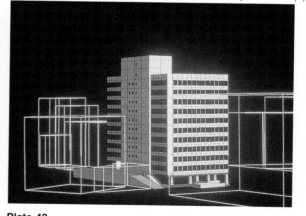

Plate 43
Solids and color shading used with wireframe to view the building and its surroundings. (Courtesy McDonnell Douglas Information Systems Group.)

Plate 42
Solids and color shading used to realistically show how the building will appear. (Courtesy McDonnell Douglas Information Systems Group.)

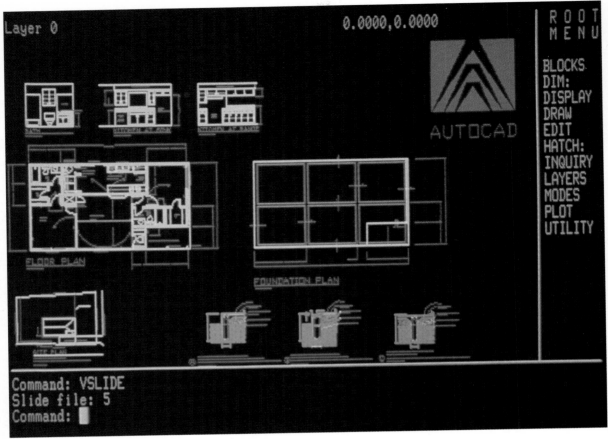

Plate 44
Two-dimensional layout and detail of a house plan. (Courtesy Autodesk, Inc.)

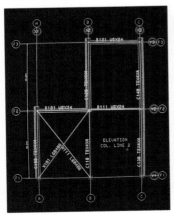

Plate 45
Using these base plans, the engineer graphically inputs a structural grid, structural geometry, and member properties without typing in coordinates of data. (Courtesy McDonnell Douglas Information Systems Group.)

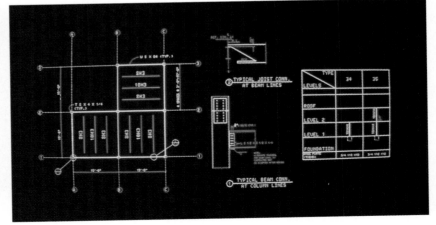

Plate 46
Member profiles can be graphically checked before proceeding with analysis. After the structural analysis is performed, results can be displayed using moment, sheer, axial force, and deflected shape diagrams. (Courtesy McDonnell Douglas Information Systems Group.)

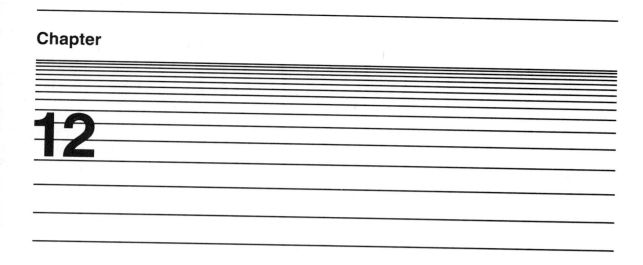

Chapter

12

Computer-Aided Manufacturing

Objectives

Upon completing this chapter the reader will be able to do the following:

- List the uses and reasons for the integration of computers into the manufacturing cycle

- Explain the advantages of using a common database for the design, drafting, machining, and manufacturing processes

- Discuss the role of CADD in NC part programming

- Describe the use of CADD in robot simulation and workcell management

- List the types of machining processes that can be programmed on a CAD/CAM system and what type of simulation is normally available

- Define the term computer-aided manufacturing and how it relates to computer-integrated manufacturing

Introduction

The manufacturing portion of CAD/CAM has been traditionally restricted to NC programming. In the 1990s, the role of CAM in a CAD/CAM environment will take on increased importance, especially as an integrator in helping firms achieve the benefits of **computer-integrated manufacturing (CIM)**.

The CIM concept encompasses many manufacturing, computer-based automation applications. CIM is a system whose primary inputs are product requirements, and whose outputs are finished products. CIM comprises a combination of software and hardware for product design, for production planning/control, and for production processes.

CAD/CAM is an excellent CIM integrator for computer-based applications in manufacturing, especially NC programming and robotics (Figure 12–1). CAD/CAM's integration ability depends on a common engineering and manufacturing *database*. This database allows engineering to define a product model (part design) and the manufacturing department to use that same model definition to produce the product (Figure 12–2).

Computer-Aided Manufacturing

CADD is the process that uses a computer to help create or modify a design. *Computer-aided manufacturing (CAM) is the process that uses a computer to manage and control the operations of a manufacturing facility.* CAM includes **numerical control (NC)** for machining operations, tool and fixture design and set up, and industrial robots in the manufacturing process. The integration of computer-aided design and computer-aided manufacturing eliminates duplication of effort by the engineering/design and manufacturing or production departments. An engineering drawing created on a graphics terminal defines the product geometry (points, lines, planes, etc.), which otherwise must be manually derived from the drawing by the manufacturing department before the product is produced. Figure 12–3 shows a diagramic layout of a complete CAD/CAM integrated system.

CAM speeds the manufacturing process since it uses the same common database initially created in the design and drafting cycle. This database, representing the part (model) design, is used by the manufacturing group. The system serves all applications, promotes standardization to enhance management control, accumulates (rather than randomly collects) manufacturing information, and reduces redundancy and errors.

The production process is computerized from the original graphics input through the manufacturing of the part on a numerically controlled machine (Figure 12–3). Shop production drawings have been eliminated entirely with this process. By obtaining the product geometry directly from the engineering data, the NC programmer can extract accurate geometric data replicating the engineer's definition of the part to be manufactured.

Many design-through-manufacture processes require skilled labor which is, and probably will continue to be, in short supply. One of the major

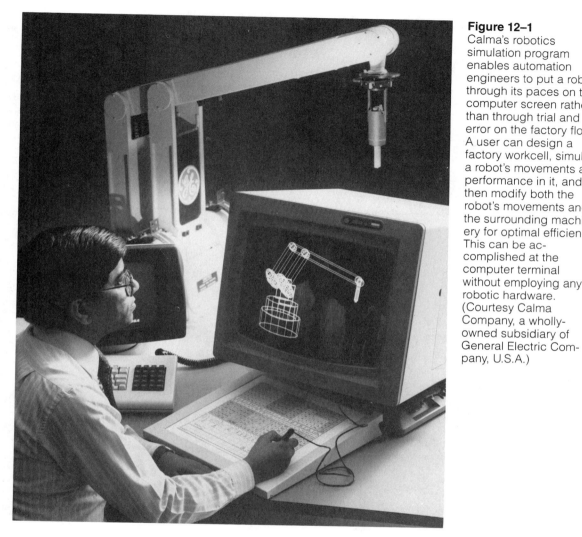

Figure 12–1
Calma's robotics simulation program enables automation engineers to put a robot through its paces on the computer screen rather than through trial and error on the factory floor. A user can design a factory workcell, simulate a robot's movements and performance in it, and then modify both the robot's movements and the surrounding machinery for optimal efficiency. This can be accomplished at the computer terminal without employing any robotic hardware. (Courtesy Calma Company, a wholly-owned subsidiary of General Electric Company, U.S.A.)

goals of the CAD/CAM system is to transfer the experience and skills of a few individuals to the database. This provides less experienced personnel with access to technical information.

Using a CAD/CAM system, the engineer or designer applies the CADD features to create a model of the part. Then, using the information stored in the database, the manufacturing engineer applies the CAM capabilities. A CADD system may have a variety of specialized CAM capabilities including the following:

Figure 12–2
The part database created during the design phase is used by all groups associated with the manufacturing process. (Reprinted with permission from Computervision Corporation, Bedford, Massachusetts)

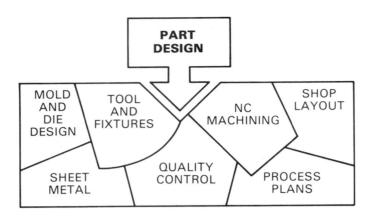

Figure 12–3
CAD/CAM integrated configuration. (Courtesy Lockheed-California Co.)

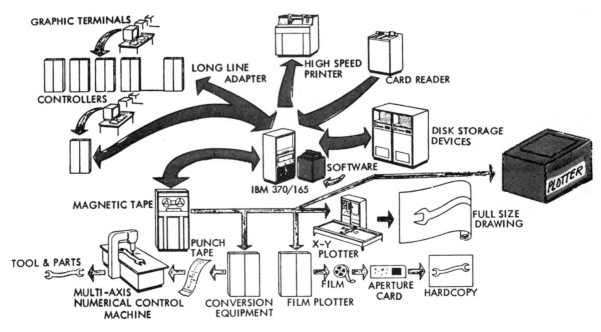

- Group Technology

- Process Planning

- Shop Layout

- Numerical Control (NC) of machining operations

- NC postprocessing

- Sheet metal applications

- Tool and fixture design

- Mold design and testing

- Technical publications and manufacturing documentation

Computer-Aided Manufacturing Systems

To use computer-aided manufacturing, the following steps must be accomplished:

1. *Process Planning.* The engineering drawing of the part to be tooled must be interpreted in terms of the manufacturing processes to be used. This step is referred to as process planning, and it should be given thought and consideration before part programming is begun.

2. *Part Programming.* A part programmer plans the process for the portions of the job to be accomplished by numerical control. Part programmers are knowledgeable about the machining process and they have been trained to program for numerical control. They are responsible for planning the sequence of machining steps to be performed by NC and to document these in a special format. There are two ways to program for NC:

- *Manual Part Programming*

- *Computer-Assisted Part Programming*

In **manual part programming**, the machining instructions are prepared on a form called a part program manuscript. The manuscript is a listing of the relative cutter positions which must be followed to machine the part. In *computer-assisted part programming*, much of the tedious computational work required in manual part programming is transferred to the computer. This is especially advantageous for complex part geometries and jobs with many machining steps. Use of the computer in these situations results in significant savings in part programming time.

3. *Transfer Media Preparation.* Punched tape is the classic medium for transferring a part program from a computer to an NC machine (Figure 12–4). Floppy disks are also being used as a major transfer medium. In computer-assisted part programming, such as the NC programmer software package that uses AutoCAD as a basis for its program (Figure 12–5), the computer interprets the list of part programming instructions, performs the necessary calculations to convert this into a detailed set of machine tool motion commands, and then develops a chosen transfer medium containing the NC data for the specific NC machine.

4. *Verification.* After the transfer medium has been prepared, the accuracy of the program is checked. Sometimes the program is checked by plotting the tool movements on paper. In this way, major errors in the program can be discovered. The "acid test" of the part program is making a trial part on the machine tool. A foam or plastic material is sometimes used for this test. Three-dimensional CADD Systems with CAD/CAM capabilities may allow verification of tool paths and cutter motion in three-dimensions on the display, eliminating the need for a test using the actual machine.

5. *Production.* The final step in the CAM procedure is to use the NC program in production. This involves ordering the rough parts, specifying and preparing the tooling and any special fixturing that may be required, and setting up the NC machine tool for the job. The machine tool operator's function during production is to load the data in the machine and establish the starting position of the cutting tool relative to the rough part. The NC system then takes over and the part is machined according to the instructions on the transfer medium. When the part is completed, the operator removes it from the machine and loads the next part. In more automated operations, a programmable robot performs this task instead of an operator.

Figure 12–4
Punched tape (left), punched card (center), and magnetic tape (right) are used for NC data input.

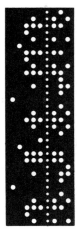

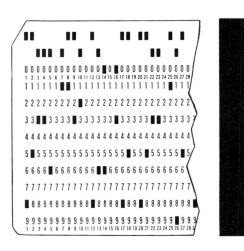

part. In more automated operations, a programmable robot performs this task instead of an operator.

Introduction to Numerical Control

Many of the achievements in computer-aided design and manufacturing have a common origin in numerical control (NC).

Numerical control (NC) can be defined as a form of programmable automation, in which the process is controlled by numbers, letters, and symbols. In NC, the numbers form a program of instructions designed for a particular part or job. When the job changes, the program of instructions is changed. This capability to change the program for each new job is what gives NC its flexibility. It is much easier to write new programs than to make major changes in the production equipment.

NC technology has been applied to a wide variety of operations including drafting, assembly, inspection, sheet metal pressworking, and spot welding. Numerical control finds a major application in flat pattern machining processes. The machined parts are designed in various sizes and shapes. Most machined parts produced in industry today are made in small- to medium-size batches. To produce each part, a sequence of drilling operations or a series of cutting operations may be required. The flexibility of NC is the primary reason for the tremendous growth of numerical control in industry over the last 25 years.

Basic Components of a Numerical Control System

An operational CAD/CAM numerical control system consists of the following three basic components (Figure 12–5):

1. Computer-aided design system

2. Computer-aided manufacturing system

3. Machine tool postprocessor

The description of the part developed with the computer-aided design system is the input to the computer-aided manufacturing system, which in turn commands the machine tool postprocessor to develop the machine instructions.

Figures 12–6 through 12–12 show a typical sequence of design, analysis, NC simulation, and manufacturing for a spindle. The menu (Figure 12–6) is used to manage the engineering data needed to model and test the part. The solid model (Figure 12–7) is used to assist the designer in creating, analyzing,

Figure 12–5
NC dedicated software consisting of AutoCAD graphics software, the NC PROGRAMMER NC software, and a postprocessor. (Courtesy NC MicroProducts Inc.)

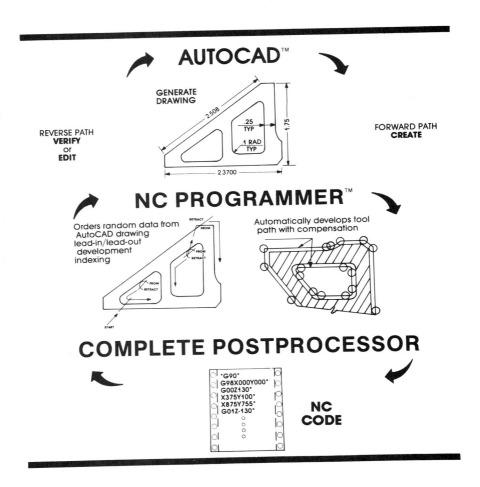

and visually displaying the part. The model can be rotated, viewed from any angle, or exploded as needed (Figure 12–8). Finite element analysis packages can generate a mesh of the part from the geometry (Figure 12–9).

Cutter paths for NC machining are defined and modified by the part programmer (Figure 12–10). Output from the postprocessor can then be used for NC machining of the actual part (Figure 12–11).

The finished assembly is reviewed on the CADD station (Figure 12-12). Plates 22 through 33 show a similar example in the computer-assisted design and manufacturing for a connecting rod.

Numerical Control (NC) Part Programming in Three-Dimensions

Computer-aided design uses language easily understood by machine shop personnel. This eases the problem of "computer shock" and eliminates the

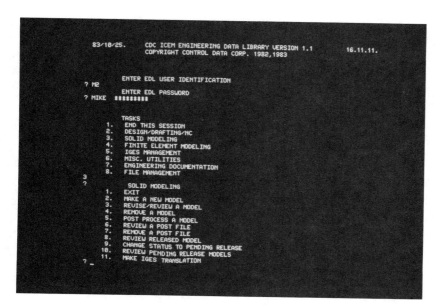

Figure 12–6
Task menu from Control Data's ICEM (Integrated Computer-aided Engineering and Manufacturing) engineering library. (Courtesy Control Data Corp.)

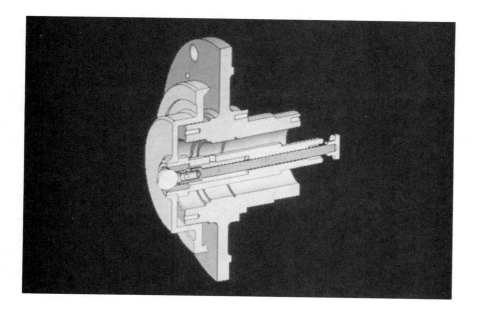

Figure 12–7
Solid modeler software help create, analyze, and visualize the part geometry. (Courtesy Control Data Corp.)

Figure 12–8
The solid model of the
assembly can be rotated,
exploded, and viewed
from any angle. (Courtesy
Control Data Corp.)

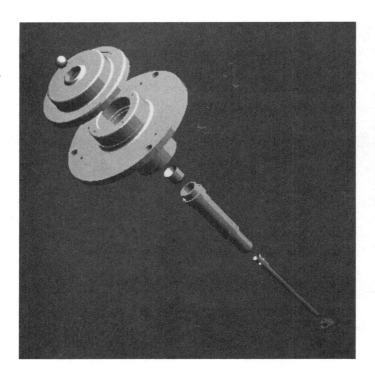

Figure 12–9
A finite element model is
generated for common
geometry and analyzed
to insure that it meets
design criteria. (Courtesy
Control Data Corp.)

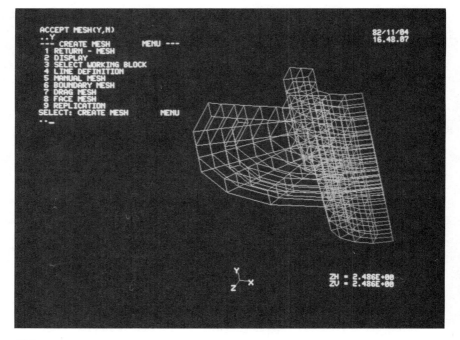

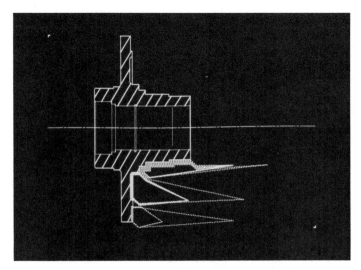

Figure 12–10
Cutter paths for numerical control machining can be defined and modified at the CADD terminal. (Courtesy Control Data Corp.)

Figure 12–11
Numerical output can be used for NC machining of the actual part. (Courtesy Control Data Corp.)

427

Figure 12–12
Finished assembly
review. (Courtesy Control
Data Corp.)

need to learn an alien language. Since the geometry of the part is defined in the CADD database, there is no need to extract the part geometry from the drawings. The geometry already exists, precisely as the designer specified it. In NC part programming, the graphics display and interactivity of the system eliminate the need to imagine the cutter path, since the designer is provided with visual verification of every step in the process (Figure 12–10).

Many three-dimensional CADD systems provide this graphic approach to numerical control. As has been stated, NC involves creating the toolpath and machine instructions for a variety of machining operations. It is a technique that creates, on punched tape or other media (Figure 12–4), complete instructions for the operation of a machine. NC machines perform machining operations automatically by using instructions contained on punched tape or other media. Many three-dimensional CADD systems have NC capabilities that include:

- Defining cutting tools and then generating cutting paths, automatically or interactively (Figure 12–10).

- Simulation and verification of toolpaths on the graphics display using computer dynamics.

- Changing the machine instructions, through postprocessors, for specific machines.

Using CADD for the NC database frees the manufacturing engineer from the costly, time-consuming task of manual parts programming. After a designer develops and stores a part design in the common database, it can be retrieved and used to create the tooling information and the fixtures needed to produce the part. Then, an NC programmer uses all of the information stored in the database to create NC programs on the CADD system to produce complete, error-free instructions.

Once a part is designed and stored in the database, the manufacturing engineer simply calls up the part (model) on the display (Figure 12–7). The engineer uses the model to generate toolpaths that can be seen graphically in either two or three dimensions (Figure 12–10). The model can be either a wireframe representation of the part or have defined surfaces which allow for the machining of more complex shapes.

The engineer defines cutting tools, creates a tool library, and retrieves these tools later to create toolpath information. CAM packages support most types of cutting tools; therefore, the engineer can describe many types of generally used cutting tools (flat, ball, tapered). The CAM system allows for definition of machining characteristics such as retract and clearance plane, cutting depth, feed rate (rate of travel), and spindle speed (rate of spindle rotation).

Machining Operations

CAM systems allow a variety of machining operations ranging from simple 2-axis point-to-point functions to complex 5-axis machining. These operations may include drilling, punching, milling, turning, profiling, pocketing, surface machining, and flame cutting (Figure 12–13). The types of parts that may be produced on NC equipment from output generated by CAD/CAM systems include:

- Irregular or uniquely machined parts

- Two-dimensional parts created by point-to-point operations

- Lathe parts produced by turning operations

- Two-and-one-half–dimensional parts which may require pocketing and profiling operations

- Three-dimensional parts produced by using all of the NC operations provided on the CAD/CAM system

Pocketing is the process of completely removing material within a bounded area (Figure 12–14). Machine pocket programs provide automatic pocketing on a CADD system by generating a toolpath to remove the material contained within a closed boundary. Capabilities typically include multiple-base rough cutting, multiple side cutting, a designer-specified final finishing pass, and islands defined within a pocket (Figure 12–13).

Figure 12–13
NC toolpaths. Six examples of toolpath generation are shown here: Absolute machining is a totally operator controlled toolpath definition process for milling, drilling, and lathe operations. Pocketing (with islands) is an operation where the user defines the part's boundaries and other machining parameters. Lace cutting is a surface machining operation creating a laced toolpath for pocketing and milling. Point-to-point automatically generates a toolpath for specified drilling locations. Profiling automatically generates toolpaths for contour milling inside or outside of part. Machining intersections automatically generate multiple surface machining toolpaths. (Reprinted with permission from Computervision Corporation, Bedford, Massachusetts)

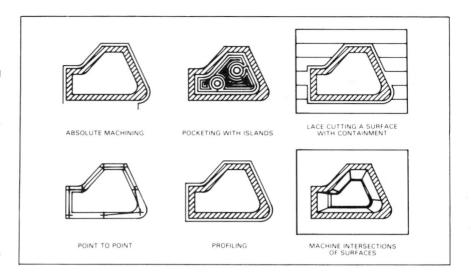

Many CADD NC packagers offer *profiling* which is automatically generating a continuously contoured toolpath around a boundary (Figure 12–14). The cutting tool moves outside or inside a profile (Figure 12–13). Capabilities include multiple-base rough cutting, multiple-side rough cutting, and a designer-specified final finishing pass.

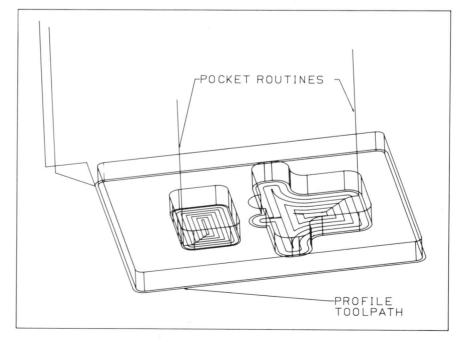

Figure 12–14
A variety of toolpaths can be created including profiling and pocketing. (Reprinted with permission from Computervision Corporation, Bedford, Massachusetts)

Three-Dimensional Parts

Manufacturing engineers work with real three-dimensional objects as well as two-dimensional paper representations. Most parts have surfaces, some as complex as the surface of an automobile body, others as simple as a rectangular-shaped gearbox housing. With three-dimensional CADD, a designer can view a part with surfaces, as it would actually appear, without building a prototype part. The ability to examine, manipulate, and add other entities to any surface at any orientation eliminates the trial and error associated with manufacturing engineering. Better design and more imaginative manufacturing processes are possible with this three-dimensional capability.

Toolpath Simulation and Verification

Many CADD systems allow accurate and realistic verification of both two- and three-dimensional toolpaths without cutting metal. The engineer can simulate and visually verify the toolpath on the display (Figure 12–10). The toolpath seen on the display may show the tool and holder actually moving along the part from any viewing angle. This permits the designer to check for toolpath correctness and clearance of tools, parts, and fixtures (see Plates 22 through 33).

A variety of output options are available with CADD. Once toolpaths are created, they may be edited and assembled into sets, machining statements may be added, and then toolpaths may be output to a specific machine or direct numerical control (DNC). Toolpaths may also be transformed into APT or COMPACT 11 for processing through a mainframe NC processor.

Tools, Fixtures, and Mold Design

In general, a *tool* is a piece of equipment that helps create a finished part. It may be anything that must be designed and/or made in order to manufacture the part. CADD systems may support the design and manufacture of the following tools:

1. Molds that are used to form a variety of plastic parts for consumer, industrial, and medical applications (Figure 12–15).

2. Dies that are used to forge, cast, extrude, and stamp materials while in various physical states, solid through fluid.

3. Tooling that is the individual component of mold or die, including a cavity, nest, core, punch, bushing, slide, or sleeve.

Fixtures are used to hold and locate parts of assemblies during machining or other manufacturing operations. The accuracy of the product being produced determines the precision with which a fixture is designed. CADD assists in production integrating design-through-manufacturing of manufactured components.

CAD/CAM is a major component in tool/fixture design and manufacturing and its influence is steadily growing. CADD increases productivity by:

1. Integrating design and manufacture through a common database.

2. Reducing design time with standard CADD graphic construction features.

3. Allowing the building of a parts library to eliminate duplication of efforts.

4. Enhancing manufacturing verification with features such as dynamic motion and toolpath stimulation.

5. Interfacing to quality control functions such as coordinate measuring machines and shadow graph machines.

To design and manufacture a finished part efficiently, product design engineers must work with tool and fixture designers as well as manufacturing engineers. CADD promotes this interaction by providing one common database for the product design and the associated tool/fixture design, manufacture, and production. When designing a tool or fixture, the manufacturing engineer retrieves the part design from the database to determine how the tool or fixture should be built to produce the finished product. The tool or fixture is designed directly on the system (see Plate 34).

Since duplicating the design for CAM-related purposes is eliminated, the common CADD database saves time for the manufacturing engineer. This also helps eliminate errors caused by misinterpreting design information. A CADD system handles large amounts of information which the engineer uses to determine complex relationships between the tool/fixture and the part. The visual representation of the tool/fixture on the display, as it relates to the part, provides an important link between engineering and manufacturing. This eliminates the tedious work of interpreting the detailed part drawing and then manually calculating individual fits and tolerances of the tool or fixture required to produce the finished part. The tool fixture design is modified and updated easily if product design changes are necessary.

Once the tool fixture is designed, the engineer creates a detail drawing to provide a geometric description of the part. Detail drawings, an integral part of all steps in the design-through-manufacturing process, can represent the tool/fixture design in any view and include dimensions, surfaces, hidden lines, and other appearance control features. These drawings may be used for marketing, design, review, and manufacturing approval, or as input to the documentation, purchasing, and production departments.

To determine the materials needed to produce a tool/fixture designed on the system, CADD can automatically output a bill of materials for the purchasing department. A bill of materials lists quantities and associated information needed to manufacture the product(s).

Visual Simulation to Verify Tool and Fixture Design

CADD systems can provide a unique way to examine the tool fixture after it is designed. For example, if it is necessary to provide clearances between the tool fixture and the part (Figure 12–15), the designer can check and verify the minimum clearance needed by zooming the view on the graphics display. This ensures optimum use of materials. Color is used to enhance the graphics display and is particularly useful for the engineering evaluation involved in tool and fixture design. The engineer uses color to discriminate components for easier viewing and highlighting.

To evaluate a tool design, a designer using a CADD system can generate a toolpath (cutter path) and visually simulate the movement of a cutting tool around a part. Using this capability, the engineer watches the simulated cutter move on the display screen to verify the result of the toolpath definition. This reduces costs for test machining, machine setup, and prototype creation by eliminating reruns. Process planners can then use this information to create process instructions and plans with the same part (Figure 12–16).

Mold Design Using CAD/CAM   Figures 12–17 through 12–20 show an example of a part which was created on a CADD system (Figure 12–16). The

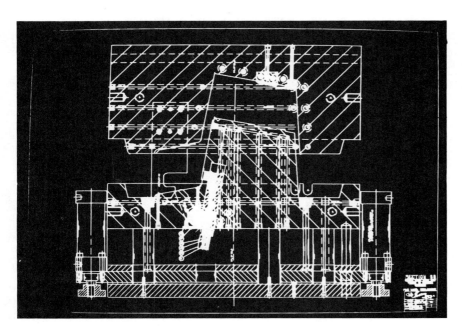

Figure 12–15
Simulation of molding process. (Reprinted with permission from Computervision Corporation, Bedford, Massachusetts)

mold for the part being machined (Figure 12–18) is shown complete in Figure 12–19. This same process is shown in Figures 12–20 through 12–22. Here the shoe was designed and displayed on a CRT using a mesh model. The mold is also designed on the system (Figure 12–21) and is being machined in Figure 12–22.

Design Analysis

A CAD/CAM system can be used to calculate mass properties including weight, volume, and center of gravity. It also creates a finite element model of a tool/fixture for checking its structural integrity. Finite element modeling is useful for heat dissipation and stress analysis. As integral parts of a CADD system, finite element modeling and mass properties analysis take advantage of system graphics and dynamics features.

Robotics

Robotics is the integration of computer-controlled robots in the manufacturing process. Industrial robots are used to move, manipulate, position, weld, machine, and do a variety of other manufacturing processes that formerly required unskilled and semi-skilled manual laborers.

Figure 12–16
Production planning.
(Reprinted with permission from Computervision Corporation, Bedford, Massachusetts)

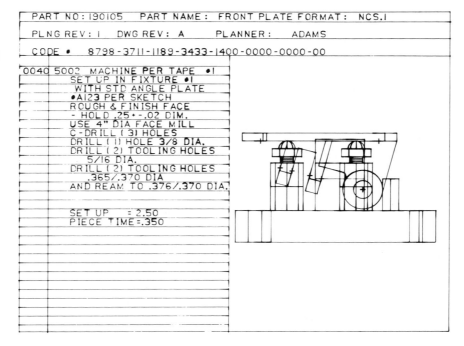

Figure 12–17
Computer design of
molded part. (Courtesy
CAMAX Systems Inc.)

Figure 12–18
Mold, for part shown in
Figure 12–17, being
machined. (Courtesy
CAMAX Systems Inc.)

Figure 12–19
Finished part and mold.
(Courtesy CAMAX
Systems Inc.)

Robots are controlled by a microprocessor and are composed of a separate stand-alone computer station, the robot mechanism itself, and an electrical hydraulic power unit (Figure 12–23).

The improvement in productivity and product quality in the next decade largely depends on new manufacturing technologies. Among emerging manufacturing automation technologies, robotics is considered one of the best bets for achieving these objectives. Robotics will also reduce costs, and may allow many companies to remain competitive in their industries.

Figure 12–20
Mesh model of a shoe
design. (Courtesy
CAMAX Systems Inc.)

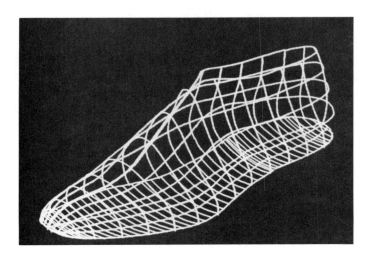

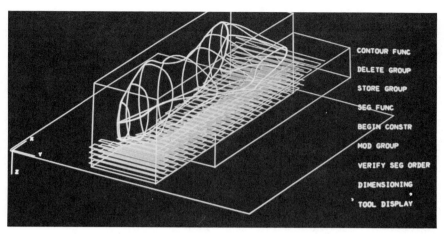

Figure 12–21
Shoe design shown on a display. (Courtesy CAMAX Systems Inc.)

The Robot Institute of America defines a robot as "a reprogrammable, multifunction manipulator designed to move material, parts, tools, or specialized devices through variable, programmed motions for the performance of a variety of tasks." This definition can be expanded to include the control and synchronization of the equipment that the robot works with, a capability that can eliminate the need for humans to work in an environment that may be hazardous. Since a robot is capable of being programmed to automatically perform different tasks, it is a form of programmable automation.

Figure 12–22
NC machining of a shoe mold design. (Courtesy CAMAX Systems Inc.)

Figure 12–23
Automatix Industrial
Robot.

Robotic Systems

The functional center of a robotic-automatic **workcell** is the robot. The major components of robotics are discussed here, as well as the technological trends that have resulted in the integration of CAD/CAM and robotics.

The Controller   The controller orchestrates the actions of the robot and stores the sequence of moves or operations.

Robot controllers have evolved in sophistication from mechanical to pneumatic, then to electrical, and finally to computerized. In each evolutionary step, the controller is able to direct the robot to do more complex tasks. Computerized controls also increase programmability.

The Manipulator   Robotic programming and simulation must consider the variety of robotic configurations including Cartesian, polar, cylindrical, and rotary. Each configuration has its own merits. For example, polar and cylindrical types can service a larger work space with a relatively small foundation.

Each joint of a robot can have either a translation or rotational movement. The sum of these motion capabilities is referred to as *degrees of freedom* for the robot. For example, the Unimation Puma robot may be a manipulator with either five or six degrees of freedom, depending on the model. The greater the degrees of freedom, the greater the robot's motion flexibility. The robot's cost increases with degrees of freedom, as does its programming complexity (see Plates 15, 35, and 36).

Manipulators may be servo- or nonservo-controlled. Nonservo means limited sequence and implies simple controls and mechanical-type programming. Motion is only possible by setting a limited number of mechanical stops. Servo robots can move along a continuous path or in a point-to-point fashion, and require greater control and programming sophistication.

Programming a Robot

The definition of robotics includes the term *reprogrammable*. Programming a robot allows the operator to put it to work for a variety of work tasks. The robotic programmer is concerned with defining the motion of the end effector or gripper. The gripper grasps parts and tools required to accomplish the automated task.

Nonservo, limited-sequence (pick-and-place) robots have the simplest type of programming — adjustable limit stops. Combined with programmable logic controllers, these robots can sample inputs and outputs in the environment, and respond with limited flexibility. Since this method of programming requires the use of the robot and its work environment, we refer to it as on-line programming. The major disadvantage is that the robot is idle and not doing production work during programming.

Programming servo-controlled robots is more sophisticated. The controller is usually a computer or microprocessor. Here, continuous path and complex point-to-point motions are possible. Two methods are in use today: the *teach method* and *off-line programming* using a robotic language.

The Teach Method   The teach method consists of walking the robot through its paces. An operator does this with a teach pendant — a box with switches that control joint or arm movements.

An operator manually positions the robot gripper and records its position. Repeating this operation for a sequence of positions, the operator creates a program that moves the gripper from one position to the next in the given sequence. There are several limitations of this method:

- The robot must be taken out of production to be programmed.

- Programming is tedious if many points are required.

- There is no way to predict motion between recorded points.

The intermediate motion requires the solution of complex mathematical equations for motion prediction.

Off-Line Programming   The development of robotic languages such as RAIL (Automatix, Inc.) and VAL (Unimation, Inc.) is a big step forward for programming servo-controlled robots. The programmer creates a computer program in the same manner that the NC programmer creates an Automatically Programmed Tool (**APT**) program. The APT program is used to prepare numerical control tapes. This robot program can be input to the controller and complex robotic operations performed.

CAD/CAM Robotic Applications

The integration of CAD/CAM and robotics results in increased productivity for robotic implementation activities. CAD/CAM robotic applications include:

- Robotic workcell design
- Robotic workcell programming
- Robotic workcell simulation

The robotic workcell contains all the physical equipment needed to create a functioning robot application (Figure 12–24). Besides the robot, a workcell can have special fixturing, automated machines (NC machines, coordinate measuring machines, or visual inspection equipment), material handling devices, part presentation equipment, and robot grippers.

The equipment in the workcell must be arranged so that the robot work envelope (Figure 12–25) includes all required device areas. CAD/CAM is perfect for designing the equipment layout. Libraries of workcell components can be stored on the CAD/CAM system and recalled when needed. For example, a robot library could contain commercial robots and their work envelopes (Figure 12–1).

CAD/CAM workcell design results in many benefits. First, the design activity is more productive and design time and costs are reduced. Second, CAD/CAM for workcell layout allows more alternatives to be considered, resulting in an optimal layout. Third, the lead time to design and lay out the cell is reduced. Fourth, the quality of the designed components and the overall cell is increased.

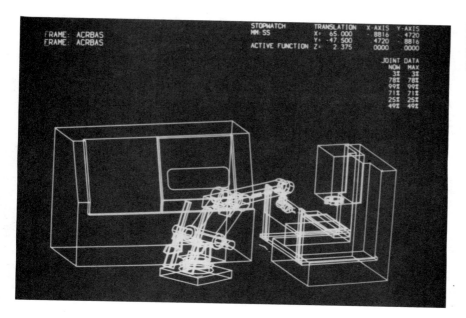

Figure 12–24
Robot work cell simulation. (Courtesy Evans & Sutherland)

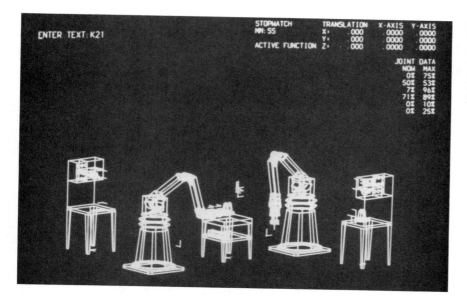

Figure 12–25
Robot and related machinery workcell evaluation simulation shown on a display. (Courtesy Evans & Sutherland)

Graphic robotic simulation (Plates 13, 14, and 16) is defined as simulating the programmed robot path. Simulation checks whether or not the robot can position its end effector to the positions and orientations specified during programming. It is possible that the robot's end effector cannot assume the desired position and orientation required, so revision of the path or workcell may be required. Also, the robot's degree of freedom (Figure 12–26) may not be sufficient to accomplish a given task. Simulation creates the actual robot trajectory using end-effector positions available from graphic robotic programming. Computervision's Robographix system is one of the first graphic robotic programming and simulation systems to be totally integrated into a turnkey CAD/CAM system.

The following activities can be performed on a CAD/CAM system using a common engineering and manufacturing database:

- Engineering designs the product, components, or parts that are manufactured with the robot.

- Process engineering lays out the robotic workcell and evaluates alternative robot selections and cell configurations.

- Tool engineering designs all fixturing and special equipment needed for the workcell.

Figure 12–26
Robot simulation of arm movement. (Courtesy Evans & Sutherland)

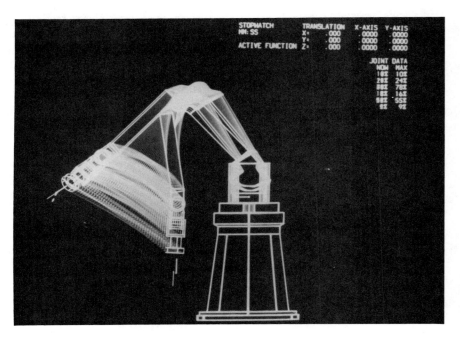

- The robot can be programmed and simulated using the workcell model.

- Other automated equipment such as NC machines and coordinate measuring machines, which are required in the workcell, can be programmed.

- The machine programs for the robot and NC machine can be directly transferred from the designer system to the workcell.

Robotics represents the final stage in the engineering, design, drafting, manufacturing, and production sequence. The computer and its related technology play an important and essential part in the present and future of industrial design. From the days of T-squares and wooden pencils, the technology of engineering design techniques has been continuously evolving, making the process of product design and production increasingly more creative and streamlined. Though the need for manual methods of drafting and drawing will never totally disappear, the use of computer-assisted methods will eventually replace a majority of manual techniques in the near future.

Information for much of this chapter was derived from material provided by Computervision Corporation and NC MicroProducts Company.

GLOSSARY

APT   Automatically Programmed Tools. A computer language used to program numerically controlled machine tools.

CAM (COMPUTER-AIDED MANUFACTURING)   A process employing computer technology to manage and control the operations of a manufacturing facility.

CL FILE (CUTTER LOCATION FILE)   Output of an APT or graphics system that provides X, Y, and Z coordinates and NC information for machine tool processing.

COMPUTER-INTEGRATED MANUFACTURING (CIM)   A totally automated factory in which all manufacturing processes are integrated and controlled by a computer system.

COMPUTER NUMERICAL CONTROL (CNC)   Using a computer to store numerical control instructions, generated by a CADD system, to control a machine.

DATABASE   An organized collection of standard parts libraries, completed designs, documentation, and computer programs.

DESIGN AUTOMATION (DA)   Using a computer to automate portions of the design process.

DIRECT NUMERICAL CONTROL (DNC)   Using a shared computer to distribute part program data to remote machine tools.

DYNAMIC MOVEMENT   The ability to zoom, scroll, and rotate the image on the screen interactively.

FINITE ELEMENT ANALYSIS (FEA)   The determination of the structural integrity of a part by mathematical simulation of the part and the forces acting on the part.

FINITE ELEMENT MODELING (FEM)   The creation of a mathematical model of a part for input to a finite element analysis program.

INTEGRATED SYSTEM   A CADD system that integrates the entire product development cycle — analysis, design, and fabrication — into a single system.

INTELLIGENT ROBOT   A robot that can make decisions by using its sensing and recognizing capabilities.

NUMERICAL CONTROL (NC)   The control of machine tools, drafting machines, and plotters by punched paper or magnetic tape encoded with the proper information to cut a part or draw a figure.

ROBOTICS   The use of computer controlled robots to automate manufacturing processes such as welding, material handling, painting, and assembly.

SURFACE MACHINING   The ability to output 3-, 4-, and 5-axis NC toolpaths using three-dimensional surface definition capabilities (e.g., ruled surfaces, tabulated cylinders, and surfaces of revolution).

TOOL PATH   A trace of the movement of the tip of a numerical control cutting tool that is used to guide or control machining equipment.

QUIZ

True or False

1. Robots can be programmed and their movements verified without touching the actual robot hardware.

2. NC is a form of programmable automation controlled by numbers, letters, or symbols.

3. Postprocessors are not necessary for running an NC program on a specific machine tool.

4. Pocketing is the process of removing material from the outer boundaries of a part.

5. A true CAD/CAM system can create a common database that is then used to derive part geometry for all areas of manufacturing and design.

6. A mold and a die can be considered "tools."

7. Cutter paths can be simulated on two-dimensional and three-dimensional CADD systems.

8. NC machines derive their operating instructions from numeric codes transferred to the machine by means of punched tape, punched cards, or some form of floppy disk or magnetic tape.

Fill in the Blank

9. Machining a continuous toolpath about a part is called
_____ .

10. Toolpaths can be _____ and _____ on the display.

11. Robot _____ _____ simulation helps insure accurate movement of the robot and its relation to the operation and surrounding equipment.

12. _____ _____ for NC machining can be defined and altered on the display before the actual machining operation.

13. _____ to _____ operations for two-dimensional parts lend themselves to NC machining.

14. The manufacturing portion of CAD/CAM was originally restricted to
_____ _____ .

15. The creation of a common _____ enables the part geometry to be used by many departments.

16. Design analysis can include calculating mass, _____ ,
_____ , and _____ of a tool or fixture.

Answer the Following

17. What is CIM and how is it affecting the factory of the present and of the future? What are some futuristic projections for CIM?

18. Define CAM as it relates to and influences NC programming.

19. What are robots and how are they being used in industry? What type of tasks are they doing and why?

20. What part does CADD play in the total process of CAM? How does the use of a common database affect the design-through-manufacturing process?

21. How can CADD be used in verification? Discuss its uses and effects on CAM in general. Mention NC, tooling design, mold design, and robotics in your evaluation.

22. What are three major components of a CAD/CAM NC system? How do they relate to one another?

23. Describe the difference between the *teach method* and *off-line programming*.

24. What is a workcell and how can CADD help in its overall efficiency?

Chapter

13

CADD Industrial Applications

Objectives

Upon completion of this chapter the reader will be able to do the following:

- List the major areas of engineering design and drafting that use CADD.

- Explain why CADD has been accepted in such widely diverse application fields as civil-mapping and electronic PCB layout.

- Describe the use of color in CADD generated graphics for design and drafting applications areas.

- Identify other engineering and nontechnical areas where CADD could be used in design and graphics generation.

- Discuss the difference between design and drafting when using CADD for mechanical applications.

- Give a short overview of how CADD has affected the electronics field.

Introduction

A typical CADD **application software** package does not require that the designer be a computer programmer. CADD systems are designed to free the designers from the time-consuming task of programming so that they can concentrate on the design capabilities of the system. On the other hand, any person using an application program must be familiar with the standards and the conventions used in that technical field. It is very important for the beginning drafter to understand that, no matter what the level of sophistication, the hardware and the software are only there to aid the user in design and drafting tasks. The drafter must know about the application and what procedures are applicable to that area. Excellent software packages have been developed for civil and mapping, structural, architectural, piping, mechanical, electronic, technical illustration, and a variety of other areas. The use of CADD in these technical areas has enhanced design and streamlined drafting, but the drafter, designer, or engineer must still know all of the particulars of the application area. CADD is a tool which can only be cost effective in the hands of a knowledgeable, well-educated user.

This chapter is meant to only acquaint the student with the many uses of CADD in industry. There are a number of excellent texts on each technical field and some texts totally dedicated to the use of CADD in that application area. Therefore, it would serve no purpose to give more than an overview within the limited space of this text. Note that the mechanical and electronic areas are covered more extensively than the other fields.

Generally, the manufacturer of the CAD/CAM system supplies programs for the creation of two- and three-dimensional drawings at a basic level. Additional programs may be supplied by the manufacturer to do engineering analysis or help the designers learn special system functions. A typical drawing software package allows the designer to construct all the traditional drafting graphics using standard conventions and practices. The difference lies in the automated capabilities embedded in the system and the availability of specific applications programs. Some CADD companies offer a general CADD software package that can be used to construct symbols, menus, standards and conventions for any engineering area. This type of software allows other venders of applications programs to write software for a technical area such as PCB design, architecture, etc., using the generic software as the base. Other CADD systems are totally dedicated to one or just a limited amount of applications. As an example, many computer-aided engineering CADD systems are dedicated to integrated circuit design. Other CADD software packages are limited to PCB design or mechanical drafting.

It would be an excellent exercise for the student to investigate what other areas of industry and business utilize CADD capabilities. For instance, chemists are using CADD to create new drugs. This field is actually called Computer-Aided Drug Design. The 1985 Indianapolis 500 winner drove a car that was designed on a CADD system. CADD systems are also used to generate land planning drawings (Figure 13–1). Once a student starts to look into the present uses of CADD, the future possibilities seem unlimited.

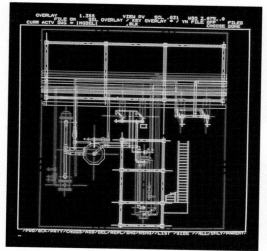

Plate 47
Piping design project modeled in three dimensions.
(Courtesy McDonnell Douglas Information Systems
Group.)

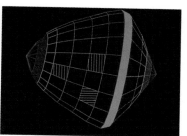

Plate 48
Wireframe model showing
different surface textures.
(Courtesy Megatek Corp.)

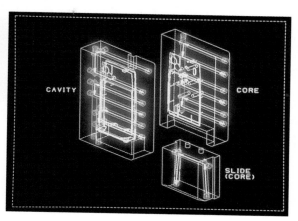

CAVITY

CORE

SLIDE
(CORE)

Plate 49
Three-dimensional wireframe of plastic mold design.
(Courtesy Calma Co., a wholly owned subsidiary of
General Electric Co., U.S.A.)

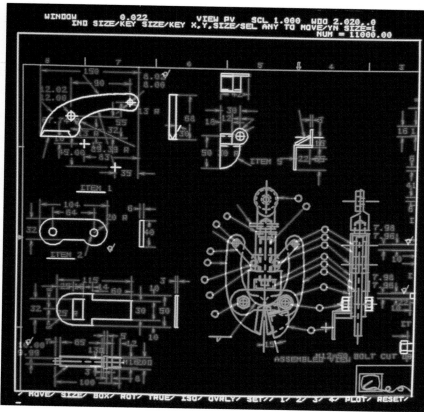

Plate 50
Assembly and detail drawing
of mechanical part. (Courtesy
Lockheed-California Co.)

Plate 51
Formula 1 race car, designed on AutoCAD by Autodesk, Inc.
Drawing courtesy of BNW Inc., Los Gatos, California. (Courtesy
Autodesk, Inc.)

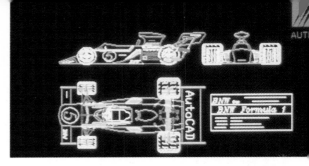

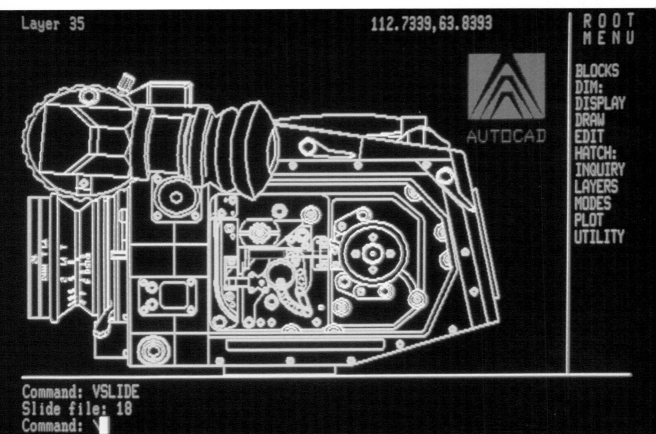

Plate 52
Mechanical layout of a 35-millimeter camera. Designed
on AutoCAD by Autodesk, Inc. Drawing courtesy of
Ultracam Camera Corp. Los Angeles, California.
(Courtesy Autodesk, Inc.)

Plate 53
Travel industry logo, designed on AutoCAD by
Autodesk, Inc. Drawing courtesy of Ed Dadey,
Marquette, Nebraska. (Courtesy Autodesk, Inc.)

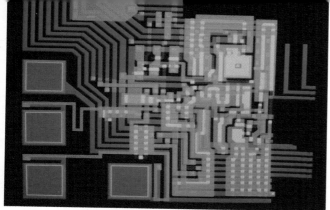

Plate 54
IC Layout. (Courtesy Calma Co.,
a wholly owned subsidiary of
General Electric Co., U.S.A.)

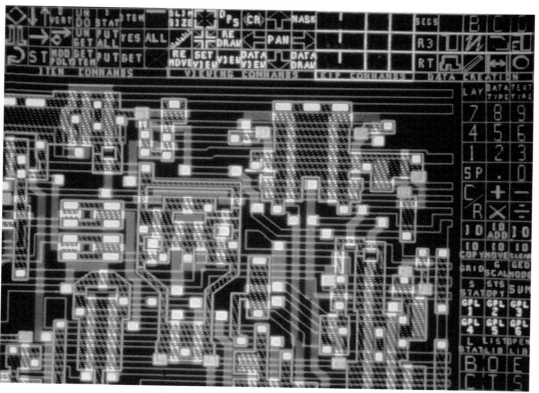

Plate 55
Electronic design using CADD.
(Courtesy Calma Co., a wholly owned
subsidiary of General Electric Co., U.S.A.)

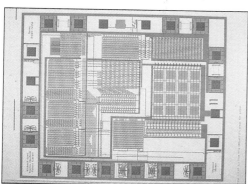

Plate 56
Integrated circuit color plot. (Courtesy Versatec)

Plate 57
Automatic component
placement using CADD.
(Courtesy Intergraph Corp.)

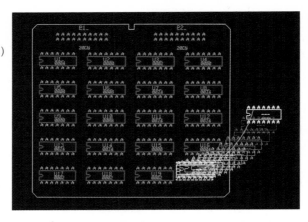

Plate 58
Automatic routing of circuit
board traces using CADD.
(Courtesy Intergraph Corp.)

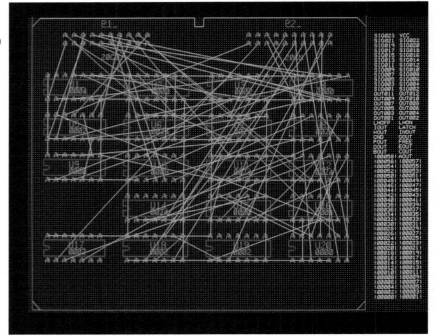

Plate 59
Component layout.
Designed on AutoCAD by
Autodesk, Inc. (Courtesy
Autodesk, Inc.)

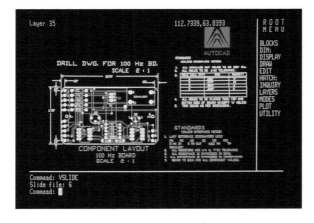

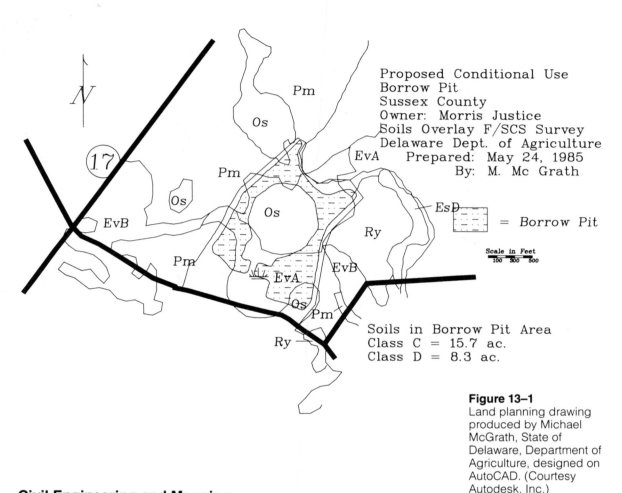

Figure 13-1

Land planning drawing produced by Michael McGrath, State of Delaware, Department of Agriculture, designed on AutoCAD. (Courtesy Autodesk, Inc.)

Civil Engineering and Mapping

Civil engineering and mapping features may include site selection, site preparation, digital terrain modeling, earthwork calculations and contour mapping. The civil drawing in Figure 13-2 shows the existing elevations (contours) and the proposed building, parking lot and landscaping for an architectural project. Mapping capabilities may include allowing utility companies and municipalities to plan distribution networks and to accurately manage assets widely distributed throughout large geographic areas.

Plates 37 through 40 show civil-mapping applications. Note the extensive use of color to separate contour levels and other drawing elements. In this series of plates we see how contour maps are developed for the civil engineer to experiment with alternative horizontal alignments (Plate 37). The

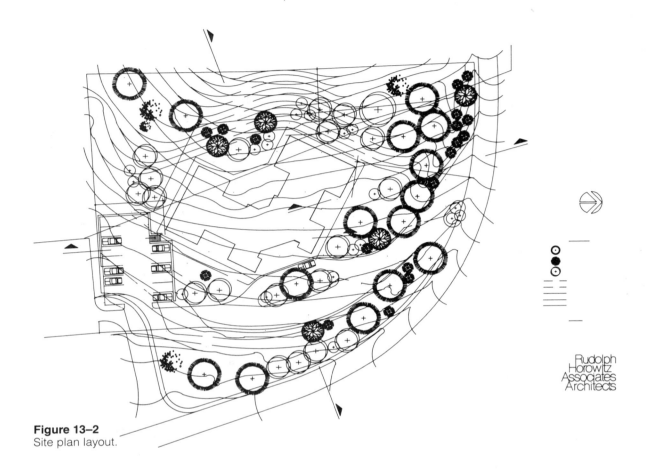

Rudolph
Horowitz
Associates
Architects

Figure 13–2
Site plan layout.

existing ground profile can be automatically generated along a selected horizontal alignment (Plate 38).

The roadway cross-section is shown in the final plate of this series (Plate
39). Here graphic options provide a variety of mechanisms for evaluating the
design, including cross-section plots, mass haul diagrams, etc.

Figure 13–3 shows a wastewater collection system. The CADD system
provides a tool for analysis and design coupled with actual cost estimates.
You can automatically design and estimate costs of a collection system by
selecting the minimum pipe sizes required and the minimum pipe slope, by
calculating flow line and excavation data, and by segregating the quantities
into bid item costs for the specified layout and flows input to each manhole.
This design tool allows the engineer to process several layouts and system
modifications, including full cost estimates, in less time than would be spent
to design one layout conventionally without cost estimates.

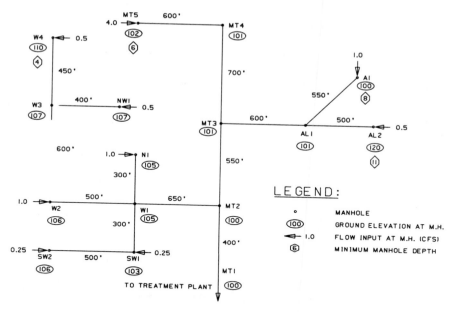

Figure 13–3
Wastewater collection system.

Architectural and Structural

Applications for building design on a CADD system include architectural design, space planning, plumbing layout, ductwork, and structural design. Most systems facilitate the integration of such disciplines and permit the designer to develop several design alternatives for a particular project.

In Figure 13–4, a floor plan was created using a two-dimensional CADD system. The detail showing an enlarged section of a wall design (Figure 13–5) and the drop cleanout detail (Figure 13–6) are examples of CADD applications for architectural projects. In Plate 41, a perspective is shown of a building. In Plate 42, solids and color shading are used to show how the building would appear realistically. This eliminates the need to physically model the building or do a technical illustration rendering.

Color and shading can also be used in conjunction with wireframe modeling to view how a building will fit into its surroundings (Plate 43). A residential floor plan, site plan, foundation plan, and kitchen and bath details are shown on the same display (Plate 44). This drawing was composed on an AutoCad two-dimensional system. Note the extensive use of color. Office planning (Figures 13–7 and 13–8), can be expedited with CADD; structural drawings and details can be produced quickly and easily (Figure 13–9).

Structural design, layout, and detailing are important applications where CADD has been used effectively in the building industry to improve design and decrease drafting time. Plates 45 and 46 show structural design

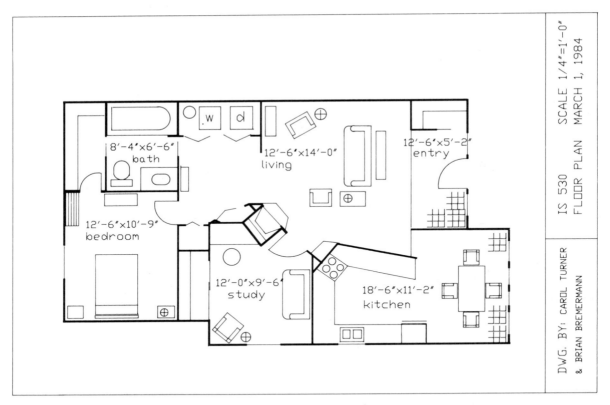

Figure 13–4
Floor plan.

Within the floor plan:

8'-4"x6'-6"
bath

12'-6"x14'-0"
living

12'-6"x5'-2"
entry

12'-6"x10'-9"
bedroom

12'-0"x9'-6"
study

18'-6"x11'-2"
kitchen

IS 530   SCALE 1/4"=1'-0"
FLOOR PLAN   MARCH 1, 1984

DWG. BY: CAROL TURNER
& BRIAN BREMERMANN

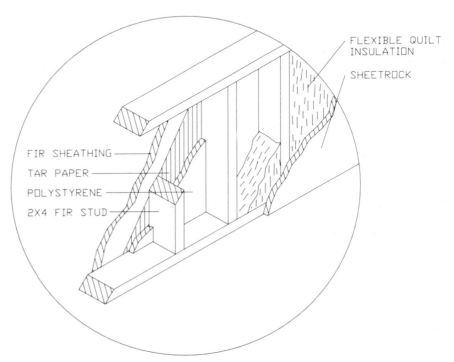

FLEXIBLE QUILT
INSULATION

SHEETROCK

FIR SHEATHING

TAR PAPER

POLYSTYRENE

2X4 FIR STUD

Figure 13–5
Wall detail. (AutoCAD
drawing Courtesy Peter
Barnett, Autodesk, Inc.)

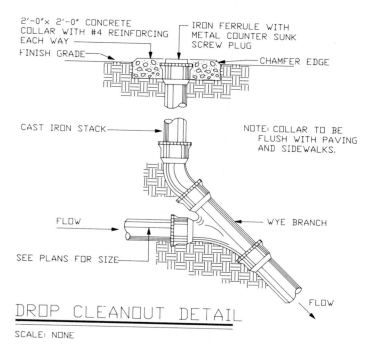

2'-0"x 2'-0" CONCRETE
COLLAR WITH #4 REINFORCING
EACH WAY
FINISH GRADE

IRON FERRULE WITH
METAL COUNTER SUNK
SCREW PLUG

CHAMFER EDGE

CAST IRON STACK

NOTE: COLLAR TO BE
FLUSH WITH PAVING
AND SIDEWALKS.

FLOW

WYE BRANCH

SEE PLANS FOR SIZE

FLOW

DROP CLEANOUT DETAIL
SCALE: NONE

Figure 13–6
Drop cleanout detail.
(AutoCAD Drawing
Courtesy CADplus
Products)

on a CADD terminal. The engineer graphically inputs the structural grid, geometry, and member properties (Plate 45). The member profiles can then be graphically checked before analysis begins. After the structural analysis is performed, the results can be displayed using moment, sheer, axial force, and deflected shape diagrams (Plate 46). Note that color and layering are used for analysis and to differentiate between structural element types and sizes.

Piping and Plant Design

With a high-level three-dimensional CADD system, designs for process and power plants can be created as a true three-dimensional model on the system (Plate 47). This model facilitates revisions, graphics manipulations, and analysis such as piping interference checks. These checks pinpoint interferences between plant components early in the design cycle. The three-dimensional model provides hidden line removal to enhance the visual representation of the model and pipeline from-to reports. The designer can recognize and rectify potential plant problems early in the design phase, eliminating costly and time-consuming construction delays.

Traditionally, many plant design projects were physically modeled (Figure 13–10). Though the physical model has not totally disappeared, the use of CADD has eliminated a portion of this once vibrant industry.

OFFICE SPACE PLANNING

OPTION 1

OPTION 2

Figure 13–7
Office space planning.
(AutoCAD drawing
Courtesy Autodesk, Inc.)

Piping drawings can also be generated using two-dimensional CADD systems (Figures 13–11 and 13–12). Here two-dimensional process flow diagrams were generated using Engineering Model Associate's EMACAD software program.

A wide range of drawings and reports can be extracted directly from the database using three-dimensional plant design CADD programs. Some examples are flow diagrams, isometrics, spools, pipe fabrications, pipe supports, plan, elevation, and section drawings, solid views, from-to lists, bills-of-material, and formatted lists. A computer-aided drafting and design system can generate all forms of graphical documentation for a piping project. Low-end systems are normally limited to the generation of two-dimensional flow diagrams (Figures 13–11 and 13–12), piping isometrics, and other types of simple projections. A mid- to high-level system will do these simple tasks along with construction of plan, elevation, and section layout drawings and actually "model" directly on the screen.

Plate 47 shows the plan view of a petrochemical plant computer model. The plan, elevation, and section drawing is actually a to-scale computer

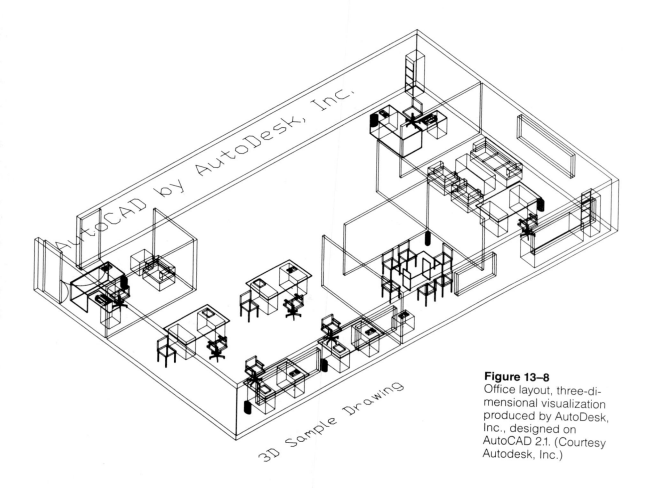

Figure 13–8
Office layout, three-dimensional visualization produced by AutoDesk, Inc., designed on AutoCAD 2.1. (Courtesy Autodesk, Inc.)

model defined in three-dimensional space through coordinates and specific piping and component data. With some systems, the designer automatically generates complete isometric spools from the computer model (Figure 13–13). Other systems require that the isometric be constructed via commands and a menu. In some cases, fabrication drawings are extracted from the isometric along with a bill-of-material.

The commands in Table 13–1 are initiated using the digitizer and menu overlay. Though each CADD system has a different command structure, they generally have similar functions. These commands are from Calma's plant design software program.

Symbols on the menu can be placed on the drawing with an electronic pen and menu (Figure 13–14). Note that menus are easily tailored to meet individual company needs and standards. The long-radius elbow (Figure 13–15) is an example of a piping component that has been placed in the

Figure 13–9
Structural footing section drawing produced by AE Microsystems, Inc., Cincinnati, Ohio, designed on AutoCAD. (Courtesy Autodesk, Inc.)

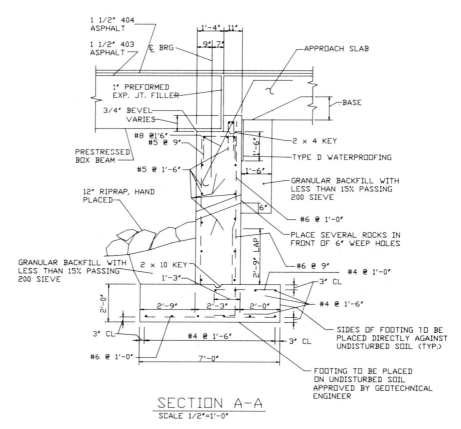

SECTION A–A
SCALE 1/2"=1'-0"

database and is available for instant recall. In Figure 13–16, a heat exchanger has been modeled and is inserted in the plant design shown in Figure 13–17. The vessel is shown with the pipes attached to it. The exchanger was created as a three-dimensional design but saved and reused as a symbol.

At present, the cost effectiveness of CADD design and drafting of piping systems is available to even the small design firm. The future will see a majority of the piping drafting and design done on these interactive devices.

Mechanical Design

CADD systems provide the designer with a means to explore many mechanical design ideas. Since exploring CADD design alternatives is much faster than manual exploration, more exploration is possible in the same amount of time. These designs are eventually refined into one finished model (Plate 48).

Figure 13–10
Industrial model of
process plant. (Courtesy
Engineering Model
Associates)

CADD allows you to create both two- and three-dimensional models which are easily constructed and manipulated. Model geometry created on the system is a true model, not just a representation of it. Plate 49 shows the design of a mold.

Some of the graphics manipulation tools available to mechanical designers include rotation, scaling, and placement, as well as *rubberbanding* and *dragging*. Rubberbanding gives the designer the capability to stretch a line to a desired location. Dragging gives the designer the capability to move elements around on the display screen. Three-dimensional mechanical software packages also provide methods to cut an object with a plane at any orientation and to create any desired cross-section for detail drawings and analysis. Any surface intersection can be defined for detailing. Exploded views can be generated from the three-dimensional model (Figure 13–18).

The previously created three-dimensional model geometry serves as the basis for detail drawings and design layouts (Figure 13–19 and Plate 50). Using the model's geometry, the designer can obtain any view or section of the model and at any scale. CADD allows the designer to measure, verify,

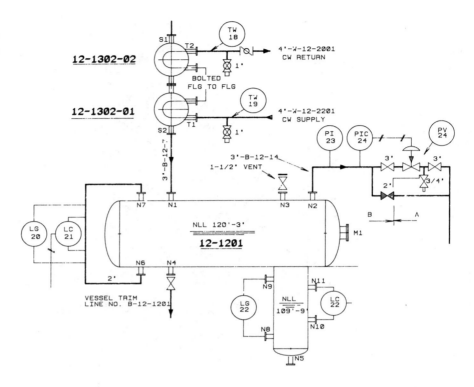

Figure 13–11
Process flow diagram of a vessel area. (Courtesy Engineering Model Associates)

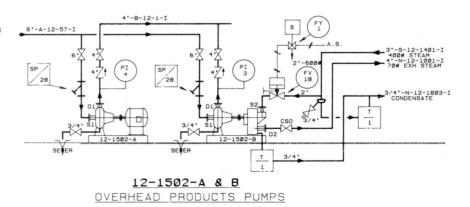

Figure 13–12
Process flow diagrams of pump station overhead products pumps. (Courtesy Engineering Model Associates)

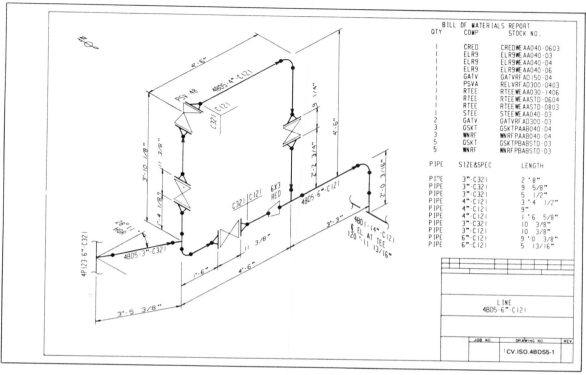

Figure 13–13
Isometric dimensioning
with bill of materials.
(Reprinted with permis-
sion from Computervision
Corporation, Bedford,
Massachusetts)

Table 13–1

Command	Function
PLADDNME	Add names to piping items
PLAUTOSYM	Automatically display isometric symbols
PLBEND	Generate bends
PLBOM	Generate bill of materials
PLCROSS	Generate crosses
PLDMP	Generate parallel isometric dimensions
PLELBOW	Generate 45 and 90 degree elbows
PLFLANGE	Generate flanges
PLGENPL	Generate basic pipeline
PLLBLBOP	Generate labels for BOP elevations
PLNORTH	Place isometric north symbol on picture
PLSYMBOL	Display isometric symbols for fittings & valves
PLTEE	Generate tees
PLVALVE	Generate valves

Figure 13–14
Piping menu. (Reprinted with permission from Computervision Corporation, Bedford, Massachusetts)

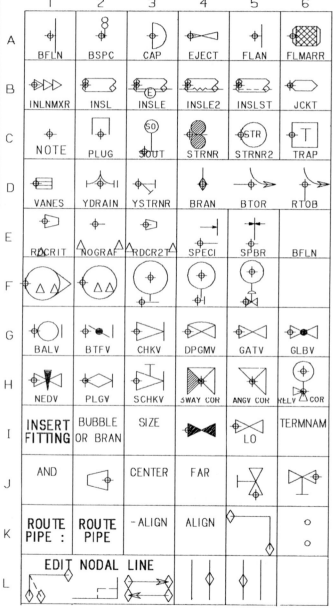

ACTIVATE PART : CVPD.P.KEYFILE.PART
RESTORE KEYFILE : KEYFILE.CVPD.P.KEYFILE.KEYS

	1	2	3	4	5	6
A	BFLN	BSPC	CAP	EJECT	FLAN	FLMARR
B	INLNMXR	INSL	INSLE	INSLE2	INSLST	JCKT
C	NOTE	PLUG	SPOUT	STRNR	STRNR2	TRAP
D	VANES	YDRAIN	YSTRNR	BRAN	BTOR	RTOB
E	RDCRIT	NOGRAF	RDCR2T	SPECI	SPBR	BFLN
F						
G	BALV	BTFV	CHKV	DPGMV	GATV	GLBV
H	NEDV	PLGV	SCHKV	3WAY COR	ANGV COR	RELV COR
I	INSERT FITTING	BUBBLE OR BRAN	SIZE		LO	TERMNAM
J	AND		CENTER	FAR		
K	ROUTE PIPE :	ROUTE PIPE	-ALIGN	ALIGN		o
L	EDIT NODAL LINE					

460

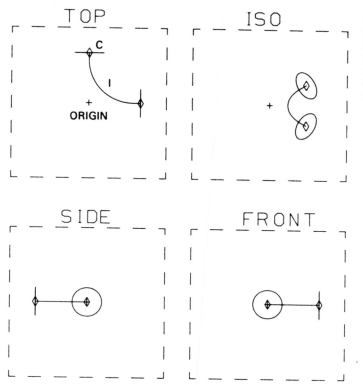

Figure 13–15
90 degree long radius,
long-tangent elbow.
(Reprinted with permis-
sion from Computervision
Corporation, Bedford,
Massachusetts)

and modify design geometry. In addition, modifications can be made to this geometry for visual clarification and presentation purposes. These changes will not affect the model's database, only the model's visual appearance. In Figure 13–20, the designer is "drawing" directly on the CRT using a light pen to create a mechanical design of an airplane.

Mechanical software has many drafting and dimensional capabilities to add dimensional information, notes, and labels to drawings. Figure 13–21 shows the dimensioning section of a mechanical design and detailing menu.

The designer can also manipulate drawings of the model for aesthetic reasons or for visual clarification. These manipulation features include choosing a variety of line fonts (patterns), erasing hidden lines, defining any type or number of views, inserting dual dimensions, defining ANSI, JIS, or ISO standards, sectioning, and crosshatching. Dimensions can be in English or metric units of measurement. In some systems, dimensional information is associative. ***Associativity means that if a designer changes or modifies geometry in the model, the dimensions will automatically be updated to reflect those changes in the detail drawings***. Associativity also

Figure 13–16
Heat exchanger after
detailing is done by the
generate detail com-
mand. (Reprinted with
permission from Com-
putervision Corporation,
Bedford, Massachusetts)

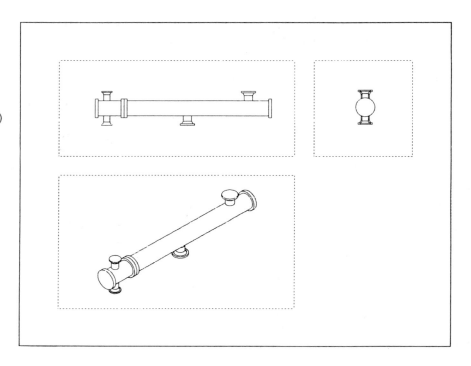

Figure 13–17
Heat exchanger with
pipes routed. (Reprinted
with permission from
Computervision
Corporation, Bedford,
Massachusetts)

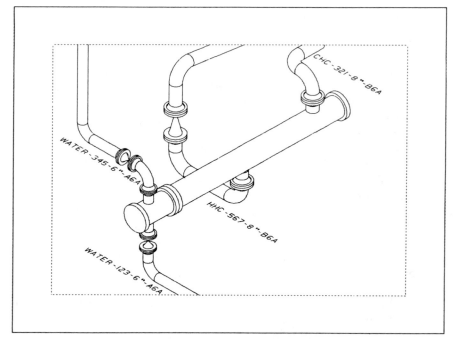

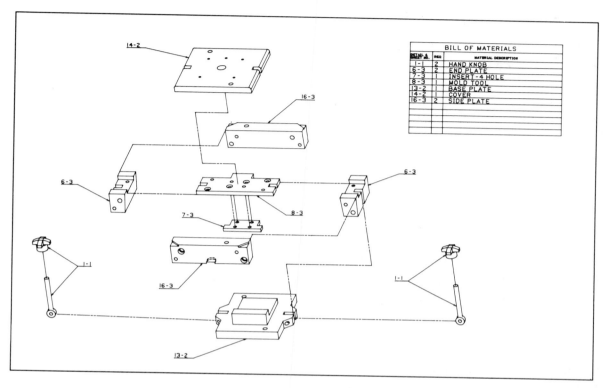

BILL OF MATERIALS		
DETAIL #	REQ	MATERIAL DESCRIPTION
1-1	2	HAND KNOB
6-3	2	END PLATE
7-3	1	INSERT-4 HOLE
8-3	1	MOLD TOOL
13-2	1	BASE PLATE
14-2	1	COVER
16-3	2	SIDE PLATE

Figure 13–18
Technical illustrations and assembly drawings can be produced using the CADDS 4 designer V systems. (Reprinted with permission from Computervision Corporation, Bedford, Massachusetts)

involves being able to carry out design change specifications all the way to the manufacturing side of the product; i.e., changes to the database could automatically update NC files and quality control features as well as inventory and other items attached to the database. An entire labor force of a plant can be trained in the use of the CAD/CAM system as a total control device. Any information that is "tagged" to the database can be used by any of the employees within the plant. Some employees have more access than others, however; the system would be used as a complete control device from design through manufacturing and shipping and storage.

Figures 13–22 through 13–28 show the design and detailing of a mechanical assembly. The three-dimensional wireframe model is created first and then each piece is detailed separately. Since the system revises designs and dimensions easily, design modification is expedited with CADD (Figures 13–27 and 13–28). Two-dimensional mechanical drawing packages are also widely used where three-dimensional modeling is either not needed or is too costly.

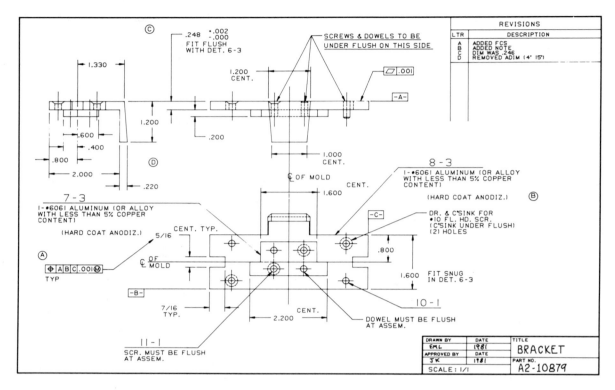

Figure 13–19
Drafting-CADDS 4
provides a total capability
for creation and genera-
tion of detail drawings.
(Reprinted with permis-
sion from Computervision
Corporation, Bedford,
Massachusetts)

Finite Element Analysis of Structures

Static structures are mechanical parts or assemblies which do not have functionally moving parts. Examples of such structures are building frames,
bridges, and chassis. The design of structures generally involves three
stages:

1. Preliminary design, during which the essential dimensions and shapes
are determined and preliminary stress calculations are made.

2. Design detailing, during which all subparts, if any, are detailed and the
manufacturing and assembly process is defined.

Figure 13–20
CADAM CADD system.
(Courtesy Lockheed-
California Company)

3. Design verification, which involves a detailed analysis of the reliability and functionality of the structure. The extent of design verification depends largely on the complexity and functional importance of the designed structure.

Most CADD systems significantly aid the design engineer in detailing and verifying the function and mechanical resistance of complex parts by employing finite element analysis methods interfaced to the three-dimensional model of the structure. Finite element analysis methods may be set up to calculate thermal stresses in addition to loads or to model the behavior of the construction material, usually steel, in its elastic or elasto-plastic domain.

The weakness of current generation mechanical CADD systems, however, lies in their lack of simple and easy-to-use tools for preliminary design, when speed and versatility are more important than precision in geometric construction and in mechanical strength calculations. In this first design phase, mechanical engineers need sketching capability rather than exact geometry creation and relatively simple, "engineering handbook"-style formulae as opposed to the very precise, but tedious, FEM method.

One of the most important tasks handled by a CADD system is the updating of existing mechanical designs and drawings since it can be accomplished quickly and easily compared to manual methods.

Figure 13–21
Dimensioning section of
a mechanical menu.
(Courtesy Computervi-
sion Corp.)

Technical Illustration

Technical illustration can be done with a two-dimensional or three-dimensional system. The fact that the original three-dimensional model database can be used to generate the illustration instead of redrawing the part is an advantage of the three-dimensional system. The generation of sales literature is also expedited with the use of CADD, especially when the different departments within a company can all share a common three-dimensional database. Figure 13–29 is an example of a technical illustration drawn with a two-dimensional system using isometric construction. Plates 51, 52, and 53 are examples of the technical illustrations one can create with a CADD system's color and layering capabilities.

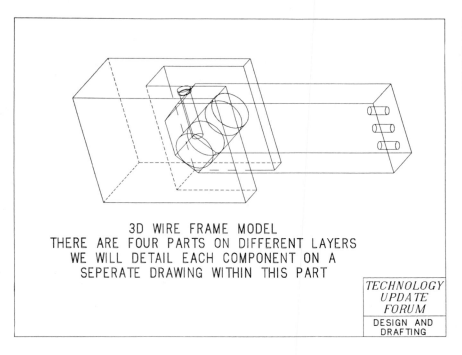

TECHNOLOGY
UPDATE
FORUM
DESIGN AND
DRAFTING

Figure 13–22
Mechanical wireframe model. (Reprinted with permission from Computervision Corporation, Bedford, Massachusetts)

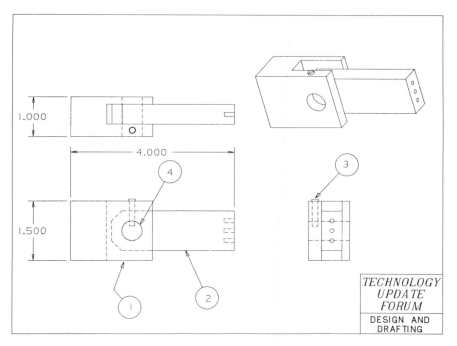

TECHNOLOGY
UPDATE
FORUM
DESIGN AND
DRAFTING

Figure 13–23
Mechanical assembly. (Reprinted with permission from Computervision Corporation, Bedford, Massachusetts)

Figure 13–24
Link detail. (Reprinted
with permission from
Computervision Corpora-
tion, Bedford, Mas-
sachusetts)

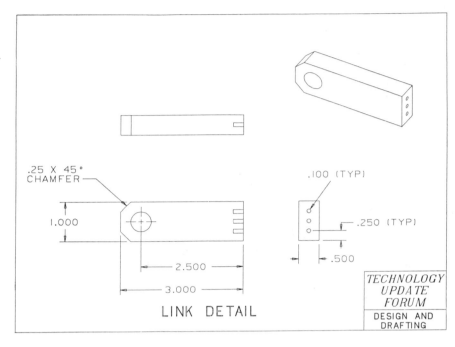

LINK DETAIL

TECHNOLOGY
UPDATE
FORUM

DESIGN AND
DRAFTING

Figure 13–25
Block detail. (Reprinted
with permission from
Computervision Corpora-
tion, Bedford, Mas-
sachusetts)

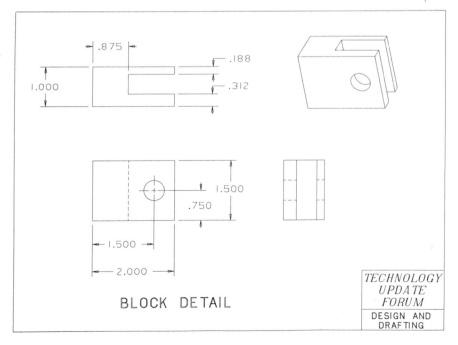

BLOCK DETAIL

TECHNOLOGY
UPDATE
FORUM

DESIGN AND
DRAFTING

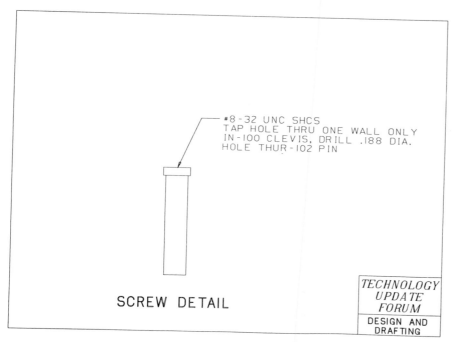

#8-32 UNC SHCS
TAP HOLE THRU ONE WALL ONLY
IN-100 CLEVIS, DRILL .188 DIA.
HOLE THUR-102 PIN

SCREW DETAIL

TECHNOLOGY
UPDATE
FORUM

DESIGN AND
DRAFTING

Figure 13–26
Screw detail. (Reprinted with permission from Computervision Corporation, Bedford, Massachusetts)

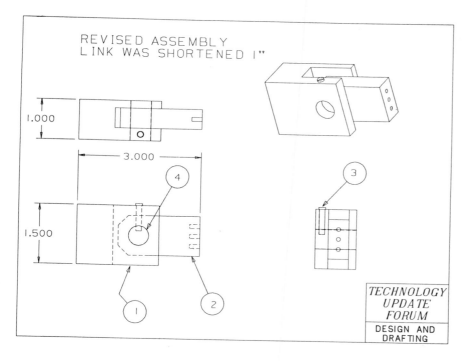

REVISED ASSEMBLY
LINK WAS SHORTENED 1"

1.000

3.000

1.500

TECHNOLOGY
UPDATE
FORUM

DESIGN AND
DRAFTING

Figure 13–27
Revised assembly link (shortened 1 inch). (Reprinted with permission from Computervision Corporation, Bedford, Massachusetts)

Figure 13–28
Updated link detail.
(Reprinted with permis-
sion from Computervision
Corporation, Bedford,
Massachusetts)

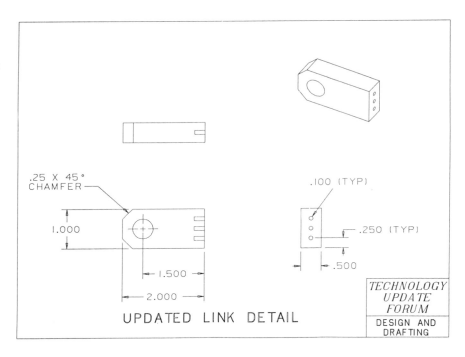

Figure 13–29
Technical illustration of
drafting machine.
(AutoCAD drawing
courtesy CADD North-
west, Inc.)

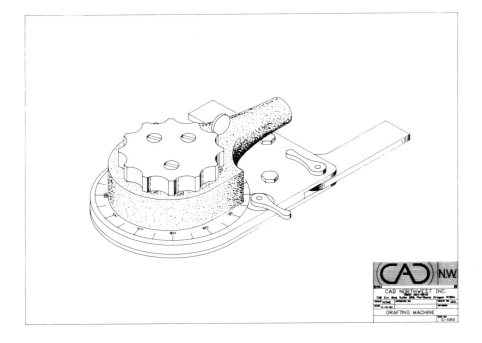

Electronics

The production of electronic products involves many distinct but related operations: circuit design and development, **printed circuit board** (PCB) design (Figure 13–30), **integrated circuit** (IC) layout (Figure 13–31), mechanical design, manufacturing, assembly, and testing.

One of the most important applications for CADD is integrated circuit and printed circuit board design and documentation. CADD increases productivity by automating and integrating the key steps in the design and production of printed circuit boards (Figure 13–30). The typical PCB program uses automatic and manual editing modes to design the entire board from the drawing of the schematic to the final manufacturing and testing stages. Schematics, text, and board geometry are entered interactively into the system. Automatic assignment, placement, and routing routines are used to complete the design of the board. A variety of PC board sizes and types can be designed. Manual input can be used to override the automatic routines.

The automatic routing of PC boards is complemented by software to automatically place components on the board. Because of the increasing density of boards and complexity of circuits, this is an important feature for development. The CADD system also provides control tapes for numerically controlled drilling and insertion machines.

A CADD system automates and integrates the key steps in the design, documentation, and design rules checking of wiring diagrams. It reduces the time and expense in capturing, checking, updating, and extracting design information. This capability is applied to many types of diagrams: elementary (ladder), schematic, wire harness, and interconnection. Designs are developed faster, with fewer errors, and with higher quality.

For the development department, there are special problems both in design and in preparing the necessary documentation for manufacturing. Each operation in development poses specific design problems: developing the circuit requires calculation of a theoretical solution, followed by breadboarding, testing, and refining. Designing the printed board entails overcoming spatial restrictions and layout constraints; designing the equipment housing requires consideration of cooling arrangements, protecting against shocks or vibrations, providing easy access for servicing and, at the same time, satisfying styling requirements.

Printed Circuit Board Design

To illustrate how a CADD system is used in the development process, we will take a look at the design of a **printed circuit board**.

Designing a PCB using manual drawing or taping methods is a very tedious and time-consuming task. Having first prepared all the necessary information for the layout, a skilled drafter finds a suitable component placement solution within spatial restrictions and design constraints. The drafter

Figure 13–30
Calma's GDSII/32 CADD workstation for designers and manufacturers. (Courtesy Calma Company, a wholly-owned subsidiary of General Electric Company, U.S.A.)

Figure 13–31
Calma's CARDS II lays out printed circuit boards with speed, power and accuracy. Designers are free to apply their time to exploring design options while the enhanced editing capabilities and higher resolution make it easy to pack dense circuitry into smaller and more cost-effective spaces. (Courtesy Calma Company, a wholly-owned subsidiary of General Electric Company, U.S.A.)

then creates a tracking pattern for hundreds, possibly thousands, of connections, all the time working to a high degree of accuracy to avoid dimensional spacing errors. The completed design is manually checked for spacing errors, for connectivity errors (by comparing it against the circuit diagram), and for artwork quality. Finally, when the board is ready to manufacture, drive tapes are programmed for any NC manufacturing and testing machines to be used.

A schematic drawing package includes many aids to ensure fast schematic layout. The circuit layout is carried out at a design station. The interaction with the graphics display is via the keyboard and tablet (with stylus). Options are displayed on the graphics screen and the designer selects the appropriate option from the menu (Figure 13–32). The designer is provided with various capabilities to assist his or her efforts throughout the layout. The designer will ZOOM or WINDOW into selected areas of the drawing; different items are set to different colors; and certain items are made invisible to reduce the amount of data displayed and assist clarity. Automatic layout is available on some CADD systems; this allows for nongridded input of symbols and nodal lines directly from an engineer's sketch (Figure 13–33). Automatic layout aligns symbols and lines on the grid producing the first document automatically (Figure 13–34).

Schematic design symbols are called from the library and placed on the screen interactively using the tablet and stylus. The designer moves and/or rotates symbols as required. Subcircuits from previous work are stored and used in the same way, providing a good starting point for new schematics. The designer defines the point-to-point connection pattern of the symbols interactively while working at the graphics display. The interconnections are made with a choice of line widths or choice of colors to enable easy differentiation between voltage, ground, and signal connections. Text, in various sizes, is added by typing the text string on the keyboard. Once defined, the text is positioned, rotated, and mirrored on the graphics display using the tablet and stylus.

The designer reproduces repetitive areas of circuitry with ease. The designer creates the section of circuitry only once and then defines it as a subdrawing. The subdrawing is then positioned and replicated on the main drawing as required.

Once the schematic has been verified by the circuit engineer, data are transferred to a PCB application package. Data transfer includes full details on components and is correlated with the corresponding symbol or symbols on the schematic. More powerful systems allow one to verify the completed PCB against the schematic and automatically update the schematic drawing to ensure that both agree.

Routines are provided to move components interactively, rotate them, and fix them in position (Figures 13–35 and 13–36). All associated connections move with the component to enable assessment of location and rotation. Free text and component names are manipulated in a manner similar

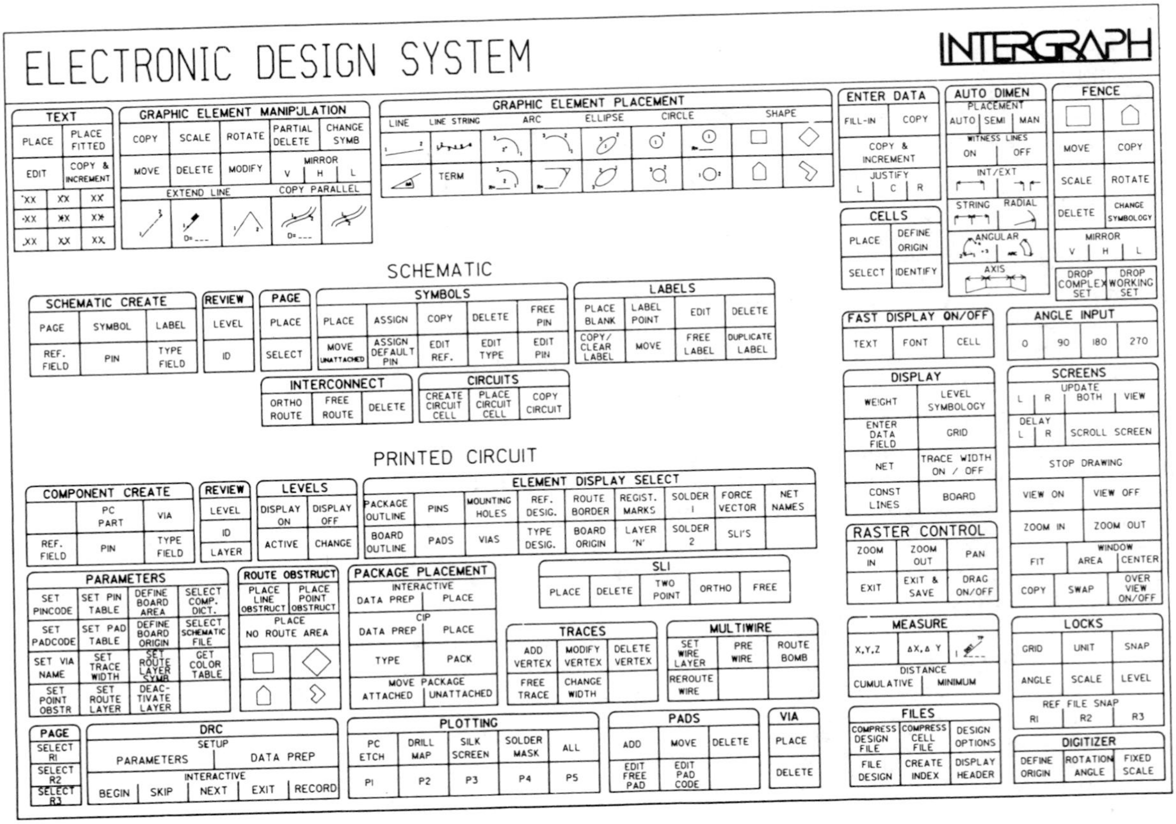

Figure 13–32
Electronic design system. (Courtesy Intergraph Corporation)

to components; they are mirrored so the text will appear on either side of the board. Most PCB design systems provide automatic component placement and automatic track routing. These routines provide significant reductions in design times.

Automatic component placement allows the designer to lay out integrated circuits and discrete components on user-defined grids. Routines are provided to swap components to improve the connection scheme. The designer has flexibility in using the placement routines; she or he fixes certain components in position and restricts the routines to operate on particular sections of the board. In addition, the designer interrupts the automatic routines to interactively place components as required.

Circuit connections are converted to tracks with interactive **routing.** The designer also modifies paths with interactive routing. Connections are displayed as straight lines (Figure 13–37) which are then converted, using the tablet and stylus, to a series of orthogonal or angled track segments. Seg-

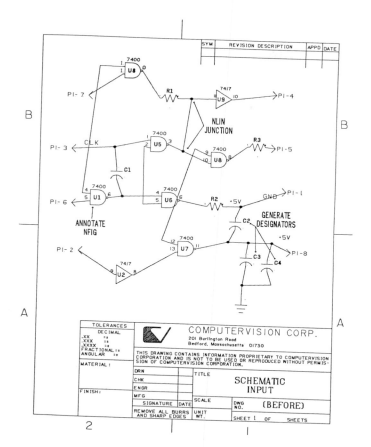

Figure 13–33
Schematic input, before.
(Reprinted with permission from Computervision Corporation, Bedford, Massachusetts)

ments can be moved and swapped between layers. Via holes are created automatically where required.

The interactive placement and routing routines provide the capability to design from start to finish. However, all of the decisions and the implementation of those decisions are done by the designer. The computer does most of the work required to do the placement and routing.

A pin-to-pin connection of all signals is used to verify connections or in conjunction with routing processes (Figure 13–38). *Rubberbanding* allows the designer to move components to see the relative location of traces on the board. This aids in the placement of components in congested areas (Figure 13–39).

The majority of circuit connections can also be converted to routes automatically. Automatic routing includes routines for routing power and ground connections, memory arrays, and the remaining signal connections.

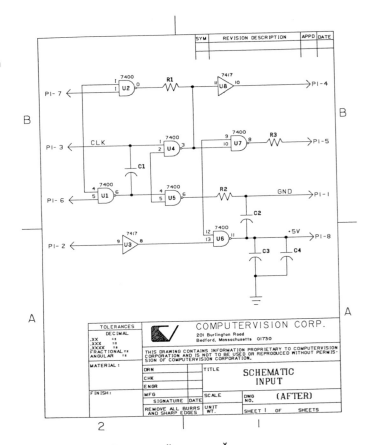

Figure 13–34
Schematic input, after.
(Reprinted with permission from Computervision Corporation, Bedford, Massachusetts)

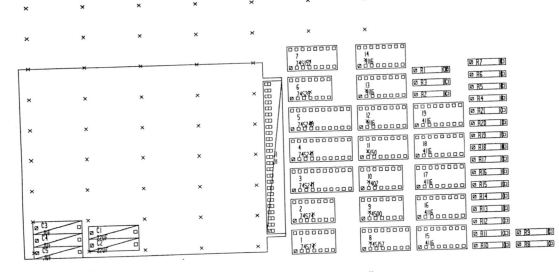

Figure 13–35
Initialized placement.
(Reprinted with permission from Computervision Corporation, Bedford, Massachusetts)

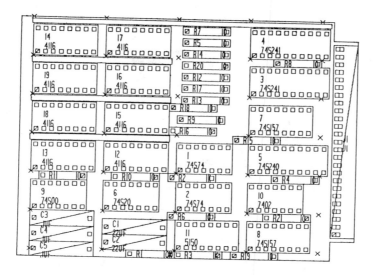

Figure 13–36
Component placement with keepouts. (Reprinted with permission from Computervision Corporation, Bedford, Massachusetts)

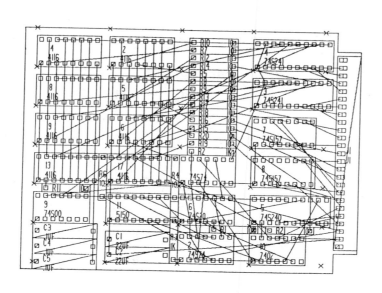

Figure 13–37
Component placement with ratsnest. (Reprinted with permission from Computervision Corporation, Bedford, Massachusetts)

Figure 13–38
Display net capability.
(Reprinted with permission from Computervision Corporation, Bedford, Massachusetts)

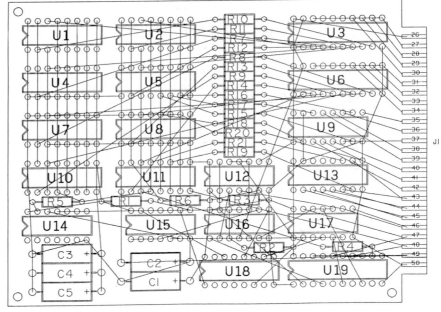

S=X.9Y.5
O=X.2Y.2

Figure 13–39
Rubberbanding of components. (Reprinted with permission from Computervision Corporation, Bedford, Massachusetts)

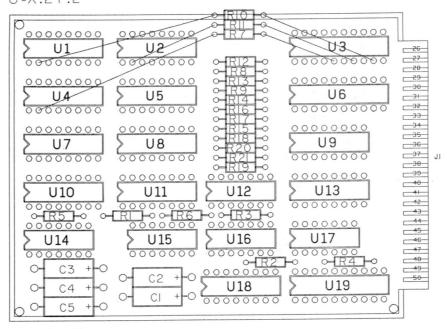

S=X.9Y.5
O=X.2Y.2

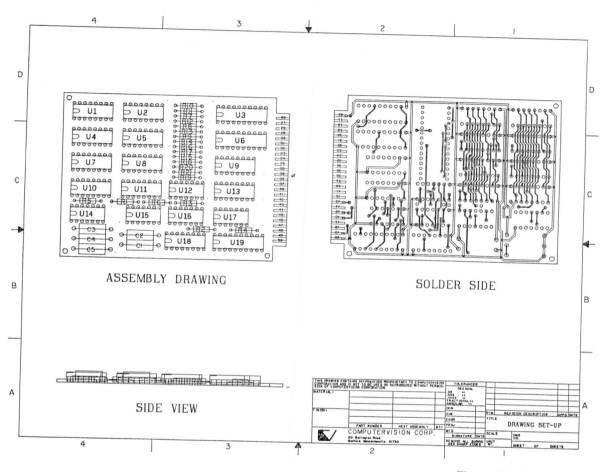

Figure 13–40
Drawing set-up. (Reprinted with permission from Computervision Corporation, Bedford, Massachusetts)

More powerful systems include **routers** specifically designed for multilayer PCBs. These routers minimize the number of via holes and prevent the insertion of vias underneath integrated circuits. The automatic routing is further enhanced by routines to do automatic gate and pen swapping.

Most systems include postprocessors to link to pen plotters, hardcopy units, and photoplotters. The pen plotters and hardcopy units provide check plots quickly at any stage in the design. Photoplotters provide high quality, one-to-one or scaled artwork for all manufacturing artwork. Assembly drawings (Figure 13–40) and a three-dimensional model (Figure 13–41) are extracted from the original design database.

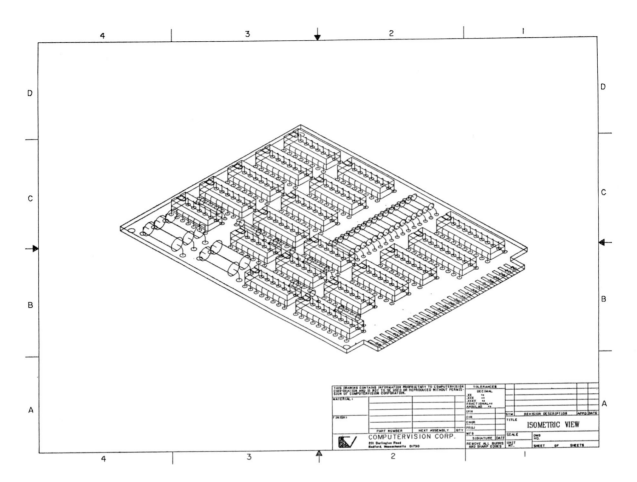

Figure 13–41
Isometric view. (Re-
printed with permission
from Computervision
Corporation, Bedford,
Massachusetts)

Output from the system does not end with manufacturing artwork. Artwork masters (Figure 13–42), solder masks (Figure 13–43), component drawings (Figure 13–44), silkscreen masters (Figure 13–45), pad masters and drill drawings (Figure 13–46), and NC drill and NC automatic component placement tapes are all generated from the original PCB design data with much of the process automated.

To complete the design cycle, the system provides design documentation with engineering reports and part listings.

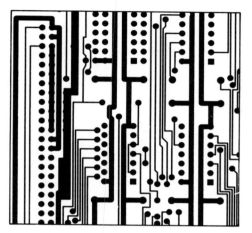

Figure 13–42
Artwork masters. One-to-one artwork masters can be generated automatically from the database, eliminating costly photo-reduction. (Courtesy Gerber System Tech.)

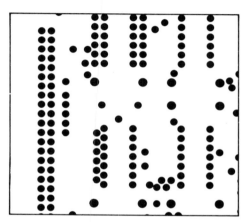

Figure 13–43
Solder masks. The solder mask is generated from the same database as the artwork master. This improves the manufacturability of the board and reduces external charges. (Courtesy System Tech.)

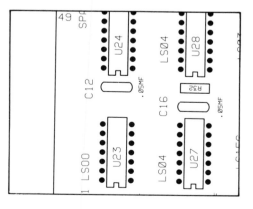

Figure 13–44
Component drawings. To aid in breadboarding prototypes or hand insertion of components, assembly drawings can be generated from the same database as the original design. (Courtesy Gerber System Tech.)

Figure 13–45
Silkscreen masters. The component layout and reference designators that are commonly created as part of the symbols can be extracted to generate a silkscreen master. (Courtesy Gerber System Tech.)

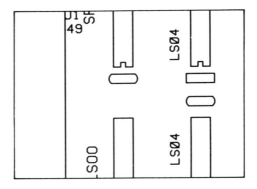

GLOSSARY

APPLICATION SOFTWARE A computer program that assists a user in performing a specific task.

ARTWORK A photoplot, photomask, pen plot, electrostatic copy, or positive or negative photographic transparency used to manufacture an IC, PC board, or other product.

ASSOCIATIVE DIMENSIONING The means by which a CADD dimensioning program automatically updates the dimensions as the geometry changes.

ASSOCIATIVITY The linking of parts, components, or elements with their attributes or with other geometric entities.

AUTOMATIC DIMENSIONING The CADD system computes the dimensions and automatically places dimensions, extension lines, and arrowheads where required.

AUTOMATIC PLACEMENT A routine that automatically packages IC optimizes the layout of components on a PC board.

AUTOMATIC ROUTE A routine that automatically determines the placement of copper on the printed circuit board to connect pins of the same signal.

BILL OF MATERIALS (BOM) A listing of all the subassemblies, parts, materials, and quantities required to manufacture an assembly or to build a plant.

CONNECTION The lines between pins, components, contacts, or circuits in printed circuit board and wiring diagram construction.

DETAIL DRAWINGS The drawing of a single part with all the dimensions and annotations necessary to completely define the part for manufacturing and inspection.

FUNCTION MENU The display or list of commands that the user can use to perform a task.

INTEGRATED CIRCUIT (IC) An electronic component which may vary in complexity from a simple logic gate to a microprocessor. An IC is usually packaged in a single substrate such as a slice of silicon, also called a *chip*.

INTEGRATED SYSTEM A CADD system that integrates the entire product development cycle—analysis, design, and fabrication—into a single system.

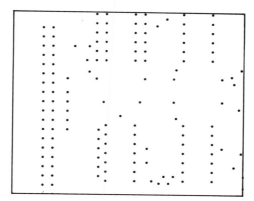

Figure 13–46
Pad masters and drill drawings. The pad master is generated from the same database as the artwork master and is used to create a drill pattern. Drill drawings with user-defined symbols representing relative hole sizes on the PC board can be generated from the same database as the artwork master with the Drill Drawing Program. (Courtesy Gerber System Tech.)

INTERFERENCE CHECKING A CADD capability that allows plant or mechanical designers to examine a three-dimensional model and automatically pinpoint interfaces between pipes, equipment, structures, or machinery.

ISOMETRIC A drawing in which the object is drawn from an oblique view so that the object appears as a solid object.

LAYER A logical concept used to distinguish subdividual group(s) of data within a given drawing; it may be thought of as a series of transparencies (overlayed) in any order without any depth.

LAYER DISCRIMINATION The selective assignment of colors to a layer, or the highlighting of entities to distinguish among data on different layers displayed on a screen.

PAD An area of plated copper on a PC board to which leads of components are soldered.

PATH The route that an interconnection takes between connections in printed circuit board design.

PATTERN GENERATION The transformation of CADD integrated circuit design information into a format for use by a photo- or electron-beam machine in producing a reticle.

ROUTER A program that automatically determines the routing path for the component connections on a PC board.

ROUTING Placing the interconnects between components on a printed circuit board or integrated circuit.

RUBBERBANDING A technique for displaying a straight line with one end fixed and the other end attached to the movable cursor.

SCHEMATIC A not-to-scale diagram of an electrical circuit.

SYMBOL A set of primitive graphic entities, lines, points, arcs, circles, and text that are grouped together as a unit.

WIRING DIAGRAM A schematic representation of all circuits and devices that shows their interconnectivity.

QUIZ

True or False

1. CADD can be used to improve and speed the design tasks associated with all engineering areas.

2. CADD finds its widest applications in the area of electronic design.

3. A three-dimensional CADD system allows greater freedom in the design stage since many variations can be tried and analyzed.

4. Without CADD, electronics development could not have reached its present state-of-the-art level.

5. Many PCB CADD packages allow for autoplacement and autorouting of printed circuit boards.

6. Technical illustrations can be generated from the model database when a three-dimensional system is used for mechanical design.

7. CADD applications are limited to traditional engineering fields.

8. Color can be used in CADD to differentiate between layers.

Fill in the Blank

9. _____ is the ability of the system to update designs and dimensions automatically after the model database has been changed.

10. Plant design and piping software packages allow for the extraction of a variety of design information and documentation including _____, _____, _____, and _____.

11. Some CADD piping programs allow for the automatic generation of piping _____ spools from the three-dimensional model without having to construct the drawing from the beginning.

12. All application software allow for the automatic placement of _____ from a menu.

13. _____ is the ability to dynamically stretch a line or shape to a desired location.

14. Two-dimensional systems normally allow for the construction of two-dimensional drawings and _____ projections.

15. The ability to move selected items and shapes about the display screen is called _____.

16. Automatic _____ allows the designer to layout the PCB on user-defined grid networks.

Answer the Following

17. Describe the difference between design "modeling" and "drafting."

18. What functions are normally carried out in the drafting mode in mechanical design?

19. How is a three-dimensional model of a piping design used to document the design?

20. Name six possible types of drawing documentation and data extraction used in three-dimensional plant design.

21. What is associativity and how does it function in changes to mechanical designs?

22. What is automatic routing and how does it help the PC designer?

23. Name six types of drawings that can be generated by CADD printed circuit design software.

24. Describe the process of PCB design using a three-dimensional CADD system.

Chapter

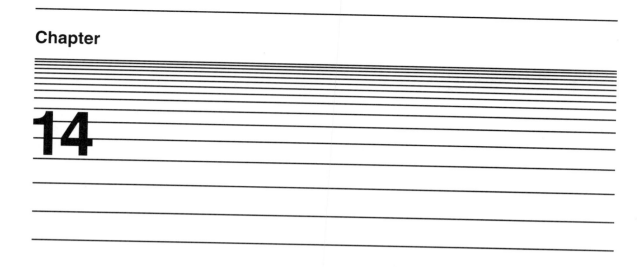

14

Engineering Workstations

Objectives

Upon completion of this chapter the reader will be able to do the following:

- Describe the various types of host-based workstations

- Understand the difference between host-based and stand-alone workstations

- Explain the role of engineering workstations in the engineering process

- Describe the role of local area networking in implementing workstations

Introduction

Workstation is a term that has many meanings in the computer industry. Traditionally, the term has been used to refer to any device used to interact with a computer system; in this sense, workstations include such devices as *dumb*, *intelligent*, and *graphics terminals*. In this book, workstation will mean a graphics terminal. This workstation can be connected to a larger computer or it can contain its own processor. If the workstation is connected to a larger computer, we call this a **host-based workstation**. When the workstation contains its own processor, we call this a *stand-alone workstation*.

Host-Based Workstations

In the past, powerful, complicated, mainframe-based CAD/CAM systems have dominated the engineering world. Figure 14–1 shows an example of a host-based mainframe CAD system. Here, a designer is using CADAM software on the old IBM 3250 workstation. The new generation of IBM 5080 workstations is now used to run CADD software (Figures 14–2 and 14–3).

CADD systems aid design by systematically storing data and drawings so engineers can edit designs without redrawing them. The most sophisticated mainframe systems — which run on supercomputers instead of general purpose machines — let engineers simulate on a workstation a prototype in action.

However, the prices of the big computers are very high and their software packages are comparably priced. Even a full-scale mainframe supports only a few CAD/CAM users compared with the number of users supported under data processing applications on the same machines. Accordingly, per-user costs of mainframe CAD/CAM systems are so high only the larger companies can justify the mainframe system.

High prices are not the only drawback of mainframe systems for computer-aided design, computer-aided manufacturing, or computer-aided engineering. When too many users get on a mainframe system at the same time, the whole system can grind to a halt. Unlike multijob systems, mainframe CAD/CAM systems have to cope with users who all want to do the

Figure 14–1
CADAM software running on the old IBM-3250 workstation. (Courtesy Lockheed-California Co.)

Figure 14-2
IBM-5080 Graphics
System.

same types of things. The choices of mainframe CAD/CAM systems are very limited. There simply aren't very many companies selling these systems.

As a result of these continuing dificulties with mainframe CAD/CAM usage, users have gone to smaller, locally controlled CAD/CAM systems. These systems use minicomputers as hosts. Some are being built from the ground up with CAD/CAM applications in mind and are very fast for their price and size (Figure 14-4).

A typical minicomputer CAD/CAM software package with drafting, designing, and machining functions costs from $100,000 to $350,000. A similar

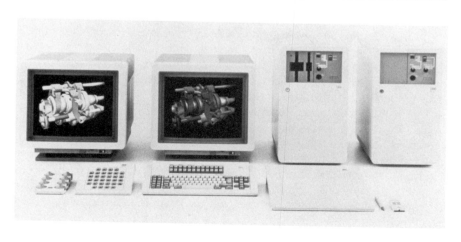

Figure 14-3
IBM-5080 system
components.

mainframe package might cost from $500,000 to $1 million or more. Since minicomputers are less powerful than mainframes, they support fewer workstations — 10 to 20 is a typical system. A large mainframe can support 50 to 200 workstations before any *degradation* in the response time. But because most engineering organizations only need a dozen or so workstations in one cluster, and because they are budget-conscious, the minicomputer-based CAD/CAM system has become the solution for many engineering companies.

Most mainframe systems share the same characteristics as shown in Figures 14–5 and 14–6. The individual designer works at a workstation, and one or more workstations are connected to a local graphics processor or controller. The local graphics processor is connected via a serial cable or teleprocessing cable with a controller at the host computer complex. The designer at his or her workstation communicates with the host computer via this cable. The software drawings created by the designer at the workstation, reside at the host.

Hardcopy drawings are obtained in one of two basic ways. If a copy of information on the display screen is needed quickly (for example, to discuss a question with a colleague), a local plot is made. Conventional hardcopies for use in approval cycles, delivery to clients, or reproduction are requested and processed via the host computer. These copies are made from the draw-

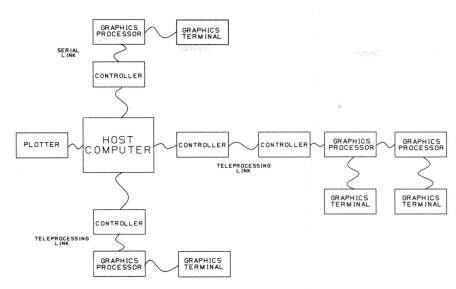

Figure 14–5
Basic host-based system components.

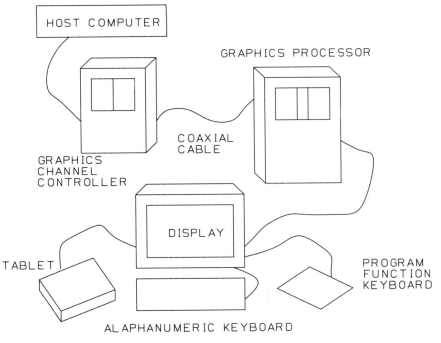

Figure 14–6
Host-based graphics system.

ings filed at the host on plotters that are located almost anywhere — near the host computer or in the same area as the workstation.

In a centralized system, all the workstations are placed in a single location. Therefore, a designer has to travel a certain distance from her or his desk — from a few feet to several thousand — to reach the workstation. In a decentralized system, there are single workstations or small clusters. Workstations are located next to a designer's drafting board or are concentrated in small clusters conveniently located with respect to various user groups.

The centralized approach offers a number of advantages. Help, whether from peers or support personnel, is more readily available because it is concentrated in one location. Access to a plotter by designers is more convenient, assuming it is located in the same area. The system is easier to control and schedule, resulting in improved usage.

There are, however, some disadvantages. Designers are away from their usual work locations, meaning time lost in travel and obtaining information from the usual work locations needed to complete the task. The designers' immediate supervisor is remote from the workstation location, complicating effective communication and supervision.

The disadvantages of the centralized approach are the strengths of the decentralized approach — namely, better supervision and easier designer access to required working materials and documentation.

Likewise, the strengths of the centralized approach are the disadvantages of decentralizing. The system itself is more difficult to manage, help is not as readily available, and obtaining hardcopy is more difficult depending on the location of the plotter. Environmental control (lighting, air conditioning, etc.) is also more difficult to maintain.

Stand-Alone Workstations

Stand-alone workstations fall somewhere between minicomputers and personal computers and share many of the characteristics of both. A typical stand-alone workstation includes a central processing unit, a high-resolution graphics display, a graphics input device, one or more storage devices (Winchester disk drive, floppy disk drive, or magnetic tape drive), communications interfaces, and a network interface. Unlike minicomputers, which typically support many users at once, stand-alone workstations are designed to be single-user systems. A CADD stand-alone workstation based on the HP 9000 computers is shown in Figure 14–7.

Instead of running data through a host CPU — whether mainframe or minicomputer — stand-alone workstations take advantage of 32-bit processors, such as the INTEL 80286 and the Motorola 68000 family, and the co-processor math chips that have been designed to work with them. The new generation processors handle the complicated floating point operations and numbercrunching involved in generating high-resolution drawings and

Figure 14–7
Hewlett-Packard's HP 9000 computer and stand-alone workstation. (Courtesy Hewlett-Packard)

sophisticated simulations. These workstations let users work locally, then upload their files to hosts or store them on hard disks. These stand-alone systems have high performance and low price tags: prices range from $30,000 to $100,000.

The sharing of resources and data is essential if the workstation is to increase productivity. Therefore, the workstations and databases are established so that the output of one process or program is the input of another. Workstations increase productivity at every stage of development, from initial product concept through manufacturing.

Compatibility is one of the most critical issues in workstation implementation. Hardware and software compatibility are both needed. Equipment in a workstation is compatible with other equipment on a network. For example, we are able to use a terminal off-line to perform pre- and postprocessing tasks, calling on the host only when intensive processing or access to a central database is needed.

Software compatibility is just as important. Ideally, workstations are able to run programs downloaded from a host without modification. More realistically, programs are run simply by recompiling source programs for the workstation.

Local area networks also play a large role in the implementation of the workstation. High-speed communication channels allow expensive resources to be shared among many workstations without performance degradation. Typically, these kinds of resources are needed for fast response but cannot be utilized continuously by a single user. Examples are large, fast plotters, supercomputers, and large central databases.

In this environment, the final design and analysis results are passed through to prototype manufacture and testing, which generate results that are fed back into the design and analysis loop; further results are fed back into prototype, and so on. In the process, better communication results between all groups involved in the product development. The factory-of-the-future concept means that the product goes from concept to manufacture on the factory floor in a completely automated sequence. Workstation implementation is the first step toward this level of automation.

The primary objective is to integrate the islands of activity, such as design, toolpath generation, or finite element mesh creation. The network of workstations provides a smooth transition from design and model development to analysis, then to toolpath generation. The system ties the design/model/manufacturing data to actual production control and other administrative functions.

The network has workstations located in key areas: design, manufacturing, quality assurance, and testing. These workstations are characterized by good drafting and design capabilities, analysis software that can operate directly on the product model, direct tie-ins to production scheduling and control, powerful NC features, and a simple and flexible human interface.

The workstations have local computer capabilities so that they can operate in a stand-alone mode. They also have network capability to communicate to a *file server* (database manager) and access the database containing the product definition (part geometry). The workstation allows each discipline to perform its own tasks while working with a production definition that is current.

Case Study

To illustrate a scenario for greater productivity, imagine an electronics engineer who is supported by a network of compatible graphics workstations, storage subsystems, and hardcopy peripherals. Displays vary from medium-resolution to very high-resolution color graphics. Each programmable workstation has a powerful general-purpose processor that can execute custom or third-party application software and a dedicated graphics processor to perform rapid graphics manipulations on the display. Graphics input devices such as joysticks, trackballs, joydisks, and mouse pointers are connected to many of the workstations, in addition to traditional keyboards.

Terminals are connected to a large mainframe via cables, while the workstations are connected to the mainframe, to peripherals, and to each other by a high-speed local area network. Each workstation can access a variety of peripherals, including mass storage devices, multipen plotters, inkjet color copiers, printers, and film recorders.

Our engineer has a medium-resolution color graphics workstation that can perform many tasks in a stand-alone mode. This engineer can also use the mainframe for large tasks that take a lot of computation and can access data from the mainframe or other workstations.

Now, follow the designer through a typical design cycle from initial concept to production (Figure 14–8). First, the workstation is used to describe the designer's idea for a new measurement instrument and to prepare a proposal for management. In this effort, the designer is aided by the word processing capability of the workstation. Then, using an interactive drawing package and mouse, he or she sketches some concept drawings on the display screen and inserts them into the text.

Rough development and manufacturing cost estimates are prepared using a spreadsheet program that runs on the workstation. The report is output onto hardcopy with the concept illustration portrayed in color. Next, a few word slides are prepared on the workstation and are output along with the design sketches onto overhead transparencies using an inkjet color copier connected to the network.

Several weeks and a few presentations later, our engineer gets approval to develop the product. Now, she or he must plan the schedule and solidify the costs. The designer uses a project planning program employing the crit-

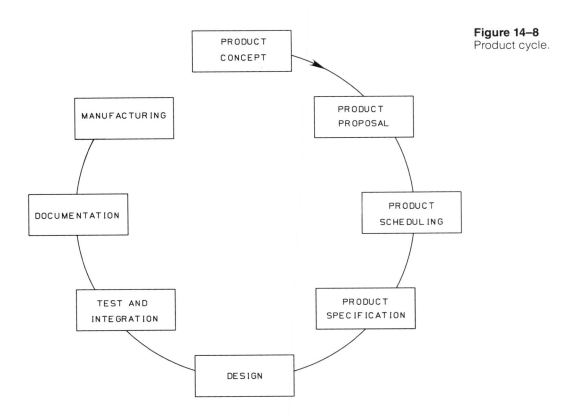

Figure 14–8
Product cycle.

ical path method to identify the project stages and coordinate support activities.

Next, specifications are written, again using the word processing and graphics capabilities. This time, however, the document is placed in a central database that resides on the network so that anyone can have immediate access to the latest version.

With the spec complete, the designer moves to a high-performance graphics design workstation to begin the circuit design. This station is shared by several engineers to better utilize its capability. Our engineer builds the circuit design by assembling a schematic diagram from an assortment of predefined component icons representing available discrete and integrated parts. In many cases, the designer merely labels part numbers and the workstation retrieves all pertinent information, such as IC type, logic equivalency, and pinout from a central database. This schematic is converted by the workstation into a database that completely describes the circuit. When the circuit is complete, the designer tests it with a circuit simulation program by sending the circuit database over the network to the mainframe. When the circuit is verified, our engineer makes a hardcopy of the schematic and sends it to evaluation engineering for analysis.

Meanwhile, the circuit board has been automatically routed by another program, and the component location diagram is transferred over the network to another workstation where a mechanical engineer will analyze the heat distribution and airflow characteristics to ensure adequate cooling. A spreadsheet program is used to find the optimum solution, one that considers total heat dissipation of all components, the required airflow at various ambient temperatures, and the cost of fans. The mechanical engineer will then use a custom program he or she has written to compute the dimensions and placements of air opening to allow proper ventilation.

Mechanical drawings of the instrument case, circuit boards, and internal support structures are created from the project database. Using a finite element mechanical modeling package on the mainframe, the rigidity of the mechanical design under vibrational stress is analyzed. The mechanical drawings will yield production and assembly drawings for the model shop, and ultimately, for the manufacturing department. These drawings are easily updated at the workstation and are available through the network.

All this time the electronics engineer is getting a head start on documentation back at her or his own workstation and is updating the project status so that timely status reports to management can be issued.

All data created in the design process are available for reference by manufacturing engineers. The whole process of getting the product to manufacturing is compacted because at each stage of the development cycle the engineer was able to function more productively. The engineer had general-purpose tools to help with all the nondesign tasks that take up a large portion of a designer's time, and he or she had the specific tools to make design time more efficient.

GLOSSARY

ACCEPTANCE TEST   A test for evaluating newly purchased hardware or software. The hardware or software must conform to predefined system specifications.

ACCESS TIME   One measure of system response. The time interval between when data are requested from storage and when those data are displayed on the screen.

BAUD RATE   A measure of the speed of signal transmission between the computer and the workstations. It is measured in bits per second.

BUS   A circuit or group of circuits that provide communications path between two or more devices.

CENTRAL PROCESSING UNIT (CPU)   The brain of a CADD system which controls the processing of information.

COMMAND   An instruction given to a processor using a menu and tablet, stylus, or alphanumeric keyboard.

COMMUNICATIONS NETWORK   A number of systems tied together to transmit data.

DATABASE   An organized collection of standard parts libraries, completed designs, documentation, and computer programs.

DEDICATED   Assigned to a single function, such as a workstation used exclusively for engineering calculations.

DEVICE   A hardware item such as a cathode ray tube, plotter, printer, or hardcopy unit.

DISK STORAGE   The use of magnetic disks as a storage device.

ERGONOMIC   Designed with the needs of the user in mind.

FILE   A named set of data on magnetic disks or tape. Also, to transfer the contents of working storage to permanent storage.

HARDCOPY   A copy on paper of what is shown on the screen; generated with an on-line printer or plotter.

HOST COMPUTER   The primary computer in a multiple computer operation.

INPUT DEVICE   Devices such as graphics tablets or keyboards that allow the user to input data into the CADD system.

INTELLIGENT TERMINAL   A workstation that contains a built-in computer, usually a microcomputer or minicomputer, and can perform some processing in a stand-alone mode.

LARGE-SCALE COMPUTER   A computer with large internal memory capacity and multiple input/output channels. Such computers can process many programs concurrently.

LOCAL AREA NETWORK (LAN)   A communications network in which all of the computers and workstations are in the same general area or building.

MAINFRAME COMPUTER   A large-scale computer.

MICROCOMPUTER   A small, relatively low-cost computer that includes a microprocessor, memory, and all necessary interface circuits.

MINICOMPUTER   A computer that is between the mainframe computers and the micro-computers in size, power, complexity, and cost.

NODE   A computer or workstation connected to a local area network.

OUTPUT   The end result of a process or series of processes, such as artwork, hardcopy, reports, and drawings.

OUTPUT DEVICE   Hardware, such as a printer or plotter, used to produce a copy of the results of the computer's processing operations.

PERIPHERALS   Devices connected to a computer such as tape drives, disks, workstations, and plotters.

PROCESSOR   The hardware components that perform arithmetic and logic operations, often called the computer.

QUEUE   A waiting list of tasks to be performed or messages to be transmitted.

RESPONSE TIME   The elapsed time from the completion of a command at a workstation to the display of the results at that workstation.

TELECOMMUNICATIONS   The transmission of signals over long distances between a computing system and remotely located devices by telephone, microwave, infrared link, fiber optics, or coaxial cable.

TURNKEY SYSTEM   A CADD system for which the vendor assumes total responsibility for building, installing, and testing all the hardware and software required to do a specific application or applications.

WINCHESTER DRIVE   A combination of a disk drive and one or more hard disks permanently sealed in a case.

WORKSTATION   The hardware by which a designer interacts with the computer, also called a *terminal*.

QUIZ

True or False

1. If a workstation is connected to a large computer, it is called a host-based workstation.

2. A stand-alone workstation is one that contains its own plotter.

3. In a host-based system, the designer communicates with the host computer through the tape drive.

4. Some systems use minicomputers that were designed especially for CAD/CAM applications.

5. In a centralized system, all the workstations are placed in a single location.

6. Stand-alone workstations cannot run programs downloaded from a host computer.

7. Stand-alone workstations have local computer capabilities.

8. Local area networks are used to tie together stand-alone workstations.

Fill in the Blank

9. A workstation can be connected to a larger _____ or it can contain its own _____.

10. Smaller, locally controlled CAD/CAM systems use _____ as hosts.

11. The designer at his or her _____ communicates with the _____ _____ via a teleprocessing link.

12. In a host-based system, drawings created by the designer at the workstation reside at the _____.

13. In a decentralized system, there are single _____ or small _____.

14. _____ _____ fall somewhere between minicomputers and personal computers.

15. The primary objective of a network of workstations is to integrate the _____ of activity.

16. Workstations have local computer capabilities so that they can operate in a _____ mode.

Answer the Following

17. Describe the difference between a centralized and decentralized system.

18. Describe the difference between a host-based system and a stand-alone system.

19. Why have many engineering firms chosen minicomputer systems instead of host-based systems?

20. How is hardcopy obtained in a host-based system?

Chapter

15

Personal Computer–Based CADD Systems

Objectives

Upon completion of this chapter the reader will be able to do the following:

- Describe how personal computer (PC)–based CADD systems differ from other CADD systems

- Discuss the advantages of PC CADD systems over other CADD systems

- Discuss the primary limitations of PC CADD systems

- Describe how a PC CADD system creates a drawing

Introduction

Personal computer–based CADD is a relatively low-cost, high-performance, mostly two-dimensional design and drafting technology that utilizes a personal computer with medium- to high-resolution display screen.

Over a dozen different personal computers (counting the IBM PC family and all 100 percent compatible machines as one) can be used for personal computer–based CADD systems. A computer suitably equipped should have 512K of RAM, a math coprocessor (this integrated circuit handles math-intensive operations for its companion CPU), and a hard disk.

Drawing regeneration on a minimal system, 384K of RAM and two floppy disks, can be painfully slow on large drawings. A hard disk can be the most important addition to the minimal system. Most of the CADD packages are large programs that use overlays and thus must refer to the disk quite often. Therefore, the speed of disk access is most important.

The math coprocessor chip helps to speed up the program's arithmetic, affecting the time it takes to draw circles, arcs, and text. The addition of the math coprocessor can increase speed by as much as 300 percent. Operating a CADD system from a keyboard alone is very slow. Input devices such as mice, digitizers, trackballs, joysticks, and light pens are recommended to achieve the greatest level of efficiency for PC-based systems.

Although some of the CADD programs support output to a few dot matrix printers, such printouts are only a quick way to preview work. Plotters with at least 14 by 17 inch paper handling are recommended for all small systems. More complex drawings, such as factory floor plans or elaborate flow charts, require a still larger unit. The lettering must fit the proportions of the drawings; a complex drawing can easily require 24 by 36 inch hard-copy in order to produce legible small print.

Personal computer–based CADD systems (Figure 15–1) have reached a level of sophistication where they can be considered legitimate professional drafting tools for small- and medium-sized design offices. The capabilities of the more competitive systems permit most ordinary drafting tasks to be completed with equal or greater efficiency than with traditional methods. There are some systems available that contain all of the features required of a fully productive CADD drafting tool.

Although the PC CADD world is just a subset of a greater universe consisting of larger workstations and host-based CADD systems, PC systems are beginning to be extremely impressive from a price/performance standpoint and can begin to be compared with the larger systems in terms of overall functionality and performance (Figure 15–2). The next generation of PCs will rival established workstation-based systems, while undercutting them in price.

Available Systems

A wide range of PC-based CADD systems are on the market, and it is not the intention of the authors to suggest that one system is better than another. Here is an overview of a few of the systems that are found at the high school and college level; this is by no means an exhaustive overview of all systems. MATC, CADAPPLE, CAD, and AutoCAD are mentioned here simply because these are the systems that many schools have purchased to serve as

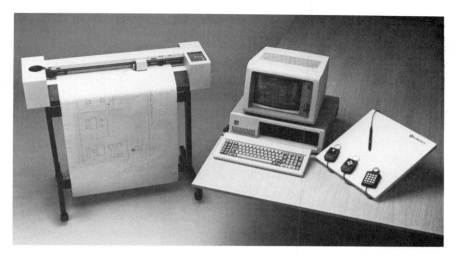

Figure 15–1
Personal computer-
based CADD system.
(Courtesy Numonics
Corp.)

trainers for CADD students. Some schools are fortunate to have workstation-
based systems, but most are relying on PC-based CADD to educate prospec-
tive drafters, designers, and engineers in the area of CADD.

Apple II computer–based systems provided the first and most cost-
effective way of introducing CADD in the classroom. CADAPPLE, from T & W
Systems, uses an 8-bit microcomputer and two floppy disk drives. It can perform many basic drafting functions, but, because of the limitations in computing power from the APPLE II, it is used mainly as a trainer and in schools.

Figure 15–2
CADD station. (Courtesy
Hewlett-Packard)

MATC is a two-dimensional training software package used to acquaint the user with Computervision's command language. Because of its extremely low price, MATC has also found its way into many schools and training programs that wish to introduce Computervision CADDS languages or just as an introduction to CADD. MATC was also originally restricted to the APPLE II Computer.

CAD can be run on a number of different personal computers but is used primarily with IBM PCs. Since these PCs have 16-bit processors, the drafting and calculating capabilities of CAD make it suitable for industrial applications confined to two-dimensional tasks and for educational institutions. A variety of industrial applications are available on VersaCAD including programs for piping, architecture, electronic, HVAC, and structural.

AutoCAD is a relatively new software addition to the PC-based CADD market and has quickly become the leading vendor of CADD stations in the world. AutoCAD can be configured with a large number of personal computers, though the IBM PC is the most common. A set of commands is given at the end of this chapter to draw a gear using AutoCAD.

Because of its popularity, AutoCAD garners support from a number of third-party products, notably Cubicomp's Model Maker. Model Maker brings solid-modeling and surface-shading capabilities to personal computer-based systems. It's not a true CADD package, but interfaces to AutoCAD and T & W Systems' VersaCAD allow users of those packages to integrate Model Maker's solid-modeling functions.

Robo System's RoboCAD PC is another package designed with general drawing and drafting application in mind. It features an easy-to-use command structure, a graphically indexed disk library, and an interface that permits the use of AutoCAD files.

While CADD software designed for personal computers is increasing in capability, stretching up to the level of bigger systems, turnkey vendors are now stretching heavy-duty miniframe- and mainframe-hosted programs down to personal computers. Turnkey systems vendors, including Auto-trol, Calma, Computervision, Tasvir, Gerber Systems, and McDonnell Douglas, have created personal computer–based software.

Advantages

PC-based systems offer autonomy and ease of maintenance. System performance does not degrade (diminish) with multiple users; and if a system goes down, only that workstation is affected.

Pricing   PC-based CADD software packages have an average initial selling price of $1000 to $2000 depending on the system (Figure 15–3). Although it may cost an additional $10,000 to purchase the hardware for a complete system for a single user, most companies already own PCs that are used for other purposes. Therefore, the software cost may be the major part of the cost for starting a CADD area in the office.

Versatility   Since they spend only about one third of their time on design and analysis tasks, the increasing use of PCs for nonCADD applications is particularly important to designers. The high cost of workstation-based systems that perform these design tasks could be somewhat offset by using PCs for all or most nondesign and analysis tasks.

Ease of Use and Specialization   PC CADD systems normally take less than a month to learn to use effectively, compared to approximately three months for workstation-based CADD and up to nine months for host-based systems. This is partially because PCs lack the complexity and advanced applications software programs normally found on larger systems. However, if the designer has prior experience using any type of CADD system, the time of training for larger CADD systems is reduced by up to 75 percent.

Training   Because of the accelerated learning speed achieved by users with previous CADD experience, low-cost PC CADD systems are used for training. Features found in both PC and large CADD systems include: layering; dimensioning; graphic operations such as translation, rotation, mirroring, and copying; computational analysis such as area, volume, distance, and

Figure 15–3
CADD system using an Apple computer and running CADAPPLE software. (Courtesy T & W Systems)

bill-of-materials generation; display functions such as panning and zooming, support for freehand sketching; file manipulation; control of line and text fonts; and other generic CADD functions. Automated dimensioning packages make PC CADD ideal for two-dimensional drafting tasks.

Drafting Decentralization   PC CADD systems are being used by companies with large systems to decrease the load on centralized CADD facilities. This use of PC CADD systems will continue to expand because many PC vendors are offering database compatibility with larger CADD systems, and many of the workstation and minicomputer vendors are supporting the PC as a terminal.

Productivity   Two-dimensional production drawing with many PC CADD systems is up to four times more productive than manual methods. Drawing revisions result in even higher gains.

Customizing   An extremely large PC vendor base allows for both hardware and software customization. Many PC software offerings permit user-defined symbol libraries, screen menus, and macros to expedite CADD drawing and database functions.

Limitations

Unrealistic Expectations   The marketing efforts of an extremely large number of PC CADD vendors have created an unrealistic level of expectation among potential users. Fierce competition among vendors has resulted in marketing claims that exceed software capabilities. It is important to understand that a cost-effective return on investment is not necessarily guaranteed by a low procurement price.

Lack of Standards   There are very few PC CADD vendors that support IGES, a program that facilitates database exchange between CADD systems. This means that moving up from a PC system to a larger system can be a problem since many systems cannot be expanded or upgraded. IGES and recent networking schemes have just begun to permit PCs to communicate with each other and with minis and mainframes.

Speed   Processing speed is limited on PC systems. Even the IBM PC/AT is still a 16-bit word machine, although arithmetic operations are performed using 32-bit words. To partially overcome this problem, the use of a math coprocessor, at least 512K of RAM memory, and hard disk storage are often recommended for CADD applications. In general, software run times on PCs are often an order of magnitude longer than with workstations and minicomputers. This is particularly true when running analysis programs such as finite element analysis where run times range from several minutes to days.

Three-Dimensionality   Although some three-dimensional software is available on PC systems, it is still either limited or quite slow for medium or larger databases. True solid modeling for mechanical applications, or even surface modeling, tends to be computationally demanding and needs at least the power of an IBM PC/AT. Some systems such as Computervision's CADDS 4X software run on the IBM AT and have three-dimensional wire-frame and surface capabilities that compare favorably with workstation-based systems as far as capabilities and speed.

Database Storage   Databases can be stored in either an integer or a float-ing-point format. Integer-based formats are not as accurate for performing graphics operations as floating-point storage, but they permit greater speed and occupy less memory space. There are several PC CADD systems that still perform arithmetic operations using integer-based numbers.

As stated before, there are some PC systems that offer all the functions to be a productive CADD drafting tool. To illustrate this functionality, a session on an AutoCAD system is included.

Introduction to AutoCAD

Here is a brief overview of AutoCAD usage. Complete operating instructions are available from Autodesk, Inc. AutoCAD provides a set of entities for use in constructing a drawing. An *entity* is a drawing element such as a line, circle, or text string. *Commands* are entered to tell AutoCAD which entity to draw. Commands can be typed on the keyboard, selected from a screen menu, or entered with a push of a button from a menu on a digitizing tablet or from a multibutton pointing device. Then, in response to prompts on the display screen, certain parameters must be supplied for the chosen entity. These parameters always include the location on the drawing where the en-tity will appear; sometimes a size or rotation angle is also required. After this information is supplied, the entity is drawn and appears on the graphics dis-play. Then, a new command to draw another entity or to perform another AutoCAD function can be entered.

Other AutoCAD functions modify the drawing in a variety of ways. En-tities can be *erased*, *moved*, or *copied* to form repeated patterns. The view of the drawing shown on the graphics display can be changed, or information about the drawing can be shown. AutoCAD also provides drawing aids that position entities accurately. When a paper copy of the drawing is needed, the designer can *plot* it on a pen plotter or printer plotter. A simple command format allows all these functions to be accomplished easily. In some cases a command is entered and the function is performed immediately. At most, the designer must follow the command with some minimal, easily entered specifications. AutoCAD prompts the designer, indicating the type of infor-mation needed. To interpret the commands in the following session use the following guide:

PICK   This is accomplished with the pointing device. Two things may be picked, a screen menu item or a position on the drawing. For the menu item, move the device to the right until the highlight cursor appears in the screen menu area, then move it up or down until the cursor is highlighted over the desired menu item. Pressing the pick button (or pressing the stylus) will pick that item. To pick a position on the drawing, move the screen cursor (cross-hairs) until it is in the desired position and press the pick button. There are many varieties of pointing devices, as well as pick mechanisms.

TYPE   This symbol will precede any data that require keyboard entry.

RETURN   This is executed by pressing the RETURN or ENTER key on your keyboard. This action will usually follow the entry of data or is used to execute a command that has selective features. At times, there may be multiple returns. This will occur when the command provides options and the tutorial will accept the option default values. It does mean, however, that a return must occur for each return.

ENCLOSE   This word indicates that you are to designate objects by enclosing them in a rectangular area or *window*. AutoCAD prompts you for two corner positions to P. After you P the first position, AutoCAD will display a "box" (window) cursor rather than normal crosshairs. At the prompt "Second point," move your cursor so that the window encloses the objects that are to be designated and then pick that position.

ORTHO on/off   A line drawing aid that limits line drawing to either horizontal or vertical.

GRID on/off   An orientation aid that displays dots on the screen in a grid format. Normally, the grid is a horizontal and vertical orientation, but it can be rotated for special applications. The spacing of the dots in the grid may be set by the designer.

This session involves drawing a gear (Figure 15–4). This would be a complex and laborious task for an experienced draftsperson. AutoCAD, with its drawing power, makes this a simple task even for a novice.

Drawing the Gear

The gear to be drawn is a *20 Degree Full Depth Involute Spur Gear* with a 3-inch pitch diameter. The various formulae for this gear are available in the Machinery's Handbook and have been used to determine the locations and lengths of the lines used to draw the gear in this exercise.

When the center circle is drawn, the first point for drawing the teeth is based on the pitch diameter of three units (radius 1.5) and a tooth addendum

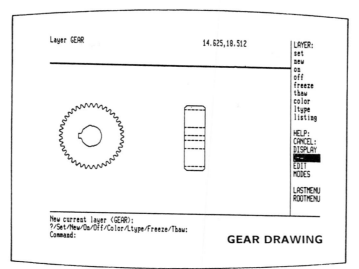

Figure 15–4
Gear drawing completed
using AutoCAD Software.
(Courtesy Autodesk, Inc.)

of .071. This point is the center of the crown of the tooth to be drawn. (We
will only draw half of the first tooth and create the full tooth with the MIRROR
command.) From the center point of the tooth crown, the upper half of the
crown, the upper side and half of the root of the tooth will be drawn (Figures
15–5, 15–6, and 15–7). With half of the tooth complete, we will mirror it across
the center line to complete a full tooth. At this point, the drawing of the gear

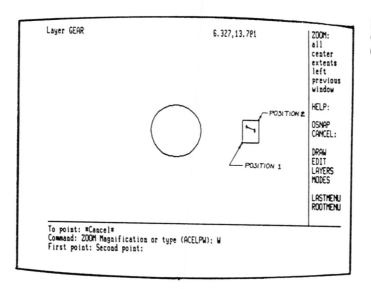

Figure 15–5
Gear drawing plate 2.
(Courtesy Autodesk, Inc.)

Figure 15–6
Gear drawing plate 3.
(Courtesy Autodesk, Inc.)

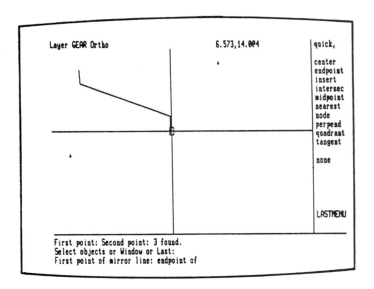

will show the centerhole and one complete tooth to the right, on the center line. The next step will be to use the ARRAY command to create a circular repetition of 40 copies of this tooth to complete the tooth structure of the gear.

We are now ready to start the drawing. The first task will be to draw the centerhole of the gear.

TYPE ACAD RETURN — This will load the AutoCAD program.

Figure 15–7
Gear drawing plate 4.
(Courtesy Autodesk, Inc.)

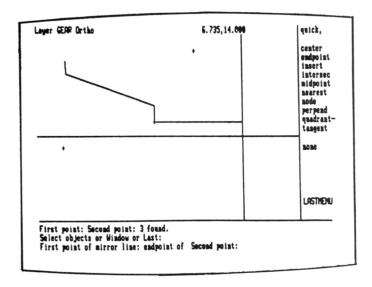

PICK DRAW

PICK CIRCLE

PICK CEN,DIA:

COMMAND: CIRCLE 3P/2P<Center point>:

The < > as used in AutoCAD indicates default. We will establish a center point.

TYPE 5,14 RETURN

The prompt asks for the circle diameter.

Prompt: D Diameter:

TYPE 1 RETURN

A small circle will be located in the upper left quadrant of the editor window. Since it is difficult to work on such a small drawing, we must make it larger. This is accomplished with the ZOOM command. ZOOM allows you to enlarge or reduce the image on the screen. Zoom is contained under display.

PICK DISPLAY

PICK ZOOM

COMMAND: ZOOM Magnification or type (ACELPW):

Several options are available to select and enlarge the circle. The easiest in this case is to use the center of the circle —

PICK center

Prompt: Center Point:

We will place the cursor over the "blip" at the center of the circle and PICK that as the center point.

Prompt: Magnification or Height <?>:

Once again we are asked how large the drawing should be magnified. The response in this case could be 5 or 5X; 5 means five times the size of the original drawing, 5X means five times the screen display. The screen display currently is the original drawing.

TYPE 5X RETURN

Now we will start drawing the gear teeth. This will be accomplished by drawing half a tooth, matching it with a mirror image and making copies of it around the circumference of the gear.

PICK DRAW

PICK LINE

The tooth will be made up of straight lines.

COMMAND: LINE From point:

TYPE 6.571,14 RETURN

The point just entered is referred to as "absolute" because the coordinates typed in indicate an absolute position in the drawing.

The next three points are relative coordinates because they are entered using a direction and distance from the last point. For example, @.0299<90 means, in this case, drawing a line from an established point .0299 units at a 90 degree angle.

Prompt: To point:

TYPE @.0299<90 RETURN

Prompt: To point:

TYPE @.17<160 RETURN

Prompt: To Point:

TYPE @.0228<94 RETURN RETURN

This half tooth is very small, so we enlarge it with the ZOOM command.

PICK DISPLAY

PICK ZOOM:

COMMAND: ZOOM Magnification or type (ACELPW):

It is easier to select this object by forming a window around it, therefore —

PICK window

The prompt line is requesting, First point: PICK a position on the screen approximately at position 1 (Figure 15–8). At the prompt Second point: move the cursor to the upper right until the window approxi-

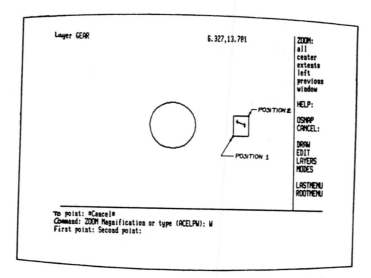

Figure 15–8
Gear drawing plate 5.
(Courtesy Autodesk, Inc.)

mates the window (Figure 15–9). Now Pick position 2. (Hereafter, this procedure will be called ENCLOSE).

Changes or revisions to drawings are classified as editing. In this case the half tooth will be reflected or "mirrored" to form a full tooth.

PICK EDIT

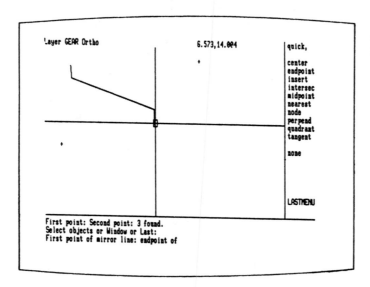

Figure 15–9
Gear Drawing plate 6.
(Courtesy Autodesk, Inc.)

The Mirror command permits you to create a mirror image of an existing object. You are required to select an object and mirror it across an axis. The axis must be horizontal or vertical and the placement of the axis line is critical. The image will be rotated around the axis line wherever you place it. If, for example, the axis line passes through the center of the object, the object will stay in the same place but will be a reversed image of the original.

PICK MIRROR:

COMMAND: MIRROR

Select objects or Window or Last:

The mirror command has selection options similar to some of those in ZOOM. The half tooth is made up of three entities, so the easiest method of selecting them is to enclose them in a window.

PICK window

Enclose all three lines as we did in the previous ZOOM command. Now completely ENCLOSE all of the lines on the screen.

RETURN

Prompt: First point of mirror line:

OSNAP permits precise geometric positions on drawing entities without precise cursor positioning. Placing this aperture or target over an entity is equivalent to having the cursor exactly on a desired position. The size of the aperture may be changed.

PICK OSNAP

OSNAP offers several options. For this application the endpoint of the line is the option desired.

PICK endpoint

Prompt: Second point:

ORTHO is one of the toggle functions previously described.

ORTHO ON

With ORTHO ON the rubberbanding line will only extend horizontally or vertically. Extend the line horizontally to the right as shown in

Figure 15–10 and PICK that position. The prompt now asks, Delete old objects? <N>. Respond with RETURN to except the default of <N> (no).

A full gear tooth has now appeared on the screen.

PICK LAST MENU PICK ROOTMENU

PICK SAVE:

COMMAND: SAVE File name <CAM>:

RETURN

We have just saved a copy of our drawing on disk.

PICK ROOTMENU

The next step is to copy the completed tooth around the circumference of the gear. This will be accomplished by making a circular array of the tooth.

PICK DISPLAY

PICK ZOOM:

COMMAND: ZOOM Magnification or type (ACELPW):

The "previous" option will cause the drawing to return to the size on the screen before the tooth was enlarged.

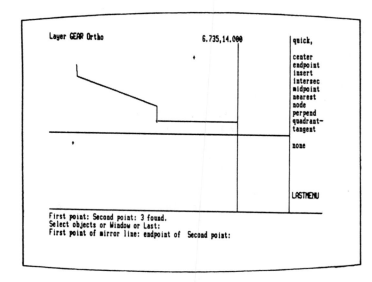

Figure 15–10
Gear Drawing plate 7.
(Courtesy Autodesk, Inc.)

PICK previous

Remember? Edit is the command used when the drawing is to be changed in some way.

PICK EDIT

PICK ARRAY:

COMMAND: ARRAY

Select objects or Window or Last:

ARRAY is the AutoCAD command that replicates entities either in a circular or rectangular pattern. This command will allow you to turn the single tooth into a complete gear. There are three entities to select, so —

PICK window

ENCLOSE the entire tooth.

RETURN

Prompt: Center point of array:

OSNAP is the command that lets you select precise geometric relationships. In this case we will locate the center of the circle.

PICK OSNAP

PICK center

Prompt: Center of:

Put the aperture over any part of the circumference of the circle and PICK that position. The next prompt will read "Angle between items (+ = CCW,-+CW):"
The gear is designed to have 40 teeth. A complete circle (360 degrees) divided by 40 = 9 degrees.

TYPE 9 RETURN

The next prompt "Number of items or - (degrees to fill):" could have two responses. The gear has 40 teeth, but it also takes 360 degrees to complete.

TYPE 40 RETURN

"Rotate objects as they are copied? (N)" gives you the option of having all teeth with the current orientation on the drawing or having them with radial orientation. Gear teeth have to radiate from the center of the gear or they just can't mesh.

TYPE Y RETURN

Try doing that manually and see how long it would take!

PICK LASTMENU

PICK LASTMENU

Toggle FLIP SCREEN

PICK DISPLAY

ORTHO ON

PICK PAN

COMMAND: PAN Displacement:

The prompt "Pan Displacement:" is requesting the distance and direction an object shall be moved on the screen. We must first establish a reference within the drawing. This is simple: PICK a reference point anywhere in the drawing.

Prompt: Second point:

TYPE @3.5<180 RETURN

Now that the front (or profile) view of the gear is complete and moved aside, the end view will be drawn. The screen should resemble Figure 15-11.

PICK DRAW

GRID ON

SNAP ON

COORDS ON

PLINE (meaning polyline) follows the same pattern as drawing lines. However, editing becomes much more efficient. We will see this soon. The rectangle that represents the side view of the gear will be drawn using a combination of absolute coordinates and relative coordinates.

Figure 15–11
Gear drawing plate 8.
(Courtesy Autodesk, Inc.)

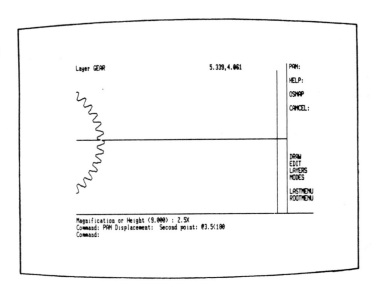

PICK PLINE:

COMMAND:PLINE

From point

TYPE 9.5,15.571 RETURN

A blip has been established at the upper right of the screen, this is the first point in the following polyline segments.

Prompt: Arc/Close/Halfwidth/Length/Undo/Width/<Endpoint of line>:

Now we move the cursor so the rubberband line extends to the right of this first point and the coordinates in the status line read 1.00< 000. PICK this position.

Prompt: Arc/Close/Halfwidth/Length/Undo/Width/<Endpoint of line>:

Now move the cursor down and to the left until the coordinates in the status line reads 1.00<180.00. PICK this position.

PICK close

Close completes a polygon by automatically drawing a line from the last established point to the first point established in the drawing sequence.

PICK EDIT

PICK CHAMFR:

Chamfer means to remove a sharp edge by cutting a little of it off at an angle.

COMMAND: CHAMFER Polyline/Distance/<Select first line>:

First select the distance from the corner for the chamfer.

PICK distance

Prompt: D Enter first chamfer distance <?>:

TYPE .1 RETURN

Prompt: Enter second chamfer distance <0.100>: accept the

default, RETURN

Prompt: Command CHAMFER Polyline/Distance/<Select

first line>:

PICK polyline

Prompt: PICK Select polyline:

Move the cursor until it is on the perimeter of the rectangle just drawn; PICK that position. All four corners were chamfered with a single command because the rectangle was a polyline (one entity).

There is a keyway to add to the centerhole of the gear. First the gear must be moved back to the screen.

PICK DISPLAY

PICK ZOOM

COMMAND: ZOOM Magnification or type (ACELPW):

PICK previous

PICK DRAW

PICK LINE

COMMAND:LINE from point:

Start with an absolute coordinate point and draw from that with relative polar coordinates.

TYPE 4625,14.125 RETURN

Prompt: To point:

Pull the rubberband line to the left until the coordinates read .250<180, and PICK that position.

Prompt: To point:

Pull the rubberband line down .250<270, and PICK that position.

Prompt: To point:

Pull the rubberband line right .250<0, and PICK that position.

RETURN

The keyway has been drawn, but a segment of arc and two line ends must be removed (see Figure 15–12).

SNAP OFF

PICK DISPLAY

PICK ZOOM:

COMMAND:ZOOM Magnification or type (ACELWP):

PICK window

Figure 15–12
Gear drawing plate 9.
(Courtesy Autodesk, Inc.)

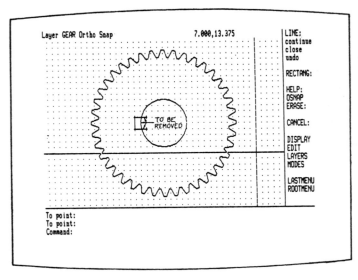

ENCLOSE an area just around the keyway.

PICK EDIT

"Change" will permit you to remove portions of lines or arcs. It has many other functions, but these are all we need now.

PICK CHANGE

COMMAND:CHANGE

Select objects or Window or Last:

PICK the upper line segment as shown in Figure 15–13 (position 1).

RETURN

Prompt: Change point (or Layer or Elevation):

PICK OSNAP

PICK intersec

This will allow us to accurately select the intersection of the center of the circle and the keyway sides.

Prompt: Intersec of

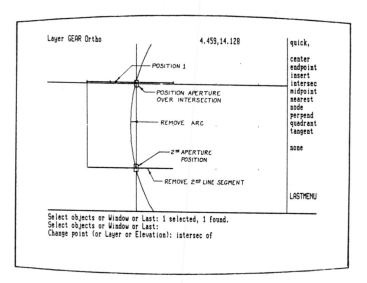

Figure 15–13

Gear drawing plate 10. (Courtesy Autodesk, Inc.)

PICK the upper line aperture position as shown in Figure 15–13 (on the same line as position 1).

PICK LASTMENU

PICK CHANGE:

COMMAND:CHANGE

Select objects or Window or Last:

PICK the lower line segment as shown in Figure 15–13 (position 2).

RETURN

Prompt: Change point (or Layer or Elevation):

PICK OSNAP

PICK intersec

Prompt: Intersec of

PICK the lower line aperture position as shown in Figure 15–10.

PICK LASTMENU

PICK LASTMENU

''Break'' will allow us to remove a portion of an entity, that is, line or circle, that lies within the entity.

PICK BREAK:

COMMAND:BREAK Select object

At the prompt BREAK Select object: PICK any position on the circumference of the circle, but not at an intersection. A second prompt will appear, Enter second point or F:

PICK 2 points (From the screen menu)

Prompt: First point:

PICK OSNAP

PICK intersec of

PICK the upper line aperture position as shown in Figure 15–13 (near position 1). Note: The top intersection was selected first because in AutoCAD, arc segments are removed in a counterclockwise direction when using the BREAK command.

Prompt: Enter second point:

PICK intersec

PICK the lower line aperture position as shown in Figure 15–13. The arc will be removed and the keyway complete. Check to see if the keyway is cleanly drawn.

PICK LASTMENU

PICK DISPLAY

PICK ZOOM:

COMMAND:ZOOM Magnification or type (ACELPW):

PICK previous

RETURN

Pressing return repeats the last command. This is convenient when we do not want to move the cursor into the screen menu area to pick the last command issued.

SNAP OFF

GRID OFF

COMMAND: ZOOM Magnification or type (ACELPW):

PICK all

PICK ZOOM:

COMMAND: ZOOM Magnification or type (ACELPW):

PICK window

Form a window. ENCLOSE both objects in the drawing. The drawing screen should have outlines similar in size and location in those in Figure 15–14.

Previously we changed layers. This permits us to draw in a different line type and color.

PICK LAYERS

PICK LAYER:

COMMAND:?/Set/New/On/Off/Color/Ltype/Freeze/Thaw:

Figure 15–14
Gear drawing plate 11.
(Courtesy Autodesk, Inc.)

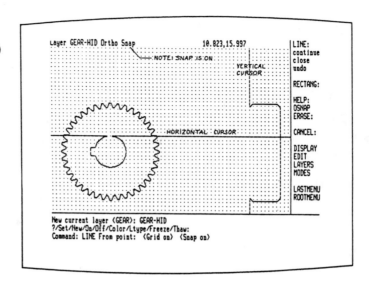

PICK set

Prompt: New Current layer:

TYPE GEAR-HID RETURN RETURN

Check the status line to confirm that the current layer is GEAR-HID.

PICK DRAW

ORTHO ON

GRID ON

SNAP ON

COORD ON

PICK LINE:

COMMAND:LINE From point:

Six horizontal hidden lines will be added to the side view of the gear. First align the horizontal cursor with the top of the centerhole and the vertical cursor with the left side of the gear, and PICK that position (see Figure 15–14). Prompt: TO point: Now PICK a position of 1.00<0 (refer to the status line) and RETURN. Note: Dotted lines in Figure 15–15 for reference only, DO NOT DRAW.

RETURN

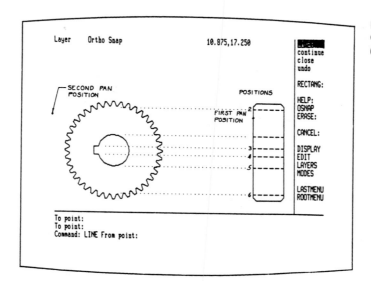

Figure 15–15
Gear Drawing plate 12.
(Courtesy Autodesk, Inc.)

COMMAND:LINE From point:

PICK position 5 as shown in Figure 15–15, and then PICK a position of 1.00<0 and RETURN.

RETURN

COMMAND:LINE From point:

PICK position 2 as shown in Figure 15–15, and then PICK a position of 1.00<0 and RETURN.

RETURN

PICK position 3 as shown in Figure 15–15, and then PICK a position of 1.00<0 and RETURN.

RETURN

COMMAND:LINE From point:

PICK position 4 as shown in Figure 15–15, and then PICK a position of 1.00<0 and RETURN.

COMMAND: LINE From point:

PICK position 5 as shown in Figure 15–15, and then PICK a position of 1.00<0 and RETURN.

COMMAND: LINE Frompoint:

Pick position 6 as shown in Figure 15–5, and then pick a position of 1.00 < 0 and RETURN.
The Gear drawing is now complete.

TYPE END RETURN

This will cause our drawing to be filed on the disk and the main menu to appear.

TYPE 0 RETURN

This procedure saves the drawing and terminates the drawing session.

GLOSSARY

AUXILIARY STORAGE Storage devices other than the main memory, also called peripheral storage (e.g., disk drives, magnetic tape).

BILL OF MATERIALS (BOM) A listing of all the subassemblies, parts, materials, and quantities required to manufacture an assembly or to build a plant.

BIT A binary digit. The smallest unit of information that can be stored and processed by a digital computer. It can only be a 0 or 1. Computers are often classified by word size in bits, such as a 16-bit or 32-bit computer.

BYTE A sequence of eight bits that are operated upon as a unit.

CAD (COMPUTER-AIDED DESIGN) A process whereby a computer assists in creating or modifying a design.

CAM (COMPUTER-AIDED MANUFACTURING) A process employing computer technology to manage and control the operations of a manufacturing facility.

COMMUNICATION LINK The physical connection, such as a telephone line, from one system to another, or from one component to another.

COMMUNICATIONS NETWORK A number of systems linked together to exchange data.

COMPUTER A data processor that can perform arithmetic and logical operations.

COMPUTER GRAPHICS A generic term applied to any discipline or activity that uses computers to generate, process, and display pictorial images.

COMPUTER-INTEGRATED MANUFACTURING (CIM) A totally automated factory in which all manufacturing processes are integrated and controlled by a computer system.

CROSS HAIRS A horizontal line intersected by a vertical line to indicate a point on the display whose coordinates are desired.

CURSOR   A special character, such as a small cross, on the screen that follows every movement of the stylus, light pen, or joystick.

DATABASE   An organized collection of standard parts libraries, completed designs, documentation, and computer programs.

DATA MANAGEMENT   The control of access to information, information storage conventions, and the use of input and output devices.

DISK   A circular plate of magnetic media on which information is stored.

DISK DRIVE   The device that reads data from or writes data onto magnetic disks.

DISK STORAGE   The use of magnetic disks as a storage device.

FINITE ELEMENT MODELING (FEM)   The creation of a mathematical model of a part for input to a finite element analysis program.

FLOPPY DISK   A flexible magnetic disk used to store data.

FONT, LINE   Repetitive patterns used to make a line more easily recognized (e.g., a solid, dashed, or dotted line).

FONT, TEXT   An assortment of characters of a given size and style.

HARDWARE   The computer, disk, magnetic tape, cathode ray tube, and other physical components that comprise a system.

HOST COMPUTER   The computer attached to a network providing services such as computation, database management, and special programs. The primary computer in a multiple computer operation.

MACRO   A combination of commands executed as a single command.

MAINFRAME   In general, a central processing unit of a large-scale computer configuration.

MAIN MEMORY   The principal data storage device of a computer system — an integral part of the computer, generally just called *memory*.

MICROCOMPUTER   A small, relatively low-cost computer that includes a microprocessor, memory, and all necessary interface circuits. Home or personal computers such as Apple, IBM PC, and TRS-80 are examples of microcomputers.

MICROPROCESSORS   A single integrated circuit that is the central processing unit of a microcomputer.

MINICOMPUTER   A computer that is between the mainframe computers and the microcomputers in size, power, complexity, and cost, generally a 32-bit computer.

MODEL   An accurate three-dimensional representation of a part, assembly, or plant designed on a CADD system and stored in the database.

MODELING   Constructing a mathematical or analytic model of a physical object or system for analysis.

PROMPT   A message or symbol appearing on the screen that informs the user of a procedural error, incorrect input to the program being executed, or the next expected action.

RANDOM ACCESS MEMORY (RAM)   A main memory storage unit that provides direct access to the stored information. Memory from which data can be retrieved regardless of input sequence.

READ ONLY MEMORY (ROM)   A storage device (memory) generally used for control programs, the content of which is not alterable.

RESPONSE TIME   The elapsed time from the completion of a command at a workstation to the display of the results at that workstation.

SOFTWARE   The computer programs, procedures, rules, and instructions that control the use of the hardware.

SOLID MODEL   Solid models represent the mass and the boundary of a complete form.

TERMINAL   A device equipped with a keyboard and some kind of display that sends and receives information over a communication channel to and from a computer.

QUIZ

True or False

1. PC CADD systems are difficult to use and take a long time to learn.

2. System performance on PC CADD systems does not degrade with multiple users.

3. Drawing production with many PC CADD systems is up to four times more productive than manual methods.

4. Most PC CADD vendors support the exchange of databases between CADD systems.

5. Although PCs are smaller and cheaper than stand-alone workstations, they are just as fast in operating speed.

6. Databases can be stored in either an integer or a floating-point format.

7. PC CADD systems offer autonomy and ease of maintenance.

8. Engineers and designers spend only about one third of their time on design and analysis tasks.

Fill in the Blank

9. PC-based systems offer _____ and ease of _____.

10. PC CADD systems normally take less than a _____ to learn to use effectively.

11. PC CADD systems are being used by multiuser system users to _____ the load on _____ CADD facilities.

12. Two-dimensional production drawing with many PC CADD systems is up to _____ times more productive than manual methods.

13. There are very few PC CADD vendors that support _____ to exchange databases between CADD systems.

14. Processing speed is _____ on PC systems.

15. Databases can be stored in either an _____ or a _____ format.

16. The capabilities of the more competitive systems permit most ordinary drafting tasks to be completed with _____ or _____ efficiency than with traditional methods.

Answer the Following

17. Explain why the processing speed on a PC CADD system is limited.

18. Why are PC CADD systems used for training?

19. Why is the lack of a standard for the exchange of databases between systems a problem with PC CADD systems?

20. What future features will enable the PC CADD system to rival workstation-based systems?

Appendix

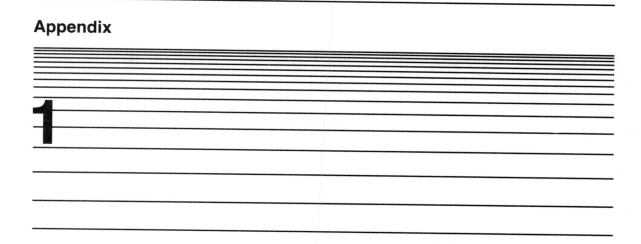

Glossary of CAD/CAM Terms

A

ABSOLUTE COORDINATES   The values of the X, Y, or Z coordinates with respect to the origin of the coordinate system.

ABSOLUTE DATA   Values representing the absolute coordinates of a point or other geometric entity on a display surface. The values may be expressed in the units of the display or of the engineering drawing.

ACCEPTANCE TEST   A test for evaluating newly purchased hardware or software. The hardware or software must conform to predefined specifications.

ACCESS   To retrieve and use a specific program or data.

ACCESS TIME   One measure of system response. The time interval between when data are requested from storage and when those data are displayed on the screen.

ACCURACY   Generally used to denote the number of digits to the right of the decimal point that can be used by a particular algorithm or system.

ACRONYM   A word made from the first letters of words in a phrase (e.g., CAD is the acronym for Computer-Aided Design).

ADDRESS   The location of data or a program in storage.

ADDRESSABLE POINT   A position on the screen that can be specified by absolute coordinates.

ADDRESSABILITY   A measure of picture resolution; the number of points that can be displayed on the screen.

AIMING DEVICE   A pattern of light activated by a light pen on the display surface to assist positioning of the pen and to describe the pen's field of view (See *cursor*).

ALGOL   ALGorithmic Oriented Language. A high-level programming language.

ALGORITHM   A set of well-defined rules or procedures for solving a problem.

ALIASING   Straight lines appear as jagged lines on a raster display if the display has low resolution.

ALPHANUMERIC DISPLAY   A display that shows letters, numbers, and special characters. It allows the designer to enter commands and to receive messages from the system.

ALPHANUMERIC KEYBOARD   A typewriterlike keyboard that allows a designer to communicate with the system.

ANALOG   Data are represented by linear movement rather than the numbers 0 and 1 as with digital.

ANNOTATION   The process of adding text, notes, or identification to a drawing, map, or diagram.

ANSI   American National Standards Institute. An association formed by industry and the U.S. government to produce and disseminate drafting and manufacturing standards.

APPLICATION SOFTWARE   A computer program that assists a user performing a specific task.

APT   Automatically Programmed Tools. A computer language used to program numerically controlled machine tools.

ARCHIVE   Placing infrequently used data in auxiliary storage.

ARRAY   A set of elements or components arranged in a pattern (e.g., a matrix).

ARTIFICIAL INTELLIGENCE   The ability of a computer to perform tasks normally associated with human intelligence, such as reasoning, learning, and self-improvement.

ARTWORK   A photoplot, photomask, pen plot, electrostatic copy, or positive or negative photographic transparency used to manufacture an IC, PC board, or other product.

ASCII   American Standard Code for Information Interchange. A standard for representing characters in the computer.

ASSEMBLER   The computer program that converts mnemonic instruction into equivalent machine language instructions.

ASSEMBLY LANGUAGE   A computer-dependent language that corresponds one-to-one with the computer machine language instructions.

ASSOCIATIVE DIMENSIONING   The means by which a CADD dimensioning program automatically updates the dimensions as the geometry changes.

ASSOCIATIVITY   The linking of parts, components, or elements with their attributes or with other geometric entities.

ATTRIBUTE   A nongraphic characteristic of a part, component, or element (e.g., length, diameter, name, volume, use, and creation date).

AUTOMATED DESIGN SYSTEM (ADS)   Another term for computer-aided design system.

AUTOMATED DRAFTING SYSTEM   Another term for computer-aided drafting system.

AUTOMATIC DIMENSIONING   The CADD system computes the dimensions and automatically places dimensions, extension lines, and arrowheads where required.

AUTOPLACEMENT (TM)   A Computervision software option that automatically packages IC elements and optimizes the layout of components on a PC board.

AUTOROUTE (TM)   A Computervision software option that automatically determines the placement of copper on the printed circuit board to connect part pins of the same signal.

AUXILIARY STORAGE   Storage devices other than the main memory, also called peripheral storage (e.g., disk drives or magnetic tape).

B

BACK ANNOTATION   Data are automatically extracted from a completed PC board and used to update the schematic. Information can also be back annotated into piping drawing and three-dimensional models.

BACKUP COPY   A copy of a file that is kept for reference in case the original file is destroyed (e.g., safe keeping).

BASIC   Beginner's All-purpose Symbolic Instruction Code. A high-level algebraic programming language.

BATCH PROCESSING   The running of a program or set of programs in a noninteractive mode.

BAUD RATE   A measure of the speed of signal transmission between the computer and the workstations. It is measured in bits per second.

BENCHMARK   A set of standards used in testing a software or hardware product or system from which a measurement can be made. Benchmarks are often run on a system to verify that it performs according to specifications.

BETA SITE   A CADD site selected for testing a new hardware or software enhancement before its sale to other customers of the vendor.

BILL OF MATERIALS (BOM)   A listing of all the subassemblies, parts, materials, and quantities required to manufacture an assembly or to build a plant.

BINARY CODE   The representation of all characters by using combinations of 0 and 1.

BIT   A binary digit. The smallest unit of information that can be stored and processed by a digital computer. It can only be a 0 or a 1. Computers are often classified by word size in bits, such as a 16-bit or 32-bit computer.

BITS PER INCH (BPI)   The number of bits of binary code that 1 inch of magnetic tape can store.

BOOT UP   To start up a computer.

BOOTSTRAP   A routine whose first few instructions load the rest of the routine into the computer from storage.

BUFFER   A software program or hardware device used to hold data, when transferring data from one device to another, if there is a difference in the time it takes the devices to process the data.

BUG   A flaw in a software program or hardware design that causes erroneous results or malfunctions.

BUS   A circuit or group of circuits that provides a communications path between two or more devices.

BYTE   A sequence of 8 bits that are operated upon as a unit.

C

CAD (COMPUTER-AIDED DESIGN)   A process whereby a computer assists in creating or modifying a design.

CAM (COMPUTER-AIDED MANUFACTURING)   A process employing computer technology to manage and control the operations of a manufacturing facility.

CARTESIAN COORDINATES   The distance of a point from any of three intersecting perpendicular planes; X, Y, Z coordinates.

CATALOG   The directory of files contained in storage.

CATHODE RAY TUBE (CRT)   A display device that creates images with a beam of electrons striking a screen.

CENTRAL PROCESSING UNIT (CPU)   The brain of a CADD system that controls the processing of information.

CHARACTER   A letter, number, or other symbol used to represent data. Symbols include the letters A through Z, numbers 0 through 9, punctuation marks, logical symbols, relational operators, and any other single symbol that may be interpreted by computer languages. A character is represented as a byte in the computer.

CHARACTERS PER SECOND (CPS)   The speed at which a device, such as a printer, can process data.

CHIP   See *integrated circuit*.

CL FILE (CUTTER LOCATION FILE)   Output of an APT or graphics system that provides X, Y, and Z coordinates and NC information for machine tool processing.

COBOL   Common Business-Oriented Language. A high-level language oriented to business applications.

CODE   A set of instructions that may be in machine language, assembly language, or a high-level language. Also may refer to an industry standard such as ANSI or ASCII.

COM   See *computer output microfilm*.

COMMAND   An instruction given to a processor using a menu and tablet, stylus, or alphanumeric keyboard.

COMMAND LANGUAGE   The language used by designers and drafters to operate a CADD system; it varies with each system.

COMMUNICATION LINK   The physical connection, such as a telephone line, from one system to another or from one component to another.

COMMUNICATIONS NETWORK   A number of systems linked together to exchange data.

COMPATIBILITY   The ability of a hardware module or software program to be used in a CADD system without modification.

COMPILER   A program that translates high-level language instructions to machine language instructions that can be understood by the CPU.

COMPONENT   A subassembly or part that goes into higher-level assemblies.

COMPUTER   A data processor that can perform arithmetic and logical operations.

COMPUTER ARCHITECTURE   The internal design of the parts of a computer system.

COMPUTER GRAPHICS   A generic term applied to any discipline or activity that uses computers to generate, process, and display pictorial images.

COMPUTER-INTEGRATED MANUFACTURING (CIM)   A totally automated factory in which all manufacturing processes are integrated and controlled by a computer system.

COMPUTER LITERACY   A basic understanding of computers and their use.

COMPUTER NETWORK   Two or more interconnected computers.

COMPUTER NUMERICAL CONTROL (NC)   Using a computer to store numerical control instructions, generated by a CADD system, to control a machine.

COMPUTER OUTPUT MICROFILM   The image of a drawing plotted on 35 mm film at a small scale by a beam of light. Microfilm containing computer-generated data; also to place computer-generated data on microfilm.

COMPUTER PROGRAM   A set of software commands that instruct the computer to perform specific operations, often called a software program or software package.

COMPUTER WORD   A sequence of bits or characters treated as a unit.

CONFIGURATION   A particular combination of computer software, hardware, and peripherals at a single installation.

CONNECT NODE   An attachment point for lines or text.

CONNECTION   The lines between pins, components, contacts, or circuits in printed circuit board and wiring diagram construction.

CONSTRUCTION PLANE   A predefined or operator-defined plane on which digitize points are projected.

CONVERSATIONAL MODE   A mode of operation for a data processing system in which each unit of input entered by the user elicits a prompt response from the computer.

COORDINATE DIMENSIONING   A system of dimensioning in which points are defined as being a specified distance and direction from a reference point.

COPY   To reproduce a design in a different location on the screen or to duplicate a file and its contents.

CPU   See *central processing unit.*

CROSS HAIRS   A horizontal line intersected by a vertical line to indicate a point on the display whose coordinates are desired.

CURSOR   A special character, such as a small cross, on the screen that follows every movement of the stylus, light pen, or joystick.

CUT PLANE A plane intersected with a three-dimensional object to derive a sectional view.

D

DATA Elements of information.

DATA BANK The total collection of information used by an organization.

DATABASE An organized collection of standard parts libraries, completed designs, documentation, and computer programs.

DATA ENTRY Data entered by an operator from an input device such as a card reader, keyboard, or disk.

DATA EXTRACT The capability to obtain information from the database.

DATA MANAGEMENT The control of access to information, information storage conventions, and the use of input and output devices.

DATA PROCESSING SYSTEM A system that accepts information, processes it in a specific manner, and produces the desired results.

DATA TABLET A graphical input device consisting of a board area capable of monitoring the position of a pen-shaped stylus.

DEBUGGING Detecting and removing programming errors (bugs) from programs.

DEDICATED Assigned to a single function, such as a workstation used exclusively for engineering calculations.

DEFAULT The predetermined value of a parameter that is automatically supplied by the system whenever that value is not specified by the user.

DELETE To erase information from the computer's memory or from storage.

DELIMITER A space, slash, asterisk, or other mark that separates data within a continuous string.

DESIGN AUTOMATION (DA) Using a computer to automate portions of the design process.

DESIGN FILE The information in a CADD database that relates to a design project.

DETAIL DRAWINGS The drawing of a single part with all the dimensions and annotations necessary to completely define the part for manufacturing and inspection.

DEVICE A hardware item such as a cathode ray tube, plotter, printer, or hardcopy unit.

DIAGNOSTICS Computer programs that test a system or its key components to detect and isolate malfunctions.

DIGIT Either 0 or 1 in binary notation; 0 through 9 in decimal notation.

DIGITAL The representation of data as combinations of the numbers 0 and 1.

DIGITIZE To convert lines and shapes into digital form.

DIGITIZER A table or tablet on which the designer moves a puck or stylus to selected points and enters coordinates for lines and shapes by pressing down the input button on the puck or stylus.

DIRECT NUMERICAL CONTROL (DNC) Using a shared computer to distribute part program data to remove machine tools.

DIRECTORY   The location on the disk where the names of files and information about them are stored.

DISK   A circular plate of magnetic media on which information is stored.

DISK DRIVE   The device that reads data from or writes data on magnetic disks.

DISK STORAGE   The use of magnetic disks as a storage device.

DISPLAY   The part of the workstation that shows the image of the data; usually refers to a cathode ray tube.

DISPLAY ELEMENTS   Points, line segments, and characters that are used to describe an object on the display.

DISPLAY GROUP   A collection of display elements that can be manipulated as a unit and that may be further combined to form larger groups.

DISPLAY IMAGE   The collection of display elements shown together on the display device.

DISPLAY MENU   A display option that allows an operator to select the next action by indicating one or more choices with an input device.

DISPLAY PARAMETERS   Data that control the appearance of graphics (e.g., choice of solid or dashed lines).

DISPLAY SPACE   The usable area of the display surface that includes all addressable points.

DOCUMENTATION   The general description, user's manual, and maintenance manual necessary to operate and maintain the system.

DOWN   The term used to describe a computer or device that is not working.

DRUM PLOTTER   An electromechanical pen plotter that draws a picture on paper or film mounted on a drum using a combination of plotting head movement and drum rotation.

DUMB TERMINAL   A terminal that can only communicate with a host computer and cannot function in a stand-alone mode.

DUMP   To transfer all the data accumulated on the system during a given period to permanent storage.

DYNAMIC MOVEMENT   The ability to zoom, scroll, and rotate the image on the screen interactively.

E

EDIT   To change, add, or delete data.

ELECTRICAL SCHEMATIC   A diagram of the logical arrangement of hardware in an electrical system that uses standard component symbols.

ELECTROSTATIC PLOTTER   Wire nibs, spaced 100 to 200 nibs per inch, that place dots where needed on a piece of paper to generate a drawing.

ELEMENT   The lowest-level design entity with an identifiable logical, electrical, or mechanical function; a basic geometric unit (e.g., point, line, arc, or circle).

EMULATION   The use of a computing system to execute programs written for another system.

ENHANCEMENTS   Software or hardware improvements, additions, or updates.

ENTITY   The fundamental building blocks that a designer uses to represent a product (e.g., arc, circle, line, text, point, line, figure, nodal line).

ERGONOMIC   Designed with the needs of the user in mind.

ERROR FILE   File generated during data processing to retain information about errors during the process.

EXECUTE   To carry out an instruction or perform a routine.

F

FAMILY OF PARTS   A collection of previously designed parts with similar geometric characteristics but differing in physical measurement.

FETCH   To locate data in storage and load it into the computer.

FIELD   A specific area in a string of characters or a record.

FIGURE   A symbol or a part that may contain other figures, attributes, and associations.

FILE   A name set of data on magnetic disk or tape; also to transfer the contents of working storage to permanent storage.

FILE MANAGEMENT SYSTEM   A software system that provides control of input, output, physical storage, and logical relationships for data files.

FILE PROTECTION   The control of access to a file without proper authority and prevention from accidental erasure of data within a file.

FILLET   A rounded corner or arc that blends together two intersection curves, lines, or surfaces.

FINITE ELEMENTS   The subdivision of a complex structure into small pieces.

FINITE ELEMENT ANALYSIS (FEA)   The determination of the structural integrity of a part by mathematic simulation of the part and the forces acting on the part.

FINITE ELEMENT MODELING (FEM)   The creation of a mathematical model of a part for input to a finite element analysis program.

FIRMWARE   Sets of instructions built into user-modifiable hardware.

FLATBED PLOTTER   An electromechanical pen plotter that draws a picture on paper, glass, or film mounted on a flat table. The plotting head moves in both axial directions.

FLICKER   The flashing on and off of the image on the screen.

FLIP   The same as mirror-image projection.

FLOPPY DISK   A flexible magnetic disk used to store data.

FLOWCHART   A graphical representation of the solution of a problem in which symbols are used to represent operations, data flow, and equipment.

FONT, LINE   Repetitive patterns used to make a line more easily recognized (e.g., a solid, dashed, or dotted line).

FONT, TEXT   An assortment of characters of a given size and style.

FORMAT   The specific arrangement of data for a list or report, a preprinted drawing border (i.e., title block and zones).

FORM FLASH   To project a constant pattern such as a report form, grid, or map as background for a display; synonymous with form overlay.

FORTRAN   FORmula TRANslation. A high-level language primarily for scientific applications that use mathematical formulas.

FULL FRAME   A display image scaled to maximize use of the viewing surface of the area of a display device.

FUNCTION KEY   An area on the digitizing tablet or a key on a box or terminal that is used to enter a command.

FUNCTION KEYBOARD   A part of the workstation that contains a number of function keys.

FUNCTION MENU   The display or list of commands that the user can use to perform a task.

G

GLITCH   Minor, often temporary, malfunction of computer hardware or software.

GRAPHIC PRIMATIVES   Simple geometric shapes such as lines, circles, cones, cylinders, ellipses, and rectangles that can be used to construct more complex shapes.

GRAPHICS   Pictorial data such as points, lines, shapes.

GRAPHICS TABLET   A surface through which coordinate points can be transmitted using a cursor or stylus; another term for a digitizing tablet.

GRID   A matrix of uniformly spaced points displayed on the screen for approximately locating and digitizing a position or placing symbols in the creation of a schematic.

H

HARDCOPY   A copy on paper of what is shown on the screen; generated with an on-line printer or plotter.

HARD DISK   A hard metal disk sealed in a disk drive and used for storage.

HARDWARE   The computer, disk, magnetic tape, cathode ray tube, and other physical components that comprise a system.

HIDDEN LINES   Line segments that would ordinarily be hidden from view in a three-dimensional display of a solid object because they are behind other items in the display.

HIERARCHY   A data structure consisting of different levels where certain objects are subdivisions of an object on a higher level.

HIGH-LEVEL LANGUAGE   A programming language that is independent of any given computer and permits the execution of a number of subroutines through a simple command (e.g., BASIC, FORTRAN, PASCAL, and COBOL).

HOST COMPUTER   The computer attached to a network providing services such as computation, database management, and special programs; the primary computer in a multiple computer operation.

I

INCHES PER SECOND (IPS)   The number of inches of magnetic tape that can be recorded or read per second or the speed of a pen plotter.

IN-HOUSE   Within an organization or company.

INITIALIZE COMPUTER   To set counters, switches, or addresses to 0 or to other starting values at the beginning of a program or routine.

INITIALIZE DISK   To prepare a disk to store information in the format of the particular operating system being used.

INPUT   To enter data or a program into the system.

INPUT DEVICE   Devices such as graphic tablets or keyboards that allow the user to input data into the CADD system.

INPUT/OUTPUT (IO)   Communications devices and the process by which communication takes place in a CADD system.

INPUT/OUTPUT CHANNEL   The path for transmitting data in and out of the central processing unit.

INQUIRY   A request for information from the computer.

INSERT   To enter entities, figures, or information into a design that is on the display.

INSTRUCTION   Line of computer programming telling the computer what to do.

INSTRUCTION SET   All the commands to which a computer will respond.

INTEGRATED CIRCUIT (IC)   An electronic component that may vary in complexity from a simple logic gate to a microprocessor. An IC is usually packaged in a single substrate as a slice of silicon, also called a chip.

INTEGRATED SYSTEM   A CADD system that integrates the entire product development cycle — analysis, design, and fabrication — into a single system.

INTELLIGENT ROBOT   A robot that can make decisions by using its sensing and recognizing capabilities.

INTELLIGENT TERMINAL   A terminal with local processing power whose characteristics can be changed under program control.

INTERACTIVE   Providing two-way instantaneous communication between a CADD system and its operators.

INTERACTIVE DISPLAY TERMINAL   A terminal consisting of one or more display devices and one or more input devices such as tablets, control balls, light pens, alphanumeric keyboards, function keys, and tape readers.

INTERACTIVE GRAPHICS   Capability to perform graphics operations directly on the computer with immediate feedback.

INTERACTIVE GRAPHICS SYSTEM   A CADD system in which the workstations are used interactively for computer-aided design and drafting; often used synonymously with CADD.

INTERCONNECTION   The connection between one display entity or connection point on a component and another. On schematic drawings, interconnections are lines that connect elements.

INTERFACE   A hardware or software link that enables two systems or a system and its peripherals to operate as a single, integrated system.

INTERFERENCE CHECKING   A CADD capability that allows plant or mechanical designers to examine a three-dimensional model and automatically pinpoint interfaces between pipes, equipment, structures, or machinery.

INTERPRETER   A software program that converts high-level language instructions to machine language instructions.

ISOMETRIC   A drawing in which the object is drawn from an oblique view so that it appears to be solid.

J

JAGGIES   The jagged or sawtoothed appearance of lines on the screen when the screen has low resolution.

JCL   Job Control Language. A problem-oriented language used to express job requirements to an operating system.

JOB   All necessary computer programs, linkages, files, and instructions for a unit of work.

JOYSTICK   A CADD data entry device that uses a hand-controlled lever to move the cursor on the screen to enter coordinates' various points.

K

K   1,024.

KEYBOARD   Resembles a typewriter and is used to enter instructions or coordinates into the computer.

KEYPUNCH   A keyboard-actuated device that punches holes in cards.

KINEMATICS   A process for simulating the motion of mechanisms to study interference, acceleration, and forces.

L

LARGE-SCALE COMPUTER   A computer with large internal memory capacity and multiple input/output channels. Such computers can process many programs concurrently.

LAYER   A logical concept used to distinguish subdividual groups of data within a given drawing, it may be thought of as a series of transparencies overlayed in any order without any depth.

LAYER DISCRIMINATION   The selective assignment of colors to a layer or the highlighting of entities to distinguish among data on different layers displayed on a screen.

LAYOUT   A to-scale drawing of the physical components and the mechanical and electrical arrangements of a part, product, or plant.

LIBRARY   A collection of symbols, components, shapes, or parts stored in the CADD database as templates for future design work on the system.

LIGHT PEN   A penlike device used in conjunction with a vector-refresh screen that identifies displayed elements from the light sources on the screen.

LINE PRINTER   A peripheral device that prints alphanumeric data one line at a time.

LINE SPEED   The rate at which signals can be transmitted over a communications line, usually measured in bauds or bits per second.

LIS (LARGE INTERACTIVE SURFACE)   An automated drafting table used to plot and/or digitize drawings; also called a digitizer table.

LOAD   To enter data into computer memory for later processing on the system.

LOCAL AREA NETWORK (LAN)   A communications network in which all of the computers and workstations are in the same general area or building.

LOG-ON   To follow the procedure by which a user begins a workstation session.

LOG-OFF To follow the procedure by which a user ends a workstation session.

LOOP A sequence of instructions that is executed repeatedly in the computer until stopped by an operator or some predetermined condition.

M

MACHINE A computer.

MACHINE INSTRUCTION An instruction that a computer can recognize and execute.

MACHINE LANGUAGE The set of instructions, in combinations of the numbers 0 and 1, used directly by a computer.

MACRO A combination of commands executed as a single command.

MAGNETIC DISK A flat, circular plate with a magnetic surface on which data can be recorded and from which data can be read. The data can be randomly accessed.

MAGNETIC DRUM A cylinder with a magnetic surface on which data can be recorded and from which data can be read.

MAGNETIC TAPE A tape with a magnetic surface on which data can be recorded and from which data can be read. The data can only be sequentially accessed. The access speed is constrained by the location of the data on the tape, the speed of the tape drive, and the density of the data on the tape.

MAINFRAME In general, the central processing unit of a large-scale computer configuration.

MAIN MEMORY The principal storage device of a computer system — an integral part of the computer; generally, just called *memory*.

MAIN STORAGE The general-purpose storage of a computer, program addressable, from which instructions can be executed and from which data can be loaded directly into registers.

MANAGEMENT INFORMATION SYSTEM (MIS) A system that can store, retrieve, process, and output data to help management in its decision-making functions.

MASS STORAGE DEVICE Auxiliary or bulk memory that can store large amounts of data readily accessible to the computer (e.g., a disk or magnetic tape).

MATRIX A two- or three-dimensional rectangular array of identical symbols or entities.

MENU A table of available commands, either on a digitizing tablet or on the screen, that can be selected instead of using the keyboard.

MEGABYTE One million bytes.

MERGE To combine two or more sets of related data into one set.

MICROCOMPUTER A small, relatively low-cost computer that includes a microprocessor, memory, and all necessary interface circuits. Home or personal computers such as Apple, IBM-PC, and TRS-80 are examples of microcomputers.

MICROPROCESSORS A single integrated circuit that is the central processing unit of a microcomputer.

MINICOMPUTER A computer that is between the mainframe computers and the microcomputers in size, power, complexity, and cost; generally, a 32-bit computer.

MIRROR-IMAGE PROJECTION   In computer graphics, the reflection of display elements or groups with respect to a specific straight line or plane; synonymous with *flip* or *reflect*.

MNEMONIC   Short words that represent complete sentences or phrases of instructions.

MODEL   An accurate three-dimensional representation of a part, assembly, or plant designed on a CADD system and stored in the database.

MODELING   Constructing a mathematical or analytical model of a physical object or system for analysis.

MODEM   MOdulator-DEModulator. A device that converts digital signals into analog signals for transmission over telephone lines. The analog signals are converted back to digital signals at the other end by another modem.

MODULARITY   The method of assembling a system by using components that can be replaced individually.

MONITOR   A display for computer output, either monochrome or full color, that is usually a cathode ray tube.

MOTHER BOARD   The large printed circuit board at the bottom of a computer to which chips, other boards, and components are attached.

MOUSE   A hand-held data entry device, about the size of a cigarette pack, that can be used without a digitizing pad. It can be used like a puck.

MULTIPROCESSOR   Computer architecture that can execute one or more computer programs using two or more processing units simultaneously.

N

NESTING   Embedding data in levels of other data so that certain routines or data can be executed or accessed continuously in loops.

NETWORK   Two or more central processing facilities that are interconnected.

NODE   A computer or workstation connected to a local area network.

NUMERICAL CONTROL (NC)   The control of machine tools, drafting machines, and plotters by punched paper or magnetic tape encoded with the proper information to cut a part or draw a figure.

NUMERIC KEYPAD   A calculator-type numeric input device that is generally part of the keyboard.

O

OFF-LINE   Equipment or devices in a system that are not under direct control of the system's computer.

ON-LINE   Equipment or devices in a system that are directly connected to and under the control of the system's computer.

OPERATING SYSTEM   The software that controls the execution of computer programs and all hardware activity; also called system software.

OPERATION   An action that a computer is instructed to perform, such as add, subtract, store, read, or write.

OPERATOR   The person who performs the input and output functions at a workstation.

ORDER   To place in sequence according to rules or standards.

ORIGIN   An *X-Y*, or *X-Y-Z* coordinate from which all figures and entity locations are referenced.

ORTHOGRAPHIC   The method of making a layout, drawing, or map in which the projecting lines are perpendicular to the plane of the drawing or map.

OUTPUT   The end result of a process or series of processes, such as artwork, hardcopy, reports, and drawings.

OUTPUT DEVICE   Hardware, such as a printer or plotter, used to produce a copy of the results of the computer's processing operations.

OVERLAY   To position one or more drawings on top of another and view them simultaneously on the screen.

P

PAD   An area of plated copper on a PC board to which leads of components are soldered.

PAINT   To fill in a bounded figure on a display using a combination of repetitive patterns or line fonts.

PAN   To scroll the view of an object on the screen.

PAPER TAPE PUNCH/READER   A peripheral device that can read or punch perforated components.

PARALLEL INTERFACE   An interface that transfers several signals at once.

PARAMETER   A variable that controls the effect and usage of a command.

PART   A product, assembly, subassembly, or component.

PART PROGRAMMING LANGUAGE   A language that describes machining operations so that they are understood by computers or controllers.

PASCAL   A high-level programming language frequently preferred by computer scientists for its more logical structure and greater power.

PASSIVE GRAPHICS   The use of a display terminal in a noninteractive mode, usually through such items as plotters and microfilm viewers.

PASSIVE MODE   A method of operating a display device that does not allow any on-line interaction or alteration.

PASSWORD   A unique string of characters that a programmer, computer operator, or user must enter to gain access to data.

PATH   The route that an interconnection takes between connections in printed circuit board design.

PATTERN GENERATION   The transformation of CADD integrated circuit design information into a format for use by photo-beam or electron-beam machines in producing a reticle.

PC   Printed circuit or, more commonly, a personal computer.

PEN PLOTTER   An electromechanical CADD output device that draws a picture on paper or film using a ballpoint pen or liquid ink.

PERFORATED TAPE   An input or output medium that uses punched holes along a continuous strip of nonmagnetic tape to record and store data.

PERFORMANCE, CRT How well the cathode ray tube meets specifications such as screen resolution, display writing speed, internal intelligence, working area, accuracy and precision.

PERFORMANCE, SYSTEM How well a system meets specifications such as speed, capacity, accuracy, and the productivity ratio of CADD versus manual methods.

PERIPHERALS Devices connected to a computer such as tape drives, disks, workstations, and plotters.

PERMANENT STORAGE The location, outside the central processing unit, where completed data is stored (e.g., a disk or tape).

PHOTOPLOTTER A device used to generate artwork photographically for PC boards.

PIXELS PICture ELements. Individual dots on a display screen that are illuminated to create an image. Pixels are evenly spaced on the display.

PL/1 Programming Language/1. A high-level programming language used in a wide range of commercial and scientific applications.

PLOT Drawing by pen, pencil, or electrostatics of a design on paper film to create a drawing.

PLOTTER An automated device used to produce accurate drawings. Plotters include electrostatic, photoplotter, and pen.

POINT An element that represents a single X-Y-Z coordinate.

POLAR COORDINATES The two numbers that locate a point by (1) its radial distance from the origin and (2) the angle that a line through this point makes with the X-axis.

POSTPROCESSOR A software program or procedure that interprets graphical data and formats it for use by an NC machine or by other computer programs.

POWER SUPPLY A transformer that reduces voltage and changes AC to DC to provide electrical power to the computer.

PREPROCESSOR A method of converting data into computer-usable form for processing and output.

PROCESSOR The hardware components that perform arithmetic and logic operations, often called the *computer*.

PROGRAM The complete sequence of instructions to the computer to perform a task.

PROM Programmable Read Only Memory. A read-only integrated circuit that can be programmed.

PROMPT A message or symbol appearing on the screen that informs the user of a procedural error, incorrect input to the program being executed, or the next expected action.

PROPERTIES Nongraphic entities that may be associated. Properties in electrical design may include component name and identification, color, wire size, pin number, lug type, and signal values.

PROTOCOL The format of signals between two computer systems or between a computer and its peripherals that allows them to communicate.

PUCK A hand-held device that enables the user to digitize a drawing placed on the digitizer surface.

Q

QUALITY CONTROL   The establishment and maintenance of standards to assure well-made products.

QUALITY ENGINEERING   The performance and interpretation of tests to measure product quality.

QUEUE   A waiting list of tasks to be performed or messages to be transmitted.

R

RANDOM ACCESS MEMORY (RAM)   A main memory storage unit that provides direct access to the stored information; memory from which data can be retrieved regardless of input sequence.

RASTER   The geometric coordinate grid dividing the display area of a display device.

RASTERIZE   The process of converting an image into a corresponding pattern of dots.

RASTER DISPLAY   A CADD workstation display in which the entire screen surface is a matrix of pixels and the image is scanned at a constant refresh rate. The bright, flicker-free image can be selectively written and erased.

RASTER SCAN   A line-by-line sweep across the entire screen surface to generate the image. The device can display a large amount of information without flicker.

READ ONLY MEMORY (ROM)   A storage device (memory) generally used for control programs, the content of which is not alterable.

REAL TIME   Immediate feedback to the user from tasks or functions executed by a CADD system. Immediate feedback through the workstation makes interactive operation of a CADD system possible.

RECORD   Related data processed as a unit.

REFLECT   The same as mirror-image projection.

REFRESH   CRT display technology requiring continuous redrawing of the display image.

REFRESH RATE   The rate at which the image on a screen is redrawn (e.g., 30 times/second or 30HZ).

RELIABILITY   The amount of time a system is running with no problems versus the down time.

REMOTE TERMINAL   An input or output peripheral located at a distance from the computer.

REPAINT   Redraw a display image on a CRT to reflect its updated status.

REPEATABILITY (OF DISPLAY DEVICE)   A measure of the hardware accuracy or the coincidence of successive retraces of a display element.

REPLICATE   To generate an exact copy of a design on the screen at any location or scale desired.

RESOLUTION   The smallest spacing between points on a graphic device at which the points can be detected as distinct.

RESPONSE TIME   The elapsed time from the completing of a command at a workstation to the display of the results at that workstation.

RESTART   To resume execution of an interrupted computer program.

RESTORE   To return a design to its original configuration after editing or modification.

ROBOTICS   The use of computer-controlled robots to automate manufacturing processes such as welding, material handling, painting, and assembly.

ROTATE   To turn a displayed image about an axis through a predefined angle.

ROUTER   A program that automatically determines the routing path for the component connections on a PC board.

ROUTINE   A computer program. A set of instructions arranged in proper sequence to cause a computer to perform a desired operation.

ROUTING   Placing the interconnects between components on a printed circuit board or integrated circuit.

RUBBERBANDING   A technique for displaying a straight line with one end fixed and the other end attached to the movable cursor.

RUN   To execute a program.

S

SATELLITE   A remote system, connected to a host system, that contains processors, memory, and mass storage to operate independently from the host.

SAVE   To transfer the data created at the workstation to a storage device.

SCALE   To enlarge or shrink an image without changing its shape.

SCHEMATIC   A not-to-scale diagram of an electrical circuit.

SCISSOR   To trim a drawing in the database so that it can be viewed on a CRT screen.

SCREEN   A computer display device, also called a *monitor* or *cathode ray tube*.

SCROLL   To automatically roll up on a screen, as on a spool, a message or drawing too large to be displayed all at once.

SECTION   To cut an object with an intersecting plane, then request generation and display of the total intersection geometry on a display surface.

SECURITY   Safeguards and procedures that can be applied to computer hardware, programs, and data to assure that access to the system is controlled.

SELECTIVE ERASE   The deletion of portions of a design without repainting the entire screen.

SEMICONDUCTOR   A material that conducts electricity and is used for the storage and transfer of computer data (e.g., silicon).

SERIAL INTERFACE   A connection that transfers data sequentially, one bit at a time.

SHAPE FILL   The automatic shading of an area on the screen.

SILICON   The basic material used in the manufacturing of computer chips. See *semiconductor*.

SILK SCREEN   Artwork used to print component placement and identification information on a printed circuit board.

SIMULATE   To imitate the behavior of a finished part under various structural and thermal loading conditions.

SOFTWARE   The computer programs, procedures, rules, and instructions that control the use of the hardware.

SOLID MODEL   Solid models represent the mass and the boundary of a complete form.

SORT   To segregate items into groups according to specified criteria (e.g., to alphabetize).

SOURCE   User-written instruction statements prior to translation by the computer into a form that can be executed by machine.

SPLINE   A smooth curve between a sequence of points in one place.

STORAGE   The physical device or location that contains all of the information on a CADD system.

STORAGE DEVICE OR STORAGE UNIT   A peripheral component in which data can be stored and later retrieved.

STORAGE TUBE   A CRT that retains an image for a considerable period of time without redrawing. It allows no selective editing or erasing.

STRING   A sequence of characters such as a word or sentence.

STYLUS   A hand-held object that provides coordinate input to the display device.

SURFACE MACHINING   The ability to output 3-, 4-, and 5-axis NC toolpaths using three-dimensional surface definition capabilities (e.g., ruled surfaces, tabulated cylinders, and surfaces of revolution).

SURFACE OF REVOLUTION   Rotation of a curve around an axis through a specified angle.

SYMBOL   A set of primitive graphic entities, lines, points, arcs, circles, and text that are grouped together as a unit. Symbols may be combined or nested to form larger symbols or drawings.

SYNTAX   The set of rules that describes the structure of statements in a computer language.

SYSTEM   All of the people, machines, and methods needed to perform a specific task.

T

TABLET   An input device that a designer can use to digitize coordinate data or enter commands into a CADD system by means of a stylus or puck, also called a *digitizing pad*.

TAPE DRIVE   The peripheral device that records and reads magnetic tape.

TELECOMMUNICATIONS   The transmission of signals over long distances between a computing system and remotely located devices by telephone, microwave, infrared link, or coaxial cable.

TELEWRITER   A typewriterlike keyboard device used to enter commands or to print system messages.

TEMPLATE   A commonly used component or part that serves as a design aid and can be subsequently traced instead of redrawn whenever needed. The CADD equivalent of a designer's template is a symbol in the symbol library.

TEMPORARY STORAGE   A location in memory for temporarily storing results of a program on the system until the results can be transferred to permanent storage, also called *working storage*.

TERMINAL   A device equipped with a keyboard and some kind of display that sends and receives information over a communication channel to and from a computer.

TEXT   Letters, numbers, and special characters.

TEXT EDITOR   A program used to create and modify text on the system.

TEXT FILE   A file stored in the system that consists entirely of text.

THROUGHPUT   The work performed by a CADD system or workstation during a given period of time; a quantitative measure of system productivity.

THUMBWHEELS   A CADD input device that uses a manually controlled vertical wheel for locating a coordinate on the Y axis, and a horizontal wheel for locating a coordinate on the X axis.

TIMESHARING   The concurrent use of a computing system in which two or more users can execute computer programs simultaneously, usually from remote terminals.

TOLERANCE   The allowed variance from a given nominal dimension.

TOOL PATH   A trace of the movement of the tip of a numerical control cutting tool that is used to guide or control machining equipment.

TRACKING   Moving a cursor across the surface of the screen with a light pen, stylus, or puck.

TRACKING SYMBOL   A symbol such as a cross, dot, angle, or square used for indicating the position of a stylus.

TRANSISTOR   An electronic switch that transmits a signal of either 0 or 1 to communicate information in binary machine language. A semiconductor device often made of silicon.

TRANSLATE   To change data from one language to another.

TRANSPORTABILITY   The ability to execute a program on different computers without major changes.

TREE   A method of file storage in which the file structure has a top level and one or more sublevels, which in turn may contain additional sublevels.

TURNAROUND TIME   The elapsed time between the start and finish of a task or project.

TURNKEY SYSTEM   A CADD system for which the vendor assumes total responsibility for building, installing, and testing all the hardware and software required to do a specific application or applications; a computer system sold in a ready-to-use state.

TUTORIAL   A message that is displayed to show the user how to perform a task.

U

UP   A term used to denote that the computer is working properly.

UPDATING   Changing a file by adding, modifying, or deleting information.

USER-FRIENDLY   A CADD system (both hardware and software) that is easy to understand and operate.

UTILITY PROGRAM   A specific system software program such as a diagnostic program, a plot program, or a sort program.

V

VECTOR   A directed line segment that has magnitude and direction.

VECTOR GENERATION   The process that determines all intermediate points between two endpoints of a line segment.

VERIFICATION   The message feedback to a display device acknowledging that an input was detected (e.g., the brightening of a display element selected by a light pen).

VERSION   A configuration control identifier that is changed whenever there are modifications or enhancements.

VIA   A hole in a printed circuit board through which a path from one layer or side is transferred to the other.

VIEW PORT   A user-selected viewing area on the screen that frames the contents of a window.

W

WAFER   A slice of silicon from which a larger number of integrated circuit chips are produced.

WINCHESTER DRIVE   A combination of a disk drive and one or more hard disks permanently sealed in a case.

WINDOW   A portion or view of a design that is framed by a view port.

WINDOWING   Proportionally enlarging a figure or portion of a figure so it fills the screen or view port.

WIRE FRAME   A picture of a three-dimensional object displayed on the screen as a series of lines that represent the edges of its surfaces. This pictures looks as if it were made from coat hangers.

WIRING DIAGRAM   A schematic representation of all circuits and devices that shows their interconnectivity.

WORD PROCESSING (WP)   The use of a special program to create, edit, store, display, and print text.

WORKING DRAWING   A detailed layout of components with complete dimensions and notes.

WORKSTATION   The hardware by which a designer interacts with the computer, also called a *terminal*.

WRITE   To copy information from main memory to a storage device.

WRITE PROTECT   A security feature that prevents existing data from being erased by new data.

Z

Z CLIPPING   The ability to specify depth parameter for a three-dimensional drawing such that all elements above or below the specified depth(s) become invisible. No change is made to the database of the part or drawing; useful in viewing cluttered or complex part geometry.

ZOOM   The successive enlargement or shrinking of the image on the screen.

2

Comparative Glossary*

	Manual Definition	**CADD Definition**
ACCURACY, DESIGN	Positional accuracy in critically tight areas determined graphically on large-scale study work-plot or manual calculations.	Positional accuracy in tight areas can be viewed graphically at any infinitely large scale and checked by requesting dimensional readout; used in interference checking.
ACCURACY, DRAFTING	Depending on scale of drawing, measure of positional accuracy of drawing elements. May be 0.01 inches (0.0254 mm) at best, if on dimensionally stable material.	Regardless of drawing scale, positional accuracy is plotted at 0.001 inches (0.0254 mm), while database coordinates are accurate to 14 decimal places.
ADD	Arithmetic or design/drafting function.	To sum, by computer, like items or parts; augment a design or drafting image with further graphic, dimensional or alphanumeric information.
ADD TEXT	Letter or type additional alphanumeric notation.	Type at workstation keyboard additional alphanumeric notation which is electronically placeable at preselected text nodes.

*Courtesy of CALMA.

	Manual Definition	**CADD Definition**
ALIGN	Place in line, as in parallel to a reference or object line.	Automatically line up design features, shapes, symbols, text, etc. parallel to a reference or object line.
ALGORITHM	A predefined sequence of steps to be taken to solve problems of a particular type; a procedure attributed to an Uzbek mathematician: Al-Khwarizmi in ninth century.	A predefined program of steps to be followed by computer to solve problems of software furnished by CADD supplier to solve typical problems.
ANNOTATE	Complement dimensioned drawing with explanatory text, labels, general notes, special notes, reference notes, subtitles, and titles.	Add explanatory text, labels, general notes, etc.; electronically copy and place repititious notation common to many symbols, drawing segments, or drawings.
ARRAY	In drafting, the alignment in X and Y of similar design entities or tabulated data.	Electronic alignment in X, Y, and Z of similar design entities or tabulated data.
ASSEMBLE	Place related units or parts into predetermined positions.	Electronically place related units or parts into predetermined positions as in arrangement and assembly drawings. Units or parts may be electronically copied from other drawings in the database.
ASSIGN	Schedule or reserve a position for an activity or a drawing segment.	Schedule or reserve a position for an activity, data, symbol or drawing segment to a layer, drawing coordinate, model, or disk memory space.
AUTO,REVISE		Revise all drawing segments, subtitles, titles, drawing numbers at each occurrence of faulty data in database; effect change with one command, on one or all drawings or documents of a set (see *Revise*).
AUXILIARY VIEW	See *View, auxiliary*.	See *View, auxiliary*.
AXIS	One of a set of three lines intersecting at a common point in space in such a way that each axis is perpendicular to the plane containing the other two.	Same as manual definition.
BASIC		A computer language: Beginners All-purpose Symbolic Instruction Code.
BATCH PROCESS		Without benefit of interactivity by CRT; digitizer; tablet or keyboard; a means for creating alphanumeric and/or graphic output from data processed by any computer.
BAUD		A unit of signaling speed equal to the number of discrete conditions or signal events per second.
BILL OF MATERIAL	A listing of parts or items required to fabricate, assemble, or erect an	A computer listing (lettered on drawing or tabulated on printer) of parts or items

	Manual Definition	**CADD Definition**
	engineering design. Also BOM or BOM list.	represented on an engineering design, automatically derived from the database.
BLANK, LINE	Erase line from drawing.	Electronically erase from view on screen, but leave in database for ultimate reuse or elimination.
BLANK, MODEL	Erase all views of a design feature on all drawings.	Electronically erase from view on screen, but leave in database for ultimate reuse, modification, or elimination.
BLANK, SCREEN		Electronically erase all data from view on screen, but leave in database for ultimate reuse, modification, or elimination.
BLANK, SUBMODEL	Erase all views of a design on all drawings.	Electronically erase from view on screen, but leave in database for ultimate reuse, modification, or elimination.
CAD		Interchangeably: Computer-aided design or computer-aided drafting; a generic term used in the United States, Europe, and Japan.
COM		Computer-output-microfilm: an electromechanical system for transforming the digital version of an engineering design directly onto 35 mm microfilm or 105 mm microfiche images.
CPU		Central Processing Unit; that section of the computer that contains the control unit, the arithmetic unit, and memory.
CARTESIAN COORDINATES	A reference system similar to engineering LEFT–RIGHT, UP–DOWN, BACK–FORWARD, system for defining a point in three-dimensional space. Compares to projection planes: FRONTAL, HORIZONTAL, PROFILE.	A reference system along X (LEFT–RIGHT), Y (UP–DOWN), and Z (BACK–FORWARD); René Descartes' X-Y-Z system for defining a point in three-dimensional space.
CATALOG	Compilation, in a printed book, of vendor's standard offerings; a reference document for designers.	Portion of the design database containing often-used vendor's or trade association's standard reference information, graphics, and dimensions.
CATHODE RAY TUBE, REFRESH		Specialized type of CRT in which screen image is formed by continuously panning electron beam over phosphor-coated tube face, *rasterization*.
CATHODE RAY TUBE, STORAGE		Specialized type of CRT in which screen image is formed by electron beam "stroking" phosphor-coated tube face.
CHECKING	Inspection or recalculation of engineering drawing data for compliance with original design, vendor's drawings, or catalog information.	Same as manual definition.

	Manual Definition	**CADD Definition**
CLASS 1 DRAWING	A designation of drawing type: NON-DIMENSIONED, NOT-TO-SCALE; usually schematic or diagrammatic.	Same as manual definition.
CLASS 2 DRAWING	A designation of drawing type: DIMENSIONED, NOT-TO-SCALE; usually with tabulated dimensions, but may be isometric (piping, etc.)	Same as manual definition, except designer has choice of electronically "rubberbanding" drawing to accurately reflect tabulated dimensions.
CLASS 3 DRAWING	A designation of drawing type: DIMENSIONED, TO SCALE.	Same as manual definition, except the three-dimensional model or submodel in database is source for two-dimensional (orthographic) views needed for working drawings.
COMPOSITE	A multilayered drawing; a series of special overlays viewable and reproducible with a base drawing to make a composite print.	Separable layers or overlays of graphic and/or alphanumeric data in the database; viewable on screen or plottable in any combination of base drawings or overlays.
DATABASE	A collection of interrelated data items that must be assembled by each application thereby causing the "reinvention of the wheel" each time the database is needed.	A collection of interrelated data items organized by a consistent scheme that allows one or more applications to process the items without regard to physical storage locations.
DELETE	Remove from document.	Remove electronically from database; selectively remove portion of symbol or drawing segment, linework or text, and automatically remove all such occurrences on any drawing or document in the database.
DESIGNER	Degreed or paraengineer who creates preliminary or working drawings and documentation from engineer's notes and sketches.	Operates input design workstations with interactive CADD processing system.
DIGITIZE	Laborious scaling and recording X-Y-Z coordinates or drawing or map elements from an origin point.	Automatically recording by pointing — X-Y-Z coordinates as in manual definition; enters graphical data into a CADD system.
DIGITIZER		Old name for CADD drafters'/designers' input workstation; a computer-oriented device for automating graphic data reduction — process called *digitizing*.
DIMENSION	Annotate drawings with lettered dimensions to denote sizes of elemental shapes and areas as well as locations.	Automated placement of dimension lines — witness lines with typed or computer-supplied dimensions to denote size of elemental shapes and areas as well as locations.
DISPLAY	Show.	Command drawing or document to appear from database on the workstation screen.
DRAFTER	U.S. government–mandated term for man or woman performing engineering	An upgraded drafter; uses CADD input or output workstations interactively to

	Manual Definition	**CADD Definition**
	drafting; formerly draftsman, draughtsman, draftswoman, draftsperson.	conduct all drafting functions.
DRAWING	Graphic representation with annotation of an engineered physical object; sketch.	Digital version of graphic and alphanumeric representation of an engineered physical object stored in database; electromechanically plotted graphic and alphanumeric representation of the object.
DRAWING, LAYER	See *Composite.*	See *Composite.*
DRAWING SEGMENT	A portion of complete drawing; may contain symbols and/or text.	A portion of complete drawing; a repeatable and electronically copied, reduced, or enlarged drawing segment for use on other drawings — with or without modification; a combination of symbols and/or text.
DRAWING STANDARDS MANUAL	Prepared by design/drafting management.	Same as manual definition, except for some special standards for CADD.
DRAWINGS SECURITY	Method for protecting original documents (tracings) from theft or unauthorized alteration; usually by controlled access.	Method for protecting digital database from theft or unauthorized copying, alteration, or accidental erasure (See *Password*).
EDIT	Review or proofread for possible revision.	Review or proofread on screen for possible revision; perform revision electronically.
EDIT STATION–CADD		Workstation for inputting design or drafting changes to existing CADD drawing or document. Changes may be redesign, revision, construction ECO, or as-built data.
ENLARGE	Make bigger than before.	Electronically causes the indicated portion of the picture to enlarge to fill screen. Operator can enlarge infinitely, until a decimal point, for example, is made to fill full 19-inch screen.
ERASE	Rub out with abrasive material (erasure); remove with moist Q-tip as with water erasable ink on mylar; remove with No. 1 and No. 2 solution as on sepia print.	Remove electronically from database.
FORTRAN		FORmula TRANslation — a computer language universally used in engineering.
FONT	A drafter's or printer's definition for unique sets of alphanumeric characters (e.g., Leroy lettering font, Futura type font).	Identifying name for lettering style or line characteristic (e.g., Leroy lettering font, Dashed line font).

	Manual Definition	**CADD Definition**
GRAPHICS COMMAND LANGUAGE	May be instructions in design/drafting manual spelling out graphic procedures, drawing composition usage, text sizes, etc.	A CADD designer's "shorthand" for communicating desired graphic actions and responses to the system.
GRID	A spaced array — graphical.	A design/drafting aid available as a placement background on the CRT screen. Grids may be square or stretch in X, Y, or Z.
HIDDEN LINE	A line on a drawing, usually shown dashed, representing an edge, contour, or surface that could be seen only if the object being drafted were transparent. May be omitted as well; must be constructed.	In three-dimensional work all hidden lines appear at first as object lines. Designer has option to "touch" each line with cursor, ask computer to make it dashed, or eliminate it from view.
HOST COMPUTER OR HOST CPU		Term usually given to a very large computer such as IBM-3081. May serve many minicomputers for data management and "number crunching."
INPUT-OUTPUT		Communication with processing system (computer). Facilities for "talking" to computer; give data, coordinates, instructions; receive answers, listings, drawings in readable form.
INTERACTIVE		A technique of designer communication in which the system immediately acknowledges and acts upon requests entered by the designer at a workstation.
ISOMETRIC	A form of drawing projection in which three faces of an object or feature are shown on three major axes 120 degrees apart and in which the angle the front edge makes with the vertical is 35 degrees. True isometrics are to-scale drawings.	Same as manual definition.
ITEM	A component of a larger grouping or assembly; part of a design; a purchased unit under a single engineering specification used in fabrication, assembly, or erection.	A two-dimensional or three-dimensional symbol (cell), or submodel, an engineering database unit under a single specification; part; an elemental portion of a cell, submodel, or model.
ITEM SELECT		A technique for selecting a symbol (cell) or submodel, including text, preparatory to executing a MOVE, COPY, or MIRROR command at the workstation.
LABEL	Hand-lettered note or "callout" identifying a drawing feature.	Computer-generated note or "callout" identifying a drawing feature.
LAYER	See *Composite*.	See *Composite*.
LETTERING, LEROY	See *Font*.	See *Font*.
LIBRARY	A cataloged collection of data.	Same as manual definition.
LINE	A visible connection between two points in space.	Same as manual definition.

	Manual Definition	**CADD Definition**
LIST		A command to request a list of items be printed by the system printer.
MACRO		Directions that generate a known set of instructions. Used to eliminate the need to write a set of instructions that are used repeatedly.
MENU		An area of the digitizing tablet reserved for an array of commands. Allows choosing the commands with the stylus.
METRICATION	The act of replacing, relettering, or recalculating nonmetric dimensions or values into SI units.	Automatic assignment and conversion of nonmetric dimensions or values into SI units, including roundoff.
MIRROR	Create, by tracing back of drawing; an opposite-hand view of a portion of a design.	Electronically command, display, or plot an opposite-hand view of a portion of a design, wherein ''mirrored'' text remains right-reading.
MIRROR, ABOUT LINE	Create opposite-hand view similar to or symmetrical about a line.	Electronically display or plot opposite-hand view; used in two-dimensional design only.
MIRROR, ABOUT PLANE	Impossible to create without redrawing.	Electronically display or plot opposite-hand view; used in three-dimensional design only.
MODEL	A three-dimensional object used to obtain physical data for drawing information.	The three-dimensional object that is being constructed electronically in the computer.
MODEM	MODulator-DEModulator; device used to send and recieve data in high-speed bulk mode over telephone lines.	Same as manual definition.
MOVE	Completely erase and redraw or trace in a different location.	Electronically move a group of items without redrawing.
ORIENT	Line up with a known axis such as X, Y, or Z.	Line up working coordinating system to base coordinate system; in three-dimensional work line up item relative to submodel or submodel to model.
ORTHOGONAL	At right angles to each other.	Same as manual definition.
ORTHOGRAPHIC-PROJECTION	The projection of a point from one plane to another.	Same as manual definition.
PAINT		Electronic drawing or lettering on the screen of a design.
PART	Elemental physical object or its symbolic representation; also, elemental portion of a drawing (i.e., point or line).	Same as manual definition; sometimes called *Item*.
PASSWORD		A word or code required to gain access to the system.
PICTURE	Any graphic representation.	The flat-plane (two-dimensional) view of a submodel or model, part of an engineering drawing to which

	Manual Definition	**CADD Definition**
		dimensions, text, and titling will be added; a "window" portion of the complete design in database.
PLOT		To get hardcopy output on a variety of plotters.
PLOTTER, BELT		Upright high-speed pen (ball point or ink) plotter capable of handling drawings up to E size.
PLOTTER, ELECTROSTATIC		A very high-speed plotter in which lines are formed by a matrix of dots.
PLOTTER, FLATBED		Large tablelike pen (ball point or ink) plotter capable of handling very long drawings.
PLOTTER, MICROFILM		Computer-Output Microfilm (COM) recorder that converts mag tape version of a drawing or document from CADD database and records a miniature version on 35 mm microfilm or 105 mm microfilm.
POINT	A visible dot to represent some coordinate in space.	Same as manual definition.
PROCESS	An orderly method for attaining a given result.	A predesigned procedure for computer to aid in attaining a given design, drafting, or documentation result.
PROCESS	To proceed, step-by-step, for attaining a given result.	Activate a predesigned software command(s) procedure to create a given result from data furnished — by computer.
REPAINT		Electronic "redraw or relettering" of latest status of a design, used right after a revision or edit has been executed, for designer to view corrections of revision or edit.
REVISE	Alter existing tracing or document by erase-replace or redraw-retype.	Alter database — electronic erase and replace, seldom redraw.
RUBBERBAND		Electronically "stretch" space between design components and have interconnected lines "stretch" also.
RULER	Scale. A tool for linear measurement. May be architect's, engineer's, mechanical (machine), or metric.	A scalelike image with the ability to be placed electronically on screen, at any location or orientation as an aid for design layout at workstation. May be marked off as architect's, engineer's, mechanical (machine), or SI metric. English and metric units are interchangeable on command.
SAVE	Keep on file.	Same as manual definition.

	Manual Definition	**CADD Definition**
SCALE, ARCHITECT'S, USA	Measuring device marked off in units varying from 1/32 to 1/2 of an English inch.	Same as manual definition.
SCALE, ENGINEER'S, USA	Measuring device marked off in units varying from 1/10 to 1/100 of an English inch.	Same as manual definition.
SCALE, MACHINE, USA	Measuring device marked off in equal units varying from 1/4 size to full size.	Same as manual definition.
SCALE, METRIC, SI	Measuring device marked off in tenths of a millimeter or centimeter.	Same as manual definition.
SCREEN	(Sometimes used to describe printers' Benday screen of dot patterns created photographically on a background site or structure drawings.)	TV-like picture tube; cathode ray tube (CRT) may be storage, vector, or raster type.
SELECT	To choose.	Identify to the computer the portion of drawing to be acted upon next.
SHIFT	To move.	Same as manual definition.
SKEW	Place at an angle off plumb or level line.	Place at an angle off plumb, level, or depth line.
SMOOTH	Drafter's refinement of plotted-point spline using French curves.	Electronic refinement of known value point curve.
SPACE	Scale off on drawing positions for repetitive symbols, drawing segments.	Electronic scaling, positioning of repetitive points, symbols, or drawing segments by typing only the overall dimension and the number of units to be repetitively spaced and placed on the screen.
SPLINE CURVE	Cumbersome pliable metal strip used to draft varying radius curves through preplotted points on drawing or template (as in Lofting).	Automatic curve-fit generator, with calculated offsets, through predetermined points for drawing or template plot (as in Lofting, Shipbuilding, or Sheetmetal).
SUBMODEL	Portion of a three-dimensional object used to obtain physical data for drawing information.	Portion of a three-dimensional object that is being constructed geometrically.
SYMBOL LIBRARY	Legend of symbols, names, and uses; key to symbols; may be plastic templates.	Digital version of symbols, by engineering discipline, instantly callable from symbol library database. Each symbol may contain associated text or preassigned space for varying text (see *Symbol, Transfer*).
SYMBOL TEMPLATE	Standard or custom, symbol cutout plastic template for tracing onto drawing; available by disciplines (e.g., piping, iso, electrical).	Not used (see *Symbol Library*).
SYMBOL, TRANSFER	"Rub-on" version of preprinted standard drafting symbols; used in photodrafting.	Digital version of standard or special symbol, library database. Electronically

	Manual Definition	**CADD Definition**
		placeable, spaceable or copyable anywhere on drawing in any orientation.
TABULAR DIMENSIONING	Listing of numerical values "keyed" to dimension letters. Used on typical details.	Same as manual definition.
TEXT NODE	Space reserved on drawing for later addition of alphanumeric characters, dimensions, etc.	A preselected space reserved on symbol (cell), drawing segment, or drawing for later addition, by keyboard typing of alphanumeric characters, dimensions, subtitles, and titles.
3-D	Three-dimensional; relates to measurable volumes in engineering.	Three-dimensional; relates to measurable volumes. $X-Y-Z$ coordinates used to make orthographic views automatically.
2-D	Two-dimensional; relates to measurable areas in engineering.	Two-dimensional; relates to measurable areas and symbols used for drawings.
TRACE	Recopy portion of repetitive drawing by tracing.	Electronically copy portion of repetitive drawing already in database.
VIEW, AUXILIARY	Planar projection of a drawing portion not perpendicular to standard orthographic projection.	Same as manual definition.
WINDOW		Portion of larger design area, filling the screen vertically and horizontally; the "distance" from which operator sees drawings or model; related to "scale."
ZOOM	A photo technique for enlarging or reducing a portion of a drawing; a TV camera technique for enlarging or reducing field of view.	An electronic enlarge/reduce technique for changing scale on screen — infinitely, up or down.

Appendix

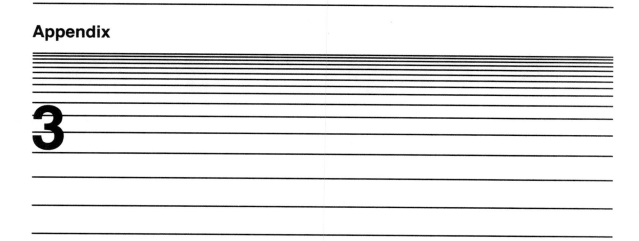

3

CADD Vendor Directory

A/E MICRO SYSTEMS, INC.
11223 Cornell Park Drive
Cincinnati, OH 45242

ADAGE, INC.
One Fortune Drive
Billerica, MA 01821

ADSI
190 East Fifth Avenue
Naperville, IL 60540

ALTEK CORPORATION
2150 Industrial Parkway
Silver Spring, MD 20904

AMERICAN COMPUTERS
AND ENG., INC.
11726 San Vicente Blvd.
Los Angeles, CA 90049

AMERICAN PROGRAMMERS
GUILD
55 Millplain Road, Suite 17-5
Danbury, CT 06811

APPA BUSINESS COMPUTERS
5864 Interface Drive
Ann Arbor, MI 48103

APOLLO COMPUTER, INC.
15 Elizabeth Drive
Chelmsford, MA 01824

APPLICON, INC.
32 Second Avenue
Burlington, MA 01803

ARTSOFT, INC.
60 South Hartford Turnpike
Wallingford, CT 06492

ATKINSON, TREMBLAY
& ASSOCIATES, INC.
1080 Beaver Hall Hill, Suite 1400
Montreal, Quebec, Canada H2Z 1S8

AUTOCAD
150 Shoreline Highway
Building B
Mill Valley, CA 94941

AUTODESK, INC.
2658 Bridgeway
Sausalito, CA 94965

AUTOMATION TECHNOLOGY
PRODUCTS
1671 Dell Avenue
Campbell, CA 95008

AUTO-TROL TECHNOLOGY
CORP.
P.O. Box 33815
Denver, CO 80233

BAUSCH & LOMB, INC.
P.O. Box 14547
Austin, TX 78761

BRUNING CAD
6111 E. Skelly Drive
Tulsa, OK 74135

CAD COUNSEL
231 East Lemon
Monrovia, CA 91016

CAD DESIGN SYSTEMS, INC.
1305 Remington Road
Schaumburg, IL 60195

CAD N.W., INC.
722 SW 2nd, Suite 208
Portland, OR 97204

CAD SYSTEMS, INC.
9086 Cypress Green Drive
Jackson, FL 32216

CADAM, INC.
2660 West Empire Avenue
Burbank, CA 91504

CADCAL PRODUCTS, INC.
9311 Eton Street
Chatsworth, CA 91311

CADGRAPH SYSTEM, INC.
P.O. Box 638
Fremont, CA 94536

CADPLUS PRODUCTS COMPANY
510 2nd Street NW, Suite 205
Albuquerque, NM 87102

CALIFORNIA COMPUTER
PRODUCTS, INC.
3320 E. La Palma Avenue
Anaheim, CA 92803

CAMAX SYSTEMS, INC.
7225 Ohms Lane
Minneapolis, MN 55435

CALMA COMPANY
501 Sycamore Drive
Milpitas, CA 95035

CASCADE GRAPHICS
DEVELOPMENT
1000 S. Grand Avenue
Santa Ana, CA 92705

CHARLES E. HILL & ASSOCIATES,
INC.
6535 E. 82nd Street, Suite 213
Indianapolis, IN 46250

CIVILSOFT
290 S. Anaheim Blvd., Suite 100
Anaheim, CA 92805

COMPUTER DETAILING
CORPORATION
301 York Road
Warminster, PA 18974

COMPUTERPLAN, INC.
920 SW 3rd Avenue
Portland, OR 97204

COMPUTERVISION CORP.
201 Burlington Road
Bedford, MA 01730

CONCAP
Sixty 98th Avenue
Oakland, CA 94603

CONE DRIVE OPERATIONS
240 East 12th Street
Traverse City, MI 49684

CONE & CONE COMPUTER
GENERATED GRAPHICS
2499 Lochaven Road
Union Lake, MI 48085

CONTROL DATA CORPORATION
HQW09F, Box O
Minneapolis, MN 55440

CUBICOMP CORPORATION
3165 Adeline Street
Berkeley, CA 94703

DARATECH, INC.
16 Myrtle Avenue
Cambridge, MA 02138

DATA DESIGN LOGIC SYSTEMS,
INC.
4800 Patrick Henry Drive
Santa Clara, CA 95054

DATA GENERAL CORPORATION
4400 Computer Drive
Westboro, MA 01580

DATAGRAPHICS SYSTEMS
P.O. Box 931
Benicia, CA 94510

DAY SOFT — CAD
2550 9th Street, Suite 113
Berkeley, CA 94710

DEMAND, INC.
7430 East Caley Avenue, Bldg. 1,
Suite 350
Englewood, CO 80111

DEVTRON, RUSSELL, INC.
500 W. Cedar Avenue
Gladwin, MI 48624

DIGICOM SYSTEMS
CORPORATION
11584 Perry Highway
Wexford, PA 15090

DIGITAL EQUIPMENT
CORPORATION
Engineering Systems Group
2 Iron Way
Marlboro, MA 01752

DISCO-TECH
P.O. Box 1659
Santa Rosa, CA 95402

ELXSI
2334 Lundy Place
San Jose, CA 95131

ENGINEERED SOFTWARE
344-L Cleveland Avenue
Tumwater, WA 98501

ENGINEERING SERVICE, INC.
21556 Telegraph Road, Box #7
Southfield, MI 48037

ENGINEERING SYSTEMS
CORPORATION
P.O. Box 80318
Baton Rouge, LA 70898

EVANS & SUTHERLAND
COMPUTER CORPORATION
580 Arapeen Drive
Salt Lake City, UT 84108

EQUITABLE LIFE LEASING CORP.
10251 Vista Sorrento Pkwy.,
Suite 300
San Diego, CA 92121

FLORIDA COMPUTER GRAPHICS,
INC.
1000 Sand Pond Road
Lake Mary, FL 32746

FORESIGHT RESOURCES
CORPORATION
34 Corporate Woods
Overland Park, KS 66210

FORMATIVE TECHNOLOGIES
The Design Center
5001 Baum Blvd.
Pittsburgh, PA 15213

GARRISON-LULL
P.O. Box 1030
New York, NY 10021

GEOCAD, INC.
P.O. Box 186, Laurel Road
Pound Ridge, NY 10576

GEORGE L. OLIVER COMPANY
P.O. Box 1842
Fremont, CA 94538

GERBER SYSTEMS
TECHNOLOGY, INC.
40 Gerber Road East
South Windsor, CT 06074

GRAFTEK, INC.
1777 Conestoga Street
Boulder, CO 80301

GT SYSTEMS
14 Bensin Drive
Melville, NY 11747

GTCO CORPORATION
1055 First Street
Rockville, MD 20850

HARRIS CORPORATION
Computer Systems Division
2101 Cypress Creek Road
Ft. Lauderdale, FL 33309

HEATH COMPANY
Hilltop Road
St. Joseph, MI 49085

HEWLETT-PACKARD
CORPORATION
16399 W. Bernardo Drive
San Diego, CA 92127

HOLGUIN & ASSOCIATES, INC.
P.O. Box 12990
El Paso, TX 79912

INFINITE GRAPHICS, INC.
4611 East Lake Street
Minneapolis, MN 55406

INTERACTIVE GRAPHICS
SERVICE CO., INC.
1479 Chain Bridge Road
McLean, VA 22101

INTERGRAPH CORPORATION
One Madison Industrial Park
Huntsville, AL 35807

INTERACTIVE COMPUTER
SYSTEMS, INC.
P.O. Box 14908
Baton Rouge, LA 70898

INTERNATIONAL BUSINESS
MACHINES CORPORATION
Direct Response Marketing
Department 72E/522
400 Parson's Pond Drive
Franklin Lakes, NJ 07417

JERGENS, INC.
19520 Nottingham Road
Cleveland, OH 44110

JEWELL TECHNOLOGIES, INC.
4451 53rd Avenue Southwest
Seattle, WA 98116

KETIV TECHNOLOGIES, INC.
3236 SW Kelly Avenue
Portland, OR 97201

KEWILL SYSTEMS
8950 Villa La Jolla Drive, #2200
La Jolla, CA 92037

LEONARD N/C SYSTEMS, INC.
6470 Federal Blvd.
Lemon Grove, CA 92045

LEONARD SYSTEMS, INC.
380-B Vernon Way
El Cajon, CA 92020

MACNEAL-SCHWENDLER CORP.
815 Colorado Boulevard
Los Angeles, CA 90041

MANUFACTURING
AND CONSULTING SERVICES
17942 Cowan
Irvine, CA 92714

MASSCOMP
One Technology Park
Westford, MA 01886

MATHEMATICAL APPLICATIONS
GROUP, INC.
3 Westchester Plaza
Elmsford, NY 10523

MATRA DATAVISION
Corporate Place I
99 South Bedford Street
Burlington, MA 01803

McDONNELL DOUGLAS
AUTOMATION CO.
Box 516
St. Louis, MO 63166

MCTel, INC.
3 Bala Plaza East, Suite 505
Bala Cynwyd, PA 19004

MEGATEK CORPORATION
9605 Scranton Road
San Diego, CA 92121

METAGRAPHICS, INC.
30 Commerce Way
Woburn, MA 01801

MICHIGAN TECH SOFTWARE,
INC.
P.O. Box 364
Houghton, MI 49931

MICRO CAD
515 Delgado Drive
Baton Rouge, LA 70808

MICRO CONTROL SYSTEMS INC.
230 Hartford Turnpike
Vernon, CT 06066

MICRO ENGINEERING
SOLUTIONS
P.O. Box 1396
Fairfield, CT 06430

MICRO-INSTALLATIONS, INC.
260 Fifth Avenue
New York, NY 10001

MICRO MENU
7235 Almond View Court
Orangevale, CA 95662

MICROCAD, INC.
181 Brewster Road
West Hartford, CT 06117

MYSTIC MANAGEMENT
SYSTEMS, INC.
380 Bayonet Street
New London, CT 06320

NC MICROPRODUCTS
P.O. Box 1930
Plano, TX 75074

NEW GEA CORPORATION
335 Oser Avenue
Hauppauge, NY 11788

NICOLET COMPUTER GRAPHICS
777 Arnold Drive
Martinez, CA 94553

NUMBER CRUNCHER
MICROSYSTEMS, INC.
1455 Hayes Street
San Francisco, CA 94117

NUMONICS CORPORATION
418 Pierce Street
Lansdale, PA 19446

OIR
240 Bear Hill Road
Waltham, MA 02154

OPTI-COPY, INC.
10930 Lackman Road
Lenexa, KS 66219

PACKAGED COMMUNICATIONS
TECH.
24 Seneca Road
Bloomfield, CT 06002

PAFEC ENGINEERING
CONSULTANTS, INC.
5401 Kingston Pike
Knoxville, TN 37919

POSTHAUER/PINCKERT CO., INC.
12138 Piping Rock
Houston, TX 77077

PRACTICAL COMPUTER
APPLICATIONS
378 Military East
Benicia, CA 94510

PRIME COMPUTER, INC.
Prime Park
Natick, MA 01760

RESULTS CONSULTANTS, INC.
6770 Lincoln Avenue, Suite 202
Lincolnwood, IL 60646

RIDGE COMPUTERS
2451 Mission College Blvd.
Santa Clara, CA 95054

ROSAL SYSTEMS LTD.
13220 St. Albert Trail 2nd floor
Edmonton, Alberta, Canada T5L
4W1

SCIENTIFIC CALCULATIONS
7635 Main Street
Fishers, NY 14453

SENSIBLE DESIGNS
10791 Tierrasanta Blvd. #104
San Diego, CA 92124

SOFTECH, INC.
460 Totten Pond Road
Waltham, MA 02254

SOURCE POINT DESIGN, INC.
5087-E South Royal Atlanta Drive
Tucker, GA 30084

SPECTRAGRAPHICS CORP.
10260 Sorrento Valley Road
San Diego, CA 92121

SPERRY COMPUTER SYSTEMS
P.O. Box 500
Blue Bell, PA 19424

SSD, INC.
1930 Shattuck Avenue
Berkeley, CA 94704

SUMMAGRAPHICS
CORPORATION
35 Brentwood Avenue
Fairfield, CT 06430

SUMMIT CAD CORPORATION
5222 FM 1960 West 102
Houston, TX 77069

SUN-FLEX CO., INC./CAD
DIVISION
20A Pimentel Court
Novato, CA 94947

SYMBOL GRAPHICS, INC.
P.O. Box 27
Corona, CA 91720

SYSTEMS UNLIMITED
OF CALIFORNIA
100 North Winchester Blvd.,
Suite 260
San Jose, CA 95128

TASVIR CORPORATION
2490 Charleston Road
Mountain View, CA 94043

TECH. & BUS.
COMMUNICATIONS, INC.
730 Boston Post Road
Sudbury, MA 01776

TECHNICAL SOFTWARE, INC.
3981 Lancaster Road
Cleveland, OH 44121

TEKTRONIX, INC.
P.O. Box 1700
Beaverton, OR 97075

TERAK CORPORATION
14151 North 76th Street
Scottsdale, AZ 85260

T&W SYSTEMS, INC.
7372 Prince Drive, Suite 106
Huntington Beach, CA 92647

THE CAD HOUSE
936 Dewing Avenue, Suite J
Lafayette, CA 94549

THE GREAT SOFTWESTERN CO.,
INC.
1405 San Gabriel Drive
Denton, TX 76205

TIMBERLINE SYSTEMS, INC.
7180 S.W. Fir Loop
Portland, OR 97223

TransformerCAD
1229 Cornwall Avenue, Suite 305
Bellingham, WA 98225

UNICAD, INC.
1695 38th Street
Boulder, CO 83301

VECTOR AUTOMATION, INC.
Village of Cross Keys
Baltimore, MD 21210

VECTOR GENERAL
21300 Oxnard Street
Woodland Hills, CA 91367

VECTOR SKETCH
GTCO Corporation
1055 First Street
Rockville, MD 20850

VERSATEC, INC.
2710 Walsh Avenue
Santa Clara, CA 95051

XCEL CONTROLS, INC.
1600 West 6th Street
Mishawaka, IN 46544

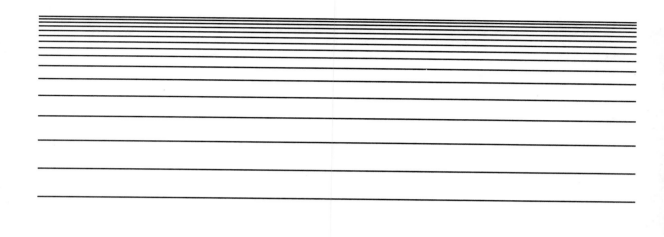

Index

WE VALUE YOUR OPINION—PLEASE SHARE IT WITH US

Merrill Publishing and our authors are most interested in your reactions to this textbook. Did it serve you well in the course? If it did, what aspects of the text were most helpful? If not, what didn't you like about it? Your comments will help us to write and develop better textbooks. We value your opinions and thank you for your help.

Text Title _____ Edition _____

Author(s) _____

Your Name (optional) _____

Address _____

City _____ State _____ Zip _____

School _____

Course Title _____

Instructor's Name _____

Your Major _____

Your Class Rank _____ Freshman _____ Sophomore _____Junior _____ Senior

_____ Graduate Student

Were you required to take this course? _____ Required _____Elective

Length of Course? _____ Quarter _____ Semester

1. Overall, how does this text compare to other texts you've used?

_____ Superior _____Better Than Most _____ Average _____Poor

2. Please rate the text in the following areas:

	Superior	Better Than Most	Average	Poor
Author's Writing Style	_____	_____	_____	_____
Readability	_____	_____	_____	_____
Organization	_____	_____	_____	_____
Accuracy	_____	_____	_____	_____
Layout and Design	_____	_____	_____	_____
Illustrations/Photos/Tables	_____	_____	_____	_____
Examples	_____	_____	_____	_____
Problems/Exercises	_____	_____	_____	_____
Topic Selection	_____	_____	_____	_____
Currentness of Coverage	_____	_____	_____	_____
Explanation of Difficult Concepts	_____	_____	_____	_____
Match-up with Course Coverage	_____	_____	_____	_____
Applications to Real Life	_____	_____	_____	_____

3. Circle those chapters you especially liked:
   1   2   3   4   5   6   7   8   9   10   11   12   13   14   15   16   17   18   19   20
   What was your favorite chapter? _____
   Comments:

4. Circle those chapters you liked least:
   1   2   3   4   5   6   7   8   9   10   11   12   13   14   15   16   17   18   19   20
   What was your least favorite chapter? _____
   Comments:

5. List any chapters your instructor did not assign. _____

6. What topics did your instructor discuss that were not covered in the text?_____

   _____

7. Were you required to buy this book? _____ Yes   _____ No

   Did you buy this book new or used? _____ New   _____ Used

   If used, how much did you pay? _____

   Do you plan to keep or sell this book? _____ Keep   _____ Sell

   If you plan to sell the book, how much do you expect to receive? _____

   Should the instructor continue to assign this book? _____ Yes   _____ No

8. Please list any other learning materials you purchased to help you in this course (e.g., study guide, lab manual).

   _____

9. What did you like most about this text? _____

   _____

10. What did you like least about this text? _____

   _____

11. General comments:

   May we quote you in our advertising? _____ Yes   _____ No

   Please mail to: Boyd Lane
                     College Division, Research Department
                     Box 508
                     1300 Alum Creek Drive
                     Columbus, Ohio 43216

   Thank you!